Classic Edition

McGRAW-HILL

LANGUAGE ARTS TODAY

Great literature is an inspiration. E.B. White's *The Trumpet of the Swan* inspired artist Don Daily to create the illustration on the cover of your book. The story begins on page 258. We hope that you enjoy the story and the illustration!

SENIOR AUTHORS

ANN McCALLUM WILLIAM STRONG TINA THOBURN

Literature Consultant Joan Glazer

McGraw-Hill School Division

New York Farmington

ACKNOWLEDGMENTS

The publisher gratefully acknowledges permission to reprint the following copyrighted material:

"Endless Search" by Alonzo Lopez from *The Whispering Wind*, edited by Terry Allen. Copyright © 1972 by The Institute of American Indian Arts. Reprinted by permission of Doubleday, a division of Bantam, Doubleday, Dell Publishing Group, Inc.

"The House Across the Street" is excerpted from *Circle of Giving* by Ellen Howard. Copyright © 1984 G. Ellen Howard. Reprinted with the permission of Atheneum Publishers, an imprint of Macmillan Publishing Company. Recorded by permission of the publisher.

"Leo and Charlie" is excerpted from *Every Living Thing* by Cynthia Rylant. Copyright © 1985 by Cynthia Rylant. Reprinted with permission of Bradbury Press, an Affiliate of Macmillan, Inc. Recorded by permission of the publisher.

"The Trumpet of the Swan" is Chapter 6 from *The Trumpet of the Swan* by E. B. White. Copyright © 1970 by E. B. White. Reprinted by permission of Harper & Row, Publishers, Inc. By permission also of Hamish Hamilton, Ltd. Recorded by permission of the publisher. Cassette permission by Joel White.

"Papa's Fish Store" (originally titled "The Fish Angel") is from *The Witch of Fourth Street and Other Stories* by Myron Levoy. Copyright © 1972 Myron Levoy. Reprinted by permission of Harper & Row, Publishers, Inc. Recorded by permission of the publisher.

"A Pocketful of Peanuts" is from *A Pocketful of Goobers: A Story About George Washington Carver* by Barbara Mitchell. Copyright © 1986 Carolrhoda Books, Inc. Reprinted and recorded by permission of Carolrhoda Books, Inc., 241 First Avenue North, Minneapolis, MN 55401.

"Many Families—One House" is excerpted from the text in ABOUT US, Volume 8 of *Childcraft—The How and Why Library*, 1989 edition © 1987 World Book, Inc. Used by permission of the publisher.

"Your Ant Is a Which" is excerpted from *Your Ant Is a Which* by Bernice Kohn Hunt. Text copyright © 1975 by Bernice Kohn; Copyright © 1976 by Bernice Kohn Hunt. Reprinted by permission of Harcourt Brace Jovanovich, Inc.

"Letters from an Animal Lover" (originally titled "Where Are the Babies?") by Tot Jones originally appeared in *Cricket* June 1986. Copyright © 1986 Tot Jones. Reprinted by permission of the author.

"A Writer Begins" is from *A Grain of Wheat* by Clyde Robert Bulla. Copyright © 1985 by Clyde Robert Bulla. Reprinted by permission of David R. Godine, Publisher.

Poems, Brief Quotations, and Excerpts

"Don't Ever Cross a Crocodile" by Kaye Starbird. Copyright 1963 by Kaye Starbird. Reprinted by permission of Ray Lincoln Literary Agency, 4 Surrey Road, Melrose Park, PA 19126.

"February Twilight" from *Collected Poems* by Sara Teasdale. Copyright 1926 by Macmillan Publishing Company. Renewed 1954 by Mamie T. Wheless. Reprinted with permission of Macmillan Publishing Company.

"The New and the Old" by Shiki is from *An Introduction to Haiku*, edited by Harold G. Henderson. Copyright © 1958 by Harold G. Henderson. Reprinted by permission of Doubleday, a division of Bantam, Doubleday, Dell Publishing Group, Inc.

Excerpt from "Mind You, Now" (and the full poem) from *I'll Read to You* by John Ciardi. Copyright © 1962 The Curtis Publishing Company (J. B. Lippincott). Reprinted by permission of the publisher.

"Song to Bring Fair Weather" from *Nootka and Quileute Music*, Bureau of American Ethnology Bulletin No. 124, by Frances Densmore. Smithsonian Institution, Washington, D.C., 1939. Reprinted by permission of the Smithsonian Institution Press.

(Acknowledgments continued on page 539.)

Cover Design: Barnett-Brandt Design
Cover Illustration: Don Daily

McGraw-Hill School Division

A Division of The ***McGraw·Hill*** *Companies*

McGraw-Hill School Division
1221 Avenue of the Americas
New York, New York 10020

Printed in the United States of America

ISBN 0-02-244302-9

1 2 3 4 5 6 7 8 006/046 02 01 00 99 98 97

Classic Edition

McGRAW-HILL

LANGUAGE ARTS TODAY

C O N T E N T S

THEME: *BEGINNINGS*

THEME: *CHOICES*

Unit 3: NOUNS 74

Language Study

Unit 4: WRITING COMPARISONS AND CONTRASTS 116

Writing

AWARD WINNING SELECTION

THEME: *MESSAGES*

Language Study

Unit 5: ACTION VERBS 150

Writing

Unit 6: WRITING LETTERS 190

THEME: *TRAVELS*

Unit 7: LINKING VERBS 222

Language Study

Unit 8: WRITING STORIES 256

Writing

AWARD WINNING SELECTION

THEME: *PICTURES*

Language Study

Unit 9: ADJECTIVES 290

Writing

Unit 10: WRITING DESCRIPTIONS 324

AWARD WINNING SELECTION

THEME: *DECISIONS*

Unit 11: PRONOUNS 356

Language Study

Unit 12: WRITING PERSUASIVE PARAGRAPHS 386

Writing

THEME: *SEARCHES*

Language Study

Unit 13: ADVERBS

Writing

Unit 14: WRITING RESEARCH REPORTS

AWARD WINNING SELECTION

WRITER'S REFERENCE

GRAMMAR OVERVIEW

Sentences

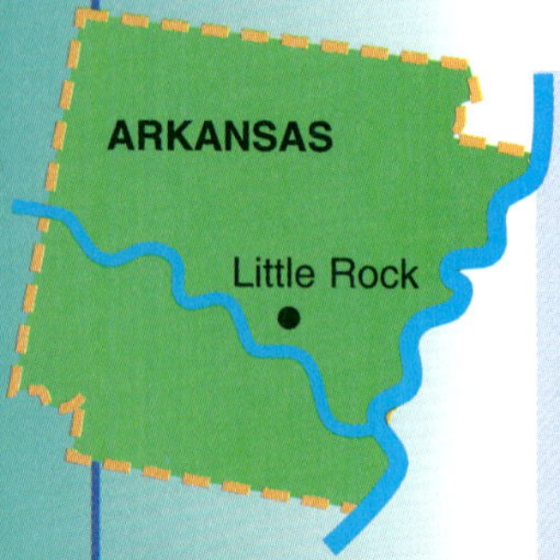

- A **sentence** is a group of words that tells a complete thought.
- A **statement** is a sentence that tells something. It ends with a **period**.
  The United States has fifty states.
- A **question** is a sentence that asks something. It ends with a **question mark**.
  Do you like your state best?
- A **command** tells or asks someone to do something. It ends with a **period**.
  Visit our state soon.
- An **exclamation** shows strong feeling. It ends with an **exclamation mark**.
  How I love my state!

Write the groups of words that make a sentence.

1. She lives in Arkansas.
2. The South.
3. A visit to North Carolina.
4. I moved here from Texas.

Write each sentence. Circle the sentences that are statements. Underline the sentences that are questions.

5. That is our neighboring state.
6. Do you like Mississippi?
7. Which state is farthest south?

Write each command or exclamation. Add the correct end punctuation.

8. How beautiful Colorado's mountains are
9. Come to Tennessee
10. I am crazy about New Jersey's beaches

Sentence Parts

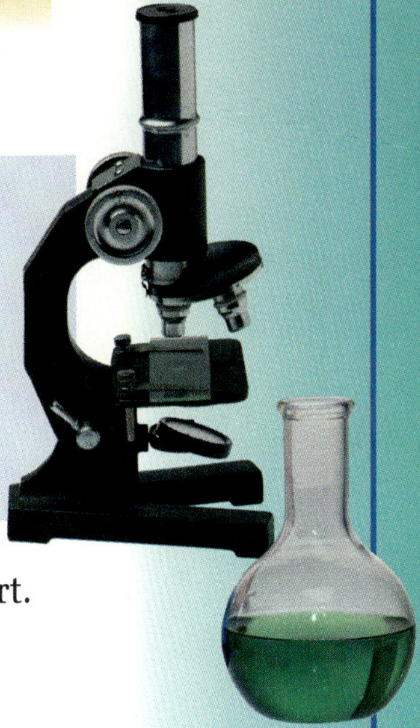

- The **subject** of a sentence tells *whom* or *what* the sentence is about.
- The **predicate** tells what the subject *does* or *is*.

subject	**predicate**
Many people	read magazines.
My friends	are good students.

Write each sentence. Draw a line under the subject part.

1. My mother reads science journals.
2. I prefer magazines about sports.
3. Our whole family likes magazines.
4. We borrow magazines from the library.
5. The library has many different kinds of magazines.

Write each sentence. Draw two lines under each predicate.

6. Sometimes we buy magazines.
7. Dad gets them at book stores.
8. I order a magazine through the mail.
9. My friends and I started our own magazine.
10. We write the articles ourselves.

Nouns

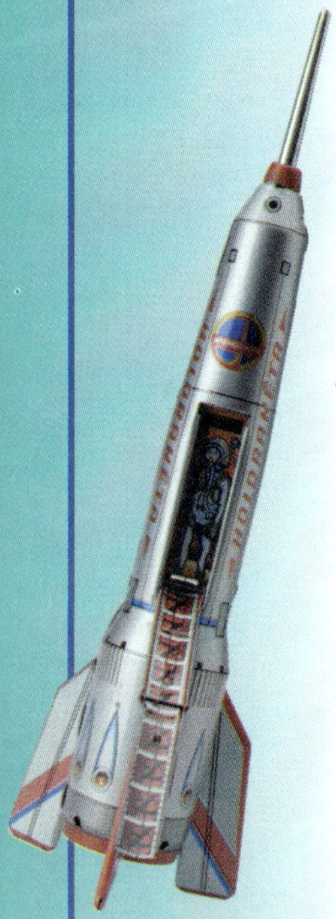

- A **noun** is a word that names a person, place, or thing.
  The **astronaut** wears a **suit**. The **space center** is nearby.
  astronaut ↓ *person*; **suit** ↓ *thing*; **space center** ↓ *place*
- Add **s** to most nouns to name more than one:
  astronaut ⟶ **astronauts**
- Add **es** to nouns that end with **s**, **ss**, **ch**, **sh**, and **x**:
  bench ⟶ **benches**
- Some nouns form their plurals in a special way:
  tooth ⟶ **teeth**
- For the plural of nouns ending in a consonant and **y**, change **y** to **i** and add **es**.
  city ⟶ **cities**

Write each sentence. Underline the nouns.

1. A satellite is going into space.
2. A rocket launches the machine.
3. Many people watch with telescopes.

Write the plural form of these singular nouns.

4. dish	**6.** box	**8.** couch
5. woman	**7.** compass	**9.** child

Write the plural form of each noun in parentheses.

10. The (mystery) of space fascinate us.
11. Many people share (memory) of the first moon walk.
12. Scientists search the (sky) for new comets.

Nouns

- A **common noun** is a noun that names any person, place, or thing. → **dog**
- A **proper noun** is a noun that names a special person, place, or thing. → **Rover**
- A **possessive noun** is a noun that shows who or what owns something.
- Add an **apostrophe** and an **s** to a singular noun to make it possessive. → **Kirby's** cat
- Add an **apostrophe** to make most plural nouns possessive. → the **girls'** pets
- Add an apostrophe and **s** to make plural nouns that don't end in **s** possessive. → **men's**

Write each noun. Write **common** or **proper** next to each noun.

1. parrot
2. American Kennel Club
3. Dogwood Drive
4. street
5. doctor
6. Dr. Chan

Write each sentence with the possessive form of the singular noun in parentheses.

7. (Katie) pet is a hermit crab.
8. The (crab) house is a shell.
9. It lives in a striped (snail) shell.

Write the plural possessive form of each phrase.

10. leashes of the dogs
11. pets of the children
12. food of the hamsters

Verbs

- An **action verb** is a word that shows action. Its **tense** tells when the action happens.
- Add **s** or **es** to most present-tense verbs when you use them with singular subjects.
- If a verb ends with a consonant and **y**, change the **y** to **i** and add **es**.
  Briana **collects** coins. She **polishes** them.
  She **carries** them in a box.
- Add **ed** to most verbs to show past tense.
  We **collected** shells last summer.
- Some verbs have special spellings to show the past tense.
  I **see**. I **saw**. I **had seen**.
- A verb in the **future tense** tells about an action that will happen. ⟶ **will collect**
- The special verb **be** does not show action.
  It **is** fun now. It **was** fun last time.

Write each sentence. Underline each verb.

1. Ted made model dinosaurs.
2. He will play with them.
3. We want models, too.
4. I have seen his models.

Write each sentence. Use the correct form of the present-tense verb in parentheses.

5. He (carry) them in a box.
6. The wind (toss) the cards all around.

Change each verb to the past tense.

7. walk
8. go
9. hurry
10. are

GRAMMAR OVERVIEW

Adjectives

- An adjective is a word that describes a noun.
  A baseball is a **large** ball.
- Add **er** to an adjective to compare two nouns.
  A soccer ball is **larger** than a baseball.
- Add **est** to an adjective to compare more than two nouns.
  A basketball is the **largest** of all.

Write each sentence. Draw one line under each adjective. Draw two lines under the noun it describes.

1. Two people are playing ball.
2. We want to start a new game.
3. My favorite sport is soccer.
4. I always give the ball a good kick.

Write the correct form of each underlined adjective. Use **er** or **est**.

5. A tennis ball is soft than a baseball.
6. A golf ball is the hard of all.
7. A beach ball is large than a basketball.
8. Which is the large ball of all?

Write the correct **er** and **est** form of each adjective.

9. young
10. old
11. dark
12. smart
13. slow
14. bright

GRAMMAR OVERVIEW

Pronouns

- A **pronoun** is a word that takes the place of one or more nouns.
- A **subject pronoun** is used as the subject of a sentence.
  Sharks and tuna are fish. ⟶ **They** are fish.
- An **object pronoun** is used after an action verb or words such as *for*, *at*, *of*, *with*, and *to*.
  Fish can smell food. ⟶ Fish can smell **it**.

Write the sentences. Underline the pronouns.

1. They went fishing.
2. I went with them.
3. She came with us.
4. We had a pole for her.

Write each sentence with the correct subject pronoun in parentheses.

5. (I, me) go to aquariums to see fish.
6. My sister and (her, she) often join me.
7. Mother and (they, them) look at the shark.
8. (He, Him) doesn't look like a killer.

Write each sentence with the correct object pronoun in parentheses.

9. The octopus fascinates _______ . (she, her)
10. She looks at _______ for a long time. (we, it)
11. The legs seem to wave at _______ . (we, us)
12. We watch _______ quietly. (them, they)

GRAMMAR OVERVIEW

Adverbs

- An **adverb** is a word that tells more about a verb.
- Some adverbs tell *when*.
  The storm began **suddenly**.
- Some adverbs tell *where*.
  Lightning flashed **there**.
- Some adverbs tell *how*.
  Thunder boomed **loudly**.

Write the sentence. Draw one line under the adverb. Draw two lines under the verb it describes.

1. The storm moved away.
2. The sky cleared slowly.
3. The sun shone brightly through the clouds.
4. Everyone went outside.

Write each sentence. Draw a line under the adverb. Write **when** if the adverb tells *when*. Write **where** if it tells *where*.

5. Later, the storm returned.
6. The lightning flashed everywhere.
7. Thunder soon followed.

Write each sentence. Make the word in parentheses tell *how*.

8. Fluffy white clouds formed ________ . (quick)
9. They danced ________ across the sky. (playful)
10. A cloud changed from a fish into a ship. (sudden) ________

UNIT 1

Sentences

In this unit you will learn about four different kinds of sentences. You can use all four kinds of sentences when you communicate with others.

Discuss Read the poem on the opposite page. What does the poem make you think about?

JOURNAL

Creative Expression The unit theme is *Beginnings.* How do you like to begin your day? Write a few sentences in your journal that tell about beginning a new day.

THEME: *BEGINNINGS*

You, whose day it is,
Make it beautiful.
Get out your rainbow colors,
So it will be beautiful.

—Nootka

1 WHAT IS A SENTENCE?

A sentence is a group of words that expresses a complete thought.

Sentences help you to put your thoughts into words. In a complete sentence the meaning is clear. No important words are missing. Your words express a complete thought. Your sentence can stand alone and make sense.

Complete Sentences	Not Sentences
The family chose the puppy with long ears.	Built a doghouse.
The puppy's name is Brewster.	Our dog Brewster.

Brewster barked at the moon.

Guided Practice

Tell which groups of words are sentences and which groups are not sentences.

Example: In the house the first night. *not a sentence*

1. Gave the puppy warm milk.
2. Robert made a bed for the puppy.
3. Began barking around midnight.
4. A ticking clock in the puppy's bed.
5. The puppy slept peacefully until morning.

?! **THINK**

■ How can I decide if a group of words is a sentence?

GRAMMAR

REMEMBER

- A **sentence** is a group of words that expresses a complete thought.

More Practice

A. Write each group of words. Next to each group write **sentence** or **not a sentence.**

Example: Puppy fun-loving. *not a sentence*

6. Dad named the puppy Brewster.
7. Changed the name to Barney.
8. My sister feeds Barney.
9. I give Barney fresh water.
10. A book about pets.
11. Barney is cute.
12. The doctor gave Barney a checkup.
13. A happy and healthy puppy.
14. Weighs six pounds.
15. Barney is a playful pet.

B. For each pair, write the group of words that is a sentence. Then read the other group. By adding your own words, make a sentence from the words.

Examples: Barney happy pup. *Barney is a happy pup.*
I love Barney. *I love Barney.*

16. One day I bought Barney a toy. Played for hours.
17. Buried his toy in the garden. I finally found the toy.
18. A cat next door. The cat chases Barney.
19. I take Barney for long walks. Tugs on the leash.
20. My mother brushes Barney. A special kind of brush.

Extra Practice, page 28

WRITING APPLICATION Sentences

Write five sentences describing an animal you once saw. Be sure to punctuate your sentences correctly.

2 DECLARATIVE AND INTERROGATIVE SENTENCES

Different kinds of sentences do different things. A **declarative sentence** makes a statement. You use a declarative sentence to tell something to someone. An **interrogative sentence** asks a question. You use an interrogative sentence when you want to know more.

Declarative Sentences
End mark: a period (**.**)
We arrived at the train station**.**
We checked our bags**.**

Interrogative Sentences
End mark: a question mark (**?**)
How many bags do you have**?**
May we sit together**?**

Begin every sentence with a **capital letter.** Notice the **punctuation mark** that ends each kind of sentence.

Guided Practice

Tell which sentences are declarative and which are interrogative. Then, tell which punctuation mark should end each sentence.

Example: Is this your first train trip
interrogative *question mark*

1. We bought our tickets yesterday
2. Do you want the seat near the window
3. Who will meet us when we arrive
4. We can have lunch on the train
5. Did you bring a sandwich
6. Are you ready to board the train

?! THINK

■ How can I decide whether a sentence is declarative or interrogative?

REMEMBER

- A **declarative sentence** makes a statement. It ends with a period.
- An **interrogative sentence** asks a question. It ends with a question mark.

More Practice

A. Write each sentence. Then write **declarative** or **interrogative** next to each to tell what kind of sentence it is.

Example: The train is ready to go. *declarative*

7. We will find our seats.
8. We are going to visit Aunt Lucy.
9. Aunt Lucy lives in Dallas, Texas.
10. Has the train started to move?
11. The train is passing a beautiful lake.
12. When will we arrive in Dallas?

B. Write each sentence correctly. Remember to use the correct end punctuation.

Example: is the train ready to go *Is the train ready to go?*

13. the train is moving
14. have you waved good-bye
15. i am glad we are sitting together
16. what book are you reading
17. i am too excited to read
18. do you feel the train slowing down
19. i hope we will arrive on time
20. can we have lunch now

Extra Practice, page 29

WRITING APPLICATION A Post Card

Imagine that you are taking a trip by train. Write a post card to a friend. Include two sentences that are statements and two sentences that are questions in your card.

GRAMMAR

3 IMPERATIVE AND EXCLAMATORY SENTENCES

You can do more with sentences than just ask questions or make statements. You can use an **imperative sentence** to tell or ask someone to do something. You can tell or ask more politely by adding the word *please* to an imperative sentence. You can use an **exclamatory sentence** when you want to show strong feeling, such as surprise, excitement, or fear.

Look at the charts below.

Imperative Sentences	Exclamatory Sentences
End mark: a period (.)	*End mark:* an exclamation mark (!)
Ring the doorbell once.	What a steep hill this is!
Please come inside.	I cannot wait to make new friends!

Guided Practice

Tell which sentences are imperative and which are exclamatory.

Example: Put our name on the mailbox. *imperative*

1. Our new neighborhood is great!
2. Please show us where the school is.
3. I have met three new friends already!
4. Meeting new people is so exciting!
5. Invite the neighbors for lunch.
6. Look at my new neighborhood.
7. The girl next door is exactly my age!

?! **THINK**

■ How can I decide if a sentence is imperative or exclamatory?

REMEMBER

- An **imperative sentence** tells or asks someone to do something. It ends with a period.
- An **exclamatory sentence** shows strong feeling. It ends with an exclamation mark.

More Practice

A. Write each sentence. Then write **imperative** or **exclamatory** next to each to tell what kind of sentence it is.

Example: What a great place this is! *exclamatory*

8. I like it very much!
9. Please come to my house this afternoon.
10. Watch out for cars.
11. Ask your friends about the park.
12. Please come skating with me.
13. What fun it is to go skating!
14. Make sure that you are home for dinner.
15. How happy I am!

B. Write each sentence. Begin each sentence with a capital letter. End it with a period or an exclamation mark.

Example: wow, you have so many books
Wow, you have so many books!

16. help me unpack my books
17. what wonderful books you have
18. please name your favorite writers
19. what luck, you like the same writers I do
20. think about joining our reading club

Extra Practice, page 30

WRITING APPLICATION A Letter

Imagine that you have moved to a new place. Write a letter to a friend. Describe your fear and excitement about meeting new people. Ask for something from your home town.

GRAMMAR

4 COMPLETE SUBJECTS AND COMPLETE PREDICATES

When you write a sentence, your words tell a complete thought. Every sentence has two important parts. The **subject** part tells you *whom* or *what* the sentence is about. The **predicate** part tells you what the subject *does* or *is*.

The subject and predicate can be one word or many words. The **complete subject** is all of the words in the subject part. The **complete predicate** is all of the words in the predicate part.

Look at the sentences below.

Complete Subject	Complete Predicate
Flowers	bloomed.
Many colorful flowers	bloomed in our garden.

Guided Practice

Tell the complete subject and the complete predicate in each sentence.

Example: Spring came early this year.
subject: Spring
predicate: came early this year

1. The warm weather surprised us.
2. The whole family worked in the garden.
3. We planted flowers by the house.
4. My father grew tomato plants from seeds.
5. The tomatoes ripened.
6. My sister and I made tomato soup.
7. The whole family loves our garden.

?! **THINK**

■ How can I identify the complete subject and the complete predicate of a sentence?

REMEMBER

- The **complete subject** includes all the words in the subject.
- The **complete predicate** includes all the words in the predicate.

More Practice

A. Write **complete subject** or **complete predicate** to tell which part of the sentence is underlined.

Example: Fall is a lovely time of year. *complete subject*

8. The turning leaves signal the beginning of fall.
9. The squirrels collect nuts for the winter.
10. A new school year starts in September.
11. The cool winds blow.
12. People wear sweaters during the day.
13. Crisp, red apples ripen on the trees.

B. Write each sentence. Draw a line between the complete subject and the complete predicate.

Example: Winter winds|make our noses cold.

14. Winter is my favorite time of the year.
15. The first snowflakes begin the season.
16. I need new mittens this year.
17. My brother complains about the winter.
18. He dislikes cold weather.
19. My sister smiles.
20. Her friends ski on the big hill.

Extra Practice, page 31

WRITING APPLICATION An Invitation

COOPERATIVE LEARNING

Work with three of your classmates to write an invitation to a party. Use complete sentences to tell your guests the important information they need to know about the party.

5 SIMPLE SUBJECTS

As you have learned, the subject part of a sentence can be one word or many words. The main word in the complete subject is called the **simple subject**. The simple subject tells exactly *whom* or *what* the sentence is about.

Look at the sentences below. The simple subject in each sentence is underlined.

Complete Subject	Complete Predicate
The Pilgrims	traveled to the New World by ship.
The first winter	was a hard one for the people.

Guided Practice

Tell the simple subject in each sentence.

Example: Ships sailed from England to the New World. *Ships*

1. Three ships landed on the Virginia coast.
2. The settlers founded a colony there.
3. The people named the colony after King James.
4. Women arrived in Jamestown after the men.
5. Many colonists died during the first year.
6. Thirty Dutch families sailed to the new land.
7. The families followed the explorer Henry Hudson.
8. Hudson claimed a river for the Dutch.
9. The river is located in New York.

?! **THINK**

■ How can I identify the simple subject of a sentence?

REMEMBER

- The **simple subject** is the main word in the complete subject.

More Practice

A. The complete subject of each sentence is underlined. Write the simple subject.

Example: Many colonists sailed across the sea to the New World. *colonists*

10. Many families built their homes beside rivers.
11. The Dutch settled along the Hudson River.
12. Some Native Americans sold Manhattan Island to them for a small amount.
13. The settlers traded with the Native Americans for furs.

B. Write the complete subject of each sentence. Then underline the simple subject.

Example: The colonists were very brave. *The colonists*

14. The Pilgrims arrived on the *Mayflower.*
15. Their ship sailed into Plymouth harbor.
16. Many settlers died during the first winter.
17. Their homes were sod huts.
18. The people elected a governor.
19. The governor wrote a report about the hardships.
20. The spring brought warmer weather.

Extra Practice, page 32

WRITING APPLICATION A Diary Entry

Imagine that you are an early American settler. Write a diary entry about your experiences. Underline the simple subject in each of your sentences. Share your diary entry with a classmate.

The Bettmann Archive

GRAMMAR

6 SIMPLE PREDICATES

You have learned that a sentence has two parts—a subject part and a predicate part. The main word in the predicate part is called the **simple predicate.** The simple predicate tells exactly what the subject *does* or *is*.

Look at the sentences below. The simple predicate in each sentence is underlined.

Complete Subject	Complete Predicate
Some families	adopt children.
They	give the children love and care.
They	provide good homes.
The families	have fun together.

Guided Practice

Tell the simple predicate in each sentence.

Example: My family adopted a new baby. *adopted*

1. The new baby has my old room.
2. We decorated the room with wallpaper.
3. A toy hangs over the crib.
4. The baby plays most of the day.
5. My mother sings to him at night.

?! THINK

- How can I identify the simple predicate of a sentence?

REMEMBER

- The **simple predicate** is the main word in the complete predicate.

More Practice

The complete predicate of each sentence is underlined. Write the simple predicate.

Example: The baby needs clothes. *needs*

6. My friend sewed clothes for the baby.
7. I stitched his name on a bib.
8. Jeremy wears the bib during meals.
9. My friend made him a stuffed bear.
10. I took a picture of the baby with the bear.
11. The bear looks bigger than the baby.
12. My father sent a copy of the picture to Aunt Carla.
13. I took another copy to school.
14. The teacher put the picture on the bulletin board.
15. Some students wrote stories about Jeremy.
16. I read the stories to my parents and sister.
17. We laughed over a story about Jeremy on Mars.
18. My mother put the stories in a scrapbook.
19. I pasted the picture to the inside cover.
20. The scrapbook is for the future.
21. My sister and I like our little brother.
22. We walk him in a stroller.
23. Our dog joins us for the walk.
24. Neighbors smile at Jeremy.
25. I feel very proud of my family.

Extra Practice, page 33

WRITING APPLICATION A Story

Find a picture of a person in a magazine. Write a story about the person. Use the photograph to illustrate your story.

7 COMPOUND SUBJECTS AND COMPOUND PREDICATES

The sentences you write can tell about two or more different persons or things and what they do. A sentence with two simple subjects joined by the word *and* has a **compound subject**. A sentence with two simple predicates joined by *and* has a **compound predicate**.

The sidewalks **and** streets|are full of people.
The parade|twists **and** turns down the street.

Some sentences can even have a compound subject *and* a compound predicate.

Boys **and** girls|clap **and** cheer for the dragon.

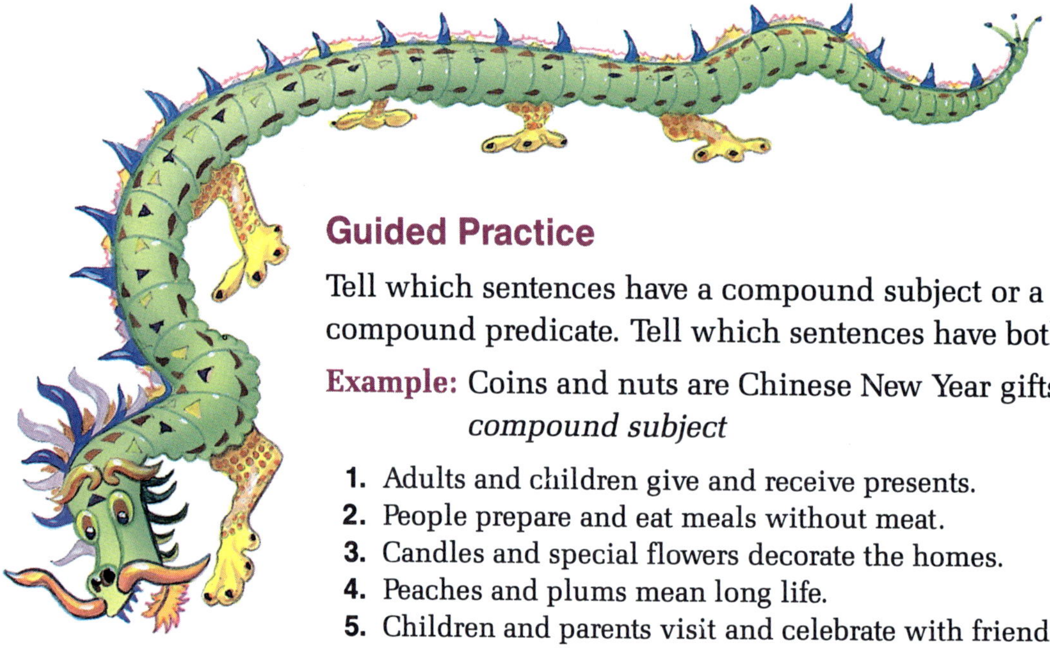

Guided Practice

Tell which sentences have a compound subject or a compound predicate. Tell which sentences have both.

Example: Coins and nuts are Chinese New Year gifts.
compound subject

1. Adults and children give and receive presents.
2. People prepare and eat meals without meat.
3. Candles and special flowers decorate the homes.
4. Peaches and plums mean long life.
5. Children and parents visit and celebrate with friends.

?! **THINK**

- How can I decide if a sentence has a compound subject, a compound predicate, or both?

REMEMBER

- A **compound subject** has two or more simple subjects.
- A **compound predicate** has two or more simple predicates.

Guided Practice

A. Write the two main words in the compound subject or the compound predicate in each sentence.

Example: We laugh and sing at holiday time. *laugh sing*

6. Excitement and joy greet the Chinese New Year.
7. Sweet nuts and rice are made into treats.
8. Strength and goodness come from the Chinese dragon.
9. Many men walk and dance under the dragon.
10. Gold and silver decorate the dragon's head.
11. The huge head shakes and jumps at the crowd.
12. Some people light and throw sparklers.

B. Write each sentence. Then, underline the two main words in each compound subject or compound predicate.

Example: Food and gifts are part of celebrations.

13. Special dances and music are part of the Nigerian New Year.
14. Farmers harvest and store their crops ahead of time.
15. Tasty food and drinks are prepared.
16. In Bolivia, people walk and ride to a New Year's fair.
17. Parents and children enjoy the fair.
18. Merchants display and sell artwork and rugs.
19. Some people buy and wear pretty scarves.
20. Tiny pots and pans decorate little dolls.

Extra Practice, page 34

WRITING APPLICATION A Dramatic Scene

Imagine that you go with friends to a New Year's celebration. What do you see, hear, and do? Write a scene for a play that tells what happens. Present your scene to the class.

GRAMMAR

8 CORRECTING RUN-ON SENTENCES

Always capitalize and punctuate your sentences correctly. A sentence is a group of words that expresses a complete thought. Sometimes, when you are writing quickly, you may let two thoughts run together without telling how the thoughts are related. This kind of sentence is called a **run-on sentence.** Look at this run-on sentence.

Light shimmers on water it moves through leafy trees.

How to Correct a Run-on Sentence

- Rewrite each complete thought as a separate sentence.
- Be sure to begin each sentence with a capital letter.
- Use the correct end punctuation for each sentence.

Example:
Light shimmers on water. It moves through leafy trees.

The Little Ballerina, Edgar Degas

Guided Practice

Tell which sentences are run-on sentences. Identify each complete thought.

Example: Our class visited a museum we saw many paintings.
run-on *Our class visited a museum.*
We saw many paintings.

1. The museum was new it had many works of art.
2. A guide gave us a tour of all the rooms.
3. She talked about the artists and their work.
4. We saw paintings we also saw sculptures.
5. Some artists sign their work I sign my drawings.

?! **THINK**

- How can I decide if a sentence is a run-on sentence?

GRAMMAR

REMEMBER

- A **run-on sentence** contains two or more sentences that should stand alone.

More Practice

Rewrite each run-on sentence correctly.

Example: The museum was nice we liked it.
The museum was nice. We liked it.

6. Our class ate lunch in the museum.
7. The meal was fancy the waiters wore white gloves.
8. We talked about art the teacher asked for opinions.
9. My favorite paintings are by Mary Cassatt.
10. She was born in America she lived in France.
11. Her paintings are very delicate they are beautiful.
12. Cassatt's paintings show mothers and children.
13. Stanley liked the paintings by Claude Monet.
14. Monet painted from nature he studied light.
15. He did a scene many times the light changed in each painting.
16. Monet painted water lilies people love these pictures.
17. The colors are red, blue, and yellow no green was used.
18. Stand back see the flowers in the pond.
19. The lilies grew in Monet's own garden.
20. Modern art surprises many people they are confused by it.
21. Some pieces are abstract they do not look like anything real.
22. Certain artists painted flat shapes others used dots of color.
23. Many modern artists have a new style.
24. Their work looks almost like photographs.
25. Peter loves these paintings he wants to buy one.

Extra Practice, Practice Plus, pages 35-37

WRITING APPLICATION A Description

Look at the photograph of the sculpture on page 16. Then, write a paragraph describing it for someone who has not seen it. Check your work for run-on sentences.

9 MECHANICS: Punctuating Sentences

As you know, every sentence must begin with a capital letter. The correct punctuation mark to use at the end of a sentence depends on what kind of a sentence it is.

Type of Sentence	End Mark	Example
Declarative Sentence ■ makes a statement	period (**.**)	Ducks lay their eggs in the spring**.**
Interrogative Sentence ■ asks a question	question mark (**?**)	Is a male duck called a drake**?**
Imperative Sentence ■ tells or asks someone to do something	period (**.**)	Please tell me about mallards**.**
Exclamatory Sentence ■ shows strong feeling	exclamation mark (**!**)	What hard work it is to build a nest**!**

Guided Practice

Tell how you would correctly punctuate each sentence.

Example: the female duck is brown *The female duck is brown.*

1. brown feathers help her to hide
2. how beautiful the drake's green feathers are
3. where do the ducks build their nests
4. a female might lay eight eggs
5. come with me to see the duck's nest
6. ducks build their nests near water

?! THINK

■ How can I decide which punctuation mark to use at the end of a sentence?

REMEMBER

- Every **sentence** must begin with a capital letter.
- **Declarative** and **imperative sentences** end with periods.
- **Interrogative sentences** end with question marks.
- **Exclamatory sentences** end with exclamation marks.

More Practice

Write each sentence correctly.

Example: the ducks are fascinating *The ducks are fascinating.*

7. watch the female duck collect twigs
8. she lines the nest with feathers
9. how soft the feathers are
10. for how long does the mother sit on her eggs
11. does she ever leave the nest
12. please help me count the eggs
13. there are four eggs here
14. when will the ducklings hatch
15. how exciting that day will be
16. please do not touch the eggs
17. a duckling is growing inside each one
18. the egg yolk provides food for the duckling
19. what part of the duckling grows first
20. look in a book for the answer
21. when does the shell become thin
22. what is the point on the duck's bill called
23. look, the ducklings are hatching
24. how weak the new ducklings look
25. when will their feathers dry

Extra Practice, page 38

WRITING APPLICATION An Announcement

Imagine that your pet duck has just hatched ducklings. Use different kinds of sentences to write an announcement about the new ducklings.

10 VOCABULARY BUILDING: Using Context Clues

You know that you can find the meaning of an unfamiliar word in a dictionary. Before looking in a dictionary, however, try to figure out the meaning of a new word by using other words in the sentence as clues.

What clues can you find in this sentence to help you guess the meaning of the word *variety?*

> The Native Americans developed a **variety** of different vegetables—corn, squash, and potatoes.

The sentence gives the names of different vegetables—*corn*, *squash*, and *potatoes*. These words give you a clue that *variety* means "a number of different things," such as vegetables.

Guided Practice

Choose the correct meaning for each underlined word.

Example: Settlers learned new skills and habits by studying Native American customs. *a.*
a. ways of doing things b. foods

1. Settlers saw Native Americans make moccasins for their feet.
   a. shirts b. shoes
2. Canoes were made of birch, tamarack, and other trees.
   a. a kind of tree b. a kind of canoe
3. Native Americans and settlers often bartered for supplies instead of using money.
   a. fought b. traded
4. Native American corn fertilized with dead fish grew faster.
   a. helped to grow b. cooked

THINK

- How can I use context clues to figure out the meaning of a word I do not know?

REMEMBER

- The words that come before and after an unfamiliar word in a sentence can be used as clues to the meaning of the word.

G R A M M A R

More Practice

A. Write the meaning of each underlined word.

Example: Many settlers lived in Native American wigwams. *a.*
a. houses b. wagons

5. Settlers used Native American snares to catch deer.
   a. clothing b. traps
6. Sumel was made from the sap inside maple trees.
   a. juice b. leaves
7. Native Americans built a weir in a stream to catch fish.
   a. bridge b. dam

B. Write each sentence. Use context clues to choose the word that correctly completes the sentence.

Example: One Native American game was _____ a hoop.
a. rolling b. running c. skipping
One Native American game was rolling a hoop.

8. Certain Native Americans made _____ whistles from clay.
   a. cloth b. paper c. pottery
9. They sailed toy _____ made of light wood.
   a. rafts b. wagons c. dolls
10. Musicians played _____ made of hollow sticks.
   a. balls b. flutes c. games

Extra Practice, page 39

WRITING APPLICATION An Explanation

COOPERATIVE LEARNING

Have you ever made a toy or invented a new game? Write a paragraph explaining how to make a toy or play a game. Read a classmate's paragraph. Did you find any new words?

GRAMMAR AND WRITING CONNECTION

Combining Sentences

When you are writing, you may want to show how the ideas in two separate sentences are related. You can show the connection between the sentences by using a comma and the word *and* to join them.

Jill's father found a new job. The family moved away.

Jill's father found a new job**, and** the family moved away.

You can use a comma and the word *but* to show a different connection.

Jill was sad to leave. She was excited about her new home.

Jill was sad to leave**, but** she was excited about her new home.

COOPERATIVE LEARNING

Working Together

With your classmates talk about each pair of sentences. Then, tell how you would join them to make a single sentence.

Example: A new company offered Andy's mother a job. She took it. *A new company offered Andy's mother a job, and she took it.*

1. The company is in France. The whole family moved there.
2. Andy took French lessons. He learned the language.
3. Andy liked the language. He found it difficult.

Revising Sentences

Andy wrote the following sentences in a letter to a friend. Help Andy revise his letter by combining each pair of sentences. Use a comma and *and* or *but* to show the connection between ideas.

4. The airport in Paris was very big. We found our luggage quickly.
5. We needed directions to the hotel. A friendly person helped us.
6. At first we stayed in a hotel. Mom and Dad soon rented a house.
7. The house is in the country. The city is not far away.
8. Mom loves her new job. I like my new school.
9. The house does not have heat. The days are very warm.
10. Dad works hard all morning. We drive to the beach in the afternoon.
11. There are huge mountains nearby. I can see them from my window.
12. France is beautiful. I miss all my friends at home.

WRITER AT WORK

Think about a place you would like to visit. Write a paragraph telling where it is and what you would do there. After writing, work with a partner to revise your work.

When you revise, join sentences that have related ideas. Use a comma and the joining word that best fits your meaning.

UNIT CHECKUP

LESSON 1

What Is a Sentence? (page 2) Write each group of words. Next to each group write **sentence** or **not a sentence.**

1. The morning sun.
2. A new day begins.
3. Chirp in the trees.
4. Drops of dew.

LESSONS 2-3

Kinds of Sentences (pages 4–7) Write each sentence. Write **declarative, imperative, interrogative,** or **exclamatory** next to each.

5. Where should we dig the garden?
6. Daisies grow best by the house.
7. Wait for me in the garden.
8. How exciting it is to start a garden!

LESSONS 4-6

Subjects and Predicates (pages 8-13) Write each sentence. Draw a line between the complete subject and the complete predicate. Then, draw one line under the simple subject. Draw two lines under the simple predicate.

9. This book begins in a funny way.
10. A shaggy dog joins a circus.
11. Three boys search for the dog.
12. Mike loses his new bicycle.
13. An elephant sits on Mike's hat.

LESSON 7

Compound Subjects and Compound Predicates (page 14) Write each sentence. Then, underline the two main words in the compound subject, in the compound predicate, or in both.

14. We read and study the recipes.
15. One pot and two bowls are needed.
16. Salt and pepper are on the shelf.
17. Jack and Lupe peel and cut the potatoes.
18. My sister and I wash and chop the celery.

LESSON 8

Correcting Run-on Sentences (page 16) Correct the run-on sentences. Write the new sentences.

19. Baseball starts in the spring our training begins in March.
20. School teams choose their players I always play first base.
21. Our first game is this weekend everyone is excited.
22. My brother practices pitches with me he is a good catcher.
23. Last year we won three games we took pictures at the games.

LESSON 9

Mechanics: Punctuating Sentences (page 18) Write each sentence correctly.

24. what a wonderful story
25. did you write it
26. show me your story plan
27. the main character is so funny

LESSON 10

Vocabulary Building: Using Context Clues (page 20) Write the correct definition of the underlined word in each sentence.

28. Some model cars look real because they are replicas of actual cars.
a. copies b. drawings

29. Read the instructions before you begin to work.
a. words telling what to do b. names of the model

30. The drawings show you how to assemble the parts of the model.
a. count b. put together

Writing Application: Sentence Mechanics (pages 2–7, 16, 18) The following paragraph contains 10 errors in mechanics. Rewrite the paragraph correctly.

31.–40.

Will you come to the fair. I know it will be fun for all? Les wants to go but Bill does not! Wow, I wouldn't miss it for the world? will the twins go if Bill does not. Perhaps the twins will go and Bill will stay at home? les is silly if he does not go to the fair!

ENRICHMENT

RAINING CATS & DOGS

An **idiom** is a saying that has a special meaning. For example, "It's raining cats and dogs" means that it is raining hard. By yourself or with a partner, suggest meanings for the idioms below. Use a dictionary if you need help. Look up the meaning of the idiom under the key word. (In these examples, the key word is the last word.)

We are in hot water.
Keep a stiff upper lip.
She has a green thumb.
Drop me a line.

PICTURE THIS

Write a message to someone in picture sentences. Use pictures in place of some words. Here is an example:

RHYME TIME

A two-line poem is called a **couplet.** The lines in a couplet usually end with words that rhyme, or sound alike. Read the couplet below quietly to yourself. Which words rhyme?

The Crocus

The golden crocus reaches up
to catch a sunbeam in her cup.

—Walter Crane

"The Crocus" tells about a flower. Think of a flower or something else in nature. Write a couplet about it. Try to make the lines rhyme.

CLUE ME IN

Form teams of three or four players each. Each team should search a dictionary for unusual words. Here are a few to get you started: *shako, umiak, ermine, borzoi.*

When you find a word that you think will stump the other team, write it in a sentence. The context, or other words in the sentence, must give a clue to the meaning of the word. For example, "The borzoi raced ahead of the other dogs."

One team begins by reading the unusual word and its context sentence. The opposite team must try to figure out the meaning of the word by using the clues in the sentence. The team that figures out the meaning of the most words wins.

Sentence Savvy

Write a round-robin story with a small group of classmates. The first person in the group writes an opening sentence. The second adds the next sentence. Continue in this manner until your story is completed. Challenge yourselves to see how many interrogative, imperative, and exclamatory sentences you can include in your story.

The Winner Is . . .

Play this game with three other players. Each of you think of a sentence. Write each word in your sentence on a separate card. Put all the cards in a pile and mix them up. Take turns selecting cards. Return the cards you cannot use to the pile. The first player to make a sentence from all the words in his or her hand wins the round.

EXTRA PRACTICE

Three levels of practice

What Is a Sentence? (page 2)

LEVEL A. Write **sentence** if the group of words is a sentence. Write **not a sentence** if it is not a sentence.

1. We go on a vacation nearly every summer.
2. Leaving tomorrow morning.
3. We plan to be gone for two weeks.
4. Driving to St. Louis.
5. My parents want to see the Gateway Arch.
6. My sisters and I.
7. Love the fabulous sights.
8. The city is interesting for tourists.
9. Watching the crowds come and go.
10. It will be the best vacation ever.

LEVEL B. For each pair, write the group of words that is a sentence.

11. Our camping trip did not start well. Big hole in the tent.
12. Large, dark storm clouds. Rain fell in the afternoon.
13. Trouble with the campfire. We could not find enough dry wood.
14. The wind blew. Running from the storm.
15. The sun finally came out. Had fun after that.
16. Watched the stars. The full moon glowed.
17. The moon was beautiful. Shone very brightly.
18. Worried for a short time. Our camping trip was a success.

LEVEL C. Add your own words to each group of words to make a complete sentence.

19. Climbed into the rowboat.
20. My aunt and uncle.
21. Our fishing rods.
22. Rowed across the lake.
23. Many small fish.
24. Tired from rowing so far.
25. All of us.

EXTRA PRACTICE

Three levels of practice

Declarative and Interrogative Sentences (page 4)

LEVEL A. Write **declarative** or **interrogative** to show what kind of sentence each one is.

1. What is the seed of an oak tree called?
2. A new oak tree grows from an acorn.
3. We have an oak tree in our backyard.
4. How many kinds of oak trees are there?
5. Our tree is a Northern Red Oak.
6. Does your tree lose its leaves?
7. How old do you think this tree is?
8. That tree was planted by my grandfather.
9. He planted several trees in our yard.
10. Do you like all of our trees?

LEVEL B. Write a period or a question mark to show how each sentence should be punctuated.

11. The seeds of a pine tree are found inside a cone
12. This sprout will someday be a large tree
13. Do pine trees stay green all year
14. Will you be planting more trees today
15. Which are the oldest trees in the world
16. Redwoods have survived for thousands of years
17. My uncle has many fruit trees on his farm
18. Have you ever picked apples or pears

LEVEL C. Write each sentence correctly.

19. we spent last weekend at the farm
20. the apple harvest was just starting
21. how many people work for your uncle
22. which foods can be made from apples
23. my aunt often serves sweet baked apples
24. my uncle makes jars of applesauce
25. how many apples are needed to make a pie

EXTRA PRACTICE

Three levels of practice

Imperative and Exclamatory Sentences (page 6)

LEVEL **A.** Write **imperative** or **exclamatory** to show what kind of sentence each one is.

1. Please teach me how to swim.
2. The water is too cold!
3. Show me how to float.
4. *Dog paddle* is such a funny name!
5. Put your face in the water.
6. How scared I was at first!
7. Don't be afraid of the water.
8. How brave you are!
9. Please give me your swimming cap.
10. Wow, her dive was really great!

LEVEL **B.** Write a period or an exclamation mark to show how each sentence should be punctuated.

11. Roller-skating is so much fun
12. Show me how to lace up the skates
13. Please hold my hand
14. What shaky knees I have
15. Tell me how you learned to skate
16. How fast everyone skates
17. Please let me practice
18. How happy I am

LEVEL **C.** Write each sentence correctly.

19. baseball is such a great sport
20. help me to learn to play the game
21. let me watch while you bat the ball
22. please tell me how to hold the bat
23. i would love to be a catcher
24. please call me before the game starts
25. wait for me at the corner of Jay Street

EXTRA PRACTICE

GRAMMAR

Three levels of practice

Complete Subjects and Complete Predicates (page 8)

LEVEL **A.** Write **subject** if the complete subject is underlined. Write **predicate** if the complete predicate is underlined.

1. Ms. Tantillo <u>teaches a painting class</u>.
2. <u>Groups of students</u> go to her studio.
3. <u>My sister</u> takes lessons on Saturdays.
4. I <u>begin my art class next month</u>.
5. My first class <u>is about watercolors</u>.
6. <u>I</u> will try painting with oils next.
7. The teacher <u>mixes her own colors</u>.
8. <u>She</u> uses a variety of brushes.
9. Her own paintings <u>are outstanding</u>.
10. <u>My paintings</u> will be as good as hers.

LEVEL **B.** Write each sentence. Draw a line between the complete subject and the complete predicate.

11. Some people build things as a hobby.
12. My mother made a birdhouse last week.
13. She cut the wood with a small saw.
14. The pieces fit together nicely.
15. We added a perch to the front.
16. The birdhouse hangs from a large tree.
17. Two little birds live in the house.
18. They bring food and twigs inside.

LEVEL **C.** Write each sentence. Add a complete subject or a complete predicate to each blank.

19. _____ plays the drums.
20. Other students _____ .
21. The teacher _____ .
22. _____ practiced all day.
23. The school band _____ .
24. _____ marches in the band.
25. The music _____ .

EXTRA PRACTICE

Three levels of practice

Simple Subjects (page 10)

LEVEL **A.** The complete subject in each sentence is underlined. Write the simple subject.

1. My cat had five kittens.
2. The kittens sleep in a box.
3. The mother cat cares for her babies.
4. The babies eat all day long.
5. My friend wants one of the kittens.
6. Her family loves animals.
7. The new kittens keep me busy.
8. Their small faces are so cute.
9. The smallest kitten is my favorite.
10. Her fluffy tail is very nice.

LEVEL **B.** Write the complete subject of each sentence. Then underline the simple subject.

11. José visited the pet store.
12. His father went with him.
13. Many pets were on display.
14. A large turtle looked at José.
15. The turtle became José's first pet.
16. José's mother named her Nina.
17. Nina laid several eggs last week.
18. The eggs will hatch soon.

LEVEL **C.** Add a simple subject to complete each sentence.

19. Our _____ have a new pet.
20. A stray _____ came to their doorstep.
21. Its _____ woke the entire family.
22. A warm _____ quieted the hungry animal.
23. A _____ was made from old blankets.
24. The youngest _____ named the dog.
25. Its _____ is Goldie.

EXTRA PRACTICE

GRAMMAR

Three levels of practice

Simple Predicates (page 12)

LEVEL A. The complete predicate in each sentence is underlined. Write the simple predicate.

1. My mother tried a new recipe yesterday.
2. She found the recipe in the newspaper.
3. The newspaper prints recipes from around the world.
4. This recipe came from India.
5. My father bought the meat and spices.
6. I selected the vegetables.
7. We combined the meat, vegetables, and spices.
8. The family ate the delicious meal.
9. We cleaned our plates.
10. Everyone loved the spicy food.

LEVEL B. Write each sentence. Then underline the simple predicate.

11. People like baby fruits and vegetables.
12. The small size makes them appealing.
13. My aunt buys little eggplants.
14. She cooks them in a sauce.
15. My grandfather enjoys baby carrots.
16. He eats them as a snack.
17. I saw tiny pineapples the other day.
18. They are the newest item at the store.

LEVEL C. Add a simple predicate to complete each sentence.

19. Judy's parents _____ a new restaurant.
20. They _____ both good cooks.
21. The menu _____ many kinds of foods.
22. I _____ the desserts best.
23. Judy's father _____ the cakes and breads.
24. Her mother _____ the main dishes.
25. My family _____ at the new restaurant.

GRAMMAR

EXTRA PRACTICE

Three levels of practice

Compound Subjects and Compound Predicates (page 14)

LEVEL **A.** Write **compound subject** or **compound predicate** to tell which part of each sentence is underlined.

1. Mom and Dad discuss the move.
2. Books and magazines fit in this box.
3. The movers wrap and pack the dishes.
4. Chairs and tables are stacked against the wall.
5. Aunt Janet covers and labels all the food.
6. The dog and cat hide in the kitchen.
7. Friends and neighbors say good-bye.
8. The moving van turns and drives away.
9. My sister and I take a last look.
10. We smile and wave at the neighbors.

LEVEL **B.** Underline the two subjects in the compound subject or the two predicates in the compound predicate.

11. The new house and yard are on the corner.
12. The van turns sharply and stops.
13. The movers unload and carry the boxes.
14. My sister skips and runs around the yard.
15. My parents and I enter the house.
16. The blue couch and chair are left in the hall.
17. The bookcase and desk fit in my room.
18. Our cat sniffs and hisses at everything.

LEVEL **C.** Think of a word to complete each compound subject or compound predicate. Then write the sentence.

19. Our big dog _____ and runs in the yard.
20. Squirrels and _____ scatter at his bark.
21. Dishes and _____ are soon unpacked.
22. Everyone makes and _____ a sandwich.
23. We quietly talk and _____ for tomorrow.
24. Our papers and _____ are in our book bags.
25. We write and _____ about our classes.

EXTRA PRACTICE

Three levels of practice

Correcting Run-on Sentences (page 16)

LEVEL A. Write **run-on** if two sentences are run together. Write **sentence** if the sentence is correct.

1. The country was new the people wanted laws.
2. Delegates gathered in Philadelphia.
3. They met in the summer it was 1787.
4. The delegates argued the weeks passed.
5. The Constitution was ready in September.
6. A nation was born the people were pleased.
7. The colonies became a great nation.
8. America grew and prospered the population grew, too.
9. Our nation became a model for others to follow.
10. We are proud to be Americans.

LEVEL B. Write each item. Draw a line between complete thoughts.

11. The meeting was secret the doors were closed.
12. George Washington came he led the meeting.
13. James Madison took notes he wrote quickly.
14. Everyone had questions ideas were exchanged.
15. Twelve states sent delegates all arrived.
16. A few delegates became angry some people left.
17. Votes were taken the ballots were counted.
18. The delegates agreed they decided on many issues.

LEVEL C. Rewrite each run-on sentence as two separate sentences.

19. Some people wanted states' rights others voted against it.
20. Delegates believed in the people they thought the people should run the government.
21. Thirty-nine delegates signed the new Constitution they took their idea to the states.
22. Some wanted a bill of rights others said it was not needed.
23. The Bill of Rights was added it was approved in 1791.
24. It was a new idea for government the idea is still strong.
25. Our nation is over 200 years old it has changed very little.

PRACTICE + PLUS

Three levels of additional practice for a difficult skill

Correcting Run-on Sentences (page 16)

LEVEL **A.** Write **run-on** if two sentences are run together. Write **sentence** if the sentence is correct.

1. My sister Joanne is learning to read.
2. We have so much fun I read aloud to her.
3. I follow the words with my finger.
4. She looks at the picture she says the words.
5. I point to letters I tell her how they sound.
6. Soon, Joanne will be reading on her own.
7. We practice handwriting in school.
8. The teacher shows us examples we write sentences.
9. Some letters are hard to form.
10. I am left-handed my mother is also left-handed.
11. We hold the paper the same way.
12. My friend writes quickly I take more time.
13. A felt pen makes writing easier.
14. The felt pen has bright blue ink.
15. The ink dries quickly this makes writing easier.
16. Some students use pencils for class work.
17. I use my pen I think it makes my work neater.
18. Writing is fun I like to write stories.
19. Are your stories fun to read?
20. My stories are very interesting I write mysteries.
21. I work hard on my stories.
22. I think about exciting events I write them down.
23. I read them to Joanne she likes them.

LEVEL **B.** Rewrite each run-on sentence as two separate sentences.

24. I stood on stage for the first time today it was very exciting.
25. My class is putting on a play we were practicing.

PRACTICE + PLUS

26. I looked out at the empty seats the room seemed so big.
27. I hope everyone will hear me the teacher says to speak up.
28. The teacher has given me breathing exercises they have helped.
29. Our costumes don't fit it's so embarrassing.
30. We will have a costume fitting the costumes will be adjusted.
31. The scenery still needs work Ned will help.
32. The stage is so empty the furniture comes tomorrow.
33. My parents will come to the play they will take pictures.
34. My friends will be there, too I hope they like the play.
35. My friend Ellen plays the piano she will like the music.
36. I know the play will be a success we are all working hard.
37. Many tickets have been sold the cast is very excited.
38. We will use the ticket money for a new curtain we really need one.
39. Our school plays are good everyone enjoys them.
40. Sometimes we perform in comedies the audience laughs so much.
41. I like to act in comedies I like to hear the audience laugh.
42. Musicals are fun, too my voice is getting better.
43. The next play will be in the summer I will try out for that one, too.

LEVEL **C.** Rewrite the following paragraph. Correct the run-on sentences. (There are 7 punctuation errors.)

44.–50. My school has a soccer team. Three of my good friends are on our soccer team I always go to the games I enjoy watching the team play. The soccer games are held on Saturday afternoon. I go to the games with Susan my friend Susan likes the games, too she hopes to be on the team one day. Everyone has fun at the games we cheer for our team our team usually wins. After the games, we go for a snack everyone congratulates the players.

EXTRA PRACTICE

Three levels of practice

Mechanics: Punctuating Sentences (page 18)

LEVEL **A.** Write **declarative**, **interrogative**, **imperative**, or **exclamatory** to show what kind of sentence each one is.

1. What a mess this room is!
2. Will you help me clean it?
3. We will need two hours to finish the job.
4. Pick up all the books first.
5. On which shelf shall I put them?
6. Please show me where you put the toys.
7. I put the toys in the closet.
8. Why did you do that?
9. The toys belong in the closet on the shelf.
10. Put the other toys in the toy chest.

LEVEL **B.** Write each sentence correctly.

11. my family is planning a yard sale
12. what a good idea that is
13. on what day will the sale start
14. how much will you charge for these books
15. please bring something to sell
16. how will the sale money be used
17. a park will be built in the vacant lot
18. how exciting a new park will be

LEVEL **C.** Write each run-on sentence as two separate sentences. Be sure to capitalize and punctuate each sentence correctly.

19. we have many chores many people will help
20. the first chore is the town park it is a mess
21. the town park is dirty who will clean it
22. what a big job cleaning the park will be how many people have volunteered
23. most of the students will help please join us if you can
24. the town lent us a big truck will we have enough trash bags
25. we plan to begin this weekend the park will look great

EXTRA PRACTICE

GRAMMAR

Three levels of practice

Vocabulary Building: Using Context Clues (page 20)

LEVEL **A.** Write each sentence. Fill in the blank with a word from the list below. Use each word only once.

Descends means "goes down."
Encounter means "meet suddenly."
Rustle means "to move quietly."
Secure means "safe."
Wily means "clever."
Drowsy means "sleepy."

1. Night begins when the sun _____ behind the hills.
2. Not all animals are asleep and _____ in the night.
3. Mice hide so they will not _____ a fox.
4. The _____ fox could outsmart a mouse.
5. A _____ owl sits quietly on the branch.
6. Leaves _____ on the ground.

LEVEL **B.** Write the meaning of the underlined word in each sentence.

7. Bats <u>emerge</u> from the cave at night.
   a. come out   b. go in
8. These <u>nocturnal</u> animals usually fly after dark.
   a. of the night   b. of the day
9. My uncle has <u>researched</u> and written about all kinds of bats.
   a. explained   b. studied
10. He says bats are good animals that <u>benefit</u> people in many ways.
   a. hurt   b. help
11. They <u>devour</u> harmful insects for food.
   a. eat   b. count

LEVEL **C.** Use context clues to choose a word from the box to complete each sentence. Write the sentence.

animals	forest
sunset	guard
dark	roots
nests	quiet

12. Gray owls build _____ in fir trees.
13. They _____ their young against enemies.
14. Owls hunt in the dark after _____ .
15. Their favorite foods are mice and other _____ .

W R I T I N G

UNIT 2

Writing Personal Narratives

Read the quotation and look at the picture on the opposite page. How do you get ideas for writing?

When you write a personal narrative, you will want your audience to share your memory of an event that was very important to you.

Focus A personal narrative tells about something that happened in your life.

What event would you like to write about? On the following pages you will read a story about an event in a writer's life. You will find some interesting photographs, too. You can use both to give you ideas for writing.

THEME: *BEGINNINGS*

I like to carry an idea in the back of my mind for a while, allowing it to develop in its own way and in its own time. One day, when the story seems complete, I begin writing. . . .

—Clyde Robert Bulla

LITERATURE

Reading Like a Writer

What do you want to be when you grow up? Do you have dreams of being an artist, a doctor, or a teacher?

Clyde Robert Bulla knew that he wanted to be a writer from the time he was a child. Nobody seemed to approve of his dream, though. How could he show his family that he was serious?

As you read the selection, look for details that show you how the author feels.

A Writer Begins

from *A Grain of Wheat*
by Clyde Robert Bulla

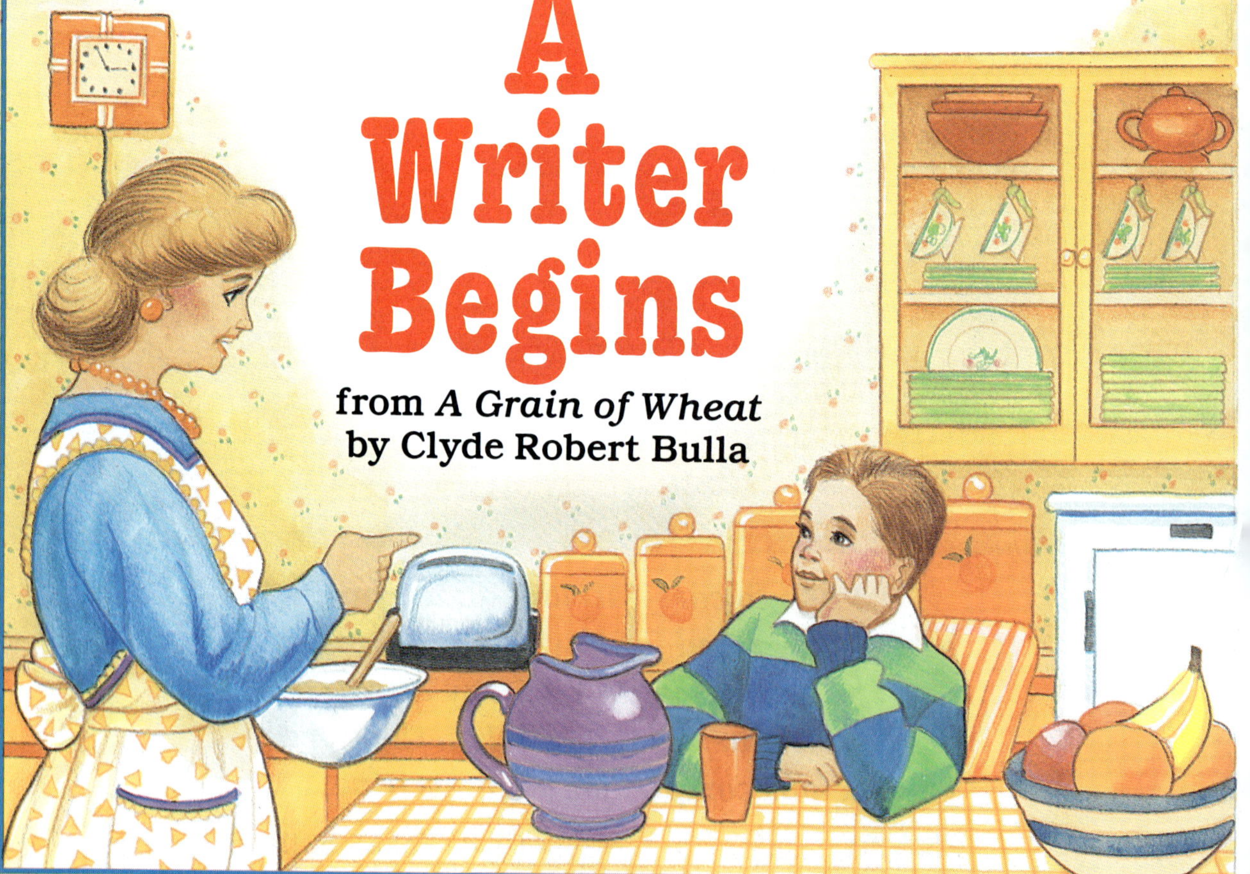

I wanted to be a writer. I was sure of that.

"I'm going to write books," I said.

My mother said, "Castles in the air."

"What does that mean?" I asked.

"It means you're having daydreams," she said. "You'll dream of doing a lot of different things, but you probably won't do any of them. As you get older, you'll change."

I went from the second grade to the third to the fourth, and I hadn't changed. I still knew what I wanted to be.

I thought about writing and talked about it. I talked too much.

My father told me he was tired of listening to me.

"You can't be a writer," he said. "What do you know about people? What have you ever done? You don't have anything to write about."

When I thought over what he had said, it seemed to me he was right. I stopped writing. But not for long.

The city nearest us was St. Joseph, Missouri. Our newspaper came from there. In the paper I read about a contest for boys and girls—"Write the story of a grain of wheat in five hundred words or less." First prize was a hundred dollars. There were five second prizes of twenty dollars each. After that there were one hundred prizes of one dollar each.

The main character is telling, or narrating, the story.

I began to write my story. It went something like this: "I am a grain of wheat. I grew in a field where the sun shone and the rain fell."

The events in the story are told in time order.

I didn't tell anyone what I was doing. When my story was finished, I made a neat copy. I mailed it in our mailbox down the road.

Time went by. I began to look for the newspaper that would tell who had won the contest. At last it came.

There was a whole page about the contest. I saw I hadn't won the first prize. I hadn't won a second prize either. That was a disappointment. I had thought I might win one of the second prizes.

I read down the long list at the bottom of the page—the names and addresses of the boys and girls who had won the one-dollar prizes. Surely my name would be there. It *had* to be!

I read more and more slowly. Only a few names were left.

And one of them was mine! "Clyde Bulla, King City, Missouri."

"I won!" I shouted.

My mother looked at my name. "That's nice," she said.

Nice? Was that all she could say?

I started to show the paper to my father. There was something in his face that stopped me. I could see he wasn't happy that I had won a prize.

My sister Corrine was there. I could see she wasn't happy either. She was sorry for me because all I had won was a dollar.

Didn't they know it wasn't the dollar that mattered?

The main character tells how he felt about winning a prize.

I had written a story that was all mine. No one had helped me. I had sent it off by myself. How many other boys and girls had sent their stories? Maybe a thousand or more. But my story had won a prize, and my name was here in the paper. I was a writer. No matter what anyone else might say, I was a writer.

A Note About the Author

You may be interested to know that the story you just read is true. At the age of ten, Clyde Robert Bulla was one of a hundred winners of a one-dollar prize awarded by a St. Joseph, Missouri, newspaper. He won the award for a story called "A Grain of Wheat." Since then, Bulla has written more than fifty books for young readers.

Thinking Like a Reader

1. If you and Clyde had been friends, would you have encouraged him to enter the writing contest? Why or why not?
2. If you won a writing contest, how would you feel? How would your family react?

Write your responses in your journal.

Thinking Like a Writer

3. How does the author help you to imagine the events that take place in the story and his feelings about them?
4. Do you like the way the story is told? What do you like about the story? What do you not like about it?

Write your responses in your journal.

Responding to

LITERATURE

Brainstorm *Vocabulary*

In "A Writer Begins," Clyde Bulla describes his own and his family's response when a story he writes wins a small prize. Think of something you did well or won—a game, a performance in a play, or a school assignment. In your journal write all the words and phrases that describe how you felt about the event. Begin to create a personal vocabulary list. You can use these words and phrases in your writing.

Talk It Over

Describe a Moment

Imagine that you have just won a contest. It can be any kind of contest you like. With a partner, imagine that you are being interviewed on the radio about winning. Describe your reasons for entering the contest. Did you expect to win? Were you and other people surprised that you won? Tell your partner about the experience.

Quick Write *A Headline*

You have imagined that you won a contest. Now imagine that the event will be reported in your local newspaper. Write a headline for the article. Try to make your headline attract your readers' attention. Use catchy words and phrases. For example, imagine that you won a baking contest.

Proud Fourth Grader Wins Mississippi Bake-Off

Write your headline on a separate sheet of paper. Keep it in your writing folder.

Idea Corner *Think of Events*

You probably have thought about exciting events that have taken place in your life. In your journal write down some of these events. Write a word or phrase after each one, telling how it made you feel. You might want to draw some pictures to illustrate one or more of the events. Write a caption for each picture.

PICTURES SEEING LIKE A WRITER

Finding Ideas for Writing

Look at the photographs on these pages. Think about what you see. What ideas for writing do the photographs give you? Write your ideas in your journal.

Los Angeles
Marathon
START

1 GROUP WRITING: A Personal Narrative

COOPERATIVE LEARNING

The **purpose** of a personal narrative is to tell about something that happened to you. Writers of a narrative think of their **audience**. What makes a personal narrative vivid and exciting for the audience?

- An Interesting Beginning Sentence
- Details About the Event
- Time Order

An Interesting Beginning Sentence

Read the personal narrative that Ben wrote. Think about what makes the underlined sentence special.

> <u>It did not take me long to like the new baby.</u> At first, I didn't even want to look at him. Why did my parents need a baby, anyway? Then, Mom pulled the blanket aside. I saw that his face was tiny. His eyes were tightly shut. Ugly, I thought. Finally, he opened his eyes. I stared at him, and after a minute he smiled and blew a bubble. I had to grin. This was Christopher. This was my new brother!

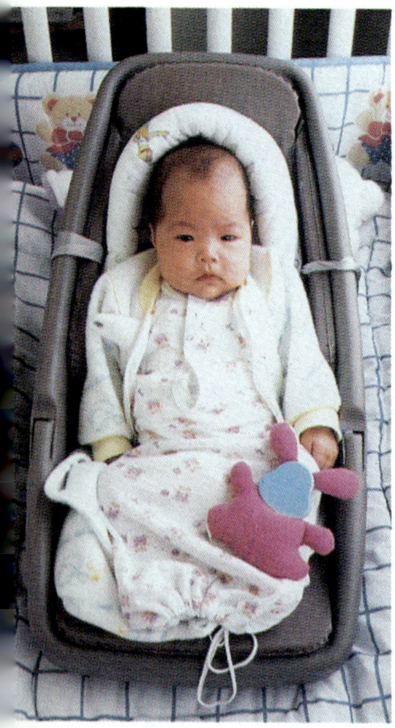

The underlined sentence begins the narrative in an interesting way. It catches the reader's attention. It also tells the **main idea**, or what the paragraph will be about.

Guided Practice: Writing an Interesting Beginning Sentence

With your class **brainstorm** about a day when something unexpected happened. Then decide on an interesting beginning sentence.

Example: My first day at the new school was not exciting until the fire bell rang.

Details About the Event

The middle of a personal narrative contains detail sentences. **Detail sentences** give specific information about the event being discussed. Detail sentences support, or say more about, the main idea.

In the paragraph on page 50, detail sentences tell why it did not take long for Ben to like the new baby. Look back at the paragraph.

- Which sentences tell what happened?
- Which sentences tell about Ben's thoughts and feelings?

Time Order

To help your readers clearly understand your experience, you may want to tell about events in the order in which they happened. To do this, you need to put your detail sentences in **time order.**

Look again at the narrative about Ben's new brother. Notice how Ben has told what happened in time order. He used time-order words to help his readers follow the events. Below are some time-order words you can use in your writing.

Time-Order Words			
first	next	then	finally

Guided Practice: Writing Details in Time Order

With your class, list details for your personal narrative. Now, write those details in complete sentences. Put the sentences in time order. Use time-order words to show the order of events.

Example:

1. First, hundreds of students marched out of the school.
2. Next, the doors closed with a clang.
3. Then, I noticed I was alone in the new school!

WRITING TOGETHER

Putting a Personal Narrative Together

With your classmates, you have thought of a topic for a personal narrative. You also have written an interesting beginning sentence and several detail sentences. Now you are ready to put your sentences together into a paragraph. Remember, a paragraph is a group of sentences that tell about one main idea.

Read your beginning sentence. Does it tell the main idea of your narrative? Read your detail sentences. Do they tell more about the day when something unexpected happened?

Here is a narrative that one student wrote. Notice how the student has put the beginning sentence and detail sentences together. The events are told in time order, and the writer has used time-order words to help her readers follow the events. How does the ending finish the narrative in a way that makes sense?

My first day at the new school was not exciting until the fire bell rang. First, hundreds of students marched out of the school. Next, the doors closed with a clang. Then, I noticed I was alone in the new school! I was afraid, but I looked for a door with a red EXIT sign above it. Finally, I pushed out into the sunlight and breathed a big sigh of relief.

Guided Practice: Writing a Personal Narrative

Write a personal narrative by putting the beginning sentence and the detail sentences that you wrote together. Remember to use time-order words to show the order of events. Add an ending that finishes your narrative in a way that makes sense.

Share your narrative with a friend. Ask your friend to suggest ways in which you can make your narrative more interesting or exciting.

Checklist: A Personal Narrative

When you write a personal narrative, you will want to keep some points in mind. A checklist will remind you of the things you want to include in the next personal narrative that you write.

Look at this checklist. Some points need to be added. Make a copy of the checklist and complete it. Keep a copy of it in your writing folder. You can use it to check yourself when you write your personal narrative.

CHECKLIST

- ✓ Purpose and ________
- ✓ Interesting beginning sentence
- ✓ Details about the event
- ✓ Time-order words
  - ■ First
  - ■ ________
  - ■ ________

WRITING TOGETHER

2 THINKING AND WRITING: Main Idea and Details

Think about what you have learned about writing a personal narrative. You know that you want to tell about something that happened to you. You also know that you want to begin in an interesting way.

A writer can begin a personal narrative by telling the main idea. The main idea may be stated in one sentence. Other sentences should be detail sentences. They should support, or tell more about, the main idea.

Look at this page from a writer's journal. The writer plans to write a personal narrative about his exciting day at the carnival. He lists many details on the page.

wild rides
cotton candy in hair
fun games
won a prize
sudden thunderstorm
called Grandma later

Thinking Like a Writer

- What sentence might the writer use to begin his narrative?
- Which details would he include and which would he leave out?

The writer wants his beginning sentence to be interesting. He also wants it to state the main idea of his paragraph. Therefore, he would begin with a sentence like this one: *I will never forget the exciting day I spent at the carnival.* His detail sentences would tell only about the carnival, not about calling Grandma later.

THINKING APPLICATION Main Idea and Details

COOPERATIVE LEARNING

Each of the writers named below is writing a personal narrative. Each has written a first sentence and has jotted down some details. Help the writers to select the best details to include in their narratives. Write the details on a separate sheet of paper. You may wish to discuss your thinking with other students.

1. Sally: My first day in ballet class was a disaster.

   forgot my ballet slippers
   stubbed my toe
   discovered I was in the wrong room
   had a sandwich for lunch

2. Andrew: The coach finally made me a pitcher.

   had been practicing my pitches
   asked the coach for a chance
   learned to hold the bat better
   pitched very well in a practice game

3. Tammy: I once had my picture in the newspaper.

   found a lost wallet
   wore my brown shoes that day
   wallet belonged to the chief of police
   reporter took our picture

4. Hernando: My last birthday was wonderful.

   have an older sister
   family made me a special dinner
   many friends signed card
   present was on my bed

3 INDEPENDENT WRITING: A Personal Narrative

Prewrite: Step 1

You have learned quite a bit about personal narratives. Now, it is time to choose a topic of your own for writing. Corrie, a student your age, wanted to write about something that had happened to her. She wanted to write a narrative that her classmates would find interesting. She chose a topic in this way.

Choosing a Topic

1. Corrie wrote a list of several events that had happened recently.
2. She carefully thought about the details of each event.
3. She chose the event that she thought was the most interesting.

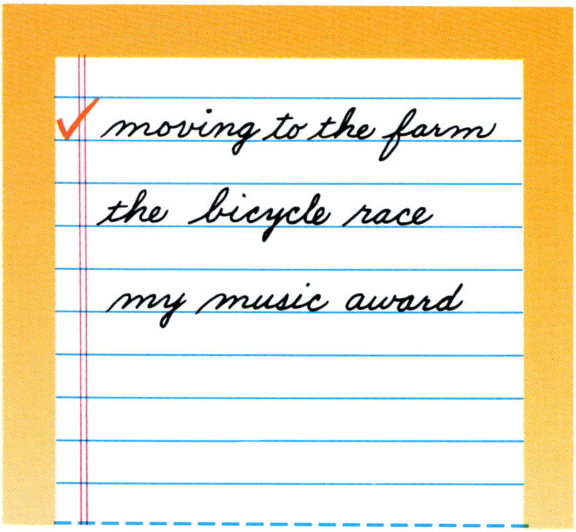

Corrie chose to write about her family's move to a farm. She decided to narrow her topic to only their arrival at their new home.

Exploring Ideas: Brainstorming Strategy

Corrie explored her topic by **brainstorming** for a main idea. She closed her eyes and thought about what was interesting about her first day on the farm. She knew that finding a new friend had made the day special. She decided to begin her narrative in this way.

The day we moved to the farm, I made a new friend.

Before beginning to write, Corrie again brainstormed for ideas. This time, she tried to recall as many details of the day as possible. She wrote those details on a **time line** to show them in time order.

After Corrie finished her time line, she reviewed it and made some changes. She wanted to make sure that the order of events in her narrative would be clear to her classmates.

Thinking Like a Writer

- What did Corrie add to her time line?
- What did she decide to move?
- Why do you think she moved that part?

YOUR TURN

JOURNAL

Think of an event that you would like to write about. Use **Pictures** or your journal as a source of ideas. Follow these steps.

- Make a list of possible events.
- Choose the one you like best.
- Narrow your topic if it is too broad.
- Brainstorm a main idea and details for your narrative.
- Think about your purpose and audience.

Make a time line. Remember, you can add to, take away from, or change the order of details on your time line at any time.

Write a First Draft: Step 2

Corrie knows what a personal narrative should include. She made a planning checklist and is ready to write her first draft.

Corrie's First Draft

The day we moved to the farm, I made a new friend. I missed my old freinds. I wandered into the barn. Inside, the barn was dark. Quiet, too. Then, I heard a funny noise what could it be. I went to look. It was a pony. I turned to run and tell Mom and dad, but they were right behind me. Finally, I knew that the pony was mine.

While Corrie was writing her first draft, she did not worry about errors. She was interested only in putting her ideas down on paper.

Planning Checklist

- Remember purpose and audience.
- Begin in an interesting way.
- Include detail sentences.
- Use time-order words.

YOUR TURN

Write your first draft. As you prepare to write, ask yourself these questions.

- What will my audience want to know?
- What is my main idea? What details can I include to support it?

TIME-OUT You might want to take some time out before you revise. That way you will be able to revise your writing with a fresh eye.

Revise: Step 3

After she had finished her first draft, Corrie read it over to herself. Then, she showed her personal narrative to a friend. She wanted some suggestions for improvement. She asked her friend if she thought the narrative could use more details.

Corrie then looked back at her planning checklist. She saw that she had forgotten one point. She checked it off so that she would remember it when she revised her narrative. Corrie now has a checklist to use as she revises her draft.

Corrie made changes to her personal narrative. Notice that she did not correct small errors. She knew that she could fix them later.

The revisions that Corrie made changed her paragraph. Turn the page. Look at Corrie's revised draft.

Revising Checklist

- Remember purpose and audience.
- Begin in an interesting way.
- ✓ Include detail sentences.
- Use time-order words.

WRITING PROCESS

Corrie's Revised Draft

The day we moved to the farm, I made a new friend. I missed my old freinds. I wandered into the barn. Inside, the barn was dark and quiet. ~~Quiet, too.~~ Then, I heard a funny noise what could it be. I went to look and saw that ~~It~~ it was a pony. I turned to run and tell Mom and dad, but they were right behind me. They were smiling. Finally, I knew that the pony was mine.

Thinking Like a Writer

WISE WORD CHOICE

- Which sentence and details did Corrie add? How do they improve the narrative?
- Which sentences did she combine? How does combining them improve her writing?

YOUR TURN

Read your first draft. Make a checklist. Ask yourself these questions.

- What makes my beginning sentence interesting? Is the main idea clear?
- Which details support the main idea? Which do not?
- How can I improve the order of my sentences?

If you wish, ask a friend to read your narrative and make suggestions. Then, revise your writing.

Proofread: Step 4

Corrie knew that her work was not complete until she proofread her personal narrative. She still had to correct her spelling, punctuation, and grammar errors. Corrie used a proofreading checklist while she proofread.

Part of Corrie's Proofread Draft

friends
I missed my old freinds. I wandered into the barn.
and quiet.
Inside, the barn was dark, Quiet, too. Then, I heard
? and saw that
a funny noise. what could it be. I went to look. It
!
was a pony. I turned to run and tell Mom and dad,
They were smiling.
but they were right behind me. Finally, I knew

YOUR TURN

Proofreading Practice

Below is a paragraph that you can use to practice your proofreading skills. Look for run-on sentences and errors in spelling and punctuation. Write the paragraph correctly on a separate sheet of paper.

> On the night of the talent show, I discovered that I love to sing? At first, I was rilly scared. In fact, I was too scared to make a sound. Then, I found the first note soon I forgot the audience. When I finished the song, everyone clapped and cheered

Proofreading Checklist

- Did I indent each paragraph?
- Did I spell words correctly?
- What punctuation errors do I need to correct?
- What capitalization errors do I need to correct?

WRITING PROCESS

Applying Your Proofreading Skills

Now, proofread your personal narrative. Read your checklist again. Review **The Grammar Connection** and **The Mechanics Connection.** Use the proofreading marks to mark changes.

THE GRAMMAR CONNECTION

Remember this rule about run-on sentences.

- A **run-on sentence** contains two or more sentences that should stand alone. You can correct a run-on sentence by writing each sentence separately.

  The weather was lovely the sky was clear and sunny.

  The weather was lovely. The sky was clear and sunny.

Check your narrative. Have you corrected any run-on sentences?

THE MECHANICS CONNECTION

Remember these rules about punctuating sentences.

- A **declarative sentence** ends with a period.
  It is snowing outside.
- An **interrogative sentence** ends with a question mark.
  Do you like snow**?**
- An **imperative sentence** ends with a period.
  Please wear a scarf if you go outside**.**
- An **exclamatory sentence** ends with an exclamation mark.
  How awful it would be to get sick**!**

Check your personal narrative. Have you punctuated your sentences correctly?

Proofreading Marks

- ¶ indent
- ∧ add
- ℯ take out
- ≡ capital letter
- / make a small letter

Publish: Step 5

Corrie decided to share her writing with her classmates in a special way. She thought of a title for her personal narrative and wrote it on a sheet of construction paper. Underneath the title she wrote her name. Then, on a separate sheet of paper, she made a neat final copy of her narrative. She stapled her title page, the page with her narrative, and a blank sheet of construction paper together to make a book.

YOUR TURN

Make a neat final copy of your personal narrative. Think of a way to share your narrative. You might find an idea in the **Sharing Suggestions** box below.

SHARING SUGGESTIONS

Present your narrative as a comic strip. Show the events as a series of pictures. Write sentences from your narrative beneath each picture.

Read your narrative into a tape recorder. Add sound effects if you like. Play the recording for your friends or family.

Create a class book of personal narratives. Illustrate the book with photographs or drawings. Ask the school librarian to display the book in the library.

4 SPEAKING AND LISTENING: Conducting an Interview

You have just written a personal narrative that expressed your feelings about an event. By conducting an interview, you can discover another person's feelings about an event. In an interview, one person asks questions about something the other person has done.

To prepare to interview someone, make a list of the questions you plan to ask. Ask *who, what, where, why, when,* and *how* questions to help the person you are interviewing remember details about the event and how he or she felt about it.

You may want to write the questions in a notebook. Leave space after each question for notes about what the person says.

Look at these questions from one interviewer's notebook.

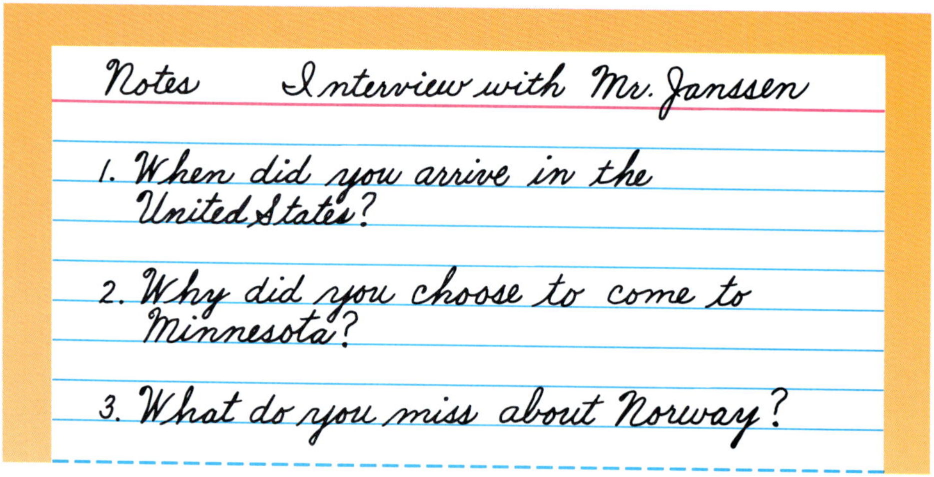
Notes Interview with Mr. Janssen

1. When did you arrive in the United States?
2. Why did you choose to come to Minnesota?
3. What do you miss about Norway?

Notice that the questions are specific. Specific questions help the person who is being interviewed to remember details about the event.

When you conduct an interview, keep these speaking guidelines in mind. They will help you to focus your interview.

SPEAKING GUIDELINES: An Interview

1. Explain why you are conducting the interview. For example, you might say you are gathering ideas for a personal narrative.
2. Ask *who*, *what*, *when*, *where*, *why*, and *how* questions. These questions will lead you to the information you want.
3. Be friendly and polite. Try to make the person you are interviewing feel at ease.
4. Listen closely to answers. Ask questions if you are not sure what the person means.
5. Thank the person when the interview is finished.

- Why is it important to be friendly and polite in an interview?
- What kinds of questions should I ask?

SPEAKING APPLICATION An Interview

Set up an interview with someone in your class. Decide on a topic, such as a trip the person has taken or a favorite day in school. Write your questions in a notebook. Leave space after each question so that you will have room to write notes about the answer. Use the speaking guidelines to help you to prepare for the interview. Your partner will be using the following listening guidelines as he or she is interviewed.

LISTENING GUIDELINES: An Interview

1. Look at the person who is interviewing you.
2. Listen carefully to the questions.
3. Think about what the interviewer wants to know.
4. Think about your answers. Are they clear? Is there anything you wish to add?

WRITING EXTENSION

5 WRITER'S RESOURCES: The Dictionary

An excellent resource for writers is the dictionary. It can help you say or spell a word. It can also tell you what a word means and how it is used in a sentence. A dictionary includes many words. The words are arranged in **alphabetical order.**

Follow these steps to find a word in the dictionary:

1. Think about the first letter of the word. Find the section of the dictionary that has words beginning with that letter.
2. Look for the correct page. Use the guide words in dark type at the top of the page to help you. **Guide words** tell you the first and last words on a page.
3. Think about the alphabet. Decide if your word comes between the guide words. If it doesn't, look on another page.

Here is one **entry word** from a dictionary. Notice that a **respelling**, or pronunciation, is printed in parentheses ( ) after the entry word. The respelling tells you how to say the word. It has special signs and letters that stand for each of the sounds in our language.

> **nar•rate** (nar′āt *or* na rāt′) *verb,* **narrated, narrating.** To tell or relate.

Look at the **pronunciation key** below. You will find a pronunciation key at the bottom of every page or every other page in a dictionary. The pronunciation key can help you read a respelling. It shows you how to say the signs for every vowel. It also gives you a sample word for each sound.

> **at**; **āpe**; **fär**; **câre**; **end**; **mē**; **it**; **īce**; **pîerce**; **hot**; **ōld**; **sông**, **fôrk**; **oil**; **out**; **up**; **ūse**; **rüle**; **pu̇ll**; **tûrn**; **chin**; **sing**; **shop**; **thin**; **this**; **hw** in **white**; **zh** in trea**s**ure. The symbol **ə** stands for the unstressed vowel sound heard in **a**bout, tak**e**n, penc**i**l, lem**o**n, and circ**u**s.

Practice

1. Copy the following chart. Then, write five words under each heading that would be found in that part of the dictionary.

	Beginning a b c d e f g	Middle h i j k l m n o p q	End r s t u v w x y z
Example	dog	keep	violin

2. Select three words from those you listed on your chart. Find the words in your dictionary. For each, write the guide words that appear on the top of the dictionary page.

Example: violin **vigor/Virginia**

3. Write the words from the pronunciation key on page 66 that help you pronounce the vowel sound in each of these words:

weigh (wā) down (doun) meal (mēl)

4. Does the word *woe* (wō) rhyme with *shoe* or *row*? Use the pronunciation key to help you answer the question.

WRITING APPLICATION Sentences

Read the following section of a personal narrative. Use a dictionary to look up the underlined words. Use each of the words in a sentence of your own. Correct the spelling of the word if necessary.

> I remember my first day wearing glasses. I did not have to squint to read the board. Also, I could recognise my friends from far away. I felt a little embarrassed about wearing glasses. However, I thought having clear vision was worth it.

6 WRITER'S RESOURCES: Dictionary Entries

As you know, a dictionary gives you information about words. One type of information it gives you is the meaning of words.

Some words have more than one meaning. The dictionary gives each meaning of the word. You will find a **1.** in front of the first meaning. You will find a **2.** in front of the second meaning, a **3.** in front of the third meaning, and so on. Sometimes, there is an example sentence to help you to understand the meaning of the word.

Look at the dictionary entry below. Notice the three meanings of the word *justice*. Also, notice the sentences that use the word and show its meanings. How do these sentences help you to better understand the meanings of *justice*?

> **justice** **1.** Fair or right treatment or action. The lawyer demanded *justice* for the innocent person. **2.** The quality or condition of being fair and right. *Justice* demands that all people be treated as equals in a court of law. **3.** A judge of the Supreme Court of the United States.
> **jus·tice** (jus′tis) *noun, plural* **justices.**

Some dictionaries tell more about a word than just its meaning. A dictionary may give you the following facts about a word:

1. how to divide the word into parts, or syllables
2. how to say, or pronounce, the word
3. how to spell the plural form of the word, especially if it requires a spelling change
4. whether the word is a noun, verb, or other part of speech, and how it is used in a sentence.

Look again at the dictionary entry above. Notice the facts it tells you about the word *justice*.

Practice

Look at this dictionary entry. Then, answer the questions. Write your answers on a separate sheet of paper.

> **nationality** **1.** The fact or condition of belonging to a particular nation. That painter's *nationality* is French. **2.** A group of people who share the same language, culture, and history. People of many *nationalities* work at the United Nations.
> **na•tion•al•i•ty** (nash′ ə nal′ i tē) *noun, plural* **nationalities.**

1. How many meanings are given for the word?
2. What sample sentence is given for the first meaning? Write the sentence.
3. How many syllables does the word have?
4. Is the word used as a noun or a verb?
5. Write the spelling of the plural form of the word.

WRITING APPLICATION A Paragraph

With a partner look up a word that you both like in the dictionary. Write the word and the information you find about it. On the same sheet of paper, write a paragraph that uses the word in a sentence. Then, share your writing.

WRITING EXTENSION

THE CURRICULUM CONNECTION

Writing About Communications

Communication means "sharing ideas." Every day we communicate with our family and friends. Although most of our daily communication takes place through conversation, we share our ideas in many ways. In addition to talking with each other, we read and write for newspapers, magazines, and books. We speak on and listen to television and radio.

Newspapers, magazines, radio, and television are part of a field called **communications**. People who work in this field do many different kinds of jobs, from writing or acting to taking pictures. They have an important responsibility, communicating information and ideas that affect our daily lives.

ACTIVITIES

Use a Resource The following words apply to jobs in the field of communications. Choose three of the words and look them up in a dictionary. Write a definition for each word and use it in a sentence.

journalist   sportscast   disk jockey   screenplay

Describe a Photograph "One picture is worth a thousand words" is a famous saying. What do you think the words mean? What can you learn from a photograph? Look at the photograph at the top of page 71. What does the photograph communicate to you? Write a paragraph describing the photograph. In the paragraph explain what the photograph tells you about the people in the picture.

Respond to Literature The picture at the top of this page was taken by Gordon Parks. He also wrote the sentences in the box below.

Gordon Parks is a photojournalist. He uses his camera to tell true stories. Many of his famous photographs were taken for *Life* magazine during the 1950s.

Read Gordon Parks's words. What do you think he is trying to say? Then, look carefully at the picture. Write a response. For example, you may wish to write a paragraph explaining how Parks's work might help to get "the bitterness out" of him. Perhaps you might choose to respond by writing a caption for the photograph. Share your response with a classmate by exchanging papers.

> My work gets the bitterness out of me. I say what I can in photography. When that's not enough, I turn to writing music, poetry, or novels.

UNIT CHECKUP

LESSON 1 **Group Writing: A Personal Narrative** (page 50) These sentences from a personal narrative are out of order. Write the sentences in correct time order.

a. Later, when I called her at home, we argued.
b. Lucy and I had a fight, but we are friends again.
c. First, she forgot to walk with me to school.
d. I hope Lucy and I stay friends forever.
e. Finally, Lucy called back and apologized.

LESSON 2 **Thinking and Writing: Main Idea and Details** (page 54) Below is the beginning sentence of a narrative. Write the details that support the beginning sentence.

The first dinner I cooked was almost a total disaster.

1. lost my homework
2. forgot to defrost the chicken
3. burned my thumb
4. dropped a tomato
5. spilled the soup
6. did not watch television

LESSON 3 **Writing a Personal Narrative** (page 56) Imagine that you will be interviewed about something funny that has happened to you. Think of an experience and make notes about it. Then, use your notes to write a personal narrative.

LESSON 4 **Speaking and Listening: An Interview** (page 64) Write three questions that you might use in an interview with your favorite TV actor or actress. Remember to ask *who, what, why, when, where,* and *how* questions.

LESSONS 5-6 **Writer's Resources: The Dictionary** (pages 66–69) Look at the following guide words. Choose the words listed below that would fall between these guide words on a dictionary page. Write the words on a separate sheet of paper.

quail/quite quell quick quote quiet quill quiver

THEME PROJECT CRAFT PROJECT

You have been thinking about beginnings. You read a story about a writer's beginnings, and you wrote a personal narrative about a new experience in your life. Here is a chance to explore beginnings in a very creative way.

Think of all the objects we throw away every day—empty containers, worn-out clothes, old newspapers, paper bags, broken toys, and many other similar items. How many of those objects could have a new beginning if we used our imaginations?

Look at the pictures below.

What do you see in the pictures? Which objects have been used in new ways? Talk with your classmates about what you see. Describe what you think someone did to turn something old into something new.

- Find an object and give it a new beginning. For example, you might turn an empty milk carton into a planter for seeds.
- You might make a spare sock into a puppet.
- Use your imagination to give your object a new and interesting beginning.
- Write a paragraph telling how to create a new object from something old.

If you wish, work with other students on this project.

GRAMMAR

UNIT 3

Nouns

In this unit you will learn about nouns. When you talk or write about people, places, or things, you are often using nouns.

Discuss Read the poem on the opposite page. What different kinds of places does the poem mention?

JOURNAL

Creative Expression The unit theme is *Choices.* Have you ever had to choose between two things that you really wanted to do? Write a few sentences in your journal about how you made your choice. Were you happy with the choice you made?

THEME: *CHOICES*

When you walk in a field,
Look down
Lest you trample
A daisy's crown!

But in a city
Look always high
And watch
The beautiful clouds go by!

—James Stephens, "When You Walk"

1 WHAT IS A NOUN?

A noun is a word that names a person, place, or thing.

The world around you is filled with people, places, and things. Nouns are words that name those people, places, and things.

Nouns	
Persons	clerk, shoppers, children
Places	store, town, department
Things	clothes, bicycle, pets

A noun may appear in any part of a sentence.

Shoppers buy new **clothes** in the **store.**
One **department** may sell **bicycles.**

Look at this sentence.

The _____ will buy a _____ from the clerk.

Any word that fits the blank correctly is a noun. How many nouns can you think of to fill each blank?

Guided Practice

Find the two nouns in each sentence. Tell whether each noun names a person, a place, or a thing.

Example: A girl bought a toy. *girl, person* *toy, thing*

1. Some stores have more than one department.
2. These stores are often found near cities.
3. Each department sells certain items.
4. One floor may display furniture.
5. Signs help the shoppers.

?! **THINK**

■ How can I decide if a word is a noun?

REMEMBER

■ A **noun** names a person, place, or thing.

More Practice

Write each sentence. Underline each noun.

Example: Long ago, more people lived on farms.
people *farms*

6. Some families shopped in the nearest town.
7. Other people lived far away from towns.
8. Stores mailed catalogs to these people.
9. Customers ordered from the catalogs.
10. Plows and dresses could be ordered.
11. Even large wagons could be bought.
12. Orders were shipped from the city.
13. Many people shopped from only one catalog.
14. A few stores serviced the whole country.
15. People now shop in different places.
16. Most large towns have malls.
17. The mall contains several stores.
18. These stores sell many things.
19. Shoppers can buy shoes or clothes in one store.
20. Customers might go to another store for a radio.
21. A gardener can find a mower for the yard.
22. A camper can find a tent and a backpack.
23. Some stores sell small pets.
24. Children can find a puppy or a hamster.
25. A large store may have a restaurant.

Extra Practice, page 102

WRITING APPLICATION A Letter

Imagine that you have been shopping in a large department store. Write a letter to a friend. Describe the things you liked. Share your writing with a classmate. Ask your classmate to circle all the nouns in your letter.

G R A M M A R

2 SINGULAR NOUNS AND PLURAL NOUNS

You know that a noun is a word that names a person, a place, or a thing. A **singular noun** names only one person, place, or thing. A **plural noun** names more than one person, place, or thing.

One **bowl** is on the tray.
Many **bowls** are on the tray.

There are certain rules for writing plural nouns. Look at the chart below.

Rules	Singular	Plural
• Add *s* to form the plural of most nouns.	tree bowl	tree**s** bowl**s**
• Add *es* to form the plural of nouns ending in *s, x, ch,* or *sh.*	bus fox sandwich bush	bus**es** fox**es** sandwich**es** bush**es**

Guided Practice

Find the nouns in each sentence. Tell which nouns are singular and which nouns are plural.

Example: The girls play a game.
girls, plural   *game, singular*

1. The picnic will be fun.
2. Many students come to the picnic.
3. The table is filled with boxes and dishes.
4. The teachers sit on the benches in the park.
5. One student eats a big sandwich.

?! **THINK**

■ How can I decide if a noun is singular or plural?

REMEMBER

- A **singular noun** names one person, place, or thing. A **plural noun** names more than one person, place, or thing.
- Most plural nouns end in *s* or *es.*

More Practice

A. Find the nouns in each sentence. Then write each noun. Label each noun **singular** or **plural.**

Example: The table was under some trees. *table, singular trees, plural*

6. The picnic was held last year.
7. Many foods were served.
8. This year, tents will be put over the tables.
9. Guests will choose from many foods.
10. One booth will serve different fruits.
11. Bunches of grapes will be displayed.
12. Students can choose a salad or a sandwich.
13. Cider and milk will be served.

B. Write the plural form of each underlined noun.

Example: Food is prepared day ahead of time. *days*

14. Food box are being stored at the school.
15. Several bus will take them to the park.
16. The picnic menu will be given out.
17. Someone has to count the glass for the drinks.
18. Many dish will be served to the guests.
19. Has anyone volunteered to cook the hamburger?
20. We hope there will not be any weather delay.

Extra Practice, page 103

WRITING APPLICATION A Menu

Plan and write a menu for a picnic lunch. List several foods. Exchange menus with a classmate. Look for plural nouns in your partner's menu.

3 MORE SINGULAR NOUNS AND PLURAL NOUNS

Some nouns that end in *y* form their plurals in a special way.

Rules	Singular	Plural
• Add *s* if a noun ends in a vowel and *y*.	boy key	boy**s** key**s**
• Change the *y* to *i* and add *es* if a noun ends in a consonant and *y*.	family country berry	famil**ies** countr**ies** berr**ies**

The boy eats the berry.

The boys eat the berries.

Guided Practice

Spell the plural form of each noun.

Example: cherry *cherries*

1. lady
2. holidays
3. daisy
4. turkey
5. company
6. fly
7. subway
8. canary
9. puppy
10. birthday

?! THINK

■ How can I decide whether to add *s* or *es* to a noun that ends in *y*?

REMEMBER

- To form the plural of nouns ending in a vowel and *y*, add **s.**
- To form the plural of nouns ending in a consonant and *y*, change the *y* to **i** and add **es.**

More Practice

A. Write the plural form of each noun.

Example: factory *factories*

11. guppy
12. bay
13. valley
14. baby
15. lily
16. jay
17. city
18. monkey

B. Complete each sentence. Write the plural form of the noun in parentheses ( ).

Example: Susan attended three _____ this month. (party) *parties*

19. Three classmates had _____ . (birthday)
20. A friend received two stuffed _____ . (puppy)
21. She really liked the _____ . (toy)
22. Girls and _____ played games. (boy)
23. Some children told _____ . (story)
24. At one party actors performed short _____ . (play)
25. At another party the children rode _____ . (donkey)

Extra Practice, page 104

WRITING APPLICATION A Description

Work with a partner. List animal names that end in *y*. Choose two animals to compare or contrast. Write a description of the animals. Here are some animal names to get you started.

pony monkey donkey stingray

With your partner, check your work. Have you spelled the plural nouns correctly?

GRAMMAR

4 MORE PLURAL NOUNS

As you know, you add *s* or *es* to singular nouns to form most plural nouns. The plural forms of some nouns do not follow a regular spelling pattern. These nouns have special plural forms.

Singular	Plural
woman	women
man	men
child	children
foot	feet

Singular	Plural
tooth	teeth
goose	geese
mouse	mice
ox	oxen

Some nouns can be used to mean both one and more than one. Their singular and plural forms are the same.

Singular	Plural
She has a pet **sheep**.	Her book is about **sheep**.
One **deer** stood nearby.	I read about three **deer**.
Have you seen a **moose**?	Two **moose** stared at me.

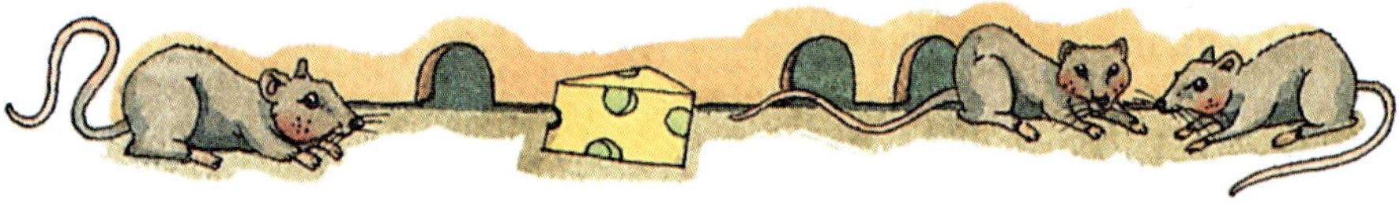

Guided Practice

Complete each sentence. Use the correct plural form of the noun in parentheses ( ).

Example: The (sheep) grazed in the meadow. *sheep*

1. Adults and (child) use the library.
2. (Man) and women can find interesting books.
3. Several books tell about raising pet (mouse).

?! **THINK**

■ How can I remember which nouns have special plural forms?

REMEMBER

- Some nouns have special plural forms.
- A few nouns have the same singular and plural forms.

More Practice

Write each sentence. Use the plural form of the noun in parentheses ( ).

Example: The library lists several books about (mouse). *mice*

4. This book shows different kinds of (goose).
5. There are even books about caring for (sheep).
6. Look in the card catalog for the titles of books about (moose).
7. Someone wants to write a report about (ox).
8. The encyclopedia article tells about (goose).
9. The magazine shows (deer) at the zoo.
10. This book is about men and (woman) who moved west in the 1800s.
11. The (child) rode in a wagon pulled by an ox.
12. I wanted a book about (tooth) for my report.
13. A runner chose several books that gave instructions for the proper care of (foot).
14. Here is a book about training (mouse)!
15. The news article is about famous (man) in sports.
16. There are two articles about (deer).
17. The class wants a story about pet (mouse).
18. The book about the (ox) was not returned.
19. Choose a book for (child) about pet geese.
20. Does the library have a book about (moose)?

Extra Practice, page 105

WRITING APPLICATION A Review

COOPERATIVE LEARNING

Write a review of one of your favorite library books. Illustrate your book review if you wish. Share your review with two of your classmates. Ask them to help you identify any special forms of plural nouns in your book review.

GRAMMAR

5 COMMON NOUNS AND PROPER NOUNS

You have learned that a noun is a word that names a person, a place, or a thing. A **common noun** names any person, place, or thing. A **proper noun** names a particular person, place, or thing.

Common Nouns	
Person	farmer, child, aunt
Place	state, beach, country
Thing	month, holiday, dog

Proper Nouns	
Person	Jack, Lisa, Aunt Julie
Place	Texas, Jones Beach, United States of America
Thing	September, Thanksgiving, Rover

Notice that a proper noun always begins with a capital letter. In a proper noun that has more than one word, each important word begins with a capital letter.

Guided Practice

Find the nouns in each sentence. Tell whether each is a common noun or a proper noun.

Example: Does Sara like apples? *Sara, proper apples, common*

1. The apple was first grown in Europe and Asia.
2. Many apples are grown in the United States.
3. Is New York known for its apples?
4. There are many orchards in Ulster County.
5. The farmers must pick the fruit by late September.

?! **THINK**

■ How can I tell whether a word is a common noun or a proper noun?

REMEMBER

- A **common noun** names any person, place, or thing.
- A **proper noun** names a special person, place, or thing.

More Practice

A. Write the nouns in each sentence. Then write **common** or **proper** next to each one to show what kind of noun it is.

Example: Many different fruits are grown in North America.
fruits, common   North America, proper

6. Many states in the United States grow apples.
7. Do apples grow in the state of Washington?
8. In America apples are often baked in pies.
9. Many people enjoy this fruit.
10. Some children bob for apples on Halloween.

B. Write each sentence correctly by capitalizing the proper nouns. Then underline any common nouns that you find.

Example: Yesterday, ted made <u>cider</u> from <u>apples</u>.   *Ted*

11. Will jan serve apples for dessert?
12. The apples from new york taste sweet.
13. Choose an apple from rhode island for tom.
14. Many apples are grown near yakima, washington.
15. The crops in the valley are picked in october.
16. By thanksgiving markets are stocked with apples.
17. The browns have an orchard near winslow hills.
18. Aunt doris hankes owns the orchard.
19. Doris walks through her orchards each monday.
20. Uncle max ships apples to texas.

Extra Practice, page 106

WRITING APPLICATION A Recipe

Find information about different kinds of oranges, potatoes, or beans. Then, choose one fruit or vegetable. Create a recipe using the fruit or vegetable of your choice.

GRAMMAR

6 SINGULAR POSSESSIVE NOUNS

You can use nouns in many different ways. Some nouns show that someone or something owns or has something. A singular noun that shows ownership is called a **singular possessive noun.**

Singular Noun	Singular Possessive Noun
The wheelchair of **Bob** is new.	**Bob's** wheelchair is new.
The hearing aid **Pam** owns helps her in class.	**Pam's** hearing aid helps her in class.
The book the **boy** has is written in Braille.	The **boy's** book is written in Braille.

Notice that by adding an **apostrophe** and **s ('s)** to a singular noun, you can make it possessive.

Guided Practice

Say each phrase another way. Use the possessive form of the underlined noun.

Example: the job of the <u>nurse</u>   *the nurse's job*

1. the help of the <u>teacher</u>
2. the research of the <u>doctor</u>
3. the leash of the <u>dog</u>
4. the telephone <u>Jerry</u> owns
5. the glasses <u>Pearl</u> has

?! **THINK**

■ How can I write the singular possessive form of a noun?

GRAMMAR

REMEMBER

- Form a singular possessive noun by adding an **apostrophe** and an **s ('s)** to a singular noun.

More Practice

A. Write each phrase in another way. Use the possessive form of the noun in dark type.

Example: the cane of the **person** *the person's cane*

6. the problem of the **man**
7. a chair belonging to **Sarah**
8. eyesight of the **dog**
9. computer used by the **boy**
10. painting done by **Donna**
11. the jacket of my **brother**
12. typewriter of our **neighbor**

B. Write each sentence. Use the singular possessive form of the noun in parentheses ( ) to complete each sentence.

Example: The _____ wheelchair is electric. (girl) *girl's*

13. A blind _____ talking books help him learn. (boy)
14. _____ dog helps him cross the street. (Sam)
15. The _____ training has helped Sam. (dog)
16. _____ car has special controls. (Bev)
17. _____ parking space is specially marked. (Joe)
18. The lights in _____ home are voice controlled. (Li)
19. _____ friends help him. (Leroy)
20. Dr. _____ note compliments Leroy. (Chou)

Extra Practice, page 107

WRITING APPLICATION An Explanation

COOPERATIVE LEARNING

Invent something that could help a handicapped person. Write a paragraph explaining how to use your invention. Share your writing with your class. Ask your classmates to point out any singular possessive nouns in your paragraph.

GRAMMAR

7 PLURAL POSSESSIVE NOUNS

Just as a singular noun can show what one person or thing owns or has, a plural noun can show what more than one person or thing owns or has. A plural noun that shows ownership is a **plural possessive noun.**

Here are two rules for forming plural possessive nouns.

- When a plural noun ends in *s,* add an apostrophe.

  voices of the singers — the singers' voices

- When a plural noun does not end in *s,* add an **apostrophe** and **s ('s).**

  bells of the sheep — the sheep**'s** bells

Guided Practice

Change each underlined plural noun to a plural possessive noun. Then, tell which word shows what the persons or things own or have.

Example: the horns of the animals — *animals' horns*

1. the votes of some people
2. the rights of all citizens
3. the decisions of all voters
4. the meeting of our classes
5. the park for many deer

?! THINK

- How can I write the plural possessive of a noun?

REMEMBER

- Add an apostrophe (') to a plural noun that ends in *s* to form the plural possessive.
- To form the plural possessive of a plural noun that does not end in *s*, add an **apostrophe** and **s ('s).**

More Practice

A. Rewrite each group of words. Use the possessive form of the noun in dark type.

Example: the topic of the **speakers** *the speakers' topic*

6. the rights of **people**
7. the choices of **voters**
8. the ideas of many **candidates**
9. the leadership of some **women**
10. the plans of those **leaders**
11. the laws of these **states**
12. the playgrounds of two **groups**
13. the wishes of many **families**
14. the ideas of some **students**
15. the hard work of all the **citizens**

B. Write the possessive form of each plural noun in parentheses ( ). Then write the sentence.

Example: Have the _____ rights been protected? (farmers)
Have the farmers' rights been protected?

16. People met to solve two _____ problems. (groups)
17. These _____ terms were not clear. (states)
18. Two _____ lands are the issue. (ranchers)
19. The _____ grazing lands are in danger. (oxen)
20. Are the _____ pens large enough? (sheep)

Extra Practice, page 108

WRITING APPLICATION A Town Law

Imagine that the parks in your town are filled with litter. Write a law that would solve this problem.

GRAMMAR

8 USING POSSESSIVE NOUNS

You use nouns often in your writing. The chart below shows the possessive forms of the different kinds of nouns you have studied.

Singular	Singular Possessive	Plural	Plural Possessive
teacher	teacher**'s**	teachers	teachers**'**
kitten	kitten**'s**	kittens	kittens**'**
child	child**'s**	children	children**'s**
man	man**'s**	men	men**'s**
deer	deer**'s**	deer	deer**'s**

Guided Practice

Find the possessive noun in each group of words. Tell whether it is a singular or a plural possessive.

Example: the child's toy *child's* *singular possessive*

1. the whales' big tails
2. the children's zoo
3. the woman's pink hat
4. the goose's baby
5. two deer's antlers

?! **THINK**

- How can I decide if a possessive noun is singular or plural?

REMEMBER

- A **singular possessive noun** is formed by adding an apostrophe and *s* **('s)** to a singular noun.
- The **plural possessive** of a plural noun that ends in *s* is formed by adding an apostrophe. An apostrophe and *s* **('s)** are added to a plural noun that does not end in *s*.

More Practice

A. Write the possessive noun in each sentence. Then, write whether it is a **singular** or **plural possessive.**

Example: The whale's tail is large. *whale's* *singular*

6. A dolphin's snout is pointed.
7. The porpoises' snouts are flat.
8. Many sea animals' habits are interesting.
9. The walruses' tricks are funny.
10. The sea otter's coat is shiny.
11. Children's shows are daily events.

B. Write the correct possessive form of each noun in parentheses ( ) to complete each sentence.

Example: Are the _____ hours listed? (zoo) *Are the zoo's hours listed?*

12. Will the _____ zoo open soon? (children)
13. The _____ cage is empty. (animal)
14. Are the _____ tails long? (monkeys)
15. Sue looked into the _____ den. (lion)
16. The _____ trunks are swinging. (elephants)
17. The two _____ tails are pretty. (peacocks)
18. Are the _____ cages nearby? (penguins)
19. The _____ pen is open. (sheep)
20. That _____ pass to the zoo is mine. (visitor)

Extra Practice, Practice Plus, pages 109-111

WRITING APPLICATION An Advertisement

Choose a favorite animal. Write an advertisement that describes the animal. Underline the possessive nouns.

9 MECHANICS: Abbreviations

Sometimes a proper noun is abbreviated. An **abbreviation** is the shortened form of a word. Most abbreviations begin with a capital letter and end with a period. Abbreviations are used in special kinds of writing, such as lists and addresses. Other abbreviations are in your **Handbook** on page 496.

Titles	Mr.	Mister	Dr.	Doctor
	Ms.	any woman	Sen.	Senator
	Mrs.	married woman	Gov.	Governor
Addresses	Ave.	Avenue	Co.	Company
	Dr.	Drive	P.O.	Post Office
Days	Mon.	Monday	Thurs.	Thursday
	Wed.	Wednesday	Sat.	Saturday
Months	Jan.	January	Sept.	September
	Apr.	April	Oct.	October

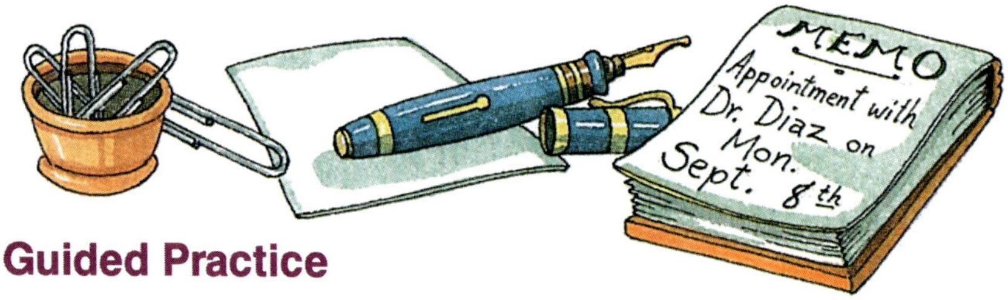

Guided Practice

Tell the abbreviation for each underlined word.

Example: Thursday afternoon *Thurs.*

1. Doctor Joan Che
2. Senator George Perez
3. Mister Mondosa
4. Post Office Box 82
5. Monday on Main Avenue

?! THINK

■ How do I recognize an abbreviation?

REMEMBER

- Most abbreviations begin with a capital letter and end with a period.

More Practice

Write the abbreviation for each underlined word. State name abbreviations are in your **Handbook** on page 496.

Example: 899 Main Street *St.*

6. Mister Stein
7. the Medi Company
8. Monday, October 3
9. 380 First Avenue
10. Doctor Tanya Simpson
11. Wednesday, April 4
12. Governor Black
13. 603 Canby Drive
14. Saturday in January
15. Senator Ellis
16. Mr. Carl Brown, Senior
17. Representative Eve Wong
18. 5 Grant Boulevard
19. 16 River Road
20. Friday, August 21
21. Tuesday, June 22
22. Post Office Box 309
23. Thomas Flynn, Junior
24. December 31, 1992
25. Thursday, February 6

Extra Practice, page 112

WRITING APPLICATION A Post Card

Imagine that you are on a vacation. Write a post card to a friend or to a relative telling him or her about something interesting that happened on your trip. Address your post card. Use abbreviations.

GRAMMAR

10 VOCABULARY BUILDING: Compound Words

Some long words are really two or more short words joined together. These words are called compound words. **Compound words** are often made by joining two nouns. Here are some examples.

Words	Compound Words
tooth + brush	toothbrush
play + ground	playground
space + craft	spacecraft

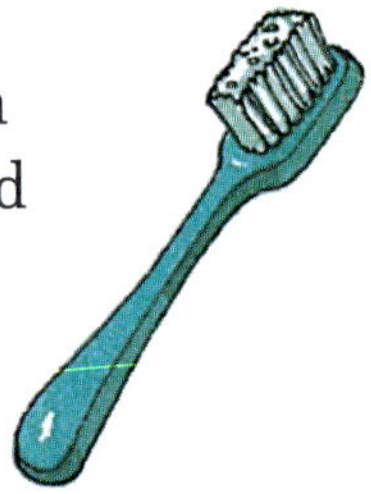

You can often figure out the meaning of a compound word from the meaning of each word in the compound.

Compound	Meanings
wallpaper	paper that covers a wall
blueberry	a berry that is blue
bookstore	a store that sells books
shoelace	a lace for tying shoes

Guided Practice

Find the compound word in each sentence. Tell which two words make up the compound word.

Example: Please ride on the sidewalk. *sidewalk* *side walk*

1. Some people make model airplanes.
2. They use sandpaper to smooth the wooden pieces.
3. Other people build models of railroads.
4. A workshop is handy for any kind of hobby.
5. List your hobby ideas in a notebook.

?! **THINK**

■ How can I tell if a word is a compound word?

REMEMBER

- A **compound word** is a word made from two or more words that are joined together.

More Practice

A. Write the compound word in each sentence. Then, write the two separate words that form the compound word.

Example: We sit in the backyard. *backyard* *back yard*

6. You may like to grow plants in a greenhouse.
7. Woodcarving is a relaxing hobby.
8. Did you build the birdhouse?
9. He used wood to make a sailboat.
10. Funny dolls can be made from clothespins.
11. The painter sketched the waterfall.
12. The artist uses a paintbrush.
13. Some people enjoy raising goldfish.
14. Others would rather sit on a riverbank and fish.
15. His fishing line hangs from the side of a rowboat.

B. Write each sentence. Change the words in parentheses ( ) to a compound word formed from the underlined words.

Example: We are making some (<u>shelves</u> to put <u>books</u> on).
We are making some bookshelves.

16. Do you own a (<u>skate</u> on a <u>board</u>)?
17. I like the (<u>ground</u> where I <u>play</u>).
18. Many people play (<u>ball</u> with a <u>basket</u>).
19. People of all ages can be (<u>mates</u> on a <u>team</u>).
20. Some skate on a (<u>walk</u> by the <u>side</u> of the street).

Extra Practice, page 113

WRITING APPLICATION A Paragraph

Write a paragraph about your favorite hobby. Then, share your paragraph with a classmate. Discuss your hobbies. Ask your partner to point out any compound words you have used.

GRAMMAR AND WRITING CONNECTION

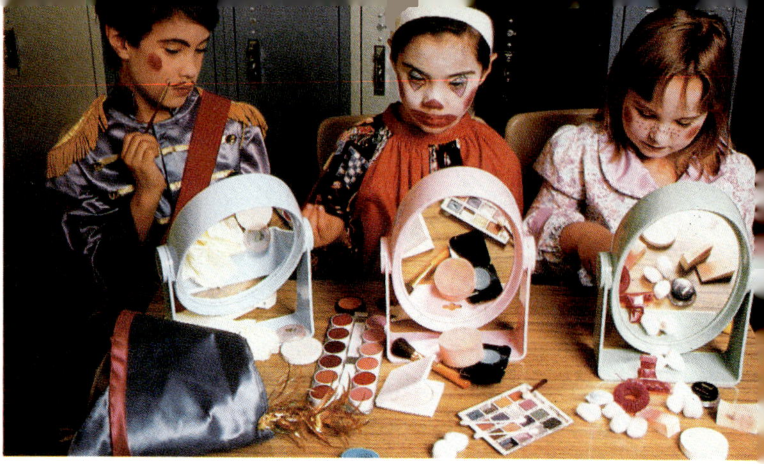

Combining Sentences

You can sometimes make your writing clearer when you combine sentences that have similar ideas. When you combine, you can use the joining word *and* or *or*. The word *and* shows that ideas are linked. The joining word *or* shows a difference between ideas.

Separate: Anita wrote about the school play.
Steve wrote about the school play.
Combined: Anita **and** Steve wrote about the school play.

Separate: Is the play a comedy?
Is the play a musical?
Combined: Is the play a comedy **or** a musical?

COOPERATIVE LEARNING

Working Together

Think about each pair of sentences. Then tell how you would combine them to make a single sentence.

Example: Joan wanted to join a school club.
Renée wanted to join a school club.
Joan and Renée wanted to join a school club.

1. The Drama Club needed new members.
The Stamp Club needed new members.
2. Joan chose the Drama Club.
Renée chose the Drama Club.
3. Is Joan a better actress?
Is Joan a better scenery painter?

Revising Sentences

Below are sentences from the story Anita wrote about the school play. Help Anita revise her story by combining the sentences. Use *and* or *or* to join the sentences.

4. Joan invited me to the dress rehearsal of the play. Renée invited me to the dress rehearsal of the play.
5. The actors wore costumes for the first time. The actors wore stage makeup for the first time.
6. The actors are ready to begin. The backstage workers are ready to begin.
7. Would the rehearsal be a success? Would the rehearsal be a failure?
8. Do my classmates prefer musicals? Do my classmates prefer serious plays?
9. Is this show a serious play? Is it a musical?
10. The play included spoken parts. It included songs.
11. Did I like the songs more? Did I like the spoken parts more?
12. My classmates would truly enjoy the show. My teacher would truly enjoy the show, too.

WRITER AT WORK

Think of a choice you have made between two things you wanted to do. Write a paragraph telling why you made the choice you did. Reread your paragraph. Combine any sentences you can. Use *and* or *or* when you combine sentences.

UNIT CHECKUP

LESSON 1 **What Is a Noun?** (page 76) Write the two nouns in each sentence. Then write **person, place,** or **thing** after each noun.

1. Children always need clothing.
2. Choose a jacket in this store.
3. A clerk is by the door.
4. The cashier helps customers.
5. Ask for a copy of the receipt.

LESSONS 2-3 **Singular Nouns and Plural Nouns** (pages 78-81) Write the correct noun in parentheses ( ) to complete each sentence.

6. My (class, classes) is planning a project.
7. Many (student, students) volunteer.
8. They choose to have many (dance, dances).
9. Lunches will be packed in (box, boxes).
10. Five (guppy, guppies) are in the tank.
11. The vase of (daisy, daisies) sits near the tank.
12. Are my (key, keys) near the vase?

LESSON 4 **More Plural Nouns** (page 82) Write each sentence correctly. Use the plural form of the noun in parentheses ( ).

13. The (child) may want another pet.
14. White (mouse) are fun to have.
15. Some people even keep (goose).
16. They might bite your (foot).
17. A farm is a good place for (sheep).

LESSON 5 **Common Nouns and Proper Nouns** (page 84) Write the nouns in each sentence. Then write **common** or **proper** next to each noun to show what kind it is.

18. A popular potato is named Monona.
19. Large crops grow in Idaho.
20. The plant first came from Peru.
21. John Jasper loves potatoes.
22. Will Sara serve yams?

LESSONS 6-8

Using Possessive Nouns (pages 86-91) Find the possessive noun in each group of words. Tell whether it is **singular** or **plural.**

23. the cat's meow
24. two deer's antlers
25. my sister's hat
26. the men's store
27. the baby's rattle

LESSON 9

Mechanics: Abbreviations (page 92) Write each group of words using the abbreviation for each underlined word.

28. Doctor Lee
29. a day in October
30. on a Monday
31. 30 Elm Avenue
32. Mister Jones
33. Post Office Box 1300
34. 15 Kendon Drive
35. December 7, 1941

LESSON 10

Vocabulary Building: Compound Words (page 94) Write the compound word in each sentence. Then, write the two words that form the compound.

36. Are the photos in the mailbox?
37. Some cameras fit into a handbag.
38. The city skyline is beautiful.
39. Take a picture of a skyscraper.
40. Snap the tugboat on the river.

Writing Application: Noun Usage (pages 76-91) There are 10 noun errors in this paragraph. Write the paragraph correctly.

41.–50.

The wilson building is at 135 wilson road in milwaukee, wisconsin. The childrens' library is located in the basement. The librarians' hours are from 9 to 5. She is there every monday through friday.

ENRICHMENT

NOUN SEARCH

You and a partner are conducting a noun search. Work together to create a list of precise nouns in general categories. For example, a general category might be animals. In that general category you might include dogs. In the category of dogs you might include two precise types—poodle and collie. Try to think of five general categories with three or more precise nouns in each.

NEVER LEAVE HOME WITHOUT IT

Select one of the following imaginary nouns and think of a product it could name. Then, make a poster with a picture of the product and instructions that tell people how to use the product.

blooster
canbam
twiktums
sippies

FLOWER POWER

The names of many flowers and other plants are really compound words. Only some of these names give clues about what the flower looks like. Choose one of the flower names below and draw a picture of the flower as you imagine it to look. Base your picture on the words that make up the name of the flower.

gooseberry	**bluebonnet**	**dogwood**
shovelweed	**foalfoot**	**milkweed**
pennyroyal	**pawpaw**	**cowslip**

CREATIVE EXPRESSION

The New and the Old

Railroad tracks; a flight
of wild geese close above them
in the moonlit night.

–Shiki

Leaves

The winds that blow–
ask them, which leaf of the tree
will be the next to go!

–Soseki

TRY IT OUT!

A **haiku** is a special type of poem. A haiku has three lines and usually has seventeen syllables. In these haiku the poets write of nature. Think of something in nature. Write a haiku about the topic you have chosen. You may wish to illustrate your haiku.

EXTRA PRACTICE

Three levels of practice

What Is a Noun? (page 76)

LEVEL **A.** Write the underlined nouns in each sentence. Then, write **person**, **place**, or **thing** next to each noun to tell what it names.

1. Young people can earn money in many ways.
2. Grocery stores need part-time helpers.
3. Clerks arrange cans on shelves.
4. Packers help customers with bags.
5. Large towns usually have malls.
6. Students can work in shops at the mall.
7. They can fill out a form for the store manager.
8. New workers must train for a few days.
9. One kind of store sells records.
10. This is a nice job for people who like music.

LEVEL **B.** Write each sentence. Underline every noun.

11. Companies often hire young people.
12. Students can work after school.
13. The boys can file papers.
14. The girls deliver messages to other offices.
15. Some people may answer telephones.
16. Most secretaries need helpers.
17. Typists can help with letters.
18. Youngsters can address envelopes.

LEVEL **C.** Write each sentence. Fill in each blank with a noun.

19. Some _____ may want to start a business.
20. One way to earn _____ is to mow _____ .
21. Many students walk other people's _____ .
22. Another service is baby-sitting for _____ .
23. Cleaning out _____ is an idea.
24. Some young people can repair _____ .
25. A few _____ are all that is needed.

EXTRA PRACTICE

Three levels of practice

Singular Nouns and Plural Nouns (page 78)

LEVEL **A.** Write the underlined nouns in each sentence. Then, write **singular** or **plural** to show what kind of noun each one is.

1. Sara likes films about animals.
2. Some people enjoy musicals.
3. They want to hear songs and see dances.
4. In some films there is an adventure.
5. The actor travels to a faraway land.
6. Each character faces many dangers.
7. At the last minute they fool the villains.
8. The last few scenes show a happy ending.
9. My friend prefers funny films.
10. Funny characters make Sara happy.

LEVEL **B.** Decide which noun in parentheses ( ) correctly completes each sentence. Then write the sentence.

11. Many people would rather see a (play, plays).
12. They like watching many (actor, actors) on stage.
13. Some (theater, theaters) are well known.
14. A play might run for several (year, years).
15. A (musical, musicals) is a popular choice.
16. People especially enjoy a (drama, dramas).
17. Some (actress, actresses) become famous.
18. An actor takes many (class, classes).

LEVEL **C.** Write each sentence correctly, using the singular or plural form of the noun in parentheses ( ).

19. Most people watch television (show).
20. There is a wide choice of (program) to see.
21. Many comedies are fun for boys and (girl).
22. A character may get into a terrible (mess).
23. There may be several (surprise) in the plot.
24. The hero has three (guess).
25. He may have to follow many (hunch).

EXTRA PRACTICE

Three levels of practice

More Singular and Plural Nouns (page 80)

LEVEL A.

Write each sentence. Then underline the plural nouns in these sentences.

1. The daisies bloomed.
2. Three bluejays chirped.
3. The summer days were peaceful.
4. Several boys played in the park.
5. Two babies sat with their mothers.
6. One baby played with toys.
7. Some families had a picnic.
8. Tom brought a bowl of cherries.
9. Later, we will ride on ponies.
10. There are many ways to have fun on a picnic.

LEVEL B.

Write the plural form of each noun.

11. factory
12. holiday
13. delivery
14. donkey
15. story
16. chimney
17. memory
18. highways

LEVEL C.

One noun in each sentence should be plural. Find that noun and write it correctly.

19. Several raccoon family lived near the road.
20. The baby were very cute.
21. They were several day old.
22. The raccoons ate berry from bushes.
23. They stayed away from their many enemy.
24. Farmers told story about the raccoons.
25. Raccoons can be as playful as monkey.

EXTRA PRACTICE

GRAMMAR

Three levels of practice

More Plural Nouns (page 82)

LEVEL A. Find the plural noun or nouns in each sentence. Write each noun.

1. Many women traveled west in 1842.
2. The children went along, too.
3. Oxen pulled the wagons.
4. Some sheep followed along.
5. A person's feet grew tired from walking.
6. Deer were hunted for food.
7. People fished for their dinners.
8. Wild geese were another source of food.
9. The men rode on horses.
10. They saw many moose.

LEVEL B. Write each sentence, using the plural form of the noun in parentheses ( ).

11. (Mouse) often got into the grain sacks.
12. They used their (tooth) to chew the fabric.
13. (Woman) carefully fastened the sacks.
14. Several (man) may have hunted together.
15. They often looked for (deer).
16. Sometimes they caught (goose).
17. The (child) usually rode in the wagons.
18. Walking made their (foot) sore.

LEVEL C. Write each sentence. Fill in each blank with the plural form of one of the words below. Use each word only once.

foot goose ox child mouse woman sheep

19. Most _____ knew how to make a campfire.
20. Small _____ probably played together.
21. They may have helped feed the _____ .
22. Tiny _____ were not welcome in the wagons.
23. _____ flying south pointed travelers in the right direction.
24. The _____ were used for their wool.
25. Travelers wore boots on their _____ .

EXTRA PRACTICE

Three levels of practice

Common Nouns and Proper Nouns (page 84)

LEVEL A.

Write the underlined nouns in each sentence. Then, write **common** or **proper** to show what kind of noun each one is.

1. The United States continues to explore space.
2. A mission to Jupiter is planned.
3. A spacecraft will be launched in November.
4. The *Galileo* will travel for six years.
5. The craft will orbit the huge planet.
6. Its journey will also take it past Venus.
7. Mars is another planet to explore.
8. Two crafts traveled to the Red Planet in 1976.
9. *Viking 2* landed on its surface in July.
10. The cameras sent color pictures back to Earth.

LEVEL B.

List the common and proper nouns in each sentence.

11. A second probe landed on Mars in September.
12. The *Observer* will be launched in 1992.
13. The shuttle will carry the craft into space.
14. The weather will be observed.
15. Neptune is the last stop for *Voyager*.
16. The Kennedy Space Center is a busy place.
17. Several spaceships went to the moon.
18. The first human to land there was Neil Armstrong.

LEVEL C.

Write each sentence correctly by capitalizing the proper nouns. Draw one line under each common noun and two lines under each proper noun.

19. The first mission took place in july 1969.
20. This mission was *apollo 11*.
21. The last landing was in december 1972.
22. eugene cernan collected rocks.
23. The module was piloted by ronald evans.
24. Most astronauts would like to go to mars.
25. The first woman in space was sally ride.

EXTRA PRACTICE

GRAMMAR

Three levels of practice

Singular Possessive Nouns (page 86)

LEVEL **A.** Write the sentence. Underline the singular possessive noun in each sentence.

1. A student's report may be about inventors.
2. An inventor's life can be interesting.
3. The teacher's suggestions are good.
4. Chester Carlson's idea was a copier.
5. Elisha Otis's invention was the elevator.
6. Cyrus McCormick's reaper saved time.
7. The farmer's harvesting time was cut in half.
8. One student's paper was about silly inventions.
9. One man's idea was very silly.
10. The class's laughter filled the halls.

LEVEL **B.** Write each sentence, using the singular possessive form of the noun in parentheses ( ).

11. A (mechanic) idea led to the pop-up toaster.
12. A (customer) burnt toast gave him the idea.
13. Charles (Strite) invention did not work at first.
14. This (inventor) solution was a timer.
15. One (man) idea for a can opener was welcome.
16. The idea for a (soldier) knife may have been used before.
17. William (Lyman) cutting wheel was safer.
18. It made the (worker) life easier.

LEVEL **C.** Rewrite each group of words. Use the singular possessive form of the noun in dark type.

19. idea of an **engineer**
20. name of the **inventor**
21. the boots of a **man**
22. first idea of this **scientist**
23. the design of **Judson**
24. the design of the **artist**
25. the radio of **Marconi**

GRAMMAR

EXTRA PRACTICE

Three levels of practice

Plural Possessive Nouns (page 88)

LEVEL **A.** Write the sentences. Underline the plural possessive noun in each sentence.

1. People's needs include clean air.
2. Drivers' car engines add to the dirt in the air.
3. Citizens' efforts can make a difference.
4. Many children's playgrounds are littered.
5. Several states' forests are full of trash.
6. Mayors' committees help with these problems.
7. One of the committees' ideas involves volunteers.
8. The volunteers' efforts help to clean the playground.
9. The supervisors' work is never finished.
10. The volunteers receive the families' thanks.

LEVEL **B.** Write each sentence. Use the plural possessive form of the noun in parentheses ( ).

11. Many wild (animals) homes are threatened.
12. The (deer) grazing land is shrinking.
13. Many (moose) territories have been invaded.
14. Some (visitors) picnic areas in national parks are closed.
15. The (rangers) job is to limit visitors.
16. Some (men) groups work with park officials.
17. The (children) zoo needs much work.
18. The (sheep) pens need repair.

LEVEL **C.** Rewrite each group of words. Use the plural possessive form of the noun in dark type.

19. education of the **children**
20. clubs of the **men**
21. groups of the **citizens**
22. cooperation of the **people**
23. actions of a few **farmers**
24. products of the **consumers**
25. rights of the **animals**

EXTRA PRACTICE

GRAMMAR

Three levels of practice

Using Possessive Nouns (page 90)

LEVEL A. Write the possessive noun in each group of words. Label the noun **singular possessive** or **plural possessive.**

1. a mouse's tail
2. her father's job
3. the kittens' mother
4. Sherri's sweater
5. the photographers' cameras
6. his sisters' friends

LEVEL B. Write the possessive form of the noun in parentheses ( ) to complete each sentence.

7. My _____ fair is over. (class)
8. All _____ projects were judged. (student)
9. That _____ model won a prize. (girl)
10. My _____ vote was counted. (teacher)
11. Each _____ ribbon was red. (winner)
12. Three _____ reports won ribbons. (boy)
13. A video about _____ habits also won. (deer)

LEVEL C. Write the plural possessive form of the singular noun in parentheses ( ) to complete each sentence.

14. The _____ dishes were in a row. (cat)
15. Four _____ toys were in the corner. (kitten)
16. The _____ pets were very cute. (girl)
17. Her _____ kittens are prize winners. (sister)
18. The _____ fur is long and fluffy. (baby)
19. Five _____ cats ran away. (boy)
20. My _____ canaries chirp at the cats. (brother)
21. The _____ coats were brushed and shiny. (dog)
22. The _____ cages were lined up in a row. (parrot)
23. Many _____ pets received a prize. (family)
24. The _____ choices were very good. (judge)
25. The _____ owners were happy. (pet)

GRAMMAR

PRACTICE + PLUS

Three levels of additional practice for a difficult skill

Using Possessive Nouns (page 90)

LEVEL A. Write these sentences. Underline the possessive noun in each sentence.

1. Ellen's favorite animals are dogs.
2. Her family's pet is a dog.
3. The dog's name is Ned.
4. Ned's only fault is his huge appetite.
5. If food drops from the table, it is the dog's.
6. Cats' appetites are much smaller.
7. Bill's cats eat all the time.
8. The cats' names are Fritz and Maggie.
9. Fritz's favorite food is fish.
10. Meat is Maggie's favorite food.
11. The animals' dishes are in the kitchen.
12. You must take care of your pet's needs.
13. Mimi's bird became ill.
14. The bird's feathers were falling out.
15. The vet's care saved the bird.
16. Other people's pets wait for the vet.
17. A woman's pet turtle is next.
18. The turtle's shell is cracked.
19. The boy's dog is in the office, too.
20. The dog's paw is hurt.

LEVEL B. Write these sentences. Include apostrophes where they are needed.

21. Carls school has a good volleyball team.
22. The teams record is nearly perfect.
23. The players skills improve with practice.
24. The teachers and schoolmates cheer the teams efforts.
25. Carls parents are proud of him.

PRACTICE + PLUS

26. Other parents pride is great, too.
27. Carls schools other teams are good, too.
28. The coachs hope is shared by the team.
29. Ruths day begins very early in the morning.
30. Her trainers instructions are very clear.
31. Her two friends cheers encourage her.
32. Their shouts attract peoples attention.
33. Her classmates applause fills the stands.
34. Many girls parents came to the stadium.
35. Mrs. Verners cheers are loudest of all.

LEVEL **C.** Rewrite these sentences. Use possessive nouns in place of the underlined phrases.

36. <u>The pen pal of Jan</u> sent her a letter.
37. <u>The name of the pen pal</u> is Tomas.
38. <u>The family of her friend</u> lives in Mexico.
39. <u>The letter of the writer</u> took a week to arrive.
40. <u>The letter of Tomas</u> and <u>the letter of Jan</u> crossed in the mail.
41. <u>The envelopes of the senders</u> contained birthday cards.
42. <u>The birthdays of the pen pals</u> are the same day.
43. <u>The parents of the children</u> plan a surprise.
44. <u>The mother of Tomas</u> bakes a big cake.
45. <u>The father of Jan</u> also bakes a cake.
46. <u>The friends of the girl</u> sing "Happy Birthday."
47. <u>The relatives of the children</u> come to the party.
48. <u>The sisters of Jan</u> give a fabulous gift.
49. <u>The friends of the parents</u> are happy for the children.
50. <u>The gifts of the relatives</u> are happily received.

EXTRA PRACTICE

Three levels of practice

Mechanics: Abbreviations (page 92)

LEVEL A. Write the correct abbreviation for the underlined word in each group of words.

1. Mister Sandoz
2. Doctor Elizabeth Blackwell
3. Governor Jane Lyons
4. Senator Harold Caraway
5. the senator from Arkansas
6. the representative from Montana
7. Downing Street
8. Pennsylvania Avenue
9. Rodeo Drive
10. Hollywood Boulevard

LEVEL B. Write each group of words. Use an abbreviation for each underlined word.

11. Broadway in October
12. Telegraph Road
13. Mardi Gras in February
14. Thanksgiving on a Thursday
15. a Tuesday in November
16. a Monday in September
17. Senator Dan Morrow
18. Holyoke, Massachusetts

LEVEL C. Write each address. Use abbreviations for as many words as you can.

19. Mister Carlos Contreras
1630 Green Boulevard
Houston, Texas 77201

20. Sylvia Levy
Post Office Box 3882
Indianapolis, Indiana 46206

21. The Jacks Toy Company
84 Conway Street
Atlanta, Georgia 30304

22. Doctor Miyoshi Tamura
631 River Road
Portland, Oregon 97308

EXTRA PRACTICE

GRAMMAR

Three levels of practice

Vocabulary Building: Compound Words (page 94)

LEVEL A.

Write the two words that form the compound word underlined in each sentence.

1. A cookbook offers many recipes.
2. We make egg dishes for breakfast.
3. Pancakes are easy to make.
4. Do you like blueberries?
5. A main ingredient might be buttermilk.
6. Do you use a tablespoon?
7. Put some water in the teakettle.
8. Please put the tablecloth on the table.
9. I like oatmeal.
10. Mix it with strawberries.

LEVEL B.

Write the compound word in each sentence. Then, write the two words that form the compound.

11. You can buy supplies at a supermarket.
12. Ask the shopkeeper for special items.
13. Put the groceries in the cupboard.
14. Do you put salt in everything?
15. The cook used a tablespoon of baking powder.
16. Applesauce can be used in many recipes.
17. Some people enjoy eating eggplant.
18. Cornbread is good with any meal.

LEVEL C.

Write each sentence. Change the words in parentheses ( ) to a compound formed from the underlined words.

19. Long ago, people used (wood for a fire) for cooking.
20. The wood was put in a (place to make fires).
21. They went to the (house for a hen) for eggs.
22. Biscuits were made of (dough that is sour).
23. They cleaned dishes in a (tub for the wash).
24. Milk was delivered to the (step before the door).
25. Cows were kept in the (yard by the barn).

MAINTENANCE

UNIT 1: Understanding Sentences

Sentences (pages 2, 4, 6) Write each group of words that is a sentence correctly. Then write **declarative, interrogative, imperative,** or **exclamatory** to tell what kind of sentence it is.

1. how do you ride a bicycle
2. taught my little brother
3. please show me what to do
4. your feet on the pedals
5. how hard it is to balance
6. squeeze the brakes gently
7. this bike has five gears
8. what kind of bike do you have
9. good for your leg muscles
10. what fun it is to ride a bike

Subjects and Predicates (pages 10, 12) Write each sentence. Draw a line between the complete subject and the complete predicate. Draw one line under the simple subject and two lines under the simple predicate.

11. My family camps in the summer.
12. We travel by car to a lake.
13. My sister likes the trips.
14. Many birds call from the trees.
15. A raccoon lives in the woodpile.
16. Our log cabin sits on the shore.

Compound Subjects and Compound Predicates (page 12) Write each sentence. Draw a line between the subject and the predicate. Then, underline the compound subject or the compound predicate.

17. The musicians play and tune their instruments.
18. The men and women in the audience clap.
19. The conductor taps and raises his baton.
20. The flutes and violins begin the melody.
21. Several dancers run and twirl onto the stage.

Correcting and Punctuating Run-on Sentences (pages 14, 16) Rewrite each run-on sentence correctly as two sentences.

22. I want to order some books I can fill out the form.
23. Please write your name on the first line your address comes next.
24. Put your Zip Code on the form it will speed up your order.
25. I will figure out the tax I am good at math.

Using Context Clues (page 18) Write the meaning of the underlined word in each sentence. Then, write the word or words you used as context clues.

26. Long ago, the shells of cowries were used as money.
    a. rocks b. sea snails
27. They were portable because they were tiny and fit in pockets.
    a. easily carried b. too heavy
28. In the 1930s, laws made legal the use of wooden nickels.
    a. criminal b. lawful
29. Today our currency—nickels, dimes, or dollar bills—is made only with metal or paper.
    a. money b. change

UNIT 3: Nouns

What Is a Noun? (page 76) Write the nouns in each sentence. Then write **person, place,** or **thing** after each noun.

30. Many birds land in our yard.
31. My mother scatters crumbs on the grass.
32. Birdseed can be bought at the store.
33. The library has many books about birds.
34. Dad built several birdhouses.

Singular Nouns and Plural Nouns (pages 78, 80, 82) Write and correctly complete each sentence with the singular or plural form of the noun in parentheses ( ).

35. How many (circus) have you seen?
36. Some shows travel in our (country).
37. The (clown) are my favorite.
38. One clown had two (monkey).
39. A monkey rode a (sheep).
40. I saw two (mouse) do tricks.
41. An elephant danced two (waltz).
42. Many (child) clapped loudly.

Singular and Plural Possessive Nouns (pages 86, 88, 90) Complete each sentence with the singular or plural possessive form of the noun in parentheses ( ).

43. A Cuban land (crab) pace is very fast.
44. The (kangaroos) powerful legs help them to leap high.
45. A (jackrabbit) jump can reach up to twenty feet.
46. (People) top running speeds are far behind many animals'.
47. Most (cheetahs) speeds reach up to seventy miles per hour.
48. By contrast, the (moose) gallop is quite slow.
49. Many (birds) flying speeds are fast.
50. A duck (hawk) flight has been clocked at 180 miles per hour.

UNIT 4

Writing Explanations

Read the quotation and look at the picture on the opposite page. How do you decide what is important to write about?

Explanations help people learn more about things. When you write an explanation, you will want to include the facts you know. Comparing and contrasting these facts is one way to help your audience understand your meaning.

Focus An explanation presents the facts about something in a clear and logical way.

What would you like to explain? In this unit you will read a story about a boy who explained something to his class. You will find some interesting photographs, too. You can use both to get some ideas for writing.

THEME: *CHOICES*

I still think the most important things that happen to us are the smallest things—eating supper together, bedtime, planting flowers, sitting on a porch on summer nights, feeding the birds. . . . those small things make the difference between a rich and good life or an empty one . . .

—Cynthia Rylant

LITERATURE

Reading Like a Writer

AWARD WINNING SELECTION

What makes you happy? What makes you sad?

Leo, the boy in this story, thinks that he will never be happy. Then, he finds a turtle, which he names Charlie, and things begin to change. Leo decides to talk about Charlie in a report he gives in school. Leo's choice of topics is a good one, as you will discover.

As you read the story, notice how the author tells you about Leo and Charlie. Also, notice when she compares or contrasts different things.

Leo & Charlie

from

Every Living Thing

by Cynthia Rylant

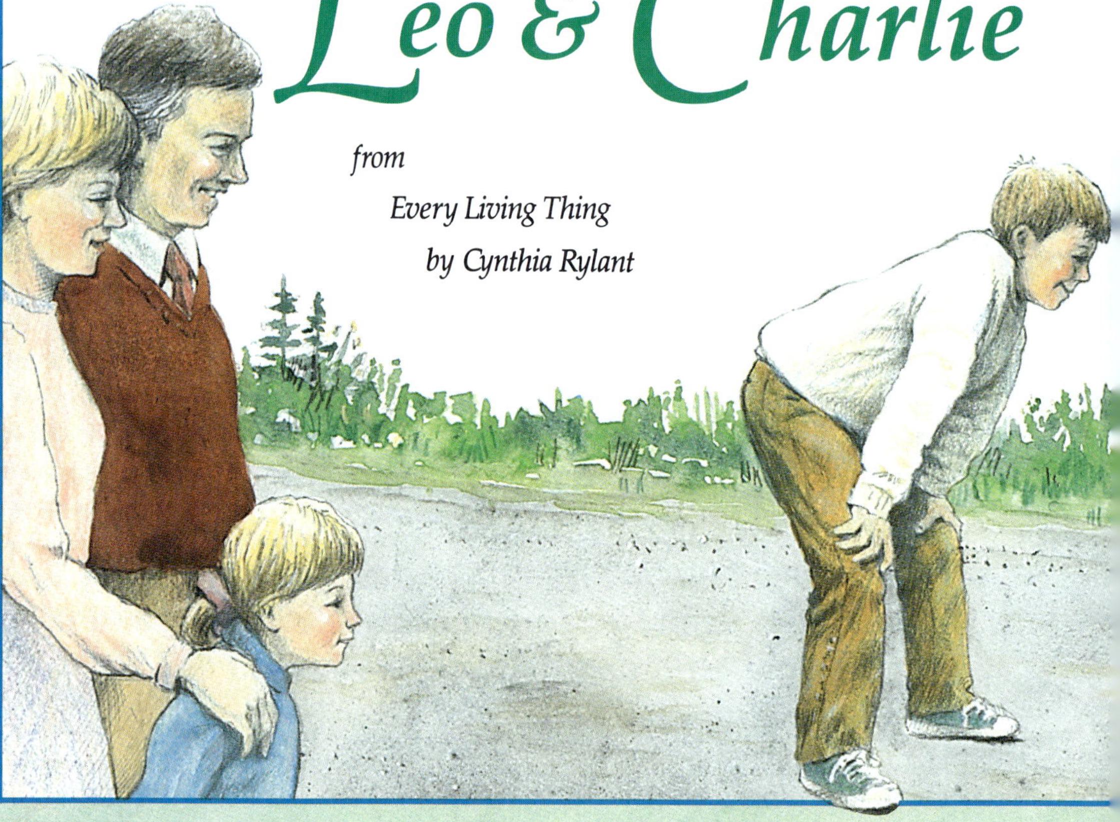

Leo was the first one to spot the turtle, so he was the one who got to keep it. They had all been in the car, driving up Tyler Mountain to church, when Leo shouted, "There's a turtle!" and everyone's head jerked with the stop.

Leo's father grumbled something about turtle soup, but Leo's mother was sympathetic toward turtles, so Leo was allowed to pick it up off the highway and bring it home. Both his little sisters squealed when the animal stuck its ugly head out to look at them, and they thought its claws horrifying, but Leo loved it from the start. He named it Charlie.

The dogs at Leo's house had always belonged more to Leo's father than to anyone else, and the cat thought she belonged to no one but herself, so Leo was grateful for a pet of his own. He settled Charlie in a cardboard box, threw in some lettuce and radishes, and declared himself a happy boy.

Leo adored Charlie, and the turtle was hugged and kissed as if he were a baby. Leo liked to fit Charlie's shell on his shoulder under his left ear, just as one might carry a cat, and Charlie would poke his head into Leo's neck now and then to keep them both entertained.

Leo was ten years old the year he found Charlie. He hadn't many friends because he was slower than the rest. That was the way his father said it: "Slower than the rest." Leo was slow in reading, slow in numbers, slow in understanding nearly everything that passed before him in a classroom. As a result, in fourth

The main character is described here.

grade Leo had been separated from the rest of his classmates and placed in a room with other children who were as slow as he. Leo thought he would never get over it. He saw no way to be happy after that.

But Charlie took care of Leo's happiness, and he did it by being congenial. Charlie was the friendliest turtle anyone had ever seen. The turtle's head was always stretched out, moving left to right, trying to see what was in the world. His front and back legs moved as though he were swimming frantically in a deep sea to save himself, when all that was happening was that someone was holding him in midair. Put Charlie down and he would sniff at the air a moment, then take off as if no one had ever told him how slow he was supposed to be.

Every day, Leo came home from school, took Charlie to the backyard to let him explore and told him about the things that had happened in fifth grade. Leo wasn't sure how old Charlie was, and, though he guessed Charlie was probably a young turtle, the lines around Charlie's forehead and eyes and the clamp of his mouth made Leo think Charlie was wise the way old people are wise. So Leo talked to him privately every day.

Then one day Leo decided to take Charlie to school.

It was Prevent Forest Fires week and the whole school was making posters, watching nature films, imitating Smokey the Bear. Each member of Leo's class was assigned to give a report on Friday dealing with forests. So Leo brought Charlie.

Leo was quiet about it on the bus to school. He held the covered box tightly on his lap, secretly relieved that turtles are quiet except for an occasional hiss. Charlie rarely hissed in the morning; he was a turtle who liked to sleep in.

Leo carried the box to his classroom and placed it on the wide window sill near the radiator and beside the geraniums. His teacher called attendance and the day began.

In the middle of the morning, the forest reports began. One girl held up a poster board pasted with pictures of raccoons and squirrels, rabbits and deer, and she explained that animals died in forest fires.

The pictures were too small for anyone to see from his desk. Leo was bored.

One boy stood up and mumbled something about burnt-up trees. Then another got up and said if there were no forests, then his dad couldn't go hunting, and Leo couldn't see the connection in that at all.

Finally it was his turn. He quietly walked over to the window sill and picked up the box. He set it on the teacher's desk.

"When somebody throws a match into a forest," Leo began, "he is a murderer. He kills trees and birds and animals. Some animals, like deer, are fast runners and they might escape. But other animals"—he lifted the cover off the box—"have no hope. They are too slow. They will die." He lifted Charlie out of the box. "It isn't fair," he said, as the class gasped and giggled at what they saw. "It isn't fair for the slow ones."

Leo compares and contrasts animals to explain about forest fires.

Leo said much more. Mostly he talked about Charlie, explained what turtles were like, the things they enjoyed, what talents they possessed. He talked about Charlie the turtle and Charlie the friend, and what he said and how he said it made everyone in the class love turtles and hate forest fires. Leo's teacher had tears in her eyes.

That afternoon, the whole school assembled in the gymnasium to bring the special week to a close. A ranger in uniform made a speech, then someone dressed up like Smokey the Bear danced with two others dressed up like squirrels. Leo sat with his box and wondered if he should laugh at the dancers with everyone else. He didn't feel like it.

Finally, the school principal stood up and began a long talk. Leo's thoughts drifted off. He thought about being home, lying in his bed and drawing pictures, while Charlie hobbled all about the room.

He did not hear when someone whispered his name. Then he

jumped when he heard, "Leo! It's you!" in his ear. The boy next to him was pushing him, making him get up.

"What?" Leo asked, looking around in confusion.

"You won!" they were all saying. "Go on!"

Leo was pushed onto the floor. He saw the principal smiling at him, beckoning to him across the room. Leo's legs moved like Charlie's – quickly and forward.

Leo carried the box tightly against his chest. He shook the principal's hand. He put down the box to accept the award plaque being handed to him. It was for his presentation with Charlie. Leo had won an award for the first time in his life, and as he shook the principal's hand and blushed and said his thank-you's, he thought his heart would explode with happiness.

That night, alone in his room, holding Charlie on his shoulder, Leo felt proud. And for the first time in a long time, Leo felt *fast*.

Thinking Like a Reader

1. If you were in Leo's class, would you have liked his report on forest fires and turtles? Why?
2. Imagine that you could bring a pet to class. What kind of animal would it be? What would you say about it?

Write your responses in your journal.

Thinking Like a Writer

3. What facts about turtles does the author give you? How does she make these facts interesting?
4. The author compares Leo and Charlie. How does comparing them help her explain Leo's feelings?

Write your responses in your journal.

Responding to

LITERATURE

Brainstorm *Vocabulary*

In "Leo and Charlie" the author uses many different words to describe Charlie. Go back and find the words she uses. Write them in your journal. Put a star next to the words that you like the most. Begin to create a personal vocabulary list of describing words. You can use these words in your writing.

Talk It Over *Choose a Pet*

Imagine that you are choosing a pet. You might choose a dog, a cat, a parakeet, a goldfish, or a hamster. With a partner discuss the kind of pet you would like. You might tell about your pet's size—its height, length, and weight—and its color. You could also describe how your pet would act. Would it be friendly to strangers? Would it be quiet or frisky? Would it sleep during the day and play when it is dark? Explain how the pet is like or unlike other animals.

Quick Write *Write Instructions*

In "Talk It Over" you thought about a pet that you would like to have. Now, write a paragraph explaining to your family how to care for the pet. Tell how and when your pet should be fed. Will it need special sleeping quarters? How can your pet be trained to become a good family member?

Idea Corner

Compare and Contrast

When you **compare,** you explain how things are alike. When you **contrast,** you explain how things are different. What ideas do you have about things that can be compared and contrasted? Write your ideas in your journal. You might list pairs of things to compare and contrast, such as "parrot and parakeet" or "ocean and lake." You might list ways that two things are alike or different. You might sketch two things and circle the parts that are the same or those that are different.

Finding Ideas for Writing

Look at the photographs. How are they alike? How are they different? What ideas for writing do the photographs give you? Write your ideas in your journal.

COOPERATIVE LEARNING 1

GROUP WRITING: An Explanation

You know that comparing means telling about likenesses. Contrasting means telling about differences. **Comparing** and **contrasting** are ways to explain. When you explain, your **purpose** is to present facts to your **audience.** You tell what you know or think about something. What can make an explanation clear and interesting?

- A Topic Sentence
- Details That Compare and Contrast
- Logical Order of Details

A Topic Sentence

Read the following explanation. Look for the sentence that tells the main idea.

> Computers and typewriters are alike in some ways but different in other ways. Both a computer and a typewriter let you type your ideas. Both have keyboards and fit on the top of a desk. Unlike a typewriter, a computer lets you change words and move them around. It also saves the words you have typed.

The first sentence tells the main idea. In an explanation the sentence that tells the main idea is called the **topic sentence.** The topic sentence often comes first or last in a paragraph. In that way it states or sums up the main idea.

Guided Practice: Writing a Topic Sentence

Plan to explain how two things are alike and how they are different. Working as a class, decide on a topic. Then, write a topic sentence. Remember, your topic sentence should state your main idea.

Example: Frogs and toads are similar, but they are not exactly the same.

Details That Compare and Contrast

As you know, the topic sentence of an explanation tells the main idea. The other sentences are detail sentences. They give facts and examples that support the main idea.

Reread the paragraph about computers and typewriters. Notice that the detail sentences tell how the two kinds of machines are alike and different.

- Which sentences are detail sentences?
- What facts are you told about the two machines?

Logical Order of Details

Look again at the paragraph on page 126. Notice that the details are ordered in a logical way. First, the writer explains how computers and typewriters are alike. Then, the writer explains how they are different. When you write an explanation, think of a good way to order your ideas. One good way to order ideas when comparing and contrasting is to tell first about likenesses and then about differences.

Guided Practice: Ordering Ideas

Think of details for your explanation. As a class, make a chart like the one below. Write facts or examples that further explain your main idea.

Topic Sentence Frogs and toads are similar, but they are not exactly the same.	
Details That Compare	**Details That Contrast**
both are amphibians	toads spend more time on land
both eat insects	toads have shorter, wider bodies
both lay eggs in water	toads have thicker, bumpier skin

Discuss ways to order the details in your chart. Write detail sentences. Number them to help you remember the order.

Example: **1.** Both frogs and toads are amphibians.

Putting an Explanation Together

With your classmates you have written a topic sentence for your explanation. You have made a chart of details that show likenesses and differences. You have also decided how to order those details in your explanation.

Think about your topic sentence. Does it tell the main idea of your explanation? Look again at your detail sentences. Do they give facts or examples? Are they in a logical order?

Here is an explanation one student wrote. It explains how frogs and toads are alike and different. You have seen the parts of this explanation before. Notice how the writer has put together the topic sentence and the detail sentences.

> Frogs and toads are similar, but they are not exactly the same. Both frogs and toads are amphibians. Both eat insects and lay their eggs in water. A toad spends more time on land than a frog. Its body is shorter and wider than a frog's. Its skin is also thicker and bumpier.

This student chose to begin with the topic sentence. The student also chose to tell likenesses first and then differences.

Frog

Toad

Guided Practice: Writing an Explanation

Use your topic sentence and detail sentences to write an explanation. Put your topic sentence first or last. Include facts or examples that compare and contrast. Put these details in a logical order.

Share your explanation with a friend. Ask your friend to tell you what he or she has learned by reading your explanation.

Checklist: An Explanation

When you write an explanation, you will want to keep some points in mind. A checklist will remind you of the important points you learned in this lesson.

Look at this checklist. Some points need to be added. Make a copy of the checklist and complete it. Keep a copy of it in your writing folder. You can use it to check yourself when you write.

CHECKLIST

- ✔ Purpose and audience
- ✔ A topic sentence
- ✔ Details that ______
- ■ ______
- ■ ______
- ✔ Details that contrast
- ■ ______
- ■ ______
- ■ ______
- ✔ Logical order

2 THINKING AND WRITING: Comparing and Contrasting

Think about what you have learned about comparing and contrasting. You know that details that compare show how two things are alike. Details that contrast show how two things are different.

When a writer chooses to explain by using comparison and contrast, that writer has to decide which details to compare and which to contrast.

Look at this page from a writer's journal.

a bike and roller skates

Alike	Different	
	Bike	Roller Skates
have wheels	gets you places	easy to carry
are fun to use	is fast	used indoors and out
need to be laced or strapped on	costs more	

The writer plans to explain how bicycles and roller skates are alike and different. On the page, several details have been listed that compare and contrast a bike and roller skates.

Thinking Like a Writer

■ Which details are in the wrong place and need to be moved?

The writer needs to make clear what is alike and what is different. Two details are out of place. Only roller skates are laced or strapped on. Both a bike and roller skates can get you places.

When you write an explanation using comparison and contrast, arrange your details correctly. First, group likenesses together. Then, group differences together.

THINKING APPLICATION Comparing and Contrasting

COOPERATIVE LEARNING

Each of the writers named below is planning to write an explanation. Each plans to compare and contrast two things. Help the writers to arrange their details correctly. In each case, group details under the headings ALIKE and DIFFERENT. Write your lists on a separate sheet of paper.

1. Marguerite plans to compare and contrast cereal and toast. Here are her details:

   are quick to eat
   needs milk
   needs a toaster
   taste good

2. Joe plans to compare and contrast oak trees and pine trees. Here are his details:

   have needles
   are trees
   have leaves
   give us wood

3. Timothy plans to compare and contrast spring and fall. Here are his details:

   seasons of change
   warmer weather
   cooler weather
   clocks change

4. Callie plans to compare and contrast pencils and pens. Here are her details:

   need sharpening
   use ink
   let us write
   come in different colors

3 INDEPENDENT WRITING: An Explanation

Prewrite: Step 1

You have discovered that comparing and contrasting can help you to explain what you know or think about something. Sam, a student your age, wanted to explain by comparing and contrasting. He wanted to explain something to his after-school club. He chose a topic in this way.

Choosing a Topic

1. Sam wrote a list of pairs of things that he could compare and contrast.
2. He thought about comparing and contrasting each pair.
3. He decided on the pair he found the most interesting.

my twin cousins

✓ summer camps – good,
but only two kinds of camps

public school and private school

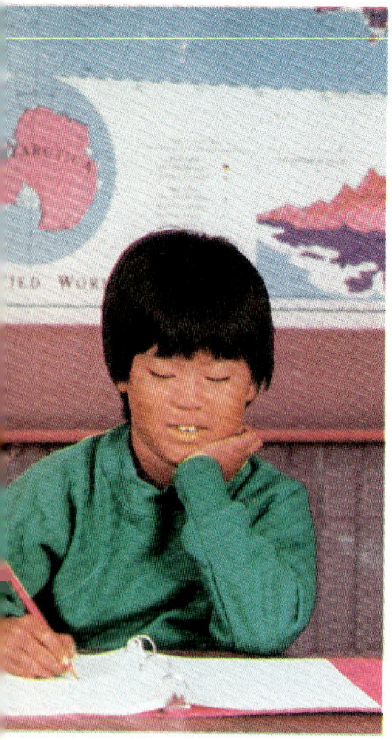

Sam liked the second pair on his list best. He found the topic interesting and had many things to say about it. He decided to narrow his topic to only two kinds of summer camps. He chose a nature camp and a baseball camp.

Exploring Ideas: Listing Strategy

Sam explored his topic by **listing** the good points of each camp. Look at Sam's lists on page 133.

Nature Camp	Baseball Camp
wildlife walks	special training
swimming	arts and crafts
campfires	swimming
arts and crafts	

Sam knew that he now had many ideas for writing.

Before beginning to write, Sam looked at his lists again. He decided to rewrite them. He wanted to make it easier to compare and contrast the two camps. Here are the new lists.

Alike	swimming, arts and crafts	
Different	Nature Camp	Baseball Camp
	wildlife walks	special baseball training
	campfires	

Thinking Like a Writer

- How did Sam change his lists?
- Why do you think Sam found the new lists more helpful?

YOUR TURN

JOURNAL

Think of two things you would like to compare and contrast. Use **Pictures** or your journal for ideas. Follow these steps.

- Make a list of pairs of items. Choose the pair you like best.
- Narrow your topic if it is too broad.
- Think of your purpose and audience.

Write a First Draft: Step 2

Sam knows what an explanation should include. He has made a planning checklist and is ready to write his first draft.

Sam's First Draft

I would like to compare and contrast Wapasakee Nature Camp and green field Baseball Camp. The nature camp offers swimming. Both campes teach arts and crafts. The baseball camp has a built-in pool. The pool is for swimming. At Wapasakee, the campers go on wildlife walks. At green field, everyone takes special training. The nature camp lets campers sleep outside around campfires.

While Sam was writing his first draft, he did not worry about errors. He was interested in getting his ideas on paper.

Planning Checklist
- Remember purpose and audience.
- Begin or end with a topic sentence.
- Include details that compare and contrast.
- Use a logical order for details.

YOUR TURN

Write your first draft. As you prepare to write, ask yourself these questions.

- What will my audience want to know?
- Which should I do first, compare or contrast?

TIME-OUT You might want to take some time out before you revise. That way you will be able to revise your writing with a fresh eye.

Revise: Step 3

After completing his first draft, Sam read it over to himself. Then, he shared his writing with a classmate. He wanted some suggestions for changes that would improve his writing.

Sam made a note to follow his classmate's advice. Then he looked back at his planning checklist. He saw that he had forgotten one point. He checked it off so that he would remember it when he revised.

Sam now has a checklist to use as he revises his draft.

Sam made some changes in his explanation. Notice, however, that he did not correct small errors. He knew that he could fix them later.

The changes Sam made improved his writing. Turn the page. Look at Sam's revised draft.

Revising Checklist

- ✓ Remember purpose and audience.
- Begin or end with a topic sentence.
- Include details that compare and contrast.
- Use a logical order for details.

WRITING PROCESS

Sam's Revised Draft

I would like to compare and contrast Wapasakee Nature Camp and green field Baseball Camp. The nature camp offers swimming in a lake. Both campes teach arts and crafts. The baseball camp has a built-in pool. ~~The pool is for~~ swimming. At Wapasakee, the campers go on wildlife walks. At green field, everyone takes special baseball training. The nature camp lets campers sleep outside around campfires. Since I like sleeping outdoors, I would like the nature camp better.

Thinking Like a Writer

WISE WORD CHOICE

- Which sentence did Sam move? Why?
- Which sentences did he combine? How does combining them improve the paragraph?
- Which sentence did he add? Why did he add it?

YOUR TURN

Read your first draft. Make a checklist. Ask yourself these questions.

- How can I make my topic sentence clearer?
- Do I use details that compare and contrast?
- How can I improve the order of my details?

If you wish, ask a friend to read your writing and make suggestions. Then, revise your first draft.

Proofread: Step 4

Sam knew that he still needed to proofread his work. He made a proofreading checklist. He used it while he proofread.

Part of Sam's Proofread Draft

I would like to compare and contrast Wapasakee Nature Camp and green field Baseball Camp. The nature camp offers swimming in a lake. Both camps campes teach arts and crafts. The baseball camp has a built-in pool. The pool is for swimming. At Wapasakee,

YOUR TURN

Proofreading Practice

Below is a paragraph that you can use to practice your proofreading skills. Find the errors. Look carefully for mistakes in plural nouns and proper nouns. Write the paragraph correctly on a separate sheet of paper.

I could not decide whether to buy the new record by tami tercel. Or a mystery story. I love mystery storys. tami tercel is one of my favorite Singers, though. I went to Book and Record jungle and compared prices. The book cost more than the record, so I bought the record. On the way home, I stopped at one of our local librarys and borrowed the book.

Proofreading Checklist

- Did I indent each paragraph?
- Did I spell all words correctly?
- What punctuation errors do I need to correct?
- What capitalization errors do I need to correct?

Applying Your Proofreading Skills

Now proofread your paragraph of comparison and contrast. Read your checklist one more time. Review **The Grammar Connection** and **The Mechanics Connection**, too. Use the proofreading marks to mark changes.

THE GRAMMAR CONNECTION

Remember these rules about plural nouns.

- If a singular noun ends with *s, ss, x, ch, sh,* or *z,* add *es* to form the plural.
  class → class**es** fox → fox**es** wish → wish**es**
- If a singular noun ends with a vowel and *y,* add *s* to form the plural. boy → boy**s** key → key**s**
- If a singular noun ends with a consonant and *y,* change the *y* to *i* and add *es* to form the plural.
  city → cit**ies** sky → sk**ies**

Check your paragraph. Have you formed plural nouns correctly?

THE MECHANICS CONNECTION

Remember these rules about capitalization.

- **Proper nouns** are nouns that name particular people, places, or things. They should begin with a capital letter.
  Amanda **F**ebruary **T**exas

Check your paragraph. Have you capitalized the proper nouns?

Proofreading Marks

¶	Indent
∧	Add
ℓ	Take out
≡	Make a capital letter
/	Make a small letter

Publish: Step 5

Sam wanted to share his explanation with his after-school club. He decided to read his writing aloud at the next meeting. To make his talk interesting, he made a display. First, he neatly copied his paragraph. Then, he glued it to a piece of poster board. On one side he added pictures of things to do at nature camp. On the other side he added pictures of things to do at sports camp.

YOUR TURN

Make a neat, final copy of your explanation. Then, think of a way to share your writing. You might find some ideas in the **Sharing Suggestions** box below.

SHARING SUGGESTIONS

Take photographs to illustrate your writing. Ask your classmates to compare and contrast your photos.

With your classmates publish a magazine. Include your writing, ads, and an eye-catching cover.

Read your writing aloud to some friends. Have a group discussion.

4 SPEAKING AND LISTENING: Talking on the Telephone

Ring. The call is for you. What are some things you need to know when you make and receive telephone calls? First, of course, it is important to be polite. Second, you need to know how to take and leave messages.

Read this telephone message. Notice the information it includes.

When you talk on the telephone, it will help you to keep the following guidelines in mind. If you wish, add other guidelines to the list. Write them on a separate sheet of paper.

SPEAKING GUIDELINES: A Telephone Conversation

1. Say "Hello" and give your name.
2. Ask to speak to the person you are calling.
3. If the person is not at home, leave a brief message.
4. Speak clearly and politely.

- What information is important in a telephone message?
- How should you speak on the telephone?

SPEAKING APPLICATION A Telephone Conversation

To practice talking on the telephone, choose a partner from your class. Imagine that you are calling someone who is not at home. Leave a message. Use the speaking guidelines to help you. Your partner will be using the following guidelines.

LISTENING GUIDELINES: A Telephone Conversation

1. Listen for the name of the caller.
2. Listen for the name of the person who is being called.
3. Listen closely to the message. Be sure you write down the caller's phone number.

W R I T I N G

EXTENSION

5 WRITER'S RESOURCES: The Library

In this unit you have written paragraphs that explain. As you know, you need facts and examples in order to explain. Where can you find facts, examples, and other types of information?

The library is a good place to find information. The library has books, magazines, newspapers, films, filmstrips, records, and tapes. Some libraries even have computers for your use.

Most libraries are divided into three main sections: fiction, nonfiction, and reference. What types of books would you find in each of these sections?

Fiction books contain made-up stories. Novels and short stories are examples of fiction. Fiction books are arranged in alphabetical order by the authors' last names. For example, a book called *The Wind in the Willows* by Kenneth Grahame would be found with other books of fiction by authors whose last names begin with *G.*

Nonfiction books contain facts and practical information. For example, a book about caring for turtles is nonfiction. Nonfiction books are grouped together by subject. Each nonfiction book has a call number. The **call number** helps you to find the book on the shelf.

Reference books also contain facts and practical information. Dictionaries, encyclopedias, atlases, and directories are reference books. You can borrow most books in a library, but you cannot borrow reference books.

Practice

A. In which part of the library would you find each book? Write **fiction**, **nonfiction**, or **reference.**

1. *Earthworms, Dirt, and Rotten Leaves* explores the life of the earthworm and its environment.
2. *The Best Bad Thing* by Yoshiko Uchida is a story about a young girl who spends her summer helping her mother's friend.
3. *Duck Boy* by Christobel Mattingly is a story about a boy named Adam, who protects a family of ducks from their enemies.
4. *The Readers' Almanac* provides information on books for children by famous authors.
5. *Carpentry for Children* tells how to make special projects.
6. *The Macmillan Illustrated Animal Encyclopedia* contains information about the creatures of the world.

B. Below is a list of fiction books. For each, write the word that would help you find the book on the library shelves.

7. *The Enormous Egg,* by Oliver Butterworth
8. *Zeely,* by Virginia Hamilton
9. *Circle of Giving,* by Ellen Howard
10. *The Silver Chair,* by C. S. Lewis

C. Below is a list of nonfiction books. For each, write the subject you would look under to find it in the library.

11. *Volcano: The Eruption and Healing of Mount St. Helens*
12. *Going to School in 1876*
13. *Shelters from Tepee to Igloo*
14. *A Snake's Body*
15. *Project Panda Watch*

WRITING APPLICATION A List

Go to your school or public library and find a fiction book, a nonfiction book, and a reference book. Copy the title of each book. Later, write the title of each book on a piece of construction paper and draw pictures to illustrate the book.

6 WRITER'S RESOURCES: The Card Catalog

How do you find a book in the library? One way is to look in the card catalog. The **card catalog** contains cards that are filed in alphabetical order. In some libraries the card catalog has been replaced by large books or by a computer. In all cases, the system works the same way.

Each book in the library is listed on a title card and on an author card. Every nonfiction book and some fiction books also have a subject card.

A **title card** shows the title of a book first. Then, it gives information, such as who wrote the book and what it is about. An **author card** lists the author of the book first. A **subject card** begins with the subject of the book.

Look at these examples of cards from the card catalog. Think about how these cards could help you to find a book.

TITLE CARD

call number

The World of Dogs

636 Racklin, Nora.
R

AUTHOR CARD

636 Racklin, Nora.
R The World of Dogs
New York: Random House, Inc., c. 1981.

SUBJECT CARD

DOGS

636 Racklin, Nora.
R The World of Dogs
New York: Random House, Inc., c. 1981.
212p. : illus.

You will notice that each card has a **call number** in the upper left-hand corner. The call number can help you to find the book. Nonfiction books are arranged on the shelves according to their call numbers.

Practice

A. Look again at the title, author, and subject cards on page 144. Use them to help you answer these questions. Write your answers on a separate sheet of paper.

1. What is the call number of the book?
2. What is the book's title?
3. Who wrote the book?
4. When was the book published?
5. How many pages does the book have?

B. Which card would you use to find each of the following books? On a separate sheet of paper, write **title card, author card,** or **subject card.**

6. A book about horses
7. A book by Scott Corbett
8. A book called *Light in the Forest*
9. A book about Martin Luther King, Jr.
10. A book called *Making Kites*
11. A book by Nicholasa Mohr
12. A book about the thirteen colonies
13. A book by Laura Ingalls Wilder
14. A book about using computers
15. A book called *The Midnight Fox*

WRITING APPLICATION A List

At your school or public library, use the card catalog to find three interesting books about one of the subjects below. On a separate sheet of paper, write the call number, title, and author of each of the three books you find.

INSECTS CRAFTS MYTHOLOGY

THE CURRICULUM CONNECTION

Writing About Health

An important part of good health is regular exercise. Exercise helps to keep bones, muscles, and organs in good working order. Exercise can even put you in a good mood.

There are many forms of exercise. You can walk, run, or swim. You can play a sport, such as baseball, basketball, or tennis. You can do calisthenics—exercises designed to strengthen specific muscles. For almost everyone, exercise should be an important part of daily life.

ACTIVITIES

Compare and Contrast Look at the soccer players in the photograph. Notice how they are moving and what muscles they are using. Look at their uniforms. On a separate sheet of paper, write sentences that explain what is alike and what is different about the players in the photograph.

Imagine a Situation Imagine that you are going to compete in the Olympics. Choose one summer sport and one winter sport in which you might like to compete. Write a paragraph comparing and contrasting the two sports.

Respond to Literature The following explanation is taken from an encyclopedia. As you read it, notice the examples of comparison and contrast. Then, respond to what you have read. Your response may be a paragraph in your journal about playing soccer or another game, a summary of the explanation, or an illustration for one of the paragraphs.

Soccer

SOCCER is the world's most popular sport. It is the national sport of most European and Latin American countries, and of many other nations. Millions of people in more than 140 countries play soccer. Soccer's most famous international competition, the World Cup Championship, is held every four years.

In a soccer game, two teams of 11 players try to kick or hit a ball into each other's goal. The team that scores the most goals wins. All the players except the goalkeepers must kick the ball or hit it with their head or body. Only the goalies can touch the ball with their hands.

Soccer as it is played today developed in England during the 1800s and quickly spread to many other countries. Until the mid-1900s, the game was not greatly popular in the United States. But today, it is one of the nation's fastest-growing sports.

In Great Britain and many other countries, soccer is called *football* or *association football.* The word *soccer* comes from *assoc.,* an abbreviation for *association.*

UNIT CHECKUP

LESSON 1 **Group Writing: An Explanation** (page 126) Rewrite this paragraph. Put the details in a logical order.

I think I am like my brother in some ways but not in other ways. Both my brother and I like to laugh. He is older and more sure of himself. I feel shy around other people. We also like the same music.

LESSON 2 **Thinking: Comparing and Contrasting** (page 130) Group these details about dogs and cats under the headings: ALIKE and DIFFERENT.

cat is small
dog is very big
both like to be petted
cat scratches the furniture
dog chews up slippers
both like to sleep on my bed

LESSON 3 **Writing an Explanation** (page 132) Imagine that you are helping a younger friend. You want to explain the ways that two things are alike and different. For example, the two things may be snow and rain, buses and trains, or crayons and chalk. Write a paragraph that compares and contrasts the two things.

LESSON 4 **Speaking and Listening: The Telephone** (page 140) List three things you should remember to listen for when you take a telephone message.

LESSONS 5-6 **Writer's Resources: The Library and the Card Catalog** (pages 142-145) You want to write a report comparing and contrasting your state and another state. Answer these questions.

1. Which reference book would help you more, a dictionary or an encyclopedia?
2. What type of card would you look for in the card catalog, a subject card or an author card?

THEME PROJECT A Taste Test

You have been thinking about choices. You read a story about a boy who chose to talk about his turtle in class. You wrote an explanation that compared and contrasted two things.

People who make commercials know we all make choices. They sometimes show us making choices in their ads. For example, some ads use taste tests to suggest that one product is better than another. You can do your own taste tests. In fact, you can do tests that use all the senses—sight, sound, taste, touch, and smell.

Think of a test you would like to do.

- First, think of two products to compare and contrast. They must be similar, such as two types of fruit juice.
- Then, decide on the kind of test you want to do. Do you want people to look at, listen to, taste, touch, or smell your products?
- Bring the items to school. Also, bring other materials you need, such as cups or paper to cover the labels. Ask for volunteers. Have them try your products and tell which one they like better.
- Write down each person's choice. After all your volunteers have done the test, show them the products they chose.
- If you wish, work in small groups on this project.

UNIT 5

Action Verbs

In this unit you will learn about action verbs. Action verbs are words like *tickle.* Action verbs can add excitement to your writing.

Discuss Read the poem on the opposite page. What are the children doing?

Creative Expression The unit theme is *Messages.* When might you need to send a message to someone? What would you like to say? In your journal, write a message to a friend.

THEME: *MESSAGES*

Whispers
tickle through your ear
telling things you like to hear.

—Myra Cohn Livingston, from "Whispers"

1 WHAT IS AN ACTION VERB?

An action verb is a word that expresses action.

You know that all sentences have a subject and a predicate. The predicate tells what the subject does or is. The main word in the predicate is the verb. Most verbs are action verbs. An **action verb** expresses an action. It tells what the subject does or did.

Subjects	Predicates
Mom and Dad	wrote a note.
Mom	put it on the table.
We	found the note.
My sister	read the note.

Read these sentences.

I _____ a note.
Dad _____ the note.

How many words can you think of that fit in the blank? Any word that fills the blank correctly is an action verb.

Guided Practice

Tell the action verb in each sentence.

Example: Maria sent the note. *sent*

1. Tom wrote a note to Stan.
2. Tom left the note in Stan's lunch box.
3. Tom asked Stan for an apple.
4. Stan found the note.
5. He gave Tom an apple.

?! THINK

- How can I decide which word in a sentence is an action verb?

REMEMBER

■ An **action verb** is a word that expresses action. An action verb shows what the subject does or did.

GRAMMAR

More Practice

A. Write each sentence. Underline each action verb.

Example: José bought a stamp.
José bought a stamp.

6. José mailed a letter to Roberto.
7. Roberto lives in Puerto Rico.
8. Roberto's family moved there last year.
9. José misses Roberto.
10. The friends send letters to each other often.
11. José writes to Roberto often.
12. Roberto answers José's letters quickly.

B. Write each sentence. Write an action verb in each blank.

Example: Mom _____ to the mailbox.
Mom went to the mailbox.

13. Mom and I _____ a letter from my sister Toby.
14. Toby _____ in San Francisco, California.
15. Toby _____ us to visit her.
16. Mom _____ me about the trip.
17. I _____ the idea very much.
18. Mom _____ to Toby.
19. She _____ Toby's invitation.
20. Mom _____ to visit Golden Gate Park.

Extra Practice, page 178

WRITING APPLICATION A Letter

Write a letter to a friend who lives far away. Tell your friend about some of the things that you enjoy doing. Exchange letters with a classmate. Then, underline all of the action verbs in each other's letters.

2 MAIN VERBS AND HELPING VERBS

Sometimes a verb may be more than one word. The **main verb** tells what the subject does or is. A verb that comes before the main verb is the **helping verb**.

Verbs Often Used As Helping Verbs

have	am	was
has	is	were
had	are	will

Read the sentences below. The main verbs are in pink. The helping verbs are in blue.

Allan is learning a new alphabet.

The alphabet was invented many years ago.

He has read many books about it.

Sarah will teach him the new letters.

Guided Practice

Tell which word in each sentence is the main verb and which is the helping verb.

Example: The student had studied many alphabets.
had *helping verb* *studied* *main verb*

1. I have learned many letters.
2. He is learning a new letter every day.
3. Some alphabets have included pictures for words.
4. One person had invented symbols for some sounds.
5. I am studying an unusual alphabet.

?! THINK

■ How can I decide which verb in a sentence is the main verb and which is the helping verb?

GRAMMAR

REMEMBER

- The **main verb** tells what the subject does or is.
- A **helping verb** helps the main verb to show an action.

More Practice

Write each sentence. Draw one line under each main verb. Draw two lines under each helping verb.

Example: The alphabet was formed long ago.

6. Twenty-six letters are included in our alphabet.
7. That alphabet had come from the Roman alphabet.
8. The Egyptians had created picture writing.
9. The picture writing is called hieroglyphics.
10. My grandmother has learned all of the symbols.
11. She will teach me their meanings.
12. Amy is studying the Greek alphabet.
13. She has written each letter on a chart.
14. Joe will read the letters in the alphabet.
15. We are learning about different alphabets.
16. Many alphabets were taken from the Greek alphabet.
17. The Greek letters are used in the other alphabets.
18. Our letter names have come from Greek.
19. My teachers are studying the first alphabet.
20. Some languages are written with signs.
21. The Chinese alphabet is written with signs.
22. Chin Lee is teaching me some Chinese signs.
23. I have learned many Chinese signs.
24. Josie has seen ancient Latin scrolls.
25. My sister is studying Latin in college.

Extra Practice, page 179

WRITING APPLICATION An Alphabet

COOPERATIVE LEARNING

Work with two or three classmates to invent your own alphabet. Then, write a few sentences that explain how your alphabet works. When you have finished, exchange your writing with someone in your group. Underline the verbs.

3 VERB TENSES

You know that a verb can express action. A verb can also tell when an action takes place. The **tense** of a verb lets you know that something is happening in the present, in the past, or in the future.

Three Main Verb Tenses

Present	Past	Future
talk, talks	talked	will talk
call, calls	called	will call

- Verbs in the **present tense** show actions that are happening now.

  John **looks** in the phone book. He **finds** the right number.

- Verbs in the **past tense** show actions that have already happened. Many verbs in the past tense end in *ed*.

  Tanya **answered** the telephone. Then, she **hung** up.

- Verbs in the **future tense** show actions that will happen. To form the future tense, use the helping verb *will*.

  Marcia **will call** Simon. She **will ask** him a question.

Guided Practice

Find the verb in each sentence. Then, tell whether it is in the present tense, in the past tense, or in the future tense.

Example: The inventor called his helper. *called past*

1. Alexander Graham Bell invented the telephone.
2. Samuel will tell us about Bell's invention.
3. Telephones help people in many ways.
4. People receive messages every day.
5. This invention benefits many people.

?! **THINK**

- How can I tell whether a verb shows the present tense, the past tense, or the future tense?

REMEMBER

- Verbs can show when actions take place.
- The **tense** of a verb tells whether an action takes place in the past, present, or future.

More Practice

A. Write each sentence. Then, write **past, present,** or **future** to show the tense of each underlined verb.

Example: Students will report on great inventors. *future*

6. Samuel chooses Alexander Graham Bell.
7. Alexander Graham Bell came from Scotland.
8. Thomas Watson helped Bell.
9. On March 10, 1876, Bell spoke on the first telephone.
10. Watson listens to the words.
11. Bell and Watson lectured about the telephone.
12. They wanted people to see the telephone.
13. Samuel will finish his report soon.

B. Write each sentence. Underline each verb. Then, write **past, present,** or **future** to show the tense.

Example: The telephone changed our lives. *past*

14. Alexander Graham Bell interests me.
15. He developed the telephone in 1876.
16. He invented other things besides the telephone.
17. Gary asked me to call him.
18. I will tell him about our assignment.
19. We will work together on our report about the telephone.
20. We will read our report to the class.

Extra Practice, page 180

WRITING APPLICATION A Telephone Conversation

Imagine a telephone conversation taking place between two people. Write the conversation they have. Then, exchange papers with a classmate. Tell whether each verb in the conversation is in the past, present, or future tense.

4 MORE ABOUT VERB TENSES

The tense of a verb tells you when an action takes place. A **present-tense** verb tells what happens now. A **past-tense** verb tells what happened in the past. A **future-tense** verb tells what will happen in the future.

Present Tense	hike	We **hike** the trail.
Past Tense	hiked	We **hiked** all day.
Future Tense	will hike	We **will hike** tomorrow.

Guided Practice

Tell which word or words in each sentence are the verbs.

Example: Sam walks in the park. *walks*

1. Greta takes the sailboat out on the lake.
2. She learned about sailboats last year.
3. The boat skims over the water.
4. Soon it will rain.
5. Greta turns the boat around.

?! THINK

■ How can I tell when the action in a sentence takes place?

REMEMBER

- A verb in the **present tense** tells what happens now.
- A verb in the **past tense** tells what has happened.
- A verb in the **future tense** tells what will happen.

More Practice

A. Write the sentences. Underline each verb. Write whether the verb is in the **present tense, past tense,** or **future tense.**

Example: I will leave for camp tomorrow. *future*

6. I like camp very much.
7. It rains here every day.
8. Yesterday, we pitched the tent between storms.
9. We usually sleep in cabins.
10. Tomorrow, we will stay in the tents.
11. We will cook dinner over the campfire.
12. I swim each morning.
13. Soon, I will help others in my class.

B. Write these sentences. Fill in the blank with the correct form of the verb in parentheses ( ).

Example: We ______ tomorrow. (leave, future) *will leave*

14. We ______ San Francisco at noon. (reach, past)
15. I ______ our luggage from the rack. (pull, present)
16. I ______ the bags to the hotel. (carry, future)
17. Soon, we ______ to the Golden Gate Bridge. (walk, future)
18. We ______ to the top of a tall building. (climb, past)
19. The cable cars ______ slowly up the hills. (move, past)
20. We ______ them later. (ride, future)

Extra Practice, page 181

WRITING APPLICATION A Post Card

Think of a place that you have visited. Write a message on a post card about the place. Exchange your message with a classmate. Underline the verbs in your classmate's message. Then tell which tense each verb is in.

5 SUBJECT-VERB AGREEMENT

In a sentence the subject and verb must work together. A verb must **agree** with the subject of a sentence. If the subject is singular, the verb must be singular. If the subject is plural, the verb must be plural.

Look at the chart below.

Making Subjects and Verbs Agree

Singular Subjects If the subject is a singular noun or *he, she,* or *it,* add **s** or **es** to the verb.	Jan **goes** to a bakery. She **sees** many cakes.
Plural Subjects If the subject is a plural noun or *I*, *we*, *you*, or *they*, **s** is not added to the verb.	The bakers **wave** at Jan. They **smile** at her.

Guided Practice

Tell which verb in parentheses ( ) correctly completes each sentence.

Example: The bakers (bake, bakes) well. *bake*

1. This baker (make, makes) many cakes.
2. The cakes (bake, bakes) for one hour.
3. People (buy, buys) the cakes.
4. The bakers (write, writes) messages in icing.
5. This message (say, says) "Happy Birthday."
6. Some cakes (say, says) "Happy Anniversary."

?! THINK

- How can I decide when to use a singular verb or a plural verb in a sentence?

REMEMBER

- If the subject of a sentence is singular, the verb must be singular.
- If the subject of a sentence is plural, the verb must be plural.

More Practice

A. Write each sentence. Use the correct present-tense verb from the pair in parentheses ( ).

Example: The bakery window (sparkle, sparkles). *sparkles*

7. We (look, looks) at the cakes in the glass cases.
8. Two people (come, comes) to buy cakes.
9. Mr. Brown (need, needs) a cake with a message.
10. He (want, wants) the message to say "Good Luck."
11. Ms. Taylor (ask, asks) for two cakes.
12. The baker (write, writes) "Happy Days" on one.
13. He (put, puts) "Welcome Home" on the other.

B. Write each sentence. Write the correct present-tense form of the verb in parentheses ( ) for each blank.

Example: We _____ all the cakes. (like) *like*

14. The girls _____ a cake that they like. (see)
15. Sue _____ the message. (check)
16. They _____ to buy the cake. (decide)
17. The cake _____ a picture of a balloon. (show)
18. The baker _____ us some cupcakes. (give)
19. He _____ us the price. (tell)
20. We _____ them for our party. (buy)

Extra Practice, Practice Plus, pages 182–184

WRITING APPLICATION A Description

Imagine that you have been asked to design a cake for a special occasion. Write a message for your cake. Then, write five sentences about your cake.

6 USING IRREGULAR VERBS I

You know that you can form the past tense of most verbs by adding the letters *ed* to the verb. Some past-tense verbs follow different rules. Verbs that do not add *ed* to form the past tense are called **irregular verbs.**

I **see** you now. I **saw** you then. I **have seen** you often.

Here are some common irregular verbs.

Present	Past	Past with *has, have,* or *had*
see	saw	seen
go	went	gone
come	came	come
run	ran	run
give	gave	given
eat	ate	eaten
write	wrote	written
drive	drove	driven
ride	rode	ridden
take	took	taken

Guided Practice

Tell which verb in parentheses ( ) completes each sentence.

Example: She (ran, run) away. *ran*

1. I have (saw, seen) that television commercial.
2. It (came, come) on at eight o'clock.
3. A clever writer (wrote, written) the script.
4. John has (went, gone) to the television studio.
5. His father (drove, driven) him there.

?! THINK

■ How can I decide which form of an irregular verb to use?

REMEMBER

- **Irregular verbs** are verbs that do not add *ed* to form the past tense.

GRAMMAR

More Practice

A. Write each sentence. Choose the correct irregular verb from the pair in parentheses ( ).

Example: The actor (ran, run) away from the crowds. *ran*

6. We (saw, seen) actors filming a commercial.
7. We (ate, eaten) lunch with the actors.
8. They had (gave, given) a good performance.
9. A woman has (took, taken) the pictures.
10. A writer had (wrote, written) the script.
11. Another actor (came, come) onto the set.
12. She had (went, gone) to Studio A by mistake.
13. Then, she had (ran, run) back to Studio B.

B. Write each sentence. Choose the correct past-tense form of the irregular verb in parentheses ( ) for each blank.

Example: The students had _____ a performance. (give) *given*

14. Some students _____ a script. (write)
15. A film crew has _____ to our school. (come)
16. Two men had _____ to set up the cameras. (go)
17. An actor has _____ onto the set. (run)
18. She _____ two bowls of a new brand of cereal. (eat)
19. The director had _____ her a script. (give)
20. Have you _____ the commercial yet? (see)

Extra Practice, page 185

WRITING APPLICATION A Television Commercial

Imagine that you and a small group of classmates are television scriptwriters. Write a script for a commercial about a product, a person, or a place. Find the irregular past-tense verbs in your work.

COOPERATIVE LEARNING

7 USING IRREGULAR VERBS II

You know that some verbs are irregular verbs. You use irregular verbs often in your speaking and writing.

I **draw** well. I **drew** a picture yesterday.
I **have drawn** many pictures.

Here is a chart that shows more irregular verbs.

Present	Past	Past with *has, have,* or *had*
fly	flew	flown
draw	drew	drawn
sing	sang	sung
swim	swam	swum
begin	began	begun
do	did	done
grow	grew	grown
throw	threw	thrown
bring	brought	brought
make	made	made

Guided Practice

Tell which verb in parentheses ( ) completes each sentence correctly.

Example: He (fly, flew) in a plane yesterday. *flew*

1. I have (drew, drawn) a picture about littering.
2. My teacher has (make, made) my picture into a poster.
3. I (did, done) a very good job.
4. I have (bring, brought) the poster to the principal.
5. She has (began, begun) to collect our posters.

?! THINK

- How can I decide which form of an irregular verb to use?

REMEMBER

- **Irregular verbs** are verbs that do not add *ed* to form the past tense.

More Practice

A. Write each sentence. Choose the correct irregular verb from the pair in parentheses ( ).

Example: The class (begin, began) the clean-up campaign.
began

6. Our teacher has (make, made) an announcement.
7. Someone had (threw, thrown) litter into the pond.
8. A scientist has (flew, flown) in to test the water.
9. Our classroom (grew, grown) quiet.
10. Mr. Lee (began, begun) to read the announcement.
11. We (drew, drawn) a picture about pollution.
12. Stacy and Taku (sang, sung) a song.
13. Our class (did, done) something about pollution.

B. Write each sentence. Use the correct past-tense form of the verb in parentheses ( ).

Example: The mayor _____ a prize to the school. (give) *gave*

14. We have _____ a project about plants and animals. (do)
15. First, we _____ a large mural. (draw)
16. Birds _____ in the sky and nested in trees. (fly)
17. Seals _____ in the water and lay on the beach. (swim)
18. Some students have _____ seeds in window boxes. (grow)
19. I have _____ my part of the mural. (begin)
20. The teacher has _____ us time to work on our project. (give)

Extra Practice, page 186

WRITING APPLICATION A Poster

Create a poster. Write a message on your poster. Exchange posters with a partner. Underline the irregular verbs in each other's messages.

GRAMMAR

8 SPELLING VERBS CORRECTLY

You know that *s* or *es* is added to some verbs to form the present tense. You also know that *ed* is added to many verbs to form the past tense. When *es* or *ed* is added, the spelling of some verbs changes.

Look at the chart below.

For verbs ending in a consonant and *y*, change the *y* to *i* and add *es* or *ed*.	cry + *es* cry + *ed*	The baby **cries.** The baby **cried.**
For verbs ending in one vowel and one consonant, double the final consonant and add *ed*.	stop + *ed*	The car **stopped.**
For verbs ending in *e*, drop the *e* and add *es* or *ed*.	care + *es* care + *ed*	She **cares** for me. She **cared** for me.

Guided Practice

Read each sentence. Spell the present-tense and past-tense form of each verb in parentheses ( ).

Example: Jean (invite) Gary for lunch. *invites* *invited*

1. Jean (hope) Gary will come early.
2. Gary (plan) to bring a secret code.
3. Jean (love) to decode messages.
4. Gary (create) interesting codes.
5. Jean (try) to figure out Gary's code.

?! **THINK**

- How can I decide if a verb in the present tense or past tense needs a spelling change?

REMEMBER

- Change the *y* to *i* before adding *es* or *ed* to verbs that end in a consonant and *y*.
- Double the final consonant and add *ed* to verbs that end in one vowel and one consonant.
- Drop the *e* and add *es* or *ed* to verbs that end in *e*.

More Practice

Write each sentence. Use the correct present-tense or past-tense form of each verb in parentheses ( ).

Example: Roz's classmates (like) to figure out secret codes. *past*
liked

6. Roz (carry) a secret code to school. *past*
7. Roz was (horrify) when she lost the code. *past*
8. She (hurry) to retrace her steps. *present*
9. She (scurry) down the path. *present*
10. Roz (worry) about finding the code. *present*
11. She found the paper and (copy) it over. *past*
12. Roz (promise) to be more careful. *present*
13. Dave (clap) his hands when he heard Roz. *past*
14. Len (stare) at the paper. *present*
15. He (try) to figure out the code. *present*
16. He (glance) at the letters again. *past*
17. He (name) each part of the code. *past*
18. Len (study) the code carefully. *present*
19. His pencil (fly) over the paper. *present*
20. He (supply) a letter for each number. *past*

Extra Practice, page 187

WRITING APPLICATION A Secret Code

Create a code of your own and write a secret message. Then, write a paragraph that explains how to use your code. Share your writing with a partner. Ask your partner to find the past-tense and present-tense verbs.

9 MECHANICS: Using the Comma

When you speak, you pause briefly between words. In order to show a reader where to pause, you must use **commas** in your writing.

Here are some rules for using commas.

- If three or more words are listed in a sentence, the list is called a **series**. Use commas to separate the items in a series. Do not use a comma after the last word in a series.

  The children sang, danced, and played games.

- Use a comma to set off a person's name when the person is being **directly addressed.**

  Cam, look at me. You see, Cam, the color is red.

- Use a comma after the words *yes, no*, and *well*.

  Yes, I am studying. No, I will not be going.
  Well, maybe I will go tomorrow.

Guided Practice

Tell where commas are needed.

Example: Yes I went to the art show. *Yes,*

1. Eric what is your painting about?
2. Yes I understand now.
3. Reggie Sally and Gail are working on a mural.

?! THINK

- How can I decide where commas should be used?

GRAMMAR

REMEMBER

- A **comma** is needed after each item in a series except after the last item.
- A **comma** is needed to set off a person's name when the person is being addressed, and after the words *yes*, *no*, and *well.*

More Practice

Write each sentence. Use commas where they are needed.

Example: Yes I enjoy painting. *Yes, I enjoy painting.*

4. They are using green white and red paint.
5. You know Alice your drawing is beautiful.
6. Kiri your painting makes me think of warm things.
7. The way you used orange red and purple is amazing.
8. Jim drew painted and hung his picture.
9. See James here is a sculpture of children.
10. They look excited joyful and carefree.
11. What message do you get from the sculpture Yoko?
12. Yes it reminds me of being happy and free.
13. Alfred what do you think?
14. Well it makes me think of springtime.
15. No I do not know who the sculptor is.
16. Well are you glad that you will visit the museum?
17. We will see paintings sculptures and drawings.
18. I want to see the drawings watercolors and oils.
19. This artist used paint crayon and torn paper.
20. The students laughed talked and sang songs on the bus.

Extra Practice, page 188

WRITING APPLICATION An Art Review

Imagine that you have been asked by a local newspaper to write your response to a new art show. Describe what you saw, what you liked, and what message you may have received from the artwork. Exchange papers with a partner. Ask your partner to make sure you have used commas correctly.

10 VOCABULARY BUILDING: Prefixes

You can change the meaning of a word by adding a word part to it. A **prefix** is a word part added to the beginning of a word. The word to which a prefix is added is called the **base word.** Prefixes change the meanings of base words.

Below is a chart of some prefixes and their meanings.

Prefix	Meaning	Base Word	New Word
un	not, opposite of	tied	untied
dis	not, opposite of	obeyed	disobeyed
mis	bad or wrong, badly or wrongly	read	misread
im	not, without	possible	impossible
in	not, without	direct	indirect
non	not, opposite of, without	fiction	nonfiction
re	again, back	write	rewrite
pre	before	view	preview

Tied

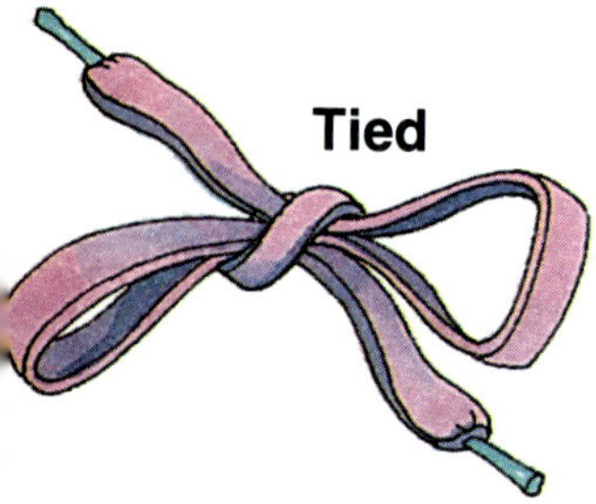

To figure out the meaning of a new word, think about the meaning of the prefix and the base word.

Untied

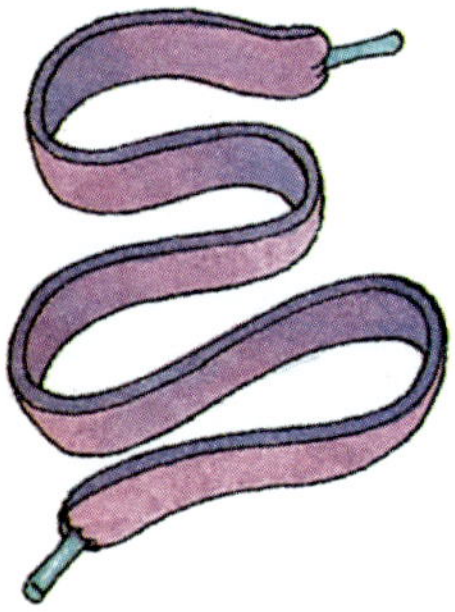

Guided Practice

Add a prefix from the chart above to each word below. Use the new word in a sentence.

Example: wrote *rewrote* *She rewrote the letter.*

1. printed
2. decorate
3. happy
4. fill
5. fire
6. tasteful
7. polite
8. honor

?! THINK

■ How can I tell the meaning of a word with a prefix?

REMEMBER

- A **prefix** is a word part added to the beginning of a base word.
- A **prefix** changes the meaning of the base word to which it is added.

More Practice

A. Write each sentence. Substitute a word with a prefix for the underlined word or words.

Example: Was that not possible? *Was that impossible?*

9. We tried to start the computer again.
10. We must have read the directions wrong.
11. This is not believable.
12. Jason is not interested in computers.
13. This floppy disk is not perfect.
14. That computer is not breakable.
15. We need to write our messages again.

B. Write each sentence. Add a prefix to each word in parentheses ( ). Use the new word to complete the sentence.

Example: We were _____ to use the computer. (able) *unable*

16. Please _____ the printer with ink. (fill)
17. Ed will _____ the directions before we begin. (view)
18. They have _____ many words. (spelled)
19. It is _____ to read them. (possible)
20. The students stared in _____ . (belief)

Extra Practice, page 189

WRITING APPLICATION A Paragraph

Develop an idea for a new computer program. Your program could make a task easier or solve a problem. Describe the program you would like to develop. Have a classmate read your writing. Ask your classmate to identify any words with prefixes.

GRAMMAR AND WRITING CONNECTION

Making Subjects and Verbs Agree

When you write, you want to make your sentences as clear as you can. You will need to be sure that your subjects and verbs agree.

Sometimes, you will want to use helping verbs in your sentences. The verbs *has, have,* and *had* are common helping verbs. In sentences with helping verbs, both the verb and the helping verb must agree with the subject.

Use *has* with a singular subject.	Sue **has** seen the air show.
Use *have* with plural subjects and *I* or *you*.	They **have** watched the pilots. I **have** watched the pilots.
Use *had* with singular or plural subjects.	The boy **had** seen the shows. The boys **had** seen the shows.

COOPERATIVE LEARNING

Working Together

Tell which helping verb correctly completes each sentence.

Example: The planes (has, have) circled above. *have*

1. I (has, have) seen many planes.
2. They (has, have) landed.
3. The planes (has, had) soared high.
4. Sara (had, have) looked at the sky.
5. She (has, have) applauded the stunt.

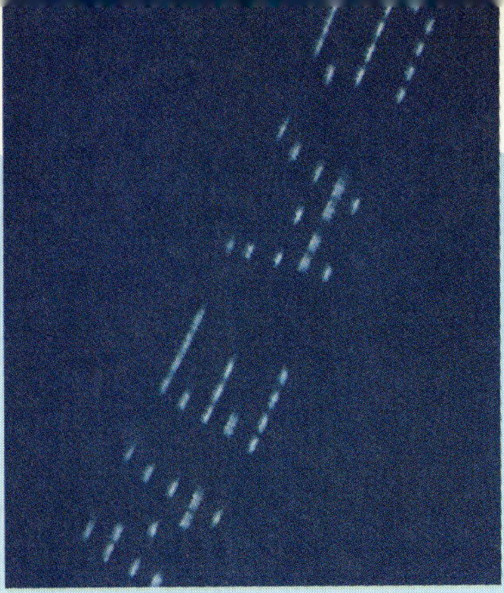

Revising Sentences

Sara wrote the following sentences about the planes that she saw. Help Sara to revise her sentences by correcting the error in subject-verb agreement in each one.

6. The planes has circled overhead.
7. I has watched white smoke coming from the engine.
8. The smoke have formed letters in the sky.
9. The letters has made words.
10. The words has told a message.
11. Skywriting have seemed like fun.
12. The pilot have known how to fly the planes.
13. Soon, the smoke have faded in the sky.
14. The messages has lasted only a few minutes.
15. They has looked pretty in the sky.
16. I has read the messages.
17. We has tried, but they faded fast.
18. The planes has landed in a nearby field.
19. We has liked the messages in the sky.
20. The show have ended.

WRITER AT WORK

Think about all the different ways in which messages are sent and received. Then, write a paragraph or a poem in which you give a message. As you revise your work, check to make sure that all subjects and verbs agree.

UNIT CHECKUP

LESSON 1

What Is an Action Verb? (page 152) Write each sentence. Draw one line under the complete predicate. Draw two lines under each action verb.

1. I mailed a letter to my friend Roxanne.
2. She lives in another state.
3. I invited her for a visit.
4. Roxanne enjoys my letters.
5. She replies quickly to each one.

LESSON 2

Main Verbs and Helping Verbs (page 154) Write each sentence. Draw one line under each main verb. Draw two lines under each helping verb.

6. Paco and Rebecca are collecting stamps.
7. They have filled an album with stamps.
8. They will show their album to other classes.
9. I have seen their collection.
10. They are giving stamps to their classmates.

LESSONS 3-4

Verb Tenses (pages 156–159) Write each sentence. Then write **past, present,** or **future** to show the tense of each underlined verb.

11. Ms. Kimura <u>will speak</u> to our class.
12. She <u>works</u> for a large company.
13. Her company <u>delivers</u> mail quickly.
14. I <u>received</u> an overnight package.
15. Ms. Kimura <u>will tell</u> us about her company.

LESSON 5

Subject-Verb Agreement (page 160) Write each sentence. Use the correct verb in parentheses ( ).

16. Jim (take, takes) a typing class.
17. They (use, uses) a chart.
18. The charts (show, shows) pictures of a keyboard.
19. Jim (know, knows) where all the keys are.
20. He (type, types) a message to Kate.

LESSONS 6-7

Using Irregular Verbs (pages 162–165) Write the correct irregular verb in parentheses ( ).

21. We (saw, seen) an interesting movie.
22. We (bring, brought) popcorn with us.
23. Have you (threw, thrown) the box away?
24. No, I have (gave, given) it to Marcy.
25. Marcy, what have you (did, done) with the box?
26. The box (fly, flew) out of my hand.
27. It (make, made) quite a mess.

LESSON 8

Spelling Verbs Correctly (page 166) Write the past tense of each verb.

28. try
29. study
30. rely
31. stop
32. plan
33. stare

LESSON 9

Mechanics: Using the Comma (page 168) Write each sentence correctly.

34. Olga have you seen Suki?
35. No but you could ask Marcos.
36. Yes I think that is a good idea.
37. Marcos I am looking for Suki Esther and Harry.
38. Look in the gym cafeteria and library.

LESSON 10

Vocabulary Building: Prefixes (page 170) Replace each underlined word or words with a word that has a prefix.

39. View your notes again.
40. My notes have not appeared!
41. It will not be possible to give my speech.
42. I am not able to find them anywhere.
43. Maybe you have placed them somewhere else.

Writing Application: Verb Usage (pages 154–165) There are 7 errors in verb usage below. Write the paragraph correctly.

44.-50. My uncle take us to the ball game. He boughted us souvenirs. He seen many games and knows where we needs to sit. I loves to go to the game. We brung food. Then we sung the national anthem.

ENRICHMENT

Where the Action Is

Play this game with a group of four or five classmates. Take turns thinking of an action verb. Pantomime the action. For instance, if you use the word *swimming,* you could pretend to be swimming underwater. Then, ask the rest of the group to try to name the action you are doing. Whoever guesses correctly can pantomime the next action. You can use these action verbs in your writing.

Sports Map

Write the word *sports* in the center of a piece of paper. Then, think of some action verbs that describe particular movements used in sports. Write them around the word *sports* and connect them with lines. Save this map for the next time you write a description.

LIGHTS, CAMERA, ACTION

Work on an action-verb mural with a group of classmates. Draw pictures of people doing many different kinds of activities. Label each drawing with an action verb.

A DIAMOND IN THE SKY

Did you know that some kinds of poems have a shape all their own? A **diamanté** is a diamond-shaped poem that is fun to write. Knowing about nouns, verbs, and adjectives will help you to write a diamanté. Look at the diamanté below. It has seven lines. Each line is made up of words of one part of speech. The nouns in the first and last lines are antonyms—words that mean the opposite of each other.

Day . . . . (one noun)
Sunny, cheery . . . . (two adjectives)
Playing, working, learning . . . . . (three *ing* verbs)
School, books, pencils, friends . . . . (four nouns)
Resting, sleeping, dreaming . . . . . (three *ing* verbs)
Dark, cozy . . . . (two adjectives)
Night . . . . (one noun)

Now write a diamanté of your own. Begin by choosing two nouns that have opposite meanings.

PICK A PAIR

Here's a game to play with two or three classmates. Write these past-tense verbs on index cards, one to a card: *given, eaten, written, driven, ridden, taken, flown, done, grown, begun.* Then make four cards each for these helping verbs: *has, have, had.* You will have twenty-two cards in all.

Shuffle the cards and give each player three cards. Put the remaining cards in a pile in front of the players. If a player has two cards that make a pair, for example *have given*, when it is that player's turn, he or she lays the two cards down and picks the top card from the pile. If the player does not have a pair, he or she also draws a card from the pile. The object of the game is to make as many past-tense verb pairs as possible and to get rid of all your cards.

GRAMMAR

EXTRA PRACTICE

Three levels of practice

What Is an Action Verb? (page 152)

LEVEL **A.** Write each sentence. The complete predicate is underlined. Find the action verb in the predicate and underline it.

1. We visited a large post office.
2. We learned about the mail.
3. We noticed some beautiful stamps.
4. George bought some unusual stamps.
5. A guide showed us around.
6. She told us many interesting things.
7. The post office provides many services.
8. People apply for passports.
9. Packages and letters move quickly on their way.
10. A letter arrived in the mail.

LEVEL **B.** Write each sentence. Draw one line under the complete predicate. Draw two lines under the action verb.

11. Karen sent me an invitation.
12. I opened it immediately.
13. She invited me to a birthday party.
14. She planned the party for next week.
15. I love birthday parties!
16. I mailed the note back to Karen.
17. I answered her invitation.
18. I bought her a lovely gift.

LEVEL **C.** Complete each sentence with an action verb. Write the sentence.

19. Jason _____ a package in the mail.
20. He _____ the package.
21. Who _____ it?
22. Jason _____ the string.
23. He _____ away the wrapping.
24. Inside he _____ another wrapped box.
25. He _____ that one.

EXTRA PRACTICE

GRAMMAR

Three levels of practice

Main Verbs and Helping Verbs (page 154)

LEVEL **A.** Write each sentence. The verbs are underlined. Write *M* above each main verb and *H* above each helping verb.

1. Justin is writing a note.
2. He will send the note to Mrs. Hill.
3. Justin had gone to her house for a visit.
4. Mrs. Hill has lived in Maine for many years.
5. She had entertained Justin and his brother.
6. The boys have returned this morning.
7. They have finished unpacking.
8. Justin has taken the note to the mailbox.
9. He has mailed it.
10. I have written a note, too.

LEVEL **B.** Write each sentence. Draw one line under each main verb. Draw two lines under the helping verb.

11. I am writing a note to my uncle.
12. I have spent two weeks in New Mexico.
13. I was staying with my uncle.
14. He has owned a ranch there for many years.
15. I had visited him once before.
16. I had ridden a horse during my visit.
17. Uncle Tito will stay with us next year.
18. He is making plans now.

LEVEL **C.** Complete each sentence. Use a helping verb in each blank.

19. Grace _____ opened her mail.
20. She _____ received two letters.
21. She _____ reading one of them.
22. Mark _____ written to thank her.
23. Grace _____ give Mark a book tomorrow.
24. He _____ thank her for the gift.
25. Mark _____ pleased with the book.

EXTRA PRACTICE

Three levels of practice

Verb Tenses (page 156)

LEVEL **A.** Write each sentence. Then, write **past, present,** or **future** to tell the tense of each underlined verb.

1. Our group works together.
2. We like the science article.
3. The article tells about weather.
4. We studied the topic.
5. Everyone reads the paper.
6. Jane will revise our writing.
7. Sam offers to type it.
8. Maybe a magazine will publish the article.
9. We hoped for a byline.
10. We will share the good news with all.

LEVEL **B.** Write each sentence. Draw a line under each verb. Then, write **past, present,** or **future** to tell the tense of each verb.

11. Sally needs an editor.
12. She edits our school newspaper.
13. She helps the other writers.
14. Sally wrote about Littlefield Zoo.
15. I will read Tom's article next.
16. Tom's article tells about new gym equipment.
17. He described each piece of equipment.
18. Next week, Sally and Tom will review a play.

LEVEL **C.** Write each sentence. Write the underlined verb in the tense shown in parentheses ( ) at the end of each sentence.

19. I receive a new issue of a magazine. (past)
20. I enjoyed reading stories about pets. (present)
21. Claire will use the magazine article. (past)
22. She gets a new magazine each month. (future)
23. We shared our magazines. (present)
24. I show Sue my article. (future)
25. Sue will like the articles about pets. (present)

EXTRA PRACTICE

GRAMMAR

Three levels of practice

More About Verb Tenses (page 158)

LEVEL **A.** Write each sentence. Draw a line under the verb. Then, write the tense of each verb.

1. Jonah will compete in the track meet.
2. He practices every day.
3. His friends timed him in the relay.
4. He jumps higher than the other team members do.
5. He will try the pole vault for the first time.
6. Last year, he tripped over the hurdles.
7. This year, he will win the race.
8. He trained for a very long time.
9. Jonah leaps high into the air.
10. He will run a very good race.

LEVEL **B.** Write these sentences. Fill in each blank with a verb from the box. Write each verb in the tense given in parentheses ( ).

11. Lisa _____ the mountain at dawn. (present)
12. She _____ early in the morning. (past)
13. Later, she _____ on the lake. (future)
14. She _____ a fish for dinner. (future)
15. Lisa _____ her firewood. (past)
16. She _____ all her meals herself. (present)

climb
catch
gather
row
start
cook

LEVEL **C.** Write these sentences. Fill in each blank with a verb of your choice. Write each verb in the tense given in parentheses ( ).

17. Ada _____ into the cave. (present)
18. Years ago, she _____ the dark. (past)
19. Now, she _____ in the dark without fear. (present)
20. She _____ for fossils. (future)
21. Last month, she _____ a perfect fossil. (past)
22. She _____ it on a shelf in her room. (past)
23. Ada _____ her fossils to friends. (future)
24. Her friends _____ her fossils. (present)
25. Ada and her friends _____ a report for the class. (past)

EXTRA PRACTICE

Three levels of practice

Subject-Verb Agreement (page 160)

LEVEL **A.** Write each sentence. Choose the verb from the pair in parentheses ( ) that agrees with the underlined subject.

1. Electricity (make, makes) a wonderful messenger.
2. The telegraph (use, uses) electricity.
3. *Telegraph* (mean, means) "write far away."
4. Some operators (write, writes) in dots and dashes.
5. Electricity (flow, flows) through a receiver.
6. Telegraphs (make, makes) strange sounds.
7. A message (travel, travels) through wires.
8. Scientists (find, finds) ways to use less wire.
9. The telegraph (meet, meets) the needs of many.
10. A messenger (deliver, delivers) the telegram.

LEVEL **B.** Write each sentence. Choose the correct verb from the pair of verbs in parentheses ( ).

11. We (see, sees) early telegraphs in the museum.
12. A guide (explain, explains) the old machines.
13. She (tell, tells) us about Morse code.
14. Some students (look, looks) at the displays.
15. Those parts (cause, causes) telegraphs to work.
16. One machine (send, sends) pictures.
17. Newspapers (use, uses) Teletype machines.
18. Messages (go, goes) all over the world.

LEVEL **C.** Fill in each blank by writing the correct present-tense form of the verb in parentheses ( ). Write the sentence.

19. Bob _____ a simple telegraph. (design)
20. He _____ a magnet. (need)
21. Sara _____ Bob with the telegraph. (help)
22. They _____ the wires to a battery. (attach)
23. They _____ on opposite sides of the room. (stand)
24. Bob _____ to Sara that he is ready. (signal)
25. They _____ out their telegraph. (try)

PRACTICE + PLUS

GRAMMAR

Three levels of additional practice for a difficult skill

Subject-Verb Agreement (page 160)

LEVEL **A.** Write each sentence. Choose the verb from the pair in parentheses ( ) that agrees with the underlined subject.

1. Victor (make, makes) a card for his mother.
2. He (write, writes) a message inside.
3. Victor (wish, wishes) his mother a happy birthday.
4. His two sisters (sign, signs) the card, too.
5. Victor's mother (tape, tapes) the card to a mirror.
6. She (smile, smiles) every time she looks at it.
7. Visitors (notice, notices) the lovely card.
8. They (call, calls) Victor an artist.
9. Victor (like, likes) his drawings very much.
10. He (show, shows) them to his friends.
11. Victor's friends (admire, admires) the work.
12. Many classmates (ask, asks) Victor for drawings.
13. The drawings (hang, hangs) on locker doors.
14. Victor (use, uses) many colors.
15. The bright colors (glow, glows).
16. We (love, loves) Victor's art.

LEVEL **B.** Write each sentence. Choose the correct verb from the pair of verbs in parentheses ( ).

17. Roxanne (want, wants) a card for her parents.
18. Her parents (enjoy, enjoys) cards at holiday time.
19. Roxanne (look, looks) at the cards in a store.
20. The cards (seem, seems) silly and dull.
21. Roxanne's aunt (think, thinks) of a good idea.
22. She (show, shows) Roxanne some old magazines.
23. Together they (cut, cuts) out letters and make words.
24. Roxanne (paste, pastes) the letters down on paper.
25. The message (read, reads) "Happy Holidays!"

PRACTICE + PLUS

26. Roxanne's parents (smile, smiles) at the card.
27. Her dad (like, likes) it very much.
28. He (tell, tells) Roxanne about another card.
29. Roxanne (laugh, laughs) when he tells her.
30. They (talk, talks) about all the cards.
31. Roxanne's aunt (come, comes) for a visit.
32. She (admire, admires) the cards.

LEVEL **C.** Fill in each blank by writing the correct present-tense form of the verb in parentheses ( ). Write the sentence.

33. Neko and Martha _____ messages to each other. (send)
34. They _____ in different states. (live)
35. Neko _____ letters to Martha. (write)
36. Martha _____ tapes to Neko. (send)
37. The tapes _____ through the mail. (travel)
38. Other friends _____ messages. (add)
39. Heather _____ songs into the tape recorder. (sing)
40. Jake _____ cartoons on the letters. (draw)
41. The children _____ the letters and tapes. (enjoy)
42. Neko _____ the tapes all together in a box. (keep)
43. Neko's box _____ with all the tapes. (overflow)
44. Martha _____ the stamps from all the letters. (collect)
45. She _____ the stamps in an album. (put)
46. Martha's friends _____ about the beautiful stamps. (comment)
47. They _____ the stamps that show sea animals. (like)
48. Martha's friend Heather _____ some stamps, too. (want)
49. Martha _____ Heather the duplicate stamps. (give)
50. Heather always _____ Martha for the stamps. (thank)

EXTRA PRACTICE

Three levels of practice

Using Irregular Verbs I (page 162)

LEVEL **A.** Write the correct past-tense form of the verb in parentheses ( ).

1. Our class (rode, ridden) in buses.
2. We (took, taken) a picnic lunch.
3. Our teacher had (gave, given) us directions.
4. The driver (went, gone) to the park.
5. We (drove, driven) through the countryside.
6. I (saw, seen) some small animals.
7. Finally, we (came, come) to the picnic grounds.
8. We (ate, eaten) our lunches under the trees.
9. We (wrote, written) a thank-you note to the driver.
10. We (ran, run) to the mailbox to send it.

LEVEL **B.** Write the correct past-tense form of the verb in parentheses ( ).

11. My family _____ a trip. (take)
12. Dad had _____ part of the way. (drive)
13. As we _____ along, we sang songs. (ride)
14. We _____ in a pretty restaurant. (eat)
15. I had _____ pictures of it in a magazine. (see)
16. My sisters had _____ shopping. (go)
17. They _____ me a shirt. (give)
18. Mom had _____ my name on it. (write)
19. Soon, we had _____ to the end of our trip. (come)

LEVEL **C.** Write each sentence. Use the correct past-tense form of one of the verbs in the Word Box to fill each blank. Use each verb only once.

write	ride	see	eat	go	give

20. Have you ever _____ a travel brochure?
21. I have _____ many brochures about the Southwest.
22. Betsy has _____ me one about Texas.
23. I have _____ to Arizona.
24. Our family _____ in a van.
25. We _____ our meals in the van.

EXTRA PRACTICE

Three levels of practice

Using Irregular Verbs II (page 164)

LEVEL **A.** Write the correct past-tense form of the verb in parentheses ( ).

1. Our class talent show has (began, begun).
2. Many students have (bring, brought) artwork.
3. Carl has (drew, drawn) a beautiful landscape.
4. Tracy and Joel (sang, sung) a song.
5. My grandmother had (flew, flown) in from Kansas.
6. Lisa and I had (wrote, written) a skit.
7. My talent has definitely (grew, grown).
8. Grandma (threw, thrown) her arms around me.
9. She (make, made) us perform our skit again.
10. We (did, done) a good job.

LEVEL **B.** Write the correct past-tense form of the verb in parentheses ( ).

11. We have _____ safety posters. (make)
12. Some students _____ traffic-safety posters. (draw)
13. I _____ a poster about pool safety. (do)
14. People _____ in a big pool. (swim)
15. A lifeguard _____ a life preserver to a boy. (throw)
16. We have _____ our posters home. (bring)
17. Next, we _____ work on a safety mural. (begin)

LEVEL **C.** Write each sentence. Use the correct past-tense form of one of the verbs in the Word Box to fill each blank. Use each verb only once.

18. In springtime we _____ to see new life.
19. Birds _____ from tree to tree.
20. They had _____ nests.
21. They _____ sweet songs.
22. Harriet has _____ some crumbs.
23. We _____ the crumbs to the birds.
24. Flowers had _____ from seeds.
25. Fish _____ in a pond.

swim
sing
bring
make
begin
grow
throw
fly

EXTRA PRACTICE

GRAMMAR

Three levels of practice

Spelling Verbs Correctly (page 166)

LEVEL **A.** Write each sentence. Choose the correct verb in parentheses ( ) to complete each sentence.

1. Gina (take, takes) dancing lessons.
2. She (try, tries) to practice every day.
3. Jerry (watch, watches) Gina.
4. He (help, helped) her make a costume.
5. Gina (worry, worried) about the size of the costume.
6. A big performance was (plan, planned).
7. Finally, Jerry (give, gives) her the costume.
8. Gina (hop, hopped) on her bicycle.
9. She (arrive, arrives) at the theater.
10. Gina (dance, danced) well that evening.

LEVEL **B.** Write each sentence. Change each present-tense verb to the past-tense form.

11. Mario attends a tennis match.
12. He watches the exciting game.
13. The players dry their hands on towels.
14. One player raises her racket.
15. She rushes to the net.
16. The other player handles the ball well.

LEVEL **C.** Write each sentence. Use the verb in parentheses ( ). The tense that you should use is shown at the end of each sentence.

17. Steven (carry) his costume carefully. *past*
18. He (hurry) to the school auditorium. *present*
19. His bike almost (fly). *present*
20. He (pull) the costume on. *present*
21. Steven (gasp) when a button came off. *past*
22. It (pop) off as he pulled his costume on. *past*
23. Mr. Gray (supply) a safety pin. *present*
24. Steven (move) onto the stage. *present*
25. The audience (clap) loudly. *past*

EXTRA PRACTICE

GRAMMAR

Three levels of practice

Mechanics: Using the Comma (page 168)

LEVEL A. Write each sentence. Add two words to each sentence to form a series.

1. Polly's favorite colors are blue, _____ , and _____ .
2. She likes to paint, _____ , and _____ .
3. Yesterday, she invited Herb, _____ , and _____ .
4. They played baseball, _____ , and _____ .
5. Polly showed them her kitten, _____ , and _____ .
6. Her pets' names are Fluffy, _____ , and _____ .

LEVEL B. Write each sentence. Add commas where they are needed.

7. Doris have you seen Timothy?
8. Yes I saw him this morning.
9. Well do you know where he is now?
10. I saw him with Lauren Maria and Igor.
11. Do you want me to try to find him Frank?
12. No I will look for him in the park.
13. He might be playing tennis soccer or volleyball.
14. Well I will walk around the park until I see him.
15. I will go to the market the library and the playground.
16. Timothy do you know where Doris is?

LEVEL C. Write each sentence. Add commas where they are needed. Write the word **correct** next to the sentences that do not need commas.

17. Les have you ever played the telephone game?
18. Yes I have played that game.
19. Well, would you like to play it now?
20. No I have to make lunch.
21. Tom Sue and Nathan are coming over.
22. Harvey, would you like to join us?
23. We will have sandwiches, milk and apples.
24. Yes I would love some milk and apples.

24. Well come in and sit down.

EXTRA PRACTICE

Three levels of practice

Vocabulary Building: Prefixes (page 170)

LEVEL **A.** Draw a line under each word that has a prefix.

1. William was unable to go to the movies.
2. Ty and I were going to preview a new film.
3. The movie was playing in a rebuilt theater.
4. I must have misunderstood the directions.
5. I reviewed the map.
6. We were unlucky because it began to snow.
7. Soon, it became impossible to see.
8. Sometimes, the weather can be unkind.
9. We retraced our steps and came home.

LEVEL **B.** Write each sentence. Replace the underlined word or words with a word that has a prefix.

10. Jenna is not interested in that book.
11. She viewed the movie before it opened.
12. Jenna had to write her report again.
13. She had not understood the directions.
14. It was not possible for her to work.
15. She spelled many words wrong.
16. She did her homework over.
17. Jenna was not happy.

LEVEL **C.** Write each sentence. Choose a prefix from the box for each word in parentheses ( ). Use the new word to complete each sentence.

im
un
re
dis
mis

18. I stared at my mother in _____ . (belief)
19. She _____ that I had won the contest. (stated)
20. It seemed _____ . (possible)
21. I have always been so _____ . (lucky)
22. I asked her if she had _____ . (understood)
23. She _____ the letter from the judges. (read)
24. My worries finally _____ . (appeared)
25. I had been about to _____ the contest. (enter)

UNIT 6

Writing Letters

Read the quotation and look at the picture on the opposite page. Talk about different ways in which people communicate and share with one another.

When you write a letter, you want to share something with a specific person.

Focus A friendly letter is a way to communicate with someone. A friendly letter has five parts. Each part gives the receiver important information.

Is there someone who would like to receive a letter from you? What would you write to that person? In this unit you will read a story about a letter writer and find some interesting photographs. You can use the story and the photographs to give you ideas for writing.

THEME: *MESSAGES*

Writing is my way of sharing. I suppose it's a very peculiar way to share, because there's no personal contact. . . . But I get letters from people who have read my books. And from what they write, I know I have touched them. We have made a bond through words.

—Marianna Mayer

LITERATURE

Reading Like a Writer

What kinds of letters do you like to write? Have you ever written a letter to explain something to a friend?

In the letters you will read, David tells his friend Hank about a mysterious situation.

As you read the letters, notice how David explains the situation to his friend.

Letters from an Animal Lover

by
Tot Jones

Tuesday

Dear Hank,

The babies are disappearing!

I've told you before about the raccoons in the woods by our house. In the three years we've lived here, they've multiplied like crazy! We now have six raccoon moms that visit us, and this year each of them had several kits (babies). The moms groom their babies all the time and watch them wrestle and run sideways like kittens. Sometimes they sleep in little piles around the deck. Their dens are scattered throughout the wooded ravine below our house.

In his letter, David shares an interesting event with a friend.

Anyway, a few nights ago I noticed that some of the babies were missing, and the moms were acting nervous. Every now and then I think I hear a noise coming from across the ravine, where the woods are pretty thick. It sounds like someone pounding.

Last night only *six* babies were here. Boy, did they ever stick close to their moms! I can't figure out what's happening to them.

More later.

David

Thursday

Dear Hank,

There are just two babies left now, and the moms only stay around for a few minutes at a time. I still hear noises coming from across the ravine, but I can't figure out what is causing them. The moms seem sad—I've got to do something!

I'll keep you posted.

David

Saturday

Dear Hank,

I found them!

This morning I couldn't stand it any longer. Right after breakfast I slid down to the bottom of the ravine and started climbing up the other side. It was pretty tough climbing, because it's steep, there's a lot of underbrush, and the ground is soft. I kept heading for the place the noise came from. When I got close to the top of the hill, I had to climb over a pile of fallen trees, and I was surprised to find a small clearing up ahead—you can't see it from our deck.

When I stopped to catch my breath, I heard some chirring from fairly close by. Chirring is the sound raccoon mothers and babies make to communicate with each other—it's like a cat's purr, but about a hundred times louder.

I kept walking, and suddenly there they were. Someone had built a huge cage out of wire fencing, and the missing babies were all crowded into it. There were bags of dog food in the cage and some small traps lying nearby. I guess the raccoon moms were too clever for the traps, so only the babies got caught. Since they were about three months old and had been raised in the wild, it would have been impossible to sell them as pets. It makes me sick to think about what the trappers were going to do to those kits—probably kill them for their pelts and tails!

David knows how to solve the problem.

I knew that the trappers might come back at any time—I had to go for help! Dad and I could return with wire cutters to free the kits.

Stumbling back down the hill and up the other side to our house didn't take very long, and fortunately Dad was home. I talked so fast that he could hardly understand me, but he finally got the message and headed for the phone to call the wildlife authorities. I found the wire cutters and took off again. Dad said he would follow me as soon as he had talked to the deputies. Since it's all city park around here, the wild animals are protected, and the trappers could be arrested.

I practically rolled down the hill and flew up the other side. My legs were beginning to feel like rubber. When I approached the clearing I kept as quiet as possible. The raccoon babies were all watching me, and no one else was in sight. I started cutting a big hole in the cage, as fast as I could. The babies huddled together on the far side. When I pulled the piece of fencing away, I expected them to leap out, but they were too scared.

Knowing how sharp their teeth are, I didn't think it would be too smart for me to crawl in and shove them out. Finally, I went to the far side of the cage and made shooing noises, and they started to climb out through the hole. In minutes they were all out and running like crazy. I knew they'd find their dens.

Then I heard someone coming. I was a bit scared, thinking the trappers might find me, so I hid behind a big tree. Fortunately it was Dad. He said Mom would show the deputies where we were.

Well, the deputies got to the clearing about twenty minutes before the trappers came back, and they arrested three guys. You

should have seen the expressions on the trappers' faces when they found an empty cage and two deputies waiting for them! I don't know what will happen to them—there's an awfully big fine, and they may end up in jail, too.

The deputies are coming back later to take the big cage apart and haul it away. They thanked me for my "vigilance on behalf of the raccoons." (Wow, how d'you like that?)

The writer tells how David feels about his experience.

Tonight all the babies are back with their moms. Boy, are they getting licked and fed! Raccoon moms can still nurse babies that are three months old. The kits probably missed a lot of meals, and now they need all the food they can get. We gave them an extra bag of marshmallows and a whole sack of nuts to celebrate. It's great to have them all back together again!

Well, it's almost time for your visit. You'd better be prepared to help spoil the babies!

See you soon.

David

Thinking Like a Reader

1. How would you have felt if you had found the caged baby raccoons?
2. What would you have done? Write three steps you would have taken.

Write your responses in your journal.

Thinking Like a Writer

3. What are some things David explained to Hank? Why do you think the author included those explanations?
4. If you were Hank, what would you write back to David?

Write your responses in your journal.

Responding to

LITERATURE

Brainstorm *Vocabulary*

In "Letters from an Animal Lover," you learned that baby raccoons are called kits. Many baby animals are called by unusual names. Find the names for the babies of three of the animals listed below. Write the names in your journal. Begin to create a personal vocabulary list of animal names.

whale	fox	goose	duck
lion	dog	pig	swan

Talk It Over
Use the Telephone

When you write a friendly letter, you share something with someone you know. When you talk on the telephone to a friend, you do the same thing. Imagine that you are David and want to tell Hank on the telephone about the missing babies. With a partner, imagine you are on the phone with Hank. Explain what happened to the baby raccoons.

Quick Write *Write a Note*

When you want to give someone a message, you can write a note. A note is a very short letter of explanation. For example, if you want to tell your parents that you had to go to the store, you might write this note.

Dear Mom and Dad,

We ran out of eggs. I have gone to the market to buy some more. I will be back in ten minutes.

Carol

Write a note that David might leave for his parents when he goes to find the baby raccoons.

Idea Corner
Think of Messages

In your journal, write the names of people who would enjoy receiving a letter from you. You might also wish to write notes or draw pictures about things you want to tell the people on your list.

PICTURES SEEING LIKE A WRITER

Finding Ideas for Writing

Look at the pictures. Think about what you see.
What ideas for writing letters do the photographs give you?
Write your ideas in your journal.

Our Pen Pals
from
California

1 GROUP WRITING: A Friendly Letter

When you write a friendly letter, your **purpose** and **audience** are very clear. Your audience might be a friend or a pen pal. Your purpose might be to explain how to do something or to let someone know how you have been or what interesting things you have been doing. What do you need to remember about friendly letters?

- Correct Letter Form
- Purpose and Audience

Correct Letter Form

Every friendly letter includes five parts. Read this letter. Notice that a comma follows the greeting and the closing.

HEADING

229 Ridgedale Road
Ithaca, NY 14851
September 4, 19–

GREETING

Dear Grandpa,

BODY

I am sending you my latest photographs with this letter. Why are these photos better that the last ones? First, I decided to stop taking pictures of everything I saw. I started looking for interesting things—a lovely sunset or a tree with red leaves against a blue sky. Next, I learned to focus the camera and to check the light. Last, I practiced taking pictures and learned from my mistakes. You will love these new photos!

CLOSING

Love,

SIGNATURE

Ruby

Parts of a Friendly Letter	
Heading	Your complete address and the date.
Greeting	Usually the word *Dear* followed by the name of the person to whom you are writing.
Body	The main part of the letter. It includes everything you want to say.
Closing	A way to say "good-bye." Some words to use are *Love, Sincerely, Your friend.*
Signature	Your name in your own handwriting.

Guided Practice: Selecting an Audience

Talk with your classmates about people to whom you might write a letter to explain something you have learned to do. You could write to a younger relative. You could write to an old friend. You could write to a pen pal in another state or another country. Write a greeting for your letter.

Purpose and Audience

Before you write a friendly letter, you should think about your **audience** and your **purpose.** Look back at Ruby's letter on page 200. Who is Ruby's audience? What is her purpose in writing the letter?

The greeting of your letter identifies your audience. The body of your letter states your purpose for writing.

Guided Practice: Deciding on a Purpose

As a class, talk about something that you have recently learned to do. Perhaps you have learned a craft or how to conduct an experiment. Imagine that you will write a letter explaining what you have learned to the person you selected in the **Guided Practice** above. Write some notes about what you will explain.

Putting a Friendly Letter Together

You have selected an audience for a friendly letter and written a greeting for it. You have made some notes to use in the body of your letter. Think about how you will begin your letter.

Here is how one student began her friendly letter.

Dear Aunt Alicia,

We learned how to make pretty designs in art class yesterday. I'll tell you how we did it.

Guided Practice: Writing a Friendly Letter

Write your letter. First, write your heading and greeting. Then, write the body of your letter. Think of a good beginning sentence. Use your notes for details. End your letter with a friendly closing and your signature.

You may wish to mail your letter. To do this, fold the letter and put it in an envelope. Address the envelope in the following way.

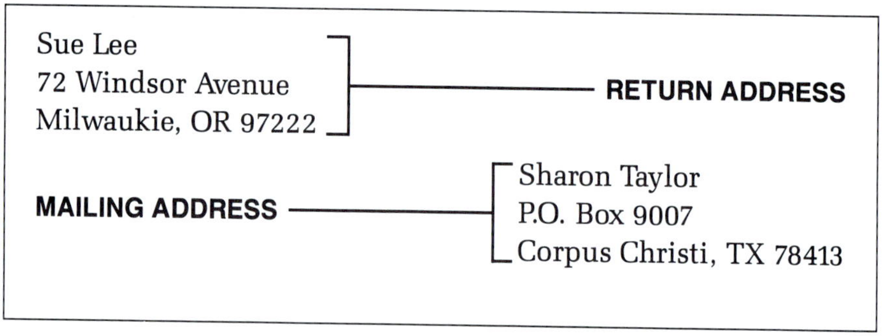

Do not forget to add a stamp. Also, see page 496 for a list of state abbreviations.

Checklist: A Friendly Letter

When you write a friendly letter, you can use a checklist. A checklist will remind you of everything you want to include in your letter.

Look at this checklist. Some points need to be added. Copy and complete the checklist. Keep it in your writing folder. You can use it whenever you write a letter.

CHECKLIST

- ✓ Purpose (to explain)
- ✓ Audience
- ■ Friend
- ■ Relative
- ✓ Parts of a friendly letter
- ■ Heading
- ■ Greeting
- ■ ______________
- ■ Closing
- ■ Signature
- ✓ Envelope
- ■ Return address
- ■ ______________

2 THINKING AND WRITING: Solving Problems

You have been reading about people who found ways to solve problems. In "Letters from an Animal Lover," David explained to Hank how he solved the problem of the missing babies. In the friendly letter on page 200, Ruby explained how she solved her picture-taking problem.

Imagine that you want to write a letter. In it you want to explain how to solve a problem. A **problem-solving chart** can help you to organize your ideas.

Here is a chart that one writer made.

Problem	Solution	Steps to follow
How to improve my grade in science	An "A" on the next test	1. Take my book home. 2. Read the chapter. 3. Take notes. 4. Review the notes. 5. Go to sleep early. 6. Try my best.

Thinking Like a Writer

- What did the writer put first in the chart?
- Why do you think the writer listed the steps in the chart?

The problem-solving chart is very clear. It shows the way the writer thinks. The writer lists the steps to help organize his or her thinking.

When you want to explain how to solve a problem, it helps to have a plan. Your plan can include these steps.

PROBLEM-SOLVING STRATEGIES

- State what the problem is.
- State a possible solution.
- List the steps to follow to solve the problem.

THINKING APPLICATION Problem Solving

Imagine that you want to explain how to solve each of the problems below. First, decide which solution makes the most sense. Write your answer on a separate sheet of paper. Then, pick the solution you chose for one problem and make a problem-solving chart like the one in the lesson.

1. You want to run for class president. What do you do?
   a. Plan a campaign.
   b. Try out for the soccer team.
   c. Stop speaking to everyone.
2. Your school's soccer team is losing every game they play. What do you do?
   a. Suggest extra practice sessions.
   b. Complain loudly.
   c. Join the other team.
3. Your sister will not help you with chores. What do you do?
   a. Take away her toys.
   b. Work out a plan to share the work.
   c. Do her chores for her.
4. You want to buy a new book to read, but you do not have enough money. What do you do?
   a. Go to the movies instead.
   b. Read a book that you have already read.
   c. Think of a way to earn extra money.

3 INDEPENDENT WRITING: A Friendly Letter

Prewrite: Step 1

You have been learning about writing friendly letters. Now you are ready to write a letter of your own. Kelly, a student your age, wanted to write a letter to her friend Donna. Here's what Kelly did.

Listing Ideas

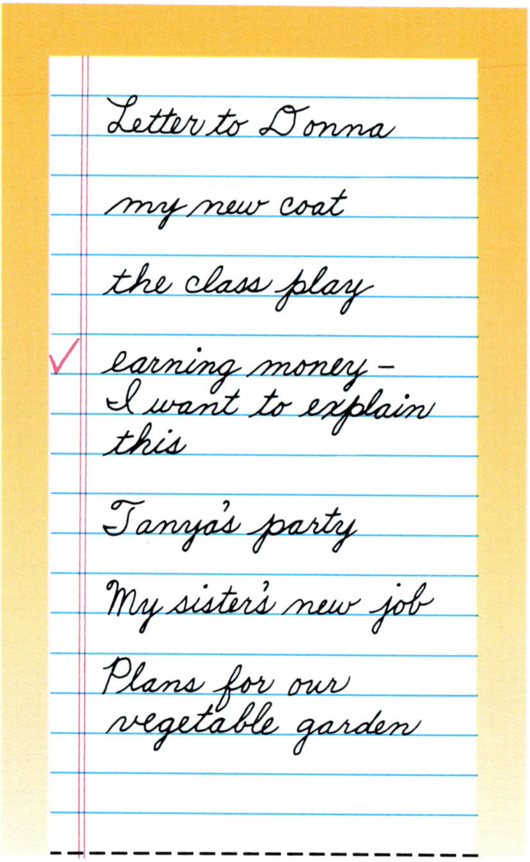

1. First, Kelly wrote a list of all the things she wanted to tell Donna.
2. Next, she thought about her **purpose** for writing.
3. Then, she looked at her list and decided on the best topic.

Kelly liked the third item on her list best. She planned to visit Donna and knew that she would need money for the trip. Kelly thought that Donna would be interested in learning how she had solved the problem of earning extra money.

Kelly's **purpose** for writing a letter to Donna was to explain how she had solved a problem—how to earn the extra money she needed for her trip.

Exploring Ideas: Charting Strategy

Kelly organized her ideas by making a **problem-solving chart.** She used the chart to plan what she would say in her letter. Here is what Kelly's chart looked like.

Problem	Solution	Steps to follow
How will I earn extra money?	Sell brownies.	1. Buy brownie ingredients. 2. Bake brownies. 3. Sell brownies at Little League games. 4. Save money.

Kelly was pleased with her chart because it helped her to organize her ideas. Kelly knew that Donna, her **audience,** would want to know how she solved her problem step-by-step.

Before beginning to write, Kelly thought about the parts of a friendly letter. She recalled that she would need a **heading, greeting, body, closing,** and **signature.**

Thinking Like a Writer

- What kind of letter does Kelly plan to write?
- Why did she make a chart?
- Does the order of her steps make sense? Why?

YOUR TURN

JOURNAL

Think of a letter you would like to send to a friend or relative. Use **Pictures** or your journal to find ideas. Explain how you solved a problem. Follow these steps.

- Decide to whom you will write.
- List ideas for the body of your letter.
- Think about your purpose for writing.
- Think about your audience.

Make a chart. State a problem, give a solution, and list the steps you will follow to solve the problem.

Write a First Draft: Step 2

Kelly knows what a friendly letter should include. She has made a checklist. Kelly is now ready to write her first draft.

Part of Kelly's First Draft

Dear Donna

I have found the greatest way to earn extra mony. I tell you about it. First, I buy ingredients for two dozen brownies. I will bake them. After ten games, I will have at least $20. I'll visit you then.

Love

Kelly

Kelly did not worry about errors in her writing. She knew she could correct and revise her letter later.

Planning Checklist

- Remember purpose and audience.
- Include all the parts of a friendly letter.
  - Heading
  - Greeting
  - Body
  - Closing
  - Signature
- Use time-order words.

YOUR TURN

Write your first draft. As you prepare to write, ask yourself these questions.

- What will my audience want to know?
- How should I organize my letter? How can I make my purpose clear?

TIME-OUT You might want to take some time out before you revise. That way you will be able to revise your writing with a fresh eye.

Revise: Step 3

After she finished her first draft, Kelly read it to herself. Then, she shared her letter with a classmate. She wanted some suggestions for improvement.

Kelly then reviewed her planning checklist. She noticed that she had forgotten one point. She checked it off so that she would remember it when she revised. Kelly now has a checklist to use as she revises her letter.

Kelly made changes to her paragraph. Notice that she did not correct small errors. She knew she could do that later.

The revisions Kelly made changed her paragraph. Turn the page. Look at her revised draft.

Revising Checklist

✓ ■ Remember purpose and audience.

■ Include all the parts of a friendly letter.
- Heading
- Greeting
- Body
- Closing
- Signature

■ Use time-order words.

WRITING PROCESS

Part of Kelly's Revised Draft

Dear Donna

,and
I have found the greatest way to earn extra mony.

must, will
I tell you about it. First, I buy ingredients for two

Then,
dozen brownies. I will bake them. After ten games,

Finally, I will
I will have at least $20. I'll visit you then.

sell them at the Little League games.

Love

Kelly

WISE WORD CHOICE

Thinking Like a Writer

- Which detail did Kelly add to her letter? How does this make her explanation clearer?
- Which time-order words did Kelly add? How do they improve the letter?
- Which sentences did she combine? How does combining them improve the letter?

YOUR TURN

Read your first draft of your friendly letter. Then ask yourself these questions.

- What will my audience need to know?
- Is my explanation clear and complete?

If you wish, ask a friend to read your letter and make suggestions. Then revise your letter.

Proofread: Step 4

Kelly knew that she needed to proofread her letter before mailing it. She used a proofreading checklist to help her.

Part of Kelly's Proofread Draft

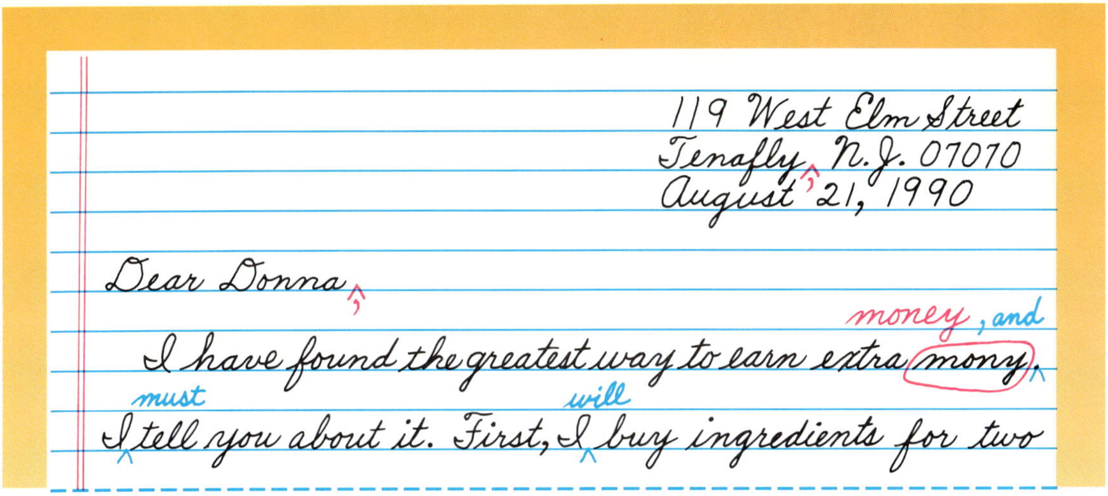
119 West Elm Street
Tenafly, N.J. 07070
August 21, 1990

Dear Donna,

money, and
I have found the greatest way to earn extra mony.
must will
I tell you about it. First, I buy ingredients for two

YOUR TURN

Proofreading Practice

Below is part of a letter that you can use to practice your proofreading skills. Find the errors. Write the letter correctly on a separate sheet of paper.

2416 Lincoln Street
Wellesley MA 02181
May 4 1991

Dear Tommy
Ron and I finished the raft! First, we got the would from the lumberyard. Then, we nailed the boreds together. I'll let you know if it floats!

Your friend
Norm

Proofreading Checklist

- Did I indent each paragraph?
- Did I spell all words correctly?
- Which punctuation errors do I need to correct?
- Which capitalization errors do I need to correct?

Applying Your Proofreading Skills

Now proofread your letter. Read your checklist one last time. Review **The Grammar Connection** and **The Mechanics Connection.** Use the proofreading marks to mark changes.

THE GRAMMAR CONNECTION

Remember these rules about verb tenses.

- If you are writing about something that is happening in the present, be sure you use *present-tense verbs.*
  She **bakes** a wheat bread today.
- If you are writing about something that happened in the past, be sure you use *past-tense verbs.*
  She **baked** raisin cookies last week.
- If you are writing about something that will happen in the future, be sure you use *future-tense verbs.*
  Next week, she **will bake** a fruit pie.

Check your letter. Are your verb tenses consistent?

THE MECHANICS CONNECTION

Remember these rules about commas.

- In the heading, use commas between the city and state and between the date and the year.
  Buffalo**,** NY 14203 February 3**,** 1991
- Use a comma after the greeting. Use a comma after the closing.
  Dear Marylou**,** Your friend**,**

Check your letter. Have you used commas correctly?

Proofreading Marks

¶ Indent
∧ Add
ℓ Take out
≡ Make a capital letter
/ Make a small letter

Publish: Step 5

Kelly knew that she wanted to mail her letter to her friend Donna. For fun, she decided to include her recipe for brownies. In her best handwriting, she copied the letter and recipe on her favorite stationery. Then, she addressed an envelope for the letter. In the top left-hand corner of the envelope, she wrote her name and address. In the center of the envelope, she wrote Donna's name and address. She put a stamp on the envelope and mailed it.

YOUR TURN

Make a neat, final copy of your letter. Think of a way to share your letter. You might find an idea in the **Sharing Suggestions** box below.

SHARING SUGGESTIONS

Address an envelope and mail your letter to your friend or relative. Perhaps you will receive a letter in return.

Illustrate your letter with step-by-step pictures. Make a classroom display of everyone's letters.

Call a friend or relative and read your letter to him or her.

4 SPEAKING AND LISTENING: Giving an Explanation

In the letter you wrote, you gave an explanation of something you did. You listed the steps you took in time order. You might have used time-order words such as *first*, *next*, *then*, and *finally*. Now you can give an explanation orally. You can give directions from your house to your school.

First, you should make a note card to organize your explanation. The note card will include only information that will help your listener understand your explanation. Make sure to put the information in a logical order.

Look at this note card.

NOTES Directions from my house to school

1. Walk down Maple Street three blocks.
2. Turn right onto Vine Street and walk two blocks.
3. Turn left onto Harbor Avenue.
4. The school is five blocks down Harbor Avenue on the right.

Notice that the steps are listed in order. Only the necessary information is included on the card.

When you give an explanation, it will help you to keep your **audience** and **purpose** in mind. Think about what your listeners will want to know. Decide what information you will need to include in your talk.

Look at the speaking guidelines below. They will help you to give a clear and interesting explanation. If you wish, add other guidelines to the list.

SPEAKING GUIDELINES: An Explanation

1. Give only necessary information.
2. Be sure your steps are in the correct order. Use time-order words.
3. Make a note card. Practice using your note card.
4. Look at your listeners.
5. Speak in a loud, clear voice.

- Why must I include only the necessary information?
- Why should I keep steps in the correct order? How do time-order words make my explanation clearer?

SPEAKING APPLICATION An Explanation

Think of the route from your house to your school. Prepare a note card telling how to get from one place to the other. Use the speaking guidelines to help you prepare. Your classmates will be using the following guidelines as they listen to your explanation.

LISTENING GUIDELINES: An Explanation

1. Listen to "see" the steps of the explanation.
2. Listen for the order of the steps.
3. Listen for the important information.
4. Write down any questions you may have.
5. Save your questions until the speaker finishes.

5 WRITER'S RESOURCES: Parts of a Book

When you explain, you give information to help someone understand something. You may already know much about the topic or you may need to find more information in a book. A book is often divided into parts. Knowing the purpose of each part can help you to find the information you need.

1. The **title page** is the first page in the book. It tells you the title, the author, and the publisher of the book.

2. The **copyright page** comes after the title page. It tells you the date the book was published.
3. The **table of contents** is in the front of the book. It lists the name or number of each chapter or unit. It also gives the page number on which each chapter or unit begins. You can find out what a book is about by looking at the table of contents.
4. The **body** of a book is like the body of a letter. It is the main part of the book. It contains all the chapters or units listed in the table of contents.
5. Some books have a **glossary**. It comes after the body. A glossary defines special words used in the book.

Glossary

pentagon A five-sided polygon
percent A fraction whose denominator is 100
perimeter The distance around a figure

6. The **index** is at the back of the book, after the glossary. It lists topics in alphabetical order. Page numbers that follow each topic tell you where to look for information.

Index

Addition 21
Angle 114
Area 230
Average 161

Practice

Use the title page, glossary, and index on these two pages to answer each question below.

1. On what page would you find information about area?
2. What is the definition of *percent*?
3. Who published the book?
4. Who is the book's author?
5. On what page would you find information about an angle?
6. What is the definition of *pentagon*?
7. Where was the book published?
8. What is the title of the book?
9. On what page would you find information about addition?
10. What is the definition of *perimeter*?

WRITING APPLICATION A List

Look in your math book. Write down its title, author, and publisher. Then, look in the index and write down the pages on which you would find information about circles.

THE CURRICULUM CONNECTION

Writing About Mathematics

When you think of mathematics, do you think of addition, subtraction, multiplication, and division? If you do, you would certainly be thinking of a very important area of mathematics. Mathematics does involve computation.

However, another very important part of mathematics is problem solving. Mathematicians solve problems by following a plan, just as you follow a plan when you write. Mathematicians may even make problem-solving charts as you did when you wrote your letter.

ACTIVITIES

Solve a Word Problem Read the following word problem. Use the facts it gives you to answer the question. Write your answer.

> Jeffrey lives across town from Tom.
> Their houses are two miles apart.
> Jeffrey can walk one mile in twenty minutes.
> How long will it take Jeffrey to walk from
> his house to Tom's house?

Design a Calendar Look at pictures of different kinds of calendars in an encyclopedia or a reference book. Use the table of contents or the index in the reference book to help you. Use the photographs you find to get ideas to design a calendar for your favorite month. Draw your calendar. Then, write a few sentences telling how to use it.

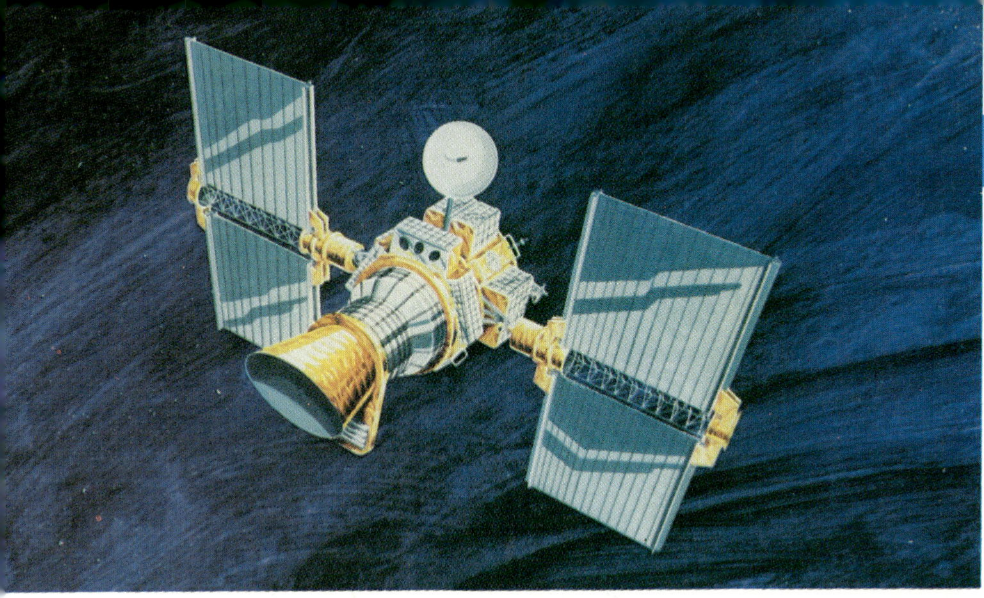

Respond to Literature The following article explains about mathematicians and problem solving. After reading the article, write a response. Your response could be a summary of the main points of the article or a poem about problem solving.

Solving Problems

Far, far above the blue and white globe of Earth, a strange machine, shaped much like a windmill, rushes out into the endless blackness of space. It is a space probe, sent from Earth to seek information about other planets. In a few months, Earth will be only a bright point of light, far behind it.

Before a space probe such as this is sent out from Earth to travel to Mars, Venus, or another planet, many problems must be worked out.

A space vehicle must be launched at a certain speed to escape the pull of gravity. The vehicle has to follow a path that will take it to where the planet is *going to be*, not to where the planet *was* when the vehicle was launched. All these complicated problems of weight, speed, and direction are figured out by people who are mathematicians.

UNIT CHECKUP

LESSON 1

Group Writing: A Friendly Letter (page 200) Look at these parts of a letter. Write the name of each part of the letter.

1. Dear Vera,
2. 42 Pleasant Road
   Jacksonville, IL 62650
   October 16, 19–
3. Sincerely,
4. Amy

LESSON 2

Thinking and Writing: Solving Problems (page 204) Imagine each of the situations below. Decide which solution is the most logical. Write your answer.

1. Your science experiment did not work. What should you do?
   a. Give up on the experiment
   b. Go over the steps with your teacher.
   c. Never return to science class.
2. You want to go swimming, but the beach is closed. What should you do?
   a. Go skiing instead.
   b. Find a swimming pool.
   c. Stay at home.

LESSON 3

Writing a Friendly Letter (page 206) Choose an author whose work you like. Write a letter to the author explaining why you enjoy reading his or her books.

LESSON 4

Speaking and Listening: An Explanation (page 214) Write a note card explaining how to play a game that your classmates will find interesting.

LESSON 5

Writer's Resources: Parts of a Book (page 216) Look in the front of this book. Find the name of the publisher, the city in which the book was published, and the date it was published. Write the information you find.

THEME PROJECT — A Code

Sending messages can be fun. As you know, writing a letter is a good way to send a message. Another way to send a message is by a secret code.

Before you can create a secret code, you have to make a plan. Usually, in a code, numbers, marks, or symbols stand for the alphabet.

Here is one kind of code. Try to decode the secret message that is written in the code.

Think of a short message that you would like to send to a friend or classmate.

- Work out a code for the message.
- Assign numbers, marks, or symbols to letters of the alphabet.
- Create a list of what symbol stands for each letter.
- Write your message.
- Send it to a friend or classmate along with the list of what the symbols stand for and a paragraph telling how to use the code.

GRAMMAR

UNIT 7

Linking Verbs

In this unit you will learn about linking verbs. Linking verbs are verbs that tell what the subject of a sentence is or is like.

Discuss Read the poem on the opposite page. What sort of advice does the poet give to campers?

JOURNAL

Creative Expression The theme of Unit 7 is *Travels.* Think of a new place you would like to visit. Is it far away? How could you get there? Write a paragraph in your journal that tells what you know about this place and what you would like to find out about it.

THEME: *TRAVELS*

Never stroll away from camp
Without a brush, a comb,
A compass, and a postage stamp
To mail yourself back home.

—John Ciardi, from "Mind You, Now"

1 WHAT IS A LINKING VERB?

A linking verb is a verb that links the subject of a sentence to a noun or an adjective in the predicate.

Often a verb expresses action. An action verb tells what the subject does or did.

A pilot **flies** the plane.
The plane **soars** high above.

Sometimes a verb does not express action. A **linking verb** does not express action.

Jack **is** a pilot.
The pilot **was** very smart.
The planes **are** jets.
The engines **were** loud.

The forms of the verb *be* are in the box below. They are often used as linking verbs.

am	was
is	were
are	

Guided Practice

Tell whether each underlined verb in the sentences below is an action verb or a linking verb.

Example: Barbara is nervous about her trip. *linking verb*

1. Barbara was ready for her trip.
2. She packed her suitcase.
3. Barbara tugged at the handle of her bag.
4. Martha is her cousin.
5. Barbara visits her every year.

?! **THINK**

- How can I decide if a verb is a linking verb or an action verb?

GRAMMAR

REMEMBER

- A **linking verb** is a verb that links the subject of a sentence to a noun or adjective in the predicate.
- A linking verb does not express action.

More Practice

A. Write each sentence. Write whether each underlined verb is an **action verb** or a **linking verb**.

Example: The telephone <u>rang</u>. *action verb*

6. Aunt Rosa <u>invited</u> Jan and Tom to her home.
7. Aunt Rosa and Uncle Marcos <u>live</u> in Mexico.
8. Jan and Tom <u>were</u> happy about the invitation.
9. They <u>are</u> curious about Mexico.
10. Jan and Tom eagerly <u>packed</u> their suitcases.
11. Uncle Marcos <u>waited</u> for them at the airport.
12. Jan and Tom <u>hugged</u> Uncle Marcos on their arrival.
13. Aunt Rosa <u>is</u> busy at home.

B. Write each sentence and underline the verb. Write whether it is an **action verb** or a **linking verb**.

Example: My vacation <u>is</u> special. *linking verb*

14. I am a lucky girl.
15. My grandfather took me with him on a trip.
16. We are in Mexico City.
17. It is the capital of Mexico.
18. Many places are very interesting.
19. Grandfather is happy here in Mexico.
20. We enjoy our vacation together.

Extra Practice, page 244

WRITING APPLICATION A Short Narrative

Write a short narrative about a trip that you have taken. The trip could be to a nearby or a faraway place.

2 LINKING VERBS IN THE PRESENT TENSE

Remember that linking verbs link the subject of a sentence to a noun or adjective in the predicate.

This book **is** good. I **am** an eager reader.
Many great books **are** interesting.

As you know, a subject can be singular or plural. A linking verb must agree with, or work with, the subject of the sentence.

Subject	Present-Tense Form of *be*
Singular Subjects	
I	am
you	are
he, she, it	is
(or singular noun)	
Plural Subjects	
we	are
you	are
they (or plural noun)	are

Guided Practice

Tell which verb in parentheses ( ) completes each sentence.

Example: These stories (is, are) funny. *are*

1. This book (is, are) terrific.
2. Eloise Greenfield (is, are) a wonderful writer.
3. Our book reports (is, are) all exciting.
4. Books about animals (is, are) my favorites.
5. I (is, am) a good reader.

?! THINK

- How can I remember which linking verb to use with the subject of a sentence?

REMEMBER

■ A **linking verb** always agrees with the subject of the sentence.

More Practice

A. Write each sentence. Use the correct linking verb in parentheses ( ) to complete each sentence.

Example: Libraries (is, are) wonderful places. *are*

6. The librarians (is, are) very helpful.
7. Sharon Bell Mathis (is, are) my favorite writer.
8. She (is, are) the author of *Sidewalk Story*.
9. The illustrations (is, are) colorful.
10. The main character (is, are) a girl named Lilly Etta.
11. She (is, are) helpful to her friends.
12. My library (is, are) special to me.
13. Books (is, are) good companions.

B. Write each sentence. Use the correct present-tense linking verb to complete the sentence.

Example: Book reports ______ fun to read. *are*

14. I ______ careful when I write a book report.
15. You ______ happy with your copy of *Jumanji*.
16. Chris Van Allsburg ______ a famous author.
17. He ______ a wonderful writer and artist.
18. His books ______ beautiful.
19. Deborah and James Howe ______ the authors of *Bunnicula*.
20. The characters in that book ______ very funny.

Extra Practice, page 245

WRITING APPLICATION A Letter

Write a letter to a relative or friend. In your letter describe a book that you have read recently. Write whether or not you liked the book. Have a classmate read your letter. Ask your partner to find the present-tense linking verbs.

3 LINKING VERBS IN THE PAST TENSE

You already know that the subject of a sentence can be singular or plural. You also know that a linking verb must agree with, or work with, the subject of the sentence.

Jo **was** chief scientist. (singular subject)
The scientists **were** ready. (plural subject)

Subject	Past-Tense Form of *be*
Singular Subjects	
I	was
you	were
he, she, it	was
(or singular noun)	
Plural Subjects	
we	were
you	were
they (or plural noun)	were

Guided Practice

Tell which past-tense linking verb in parentheses ( ) completes each sentence correctly.

Example: We (was, were) excited before lift-off. *were*

1. The spaceships (was, were) ready for take-off.
2. The captain (was, were) a good leader.
3. The stars (was, were) much brighter from the ship.
4. I (was, were) nervous about my first mission.
5. It (was, were) a great day.

?! THINK

■ How can I remember which past-tense linking verb to use with the subject of a sentence?

GRAMMAR

REMEMBER

- A **linking verb** always agrees with the subject of the sentence.

More Practice

A. Write each sentence. Use the correct linking verb in parentheses ( ) to complete each sentence.

Example: Our trip into space (was, were) about to begin. *was*

6. I (was, were) ready for the voyage.
7. You (was, were) the captain of our secret mission.
8. I (was, were) curious about deep space.
9. The navigator (was, were) good at her job.
10. The spaceship (was, were) quite comfortable.
11. You (was, were) always busy.
12. It (was, were) a long trip to Jupiter.
13. Jupiter (was, were) only one of our goals.

B. Write each sentence. Write the correct past-tense linking verb to complete the sentence.

Example: Our spaceship _____ on the launching pad. *was*

14. The spaceship _____ roomier than it looked.
15. The moon _____ the first thing we passed.
16. Some craters _____ very large.
17. The moon _____ very dark.
18. We _____ weightless in the spaceship.
19. Mars _____ next on our schedule.
20. Mars really _____ a red planet.

Extra Practice, page 246

WRITING APPLICATION A Journal Entry

COOPERATIVE LEARNING

Imagine that you took a trip in a spaceship. Write two or three journal entries. Describe what your trip was like and where you traveled. Show your journal entries to a friend. Have her or him point out the past-tense linking verbs in your writing.

GRAMMAR

4 USING LINKING VERBS

When you write, you will want to make sure that the subject of your sentence agrees, or works correctly, with the verb.

Guided Practice

Identify the correct linking verb in parentheses ( ). Tell whether it is past or present.

Example: The oxen (is, are) sleek and strong.
are *present*

1. Mary (was, were) happy about her trip to California.
2. Her home (was, were) a covered wagon.
3. The wagon (is, are) empty.
4. The horses (was, were) nervous.
5. Some wagons (is, are) full of possessions.

?! THINK

- How can I remember which form of the verb *be* to use with *I, you, we,* and other subjects?

REMEMBER

■ The verb *be* changes in the present tense and in the past tense to agree with the subject of the sentence.

GRAMMAR

More Practice

A. Write each sentence. Choose the correct form of the linking verb *be* from the verbs in parentheses ( ).

Example: Luke (was, were) a pioneer. *was*

6. Luke (was, were) ready for the journey.
7. It (is, are) a long and difficult journey.
8. His parents (is, are) Charles and Molly.
9. They (was, were) eager to begin the trip.
10. Luke (was, were) responsible for one wagon.
11. Luke's father (is, are) the leader of the train.
12. Luke's friends (is, are) Frank and Ann.
13. Their mother (was, were) also part of the train.
14. Water (is, are) scarce in the desert.
15. The pioneers (was, were) asleep when it rained.
16. Luckily, water buckets (is, are) plentiful.

The Bettmann Archive

B. Write each sentence. Write **was** or **were** to correctly complete the sentence.

Example: Wagon trains _____ a popular method of travel in the 1800s. *were*

17. A wagon train _______ often the only way to travel West.
18. Life on the trail _______ an adventure.
19. Hardships _______ frequent.
20. People _______ glad when the long journey ended.

Extra Practice, Practice Plus, pages 247–248

WRITING APPLICATION A Story

COOPERATIVE LEARNING

Imagine that you were part of a wagon train. Write a story that tells what you saw and did on your trip West. Exchange papers with a classmate. Ask your partner to find all the linking verbs in your writing.

G R A M M A R

5 CONTRACTIONS WITH *NOT*

A **contraction** is a shortened form of two words. In a contraction one or more letters are left out and an apostrophe (') takes their place. Many contractions can be formed by combining a verb with the word *not.* The apostrophe shows the place where the *o* in *not* has been left out.

Julio **is not** asleep yet. Julio **isn't** asleep yet.

The chart below shows some common contractions.

Contractions That Combine a Verb with *not*

isn't	is + not	haven't	have + not
aren't	are + not	hasn't	has + not
wasn't	was + not	hadn't	had + not
weren't	were + not	couldn't	could + not
don't	do + not	shouldn't	should + not
doesn't	does + not	wouldn't	would + not
didn't	did + not	can't	can + not
won't	will + not		

Notice that in the contraction *can't,* the apostrophe replaces the letters *n* and *o* in *not.* The verb *will* changes its spelling when it is combined with *not* in the contraction *won't.*

Guided Practice

Tell which contraction can be formed by combining each of these pairs of words.

Example: do + not *don't*

1. could not
2. will not
3. are not
4. have not
5. has not

?! THINK

■ How can I remember where to place the apostrophe when I form a contraction with the word *not*?

REMEMBER

- A **contraction** can be made by combining a verb with the word *not*. An apostrophe usually shows the place where the *o* in *not* has been left out.

More Practice

A. Write a contraction for each of the following pairs of words.

Example: will not *won't*

6. is not
7. was not
8. would not
9. did not
10. has not
11. were not
12. do not
13. are not
14. had not
15. does not
16. have not
17. should not

B. Write each sentence. Write a contraction by combining the underlined word or words.

Example: Are not the balloons colorful! *Aren't*

18. Perhaps you do not know about the Montgolfier brothers from Paris.
19. In 1793 hot air balloons had not yet been invented.
20. "It cannot be done," people said.
21. The brothers did not take no for an answer.
22. People could not believe their eyes.
23. Is not it amazing to see a balloon fly high in the air?
24. The first passengers—a sheep, a duck, and a rooster—were not afraid.
25. This flight will not be forgotten.

Extra Practice, page 249

WRITING APPLICATION A Paragraph

Imagine that you have been asked to design a new means of travel. Draw a picture of the vehicle that you invent. Then, write a paragraph that tells how it works. Exchange papers with a partner. Ask your partner to find all the contractions formed by combining verbs with *not*.

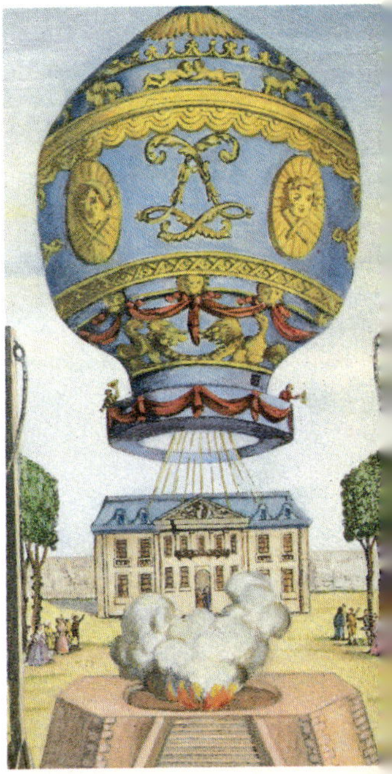

The Bettmann Archive

GRAMMAR

6 MECHANICS: Using Quotation Marks

When you write a conversation between two or more people, you must show who the speaker is by correctly using punctuation marks. When you write a speaker's exact words, it is called a **direct quotation.** Use **quotation marks** (" ") before and after a direct quotation. Never use quotation marks around the words that tell who is speaking.

Paula asked, "When can I use the new computer?"
"How impatient I am!" Paula exclaimed.
"I cannot wait," Paula said. "Let's begin right now."

Sometimes you may write what someone says without using the speaker's exact words. Do not use quotation marks when you do not use the speaker's exact words.

Paula asked when she could use the computer.
She explained that she was very impatient.

Guided Practice

Tell where quotation marks should be placed in each sentence.

Example: When can I use your computer? Jan asked.
"When can I use your computer?" Jan asked.

1. I'd like to have a computer, said Jackie.
2. Do you have computers in your school? she asked.
3. Of course we do! exclaimed Mac.
4. Paula asked, When do you think you will get your own computer?
5. Mac answered, I don't know yet.

?! **THINK**

- How do I decide where to place quotation marks when I write a conversation?

REMEMBER

- Use quotation marks before and after a speaker's exact words.

More Practice

A. Write each sentence. Add quotation marks where they are needed.

Example: Our school has a new computer, said Daryl.
"Our school has a new computer," said Daryl.

6. Computers have many uses, said Katy.
7. They help people communicate, Dennis stated.
8. People all over the world use computers, said Jo.
9. Britt asked, How were computers invented?
10. Let's go to the library to find out, said Mae.
11. We can use the library's computer, added Matt.
12. We can learn about different computers, Ray said.
13. May Ling suggested, Maybe Mr. Dean can help us.

B. Write each sentence. Add quotation marks. If a sentence does not need quotation marks, write **correct** next to it.

Example: Mike said that he will write a letter. *correct*

14. I will write it on the computer, he added.
15. Do you know what a word processor is? asked Hani.
16. Mike answered that he did not.
17. A word processor can help you write quickly, she said.
18. Mike said, I have finished my letter.
19. Now I can print it out, he added.
20. Al told Mike that he had done a good job.

Extra Practice, page 250

WRITING APPLICATION A Conversation

Draw a large computer screen. Write a conversation on the screen that might take place between you and the computer. Ask a classmate to check your quotation marks.

7 VOCABULARY BUILDING: Suffixes

You already know that you can change the meaning of a base word by adding a prefix to it. A **suffix** is a word part, too. A suffix is added to the end of a base word. When you add a suffix, you also change the meaning of the base word to which the suffix is added.

Here are some suffixes and their meanings.

Suffix	Meaning	Example
ful	full of	joy**ful**
less	without	hope**less**
ly, ily	in the manner of	quick**ly**, speed**ily**
er	one who does	work**er**
or	that which does	survey**or**
able, ible	capable of being	accept**able**, collect**ible**
y	having, being like	silk**y**
ment	the result of	agree**ment**

Guided Practice

Identify the suffix in each of these words.

Example: banker *er*

1. reporter
2. doubtful
3. guilty
4. painless
5. payment
6. thoughtful
7. actor

?! THINK

■ How can I decide if a word has a suffix?

REMEMBER

- A **suffix** is a word part that is added to the end of a base word.
- A suffix changes the meaning of the base word to which it is added.

More Practice

A. Write each word. Underline the suffix.

Example: noisily *ily*

8. sleepily
9. builder
10. fearless
11. wealthy
12. tricky
13. collectible
14. settlement
15. suddenly

B. Write each sentence. Add a suffix to each word in parentheses ( ) to complete the sentence.

Example: I completed my errands _____ . (eager)
I completed my errands eagerly.

16. One day I was a _____ at the post office. (visit)
17. Customers stood _____ at windows. (patient)
18. I gave the postal _____ my package. (work)
19. I told her my package was _____ . (break)
20. She said I should not be _____ . (fear)
21. I asked her about the _____ . (pay)
22. She figured out the cost _____ . (quick)
23. It sounded _____ to me. (reason)
24. I knew my package would arrive _____ . (safe)
25. This errand was _____ done. (easy)

Extra Practice, page 251

WRITING APPLICATION A Poem

Write a short poem about a package that gets lost in the mail. The poem can be funny or serious. Let a classmate read your poem. Ask your classmate to pick out any words that have suffixes.

GRAMMAR AND WRITING CONNECTION

Combining Sentences

Sometimes two sentences have related or connected ideas. When ideas in separate sentences are related, you can join, or combine, the sentences by using the word *and.*

Separate: The ship stopped. The ship docked.
Combined: The ship stopped **and** docked.

You can use the word *but* to show a different connection.

Separate: Liza looked toward shore. Liza saw nothing.
Combined: Liza looked toward shore **but** saw nothing.

COOPERATIVE LEARNING

Working Together

With your classmates talk about each pair of sentences. Then tell how you would join them to make a single sentence.

Example: The ferryboat lurched. It jolted the passengers.
The ferryboat lurched and jolted the passengers.

1. Liza sighted high cliffs.
   She shouted loudly.
2. Liza liked the salty spray.
   She felt a little seasick.
3. Liza enjoyed the boat ride.
   She was anxious to explore the shore.

Revising Sentences

Celia wrote the following sentences about Chris, a character in a story that she was planning. Help Celia revise her writing by combining each pair of sentences.

4. Chris left the ferryboat.
   He stood on the island.
5. The Orkney Islands were very strange.
   They were very beautiful.
6. The stores were old.
   The stores sold modern goods.
7. The wind blew constantly.
   It roared along the coast.
8. The island was treeless.
   It was covered with long grass.
9. Trees withered in the strong wind.
   They died in the strong wind.
10. Chris saw only a few cows.
    He noticed sheep everywhere.
11. The sea beat against the cliffs.
    It crashed in huge waves.
12. The ferry returned.
    It took Chris back to the mainland.

WRITER AT WORK

Think of an interesting place that you have visited or would like to visit. Write a post card describing the place. If you can, combine some sentences. Use *and* or *but* to join words. Leave out any words that repeat ideas.

UNIT CHECKUP

LESSON 1

What Is a Linking Verb? (page 224) Write each sentence and underline the verb. Then write **action verb** or **linking verb** next to each sentence.

1. Sara is happy about her trip to Asia.
2. Her parents packed the trunks.
3. Sara was always curious about Hong Kong.
4. She read books about the city.
5. Sara even wrote a book report about Hong Kong.
6. Sara showed us many pictures of the area.

LESSONS 2-3

Linking Verbs in the Present Tense and Past Tense (pages 226–229) Write each sentence. Choose the correct linking verb in parentheses ( ) to complete each sentence.

7. My suitcase (is, are) heavy.
8. They (am, are) ready for the trip.
9. I (is, am) happy about my trip.
10. Maria (is, are) glad that I will visit.
11. Max (is, are) a big help.
12. Maria and Max (is, are) my friends.
13. I (was, were) a good camper last summer.
14. My home (was, were) a summer camp.
15. The camp bus (was, were) yellow.
16. I (was, were) the leader of my dorm.
17. The two weeks (was, were) wonderful.
18. You (was, were) a good friend at camp.

LESSON 4

Using Linking Verbs (page 230) Write each sentence. Choose the correct form of the linking verb *be* in parentheses ( ).

19. This play (is, are) very popular.
20. It (was, were) the first play Chin ever saw.
21. Lara and Joy (is, are) good actresses.
22. We (was, were) comfortable in our seats.
23. Chin (is, are) curious about what he sees.
24. It (is, are) a new experience for him.

LESSON 5

Contractions with *not* (page 232) Write each sentence. Use a contraction in place of the underlined word or words.

25. Sean has not written a letter.
26. You cannot expect one from him.
27. Sean usually does not write letters.
28. I do not know exactly where he is now.
29. He will not be home for two weeks.
30. I would not worry about him.

LESSON 6

Mechanics: Using Quotation Marks (page 234) Write each sentence. Add quotation marks where they are needed.

31. Laura said, I would like to visit Quinn.
32. Nicky asked, Where does Quinn live?
33. His home is not far from here, Laura stated.
34. He lives on Oak Avenue, she added.
35. I would love to see him, too, exclaimed Nicky.
36. Here he comes now! shouted Laura and Nicky.

LESSON 7

Vocabulary Building: Suffixes (page 236) Write each sentence. Write a suffix for each word in parentheses ( ). Write the new word in the blank.

37. My _____ took our class on a picnic. (teach)
38. The countryside was _____ . (beauty)
39. We ate an _____ amount of food. (end)
40. A surprise _____ was a squirrel. (visit)
41. His arrival caused great _____ . (enjoy)
42. He fit in _____ with our group. (easy)

Writing Application: Linking Verb Usage (pages 224–231) The following paragraph contains 7 errors with linking verbs. Rewrite the paragraph correctly.

43.–50.

Reading travel books am my hobby. I is happiest when I are at the library or in a bookstore. I often imagine that I is a famous pilot like Amelia Earhart or Charles Lindbergh. They am my heroes. They was excellent pilots and famous world travelers, too. I am saving my money for the day when I is old enough for a pilot's license.

ENRICHMENT

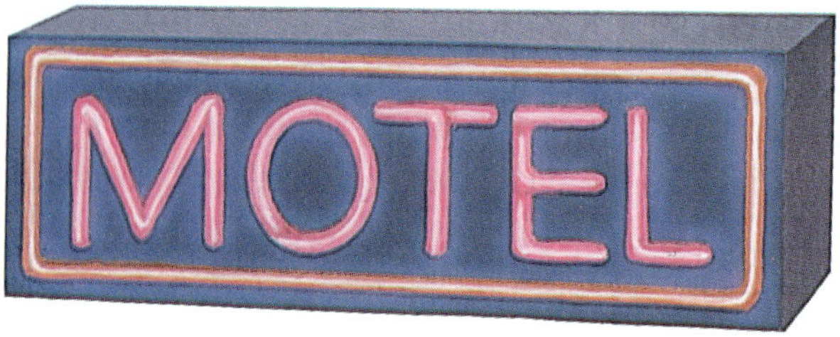

BLENDING IN

Contractions are made by joining two words together. Another kind of word, called a *blend,* is also made by joining two words. Did you know that the word *motel* is a blend? It is made from the words *motor* and *hotel.*

Play this game with a partner. Write each of these words on a separate card: *smoke, fog, breakfast, lunch, splash, spatter, news, broadcast, growl, rumble, flame, glare.*

Put the cards face down in a pile. Take turns picking one card at a time from the pile. See who can collect the most pairs to form these blends: *smog, brunch, splatter, newscast, grumble, flare.*

Use a dictionary to add more blends to your game.

THIS AND THAT

It's fun to make comparisons with word pairs.

Day is to *light* as *night* is to *dark.*

By yourself or with a partner, complete the following comparisons.

Rooster is to *chick* as *lion* is to ____ .
Thermometer is to *temperature* as *clock* is to ____ .
Seeing is to *eyes* as ____ is to *ears.*
Wrist is to *hand* as ____ is to *foot.*

Make up some comparisons of your own. Challenge a friend to complete them.

NOW AND THEN

With a group of classmates create a mural that shows some of the things you might like to be when you grow up. Label your drawings with the title of the job your picture describes. For example, you might write *Lisa will be a doctor,* or *Charles would like to be a teacher.*

SPIN A WORD

Play this game with a small group of classmates. Make suffix spinners from two paper plates. Divide the first plate into ten sections. Then write one of these words in each section: *comfort, rain, read, cheer, help, shape, care, settle, invent, teach.* Divide the second plate into eight sections and write one of these suffixes in each section: *ful, less, ly/ily, er, or, able/ible, y, ment.* Attach a cardboard arrow to each plate with a metal fastener.

The first player spins the two suffix spinners. If the arrows land on a word and a suffix that can be combined, the player must say the new word and use it in a sentence. If the player uses the word correctly, he or she receives one point. Then the other players, in turn, spin for words. The player with the highest number of points at the end of the game is the winner.

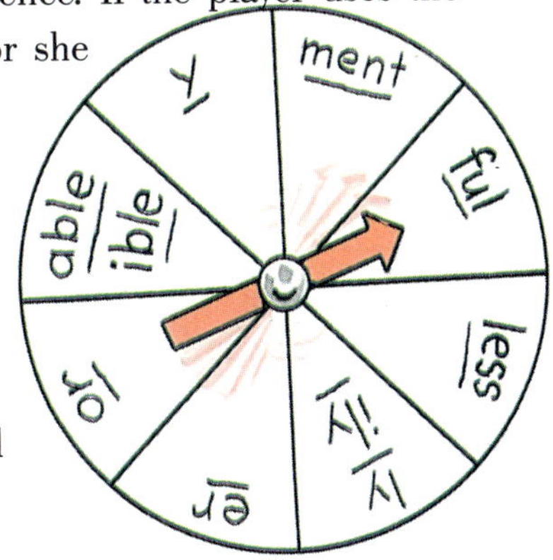

Pro-VERBS

A proverb is a short saying that tells a truth or says something wise. Most proverbs have been handed down from one generation to another. Proverbs are found in every language. Here are two that may be familiar to you.

A penny saved is a penny earned.

Don't count your chickens until they are hatched.

Make a book of proverbs. Ask relatives and neighbors to tell you their favorites. Write one proverb on each page of the book. Illustrate your collection.

EXTRA PRACTICE

Three levels of practice

What Is a Linking Verb? (page 224)

LEVEL **A.** Read each sentence. Write whether each underlined verb is a **linking verb** or an **action verb.**

1. Olan and Meg sat on the bus.
2. They waited for Chen.
3. Chen was late.
4. Chen is our group leader.
5. Chen takes us on our trips.
6. Chen is a good leader.
7. We are curious about our class trip.
8. We drove to a museum.
9. It was next to a park.
10. We liked the park very much.

LEVEL **B.** Write each sentence. Underline the verb. Then write whether it is an **action verb** or a **linking verb.**

11. We walked quickly into the museum.
12. Chen is very serious.
13. I am happy about our visit.
14. Meg sees the entrance to the exhibit.
15. The hall is very large.
16. We saw some old farm tools.
17. They were old and rusty.
18. People used them long ago.

LEVEL **C.** Write each sentence. Complete it with a linking verb.

19. Some tools _____ well preserved.
20. Many ancient objects _____ in the museum.
21. We _____ happy about seeing the displays.
22. Meg _____ sleepy.
23. It _____ time to leave.
24. The exhibit _____ too big for one visit.
25. We _____ eager for another visit.

EXTRA PRACTICE

GRAMMAR

Three levels of practice

Linking Verbs in the Present Tense (page 226)

LEVEL A. Write each sentence. Underline the present-tense linking verb in each one.

1. We are finally in Green Point Park.
2. Our class is here on a field trip.
3. Some students are together in one boat.
4. I am near the pond.
5. We are all happy.
6. It is a beautiful day.
7. Is that a chipmunk?
8. It is very cute.
9. Chipmunks are tiny animals.
10. One chipmunk is smaller than all the others.

LEVEL B. Write each sentence. Use the correct linking verb in parentheses ( ) to complete each sentence.

11. The park (is, are) full of people.
12. A playground (is, are) close to the pond.
13. My friends (is, are) still on the swings.
14. Two boys (is, are) now on the seesaw.
15. I (is, am) a good athlete.
16. Beth (is, are) also athletic.
17. We (is, are) both on a softball team.
18. (Is, Are) you the pitcher?

LEVEL C. Write each sentence. Use the correct present-tense linking verb to complete the sentence.

19. Some birds _____ also in the park.
20. _____ that a bluejay?
21. No, that bird _____ a robin.
22. I _____ a good bird-watcher.
23. There _____ many kinds of birds here.
24. Finches _____ smaller than sparrows.
25. Their nests _____ everywhere.

EXTRA PRACTICE

Three levels of practice

Linking Verbs in the Past Tense (page 228)

LEVEL A. Write each sentence. Underline the past-tense linking verb in each one.

1. Our family was ready for our trip to Japan.
2. We were very excited.
3. My sister was nervous about the plane ride.
4. Dad was uneasy about the weather.
5. The trip was ten hours long.
6. The flight attendants were helpful.
7. I was restless during the flight.
8. My brothers were tired.
9. Mom was happy at the end of the flight.
10. We were eager to begin the sight-seeing tour.

LEVEL B. Write each sentence. Use the correct linking verb in parentheses ( ) to complete each sentence.

11. Japan (was, were) full of surprises.
12. The country (was, were) really lovely.
13. The mountains (was, were) very high.
14. The sea (was, were) full of fish.
15. Certain types of fish (was, were) common.
16. Tokyo (was, were) a busy place.
17. The city (was, were) quite noisy.
18. My family (was, were) fond of sushi.

LEVEL C. Write each sentence. Write the correct past-tense linking verb to complete the sentence.

19. The Chinese _____ a strong influence in Japan.
20. The rulers in Japan _____ emperors.
21. The emperors _____ very wealthy.
22. Commodore Perry _____ an early visitor to Japan.
23. He _____ anxious to trade with the Japanese.
24. I'm sorry you _____ not with us on the trip.
25. The Japanese children _____ very much like us.

EXTRA PRACTICE

Three levels of practice

Using Linking Verbs (page 230)

LEVEL A. Write each sentence. Underline the linking verb in each sentence.

1. Margarita's parents are very nice.
2. They are helpful to us, too.
3. We were ready at noon.
4. Margarita's parents were late.
5. They are usually very prompt.
6. My watch is slow.
7. I am not very calm.
8. We were all impatient.
9. We were tired at the end of the day.
10. I was the most exhausted of all.

LEVEL B. Write each sentence. Choose the correct form of the linking verb *be* from the verbs in parentheses ( ).

11. The lions (was, were) powerful.
12. They (is, are) beautiful creatures.
13. We (was, were) the first group at the zoo.
14. The elephants (is, are) huge.
15. Their trunks (is, are) long.
16. A peacock (is, are) magnificent.
17. Its large tail (is, are) open.
18. Its feathers (was, were) beautiful.

LEVEL C. Write each sentence. Use **was** or **were** to complete each sentence correctly.

19. The giant pandas _____ very cute.
20. They _____ a gift from China.
21. It _____ a long journey for them.
22. They _____ a surprise to us.
23. One panda _____ quite large.
24. Another panda _____ asleep in the shade.
25. A baby panda _____ there, too.

PRACTICE + PLUS

Three levels of additional practice for a difficult skill

Using Linking Verbs (page 230)

LEVEL A. Write these sentences. Underline the linking verb in each sentence.

1. Karen is a good gardener.
2. Her garden is full of flowers and vegetables.
3. The tomatoes are ready for harvest.
4. They are redder than the tomatoes in the store.
5. Last year, the tomatoes were bad.
6. Karen was forgetful about weeding.
7. She is more careful this year.
8. Her tomatoes are prize winners.
9. Karen is proud of her garden.
10. The garden is a lovely place.

LEVEL B. Write each sentence. Choose the correct form of the linking verb from the pair in parentheses ( ) to complete each sentence.

11. It (is, are) Memorial Day.
12. The parks (is, are) open for swimmers.
13. Lem (is, are) always careful in the water.
14. Last year, Lem (was, were) afraid of the water.
15. Now, he (is, are) a good swimmer.
16. His parents (is, are) proud of that.
17. Lem's sisters (is, are) excellent swimmers, too.

LEVEL C. Write these sentences. Complete each sentence with a present-tense linking verb.

18. Toby's aunt _____ a scientist.
19. Some of her experiments _____ very complicated.
20. The lab _____ very modern.
21. Toby _____ interested in the equipment.
22. The lab workers _____ happy with their jobs.
23. They _____ pleased with the successful experiments.
24. The lab _____ open day and night.
25. The work done there _____ important.

EXTRA PRACTICE

GRAMMAR

Three levels of practice

Contractions with not (page 232)

LEVEL **A.** Write each sentence. Underline the contraction in each one.

1. Barney hasn't traveled to France.
2. Wouldn't you like to go there?
3. Weren't you in Paris last summer?
4. I couldn't wait for that trip.
5. Haven't you seen the Eiffel Tower?
6. Didn't you sail on a ship?
7. I don't travel by ship.
8. Traveling by ship isn't as difficult as air travel.
9. Won't you go again next spring?
10. We aren't going again next spring.

LEVEL **B.** Write each sentence. Write a contraction by combining the two underlined words.

11. Jan's friends <u>will not</u> go to Spain.
12. They <u>could not</u> get airplane tickets.
13. Jan <u>should not</u> be so upset.
14. Her parents <u>would not</u> like that.
15. It <u>has not</u> been long since I returned from Europe.
16. You <u>were not</u> in Spain last winter.
17. It <u>was not</u> yet winter when I left.

LEVEL **C.** Write each question. Then write an answer to it. Use a contraction in your answer by adding **not** to each underlined verb.

18. <u>Were</u> Debra and Scott with you?
19. <u>Have</u> they ever been to Puerto Rico?
20. <u>Does</u> Scott like spicy food?
21. <u>Will</u> you spend time in San Juan?
22. <u>Can</u> you pick up our plane tickets?
23. <u>Do</u> they know where to meet you?
24. <u>Should</u> we meet at the gate?
25. <u>Are</u> you traveling together?

EXTRA PRACTICE

Three levels of practice

Mechanics: Using Quotation Marks (page 234)

LEVEL **A.** Write each sentence. Underline the direct quotation in each one.

1. Pearl asked, "Have you heard the news?"
2. "What is the news?" asked Carlos.
3. "Kee is going on a safari," said Pearl.
4. "He is going with his uncle," added Elaine.
5. Grace exclaimed, "How exciting that is!"
6. "He will see many wild animals," remarked Phil.
7. "They will camp out in the jungle," said Jerry.
8. Ana asked, "How long will Kee be gone?"
9. "Kee will be gone one month," said Ed.
10. Eric exclaimed, "I wish I could go!"

LEVEL **B.** Write each sentence. Add quotation marks where they are needed.

11. Bo said, She is from South America.
12. Dolores asked, Which country is she from?
13. She is from Peru, Bo replied.
14. Gregg asked, What is her name?
15. Her name is Estella, said Bo.
16. She will come to school tomorrow, he added.
17. I hope she likes it here, stated Mae.

LEVEL **C.** Write each sentence. Add quotation marks. If a sentence does not need quotation marks, write **correct** next to it.

18. Where are you going? asked Sal.
19. I am going on a trip with my sister, said Hazel.
20. She added that they were going to visit their Uncle James.
21. Where does Uncle James live? Sal asked.
22. He lives in Oklahoma, said Hazel.
23. Sal asked how she would get there.
24. We are taking the train, said Hazel.
25. Have a wonderful time! exclaimed Sal.

EXTRA PRACTICE

GRAMMAR

Three levels of practice

Vocabulary Building: Suffixes (page 236)

LEVEL **A.** Write each word. Then underline the suffix.

1. hurriedly
2. hopeful
3. convertible
4. teacher
5. pointless
6. announcement
7. pitcher
8. comfortable
9. lucky
10. surveyor

LEVEL **B.** Write each base word and suffix.

Example: bossy *boss + y*

11. healthy
12. enjoyment
13. wearable
14. helpless
15. slowly
16. collectible
17. inventor

LEVEL **C.** Write each sentence. Write a suffix for each word in parentheses ( ).

18. A _____ entered the shop. (visit)
19. She looked at many _____ items. (cost)
20. A man asked if a plastic vase was _____ . (break)
21. The clerk answered _____ . (polite)
22. Two of the children had a _____ . (disagree)
23. They argued _____ . (loud)
24. The family _____ left the shop. (speed)
25. It was _____ and quiet again. (peace)

MAINTENANCE

UNIT 1: Sentences

Sentences (pages 2, 4, 6)
Write each group of words. Then write **declarative, interrogative, imperative,** or **exclamatory** next to each group. If a group of words is not a sentence, write **not a sentence.**

1. The parrot in the zoo.
2. The friendly bird says hello to everyone.
3. How funny a parrot sounds!
4. Tell me which bird speaks.
5. Can it fly to the tree?

Subjects and Predicates
(pages 8, 10, 12)
Write each sentence. Draw a line between the complete subject and the complete predicate. Then draw one line under the simple subject and two lines under the simple predicate.

6. Two classes went to an art museum.
7. A guide explained the exhibits.
8. Some students asked about the art.
9. One teacher loved the statues.
10. The tour ended much too soon.

Compound Subjects and Compound Predicates (page 14)
Write the compound subject or compound predicate in each sentence.

11. The wind whirled and howled around the house.
12. The dog ran and hid under the bed in my room.
13. My mother and father checked the windows.
14. Loud thunder and bright lightning came with the storm.
15. My sister happily clapped and loudly cheered for each boom.

Correcting and Punctuating Run-on Sentences (page 16)
Rewrite each run-on sentence as two sentences.

16. Take this trail to the waterfall is it far?
17. The trail winds along the cliff it is about a mile long.
18. How loud the water sounds how high are the falls?
19. I do not get too close to the edge I am afraid of heights.

Using Context Clues (page 20)
Write each sentence. Next, write the letter of the meaning of the underlined word in each sentence. Then, underline the word or words in each sentence that you used as context clues.

20. Everyone bought bicycles when they became a fad in the 1890s.
a. something popular b. a car

21. Many couples enjoyed the ride on the tandem bicycle.
a. for one b. for two

22. The bicycle is a major means of travel in some countries.
a. way b. unkind

23. Bicycles do not pollute the air and make it hard to breathe.
a. make clean b. make dirty

UNIT 3: Nouns

What Is a Noun? (page 76)
Write the nouns in each sentence. Capitalize the proper nouns. Then write **person**, **place**, or **thing** after each noun.

24. My friend comes from texas.
25. margo moved into the blue house.
26. The children in the neighborhood walk to parker school.
27. Some students carry books in backpacks.
28. My teacher is karen jones.

Singular Nouns and Plural Nouns (pages 78, 80, 82)
Write each sentence. Complete the sentence correctly, using the singular or plural form of the noun in parentheses ( ).

29. The farm is down that (road).
30. The farmer raises many (ox).
31. They are the best in several (county).
32. The farmer sold his (sheep).
33. Two nearby (family) bought them.
34. The four (child) will raise them as pets.

Singular and Plural Possessive Nouns (pages 86, 88)
Write the possessive form of each noun.

35. Miguel
36. women
37. deer
38. boys
39. class
40. whales
41. goose
42. people
43. children
44. monkey
45. communities
46. tooth
47. coaches
48. geese
49. babies
50. valley

MAINTENANCE

UNIT 5: Action Verbs

Action Verbs, Main Verbs, and Helping Verbs (pages 152, 154) Draw one line under the action, or main, verb. Draw two lines under each helping verb.

51. Some cars were run by steam.
52. The cars were named "Flying Teapots."
53. The steam car was known for its cleanliness.
54. The steamer was timed at a speed of over 120 miles an hour.

Verb Tenses (page 156) Write each sentence. Draw a line under the verb. Write **past, present,** or **future** to show its tense.

55. Eiffel designed a tower.
56. He built the tower with iron.
57. Many people now visit the Eiffel Tower every year.
58. Workers will repaint the tower.

Subject-Verb Agreement (page 160) Write each sentence. Use the correct form of the verb in parentheses ( ).

59. Vocal cords (make, makes) sounds.
60. Air (pass, passes) over the cords.
61. You (speak, speaks) only when you breathe out.
62. The cords (stretch, stretches) when you speak.
63. They (vibrate, vibrates) so that you can make sounds.

Using Irregular Verbs (pages 162, 164) Write each sentence. Use the correct form of the verb in parentheses ( ).

64. My aunt has (wrote, written) a new cookbook.
65. She (give, gave) my mother several recipes.
66. Aunt Maria had (begin, begun) the book when I last saw her.
67. Her last book (do, did) well.

Using the Comma (page 168) Write each sentence. Add commas where they are needed.

68. Wolves howl yap and growl.
69. Yes they talk to one another.
70. Roy watch that wolf walk.
71. Well I think it is angry.
72. You are right Carla when you say that wolves compete.

UNIT 7: Linking Verbs

What Is a Linking Verb?

(page 224) Write the verb in each sentence. Then write **action verb** or **linking verb** to tell what kind of verb it is.

73. Many birds fly south in winter.
74. Warblers go all the way to South America.
75. They are smaller than sparrows.
76. Penguins swim to winter homes.
77. Their feathers are waterproof.

Past- and Present-Tense Linking Verbs (pages 226, 228) Write each sentence. Use the correct verb in parentheses ( ).

78. Camels (is, are) desert animals.
79. A camel's hump (is, are) a storage place for fat.
80. A camel (was, were) the best carrier of desert supplies.
81. Camels (was, were) once used in the U.S. Army.
82. However, after the Civil War, the camels (was, were) no longer useful.

Contractions with *not* (page 232) Write each sentence. Use a contraction in place of the underlined word or words.

83. Albert <u>does not</u> hike.
84. He <u>would not</u> go with us.
85. We <u>will not</u> leave until in the afternoon.
86. Lee <u>has not</u> packed her lunch.
87. I <u>cannot</u> go until I find my boots.

Using Quotation Marks

(page 234) Write each sentence. Add quotation marks where they are needed.

88. Has Rosa returned from her vacation? Barb asked.
89. No, but I got a post card from her yesterday, Amy replied.
90. She will be back tomorrow, Mother said.
91. How do you know? Amy asked.
92. Her parents told me before they left, Mother answered.

Suffixes (page 236) Write the words below. Then, underline the suffix in each word.

93. actor	**97.** colorless
94. payment	**98.** lucky
95. capable	**99.** teacher
96. clearly	**100.** cheerful

WRITING

UNIT 8

Writing Stories

Read the quotation and look at the picture on the opposite page. How did E.B. White get his idea for *The Trumpet of the Swan*? Talk with a partner about the importance of a writer's imagination.

When you write a story, you will want your audience to enjoy what you have written. You will need to use your imagination.

Focus A story has a beginning, a middle, and an end. The characters in a story move the action of the story along.

What kind of story would you like to write? In this unit you will find a story about a trumpeter swan. You will find some interesting photographs, too. You can use the story and the photographs to give you ideas for writing.

THEME: *TRAVELS*

I don't know how or when the idea for The Trumpet of the Swan *occurred to me. I guess I must have wondered what it would be like to be a trumpeter swan and not be able to make a noise.*

—E.B. White

LITERATURE

Reading Like a Writer

AWARD WINNING SELECTION

We all know how it feels to prepare for a trip. Imagine that you needed to learn to fly to join your family on a trip.

The following story is about a family of swans. The swan children, called cygnets, need to learn to fly in order to travel south with their parents for the winter. The father swan, called a cob, is a kind and encouraging teacher. Sam is a boy who is a friend to the swans.

As you read the story, think about the way the author tells you about the characters, the time and place, and the events. By the end of the story, you might find yourself wishing you could fly!

from

The Trumpet of the Swan

by *E. B. White*

At the end of the summer, the cob gathered his family around him and made an announcement. "Children," he began, "I have news for you. Summer is drawing to a close. Leaves are turning red, pink, and pale yellow. Soon the leaves will fall. The time has come for us to leave this pond. The time has come for us to go."

"Go?" cried all the cygnets except Louis.

"Certainly," replied their father. "You children are old enough to learn the facts of life, and the principal fact of our life right now is this: we can't stay in this marvelous location much longer."

"Why not?" cried all the cygnets except Louis.

"Because summer is over," said the cob, "and it is the way of swans to leave their nesting site at summer's end and travel south to a milder place where the food supply is good. I know that you are all fond of this pretty pond, this marvelous marsh, these reedy shores and restful retreats. You have found life pleasant and amusing here. You have learned to dive and swim underwater. You have enjoyed our daily recreational trips when we formed in line, myself in front swimming gracefully, like a locomotive, and your charming mother bringing up the rear, like a caboose. Daylong, you have listened and learned. You have avoided the odious otter and the cruel coyote. You have listened to the little owl that says co-co-co-co. You have heard the partridge say kwit-kwit. At night you have dropped off to sleep to the sound of frogs—the voices of the night.

The setting is described here.

But these pleasures and pastimes, these adventures, these games and frolics, these beloved sights and sounds must come to an end. All things come to an end. It is time for us to go."

"Where will we go?" cried all the cygnets except Louis. "Where will we go, ko-hoh, ko-hoh? Where will we go, ko-hoh, ko-hoh?"

"We will fly south to Montana," replied the cob.

"What is Montana?" asked all the cygnets except Louis. "What is Montana – banana, banana? What is Montana – banana, banana?"

"Montana," said their father, "is a state of the Union. And there, in a lovely valley surrounded by high mountains, are the Red Rock Lakes, which nature has designed especially for swans. In these lakes you will enjoy warm water, arising from hidden springs. Here, ice never forms, no matter how cold the nights. In the Red Rock Lakes, you will find other Trumpeter Swans, as well as the lesser waterfowl – the geese and the ducks. There are few enemies. No gunners. Plenty of muskrat houses. Free grain. Games every day. What more can a swan ask, in the long, long cold of winter?"

Louis listened to all this in amazement. He wanted to ask his father how they would learn to fly and how they would find Montana even after they learned to fly. He began to worry about getting lost. But he wasn't able to ask any questions. He just had to listen.

One of his brothers spoke up.

"Father," he said, "you said we would *fly* south. I don't know *how* to fly. I've never been up in the air."

"True," replied the cob. "But flying is largely a matter of having the right attitude – plus, of course, good wing feathers. Flying consists of three parts. First, the takeoff, during which there is a lot of fuss and commotion, a lot of splashing and rapid beating of the wings. Second, the ascent, or gaining of altitude – this requires hard work and fast wing action. Third, the leveling-off, the steady elevated flight, high in air, wings beating slower now, beating strongly and regularly, carrying us swiftly and surely from zone to zone as we cry ko-hoh, ko-hoh, with all the earth stretched out far below."

"It sounds very nice," said the cygnet, "but I'm not sure I can do it. I might get dizzy way up there—if I look down."

"Don't *look* down!" said his father. "Look straight ahead. And don't lose your nerve. Besides, swans do not get dizzy—they feel wonderful in the air. They feel exalted."

"What does 'exalted' mean?" asked the cygnet.

"It means you will feel strong, glad, firm, high, proud, successful, satisfied, powerful, and elevated—as though you had conquered life and had a high purpose."

Louis's problem is introduced here.

Louis listened to all this with great attention. The idea of flying frightened him. "I won't be able to say ko-hoh," he thought. "I wonder whether a swan can fly if he has no voice and can't say ko-hoh."

"I think," said the cob, "the best plan is for me to demonstrate flying to you. I will make a short exhibition flight while you watch. Observe everything I do! Watch me pump my neck up and down before the takeoff! Watch me test the wind by turning my head this way and that! The takeoff must be *into* the wind—it's much easier that way. Listen to the noise I make trumpeting! Watch how I raise my great wings! See how I beat them furiously as I rush through the water with my feet going like mad! This frenzy will last for a couple of hundred feet, at which point I will suddenly be airborne, my wings still chopping the air with terrific force but my feet no longer touching the water! Then watch what I do! Watch how I stretch my long white elegant neck out ahead of me until it has reached its full length! Watch how I retract my feet and allow them to stream out behind, full-length, unitl they extend beyond my tail! Hear my cries as I gain the upper air and start trumpeting! See how strong and steady my wingbeat has become! Then watch me bank and turn, set my wings, and glide down! And just as I reach the pond again, watch how I shoot my feet out in front of me and use

them for the splashdown, as though they were a pair of water skis! Having watched all this, then you can join me, and your mother, too, and we will all make a practice flight together, until you get the hang of it. Then tomorrow we will do it again, and instead of returning to the pond, we will head south to Montana. Are you ready for my exhibition flight?"

"Ready!" cried all the cygnets except Louis.

"Very well, here I go!" cried the cob.

As the others watched, he swam downwind to the end of the pond, turned, tested the wind, pumped his neck up and down, trumpeted, and after a rush of two hundred feet, got into the air and began gaining altitude. His long white neck stretched out ahead. His big black feet stretched out behind. His wings had great power. The beat slowed as he settled into sustained flight. All eyes watched. Louis was more excited than he had ever been. "I wonder if I can really do it?" he thought. "Suppose I fail! Then the others will fly away, and I will be left here all alone on this deserted pond, with winter approaching, with no father, no mother, no sisters, no brothers, and no food to eat when the pond freezes over. I will die of starvation. I'm scared."

In a few minutes, the cob glided down out of the sky and skidded to a stop on the pond. They all cheered. "Ko-hoh, ko-hoh, beep beep, beep beep!" All but Louis. He had to express his approval simply by beating his wings and splashing water in his father's face.

"All right," said the cob. "You've seen how it's done. Follow me, and we'll give it a try. Extend yourselves to the utmost, do everything in the proper order, never forget for a minute that you are swans and therefore excellent fliers, and I'm sure all will be well."

They all swam downwind to the end of the pond. They pumped their necks up and down. Louis pumped his harder than any of the others. They tested the wind by turning their heads this way and

that. Suddenly the cob signaled for the start. There was a tremendous commotion—wings beating, feet racing, water churned to a froth. And presently, wonder of wonders, there were seven swans in the air—two pure white ones and five dirty gray ones. The takeoff was accomplished, and they started gaining altitude.

Louis was the first of the young cygnets to become airborne, ahead of all his brothers and sisters. The minute his feet lifted clear of the water, he knew he could fly. It was a tremendous relief—as well as a splendid sensation.

"Boy!" he said to himself. "I never knew flying could be such fun. This is great. This is sensational. This is superb. I feel exalted, and I'm not dizzy. I'll be able to get to Montana with the rest of the family. I may be defective, but at least I can fly."

The seven great birds stayed aloft about half an hour, then returned to the pond, the cob still in the lead. They all had a drink to celebrate the successful flight. Next day they were up early. It was a beautiful fall morning, with mist rising from the pond and the trees shining in all colors. Toward the end of the afternoon, as the sun sank low in the sky, the swans took off from the pond and began their journey to Montana. "This way!" cried the cob. He swung to his left and straightened out on a southerly course. The others followed, trumpeting as they went. As they passed over the camp where Sam Beaver was, Sam heard them and ran out. He stood watching as they grew smaller and smaller in the distance and finally disappeared.

"What was it?" asked his father, when Sam returned indoors.

"Swans," replied Sam. "They're headed south."

"We'd better do the same," said Mr. Beaver. "I think Shorty will be here tomorrow to take us out."

Mr. Beaver lay down on his bunk. "What kind of swans were they?" he asked.

"Trumpeters," said Sam.

"That's funny," said Mr. Beaver. "I thought Trumpeter Swans had quit migrating. I thought they spent the whole year on the Red Rock Lakes, where they are protected."

"Most of 'em do," replied Sam. "But not all of 'em."

It was bedtime. Sam got out his diary. This is what he wrote:

> I heard the swans tonight. They are headed south. It must be wonderful to fly at night. I wonder whether I'll ever see one of them again. How does a bird know how to get from where he is to where he wants to be?

Thinking Like a Reader

1. Louis has mixed feelings about learning to fly. How would you describe Louis's feelings?
2. If you were learning to fly, how would you feel? Why do you think you feel that way?

Write your responses in your journal.

Thinking Like a Writer

3. How does E.B. White let you know how Louis feels about flying?
4. Which details did the author use to do this?
5. Which details do you like best?

Write a list of the details in your journal.

Responding to LITERATURE

Brainstorm *Vocabulary*

In "The Trumpet of the Swan," E.B. White uses many words that mean the same thing. Words that have the same or almost the same meaning are called **synonyms.** Find these synonyms in the story: *go–leave, watch–observe, stretch–extend.* Write at least five words to describe a swan. Then think of a synonym for as many of the words as you can. Begin to create a personal vocabulary list. You can use these words in your writing.

Talk It Over

Describe a Person

Often the characters are what make a story special. In "The Trumpet of the Swan," Louis, the main character, is a Trumpeter Swan without a voice. Although Louis is a bird, the author has given him human qualities. Think of a person outside of school who is unusual. Describe the person to a classmate. Include details in your description so that your partner will see this person as you do.

Quick Write

Write a Character Sketch

A **character sketch** is a portrait of a character drawn with words. Write a brief character sketch about a villain in a mystery story. Write your sketch in the form of a WANTED poster. Include a physical description of your character—height, weight, hair and eye color, and any special marks, scars, or other physical characteristics that the character may have.

Idea Corner

Think of Other Characters

The **main character** is the most important character in a story, but other characters in the story help make it lively and fun to read. Louis's father, for example, is an interesting character, a character you might enjoy meeting. You probably already have some ideas about characters. In your journal, write brief descriptions of some characters you would like to write about. You may also wish to draw the characters and give them names.

PICTURES SEEING LIKE A WRITER

Finding Ideas for Writing

Look at the photographs. Think about what you see.
What ideas for stories do the photographs give you?
You may want to write your story ideas in your journal.

WRITING TOGETHER

1 GROUP WRITING: A Story

COOPERATIVE LEARNING

The **purpose** of a story is to entertain. What makes a story fun for its **audience** to read?

- Interesting Characters and Setting
- A Good Beginning, Middle, and End
- Logical Order of Events

Interesting Characters and Setting

The **characters** of a story are the people in the story. The **main character** is the most important character. The **setting** is where and when the story takes place. Read the following beginning of a story about a raft trip down the Snake River in Idaho.

Burt stared at the huge, black rubber raft. As large as it was, Burt wondered how everyone would fit in it. Mr. and Mrs. Ryder were thin, but his own father was a little overweight. The guide, Jason, was heavyset, too. Then there was the Norris family, parents and three children. They certainly would take up quite a bit of room. Burt gazed at the slow-moving water, the towering cliffs, and then back at the raft. It seemed to be getting smaller and smaller as each person stepped into it.

Guided Practice: Describing a Character

The writer has described several characters in the story above, but has not described Burt. As a class, agree on a description of Burt. Write two or three sentences that give details about Burt's appearance.

Example: Burt's brown eyes were fixed on the raft. He wore jeans and a heavy woolen shirt, and had a baseball cap on his curly black hair.

A Good Beginning, Middle, and End

A good story beginning introduces the characters and the setting. The **plot,** or the events that will take place in the story, is also introduced at the beginning of the story. The plot is developed in the middle of the story. At this point the main character usually faces a challenge or a problem. The ending of the story shows how the main character solves the problem.

Logical Order of Events

To make a story easy to follow, events must occur in a logical **order**, or sequence. The events in a story often occur in time order.

Guided Practice: Ordering Story Events

Brainstorm with your classmates to choose a problem and solution to go with the story about Burt. As a class, make a chart like the one below. Decide together on several events that lead to the story problem and write them in time order. Then choose events that lead to the solution and write them in time order.

Story middle (problem): ____________________

____

____

____

Story end (solution): ____________________

____

____

____

WRITING TOGETHER

Putting a Story Together

With your classmates, you began to put a story together. Now, you can complete your story. Use the events you have listed to tell what happens to Burt on his raft trip. Think about how you can make the events interesting to your audience. You can use varied sentences, vivid words, and dialogue.

Dialogue is the exact words a story character says. Dialogue makes a story come to life. Look back at "Off to Montana." How does the dialogue help you know how Louis is feeling? How does it give you a fuller picture of Louis's father?

Use these rules when you write dialogue.

- Put quotation marks around a speaker's exact words.
  "I'll find more food," Burt promised.
  "Wait here," Burt said. "I'll be back soon."
- Tell who is speaking.
  "Help me," shouted Mr. Ryder.
  "I'll help," Burt responded.
- Indent each time a new speaker speaks.
  Mr. Ryder thrashed about in the rushing river. As the passengers in the boat watched helplessly, the current pulled him closer and closer to the jagged rocks. "My leg!" Mr. Ryder cried. "I think it's broken."
  "Hand me that rope," Burt called to his father.
  "Here it is," Burt's father replied.

Guided Practice: Writing a Story

Use your chart of story events to help you finish the story. Include dialogue to show how the characters feel about the events that take place. End the story by having Burt solve the problem that developed in the middle of the story.

Share your story with a friend. Ask your friend to suggest ways you can make your story more entertaining.

Checklist: A Story

When you write a story, you will want to keep some points in mind. A checklist will help to remind you of things you will want to include in your story.

Look at this checklist. Some points need to be added. Make a copy of the checklist and complete it. Keep a copy of it in your writing folder. You can use it when you write your story.

CHECKLIST

- ✓ Purpose and audience
- ✓ Interesting characters and setting
- ✓ A good beginning, middle, and end
- ■ Beginning
- ■ ____________
- ■ Solution
- ✓ Logical ____________

2 THINKING AND WRITING: Understanding Sequence

Deciding on the sequence of events is an important part of writing a story. The events in a story should move logically from the beginning through the middle to the end. Events in a story are usually arranged in time order. Look at this page from a writer's journal.

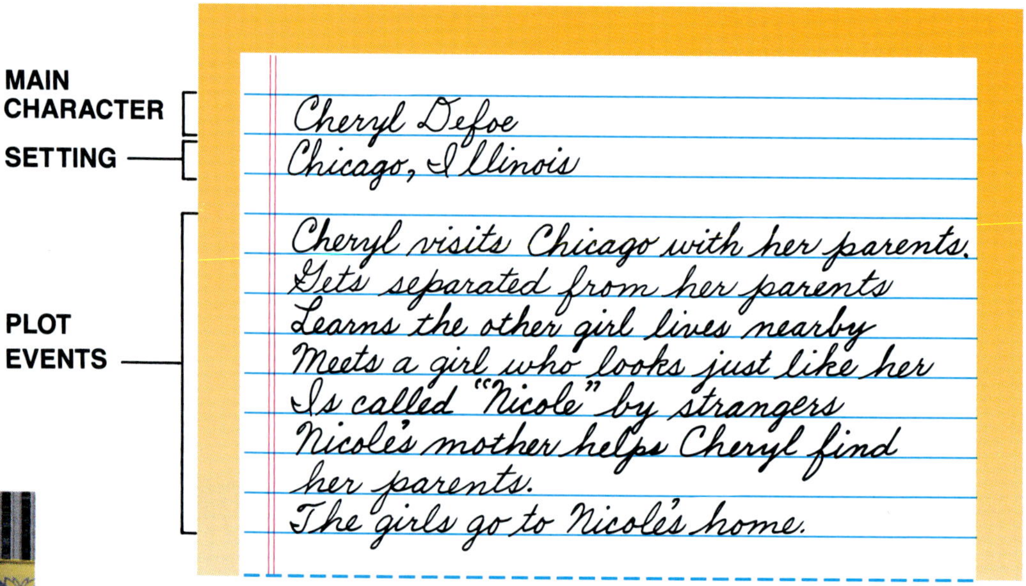

The writer wants to write a story set in Chicago. He has written the main events of the plot. He has not included time-order words, but it is obvious that certain events must occur before other events.

Thinking Like a Writer

- What is the best sequence of events for the plot?

The writer needs to put the events in the story into a logical sequence. The story concerns Cheryl, who is lost and is mistaken for Nicole. Nicole is a girl who lives in Chicago. Cheryl and Nicole meet. Nicole takes Cheryl back to her home. Then Nicole's mother helps Cheryl to find her parents.

Before you write a story, think about the events that will take place. Remember that your main character should face a problem in the middle of the story and must find a way to solve the problem. Make a list of the story events in your journal or on a separate piece of paper. Be sure that you arrange the events in a logical order, or sequence.

THINKING APPLICATION Ordering Events

COOPERATIVE LEARNING

Charlotte is planning to write a story. Read her journal entry below. Help her to put her events in a logical order. Would time order be a good way to arrange these events? Why do you think so? Write the events in the order you have chosen on a separate sheet of paper. You may wish to discuss your thinking with your classmates. In your discussions, explain why you put the events in the order that you did.

Vivian Eaglefeather
an Arizona ranch

Vivian is visiting her uncle Simon.
One afternoon, Vivian gets into the balloon basket to see what it is like.
In Simon's yard, Vivian sees a hot-air balloon.
Vivian finds a walkie-talkie in the balloon and contacts Simon.
Simon promises to take her up in the balloon.
A strong wind detaches the ties and the balloon goes up.
Simon tells her how to get the balloon down.
Vivian lands safely.

3 INDEPENDENT WRITING: A Story

Prewrite: Step 1

By now you know about the parts of a story. You are ready to write a story of your own. Manuel, a student your age, wanted to write a story for his classmates. He found his story idea this way.

Choosing an Idea

1. First, he made a list of ideas for stories he could write.
2. Next, he thought about all his ideas.
3. Last, he chose the kind of story his classmates might like best.

robots coming alive
acrobat learning new act
beginning school in a new town
✓ jewel robbery

Manuel thought a story about a jewel robbery was best. He explored his idea by making a story chart. Here is what Manuel's story chart looked like.

Exploring Ideas: Charting Strategy

CHARACTERS	Kevin, a ten-year-old boy; Senator Smith and wife; Joe, a stowaway
SETTING	A cruise ship
PLOT EVENTS	1. Mrs. Smith's jewels are missing. 2. Kevin discovers Joe on the ship. 3. Joe helps Kevin find jewels.

Manuel thought he had some good ideas. He knew his story would entertain his classmates.

Before beginning to write, Manuel thought some more about his plot. Then he added another event.

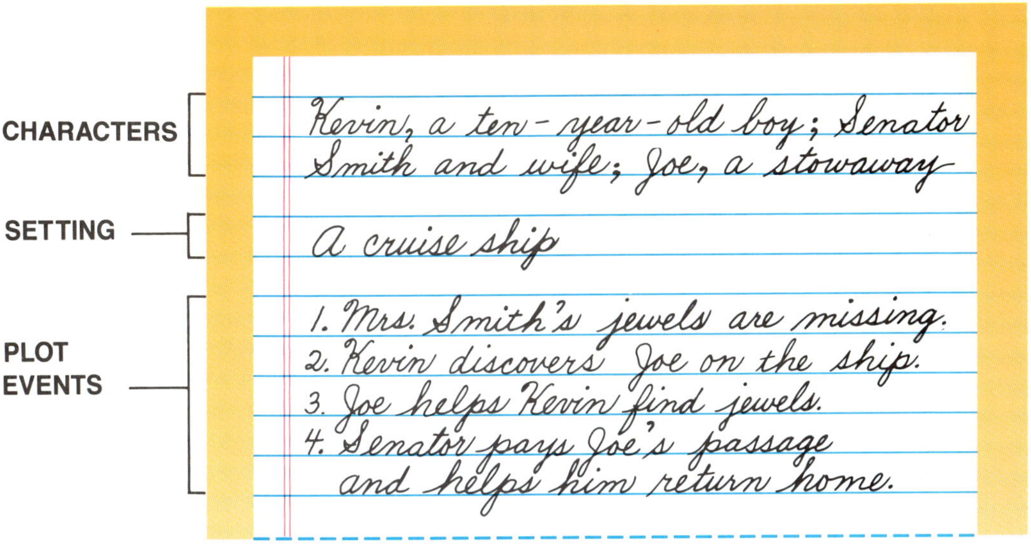

Thinking Like a Writer

- What did Manuel add?
- Why do you think he added that part? How does adding the event make his story better?

YOUR TURN

JOURNAL

Think of a story you might like to write. Use **Pictures** or your journal for ideas. Follow these steps.

- Make a list of ideas for stories.
- Choose one you like.
- Narrow your story idea if it is too broad.
- Think about your purpose and audience.

Make a story chart. Include characters and setting. Develop a plot (events in time order). Remember, you can add to or take away from your chart at any time.

Write a First Draft: Step 2

Manuel knows what to think about when he writes his story. He used a planning checklist. Manuel is now ready to write his first draft.

Part of Manuel's First Draft

Kevin had never seen any thing like this huge ship.
It had a gym a doctor's office, and many cabins.
the sea breeze was cool. It was pleasant. Kevin sat
on his deck chair. He is almost asleep when he
heard a scream. A minute later, a woman ran onto
the deck. The white-haired woman was in tears.

This is the beginning of Manuel's story. Manuel did not worry about errors while he was writing. He will revise his story later.

Planning Checklist

- Remember purpose and audience.
- Use interesting characters and setting.
- Develop a good beginning, middle, and end.
- Include dialogue.
- Use logical sequence of events (problem/solution).

YOUR TURN

Write your first draft. As you prepare to write, ask yourself these questions.

- How can I keep my audience interested in my story?
- What problem does my main character face? How does he or she solve it?

TIME-OUT You might want to take some time out before you revise. That way you will be able to revise your writing with a fresh eye.

Revise: Step 3

After he finished his first draft, Manuel read it over to himself. Then he shared his story with a classmate. He wanted some suggestions for improvement.

Manuel then looked back at his planning checklist. He noticed that he had missed one point. He put a check beside it so that he would remember it when he revised. Manuel now has a checklist to use as he revises.

Manuel made changes to the beginning of his story. Notice that he did not correct small errors. He knew that he could fix them later. The revisions Manuel made changed his paragraph. Turn the page. Look at Manuel's revised draft.

Revising Checklist

- Remember purpose and audience.
- Use interesting characters and setting.
- Develop a good beginning, middle, and end.
- ✓ Include dialogue.
- Use logical sequence of events (problem/solution).

Part of Manuel's Revised Draft

Kevin had never seen any thing like this huge ship. It had a gym a doctor's office, and many cabins. the sea breeze was cool and pleasant. Kevin sat on his deck chair. He is almost asleep when he heard a scream. A minute later, a woman ran onto the deck. It was Mrs. Smith, the senator's wife. The white-haired woman was in tears. "My diamonds are gone," Mrs. Smith cried. "I left them in my cabin and now they are gone!"

Thinking Like a Writer

WISE WORD CHOICE

- What dialogue did Manuel add? How does the dialogue improve the story?
- Which sentences did he combine? How does combining them improve the story?
- What sentence did he add? Do you like the change? Why?

YOUR TURN

Read your first draft. Make a checklist. Ask yourself these questions.

- How can I improve the description of my characters and setting?
- How can I develop my plot in a logical sequence?
- How can I use dialogue in my story?

If you wish, ask a friend to read your story and make suggestions. Then revise your story.

Proofread: Step 4

Manuel knew that his work was not complete until he proofread his story. He used a proofreading checklist while he proofread.

Part of Manuel's Proofread Draft

anything
¶ Kevin had never seen any thing like this huge ship.
It had a gym, a doctor's office, and many cabins.
and
≡ the sea breeze was cool. ~~It was~~ pleasant. Kevin sat
was
on his deck chair. He ~~is~~ almost asleep when he
heard a scream. A minute later, a woman ran onto

YOUR TURN

Proofreading Practice

Below is a section from a story that you can use to practice your proofreading skills. Find the errors. Write the section correctly on a separate sheet of paper.

Suddenly, Jenny felt very strange. She looked down at the floor and were shocked to see her feet rise several inches.

Tom, she called."What are the matter?

Tom floated around the corner of the room. He used his hands to move himself through the air.

"We have taken off, he announced. We are heading toward Mars?"

Proofreading Checklist

- Did I indent my paragraphs?
- Did I spell all words correctly?
- What punctuation errors do I need to correct?
- What capitalization errors do I need to correct?

Applying Your Proofreading Skills

Now proofread your story. Read your checklist again. Review **The Grammar Connection** and **The Mechanics Connection**, too. Use the proofreading marks to mark changes.

THE GRAMMAR CONNECTION

Remember these rules about linking verbs.

- Be sure that linking verbs are in the correct tense.
  It **is** Friday. Yesterday **was** Thursday.
- Linking verbs must agree with the singular or plural subject.
  He **is** late. They **are** late.

Check your story. Have you used linking verbs correctly?

THE MECHANICS CONNECTION

Remember these rules about using quotation marks.

- Use quotation marks before and after a speaker's exact words.
- Begin a speaker's words with a capital letter.
- Use a comma to separate the quotation from the words that tell who is speaking.
  "I will visit Texas,**"** Jim said.
  Jim said, **"**We will drive there soon.**"**

Check your story. Have you used quotation marks correctly?

Proofreading Marks

- ¶ Indent
- ∧ Add
- ℓ Take out
- ≡ Make a capital letter
- / Make a small letter

Publish: Step 5

Manuel wanted to publish his story in the school newspaper. He made a neat, final copy and sent it to the school newspaper. A month later, his story was published.

YOUR TURN

Make a neat, final copy of your story. Think of a way to share your story. You might want to use one of the ideas in the **Sharing Suggestions** box below.

SHARING SUGGESTIONS

Make a play from your story. Put on the play for the class.	Make a book out of your story. Illustrate the book.	Make a poster advertising the movie version of your story.

4 SPEAKING AND LISTENING: Telling a Story

You have just written a story. The story included characters and a setting. It had a plot with a beginning, a middle, and an end. Now you can use what you know about writing stories to tell a story.

First, you will want to make some notes to use when you tell your story. You do not have to write everything on your paper. The notes should include only the main points and some details about the characters, setting, and plot. Look at these notes.

Fire and Ice

CHARACTERS: *The King of Hibernia, the Princess Wismilda, the dragon*

SETTING: *Hibernia—kingdom of eternal snow and ice*

PLOT:
Dragon threatens kingdom; demands Wismilda as hostage.
Wismilda bravely goes to dragon.
Wismilda convinces dragon to become a pet, to use his fire to bring spring to the kingdom.

When you tell a story, you should plan it carefully. Make your listeners believe that the characters are acting out their lives as you speak. It will also help you to keep your **purpose** and **audience** in mind.

Read the speaking guidelines below. They will help you to focus your story.

SPEAKING GUIDELINES: A Story

1. Remember your **purpose** and **audience.**
2. Make notes. Practice using your notes.
3. Describe the characters and setting clearly.
4. Tell your story dramatically.
5. Use a different voice for each character.
6. Follow a logical order.
7. Look at your listeners.
8. Speak in a clear voice that your audience can hear.

- Why should I use a different voice for each character in the story?
- How does telling a story in logical order help my audience?

SPEAKING APPLICATION A Story

Think of a fairy tale that you would like to retell in your own words. Prepare notes to use when telling the story aloud. Use the speaking guidelines to help you prepare. Your classmates will be using the following guidelines as they listen to your story.

LISTENING GUIDELINES: A Story

1. Listen to "see" the characters and events as they are described.
2. Listen for details of plot and setting.
3. Listen for the dialogue between different characters.

WRITING EXTENSION

5 WRITER'S RESOURCES: The Thesaurus

Writers are careful about the words they choose. They try not to repeat a word too often, and they search for words that express exactly what they want to say.

Writers often turn to a thesaurus for help in finding words. A **thesaurus** is a reference book that gives synonyms and antonyms for many words. Remember, **synonyms** are words that have the same or almost the same meaning. **Antonyms,** on the other hand, are words with opposite meanings.

Manuel wrote this sentence in his story.

"I will reward Joe," Senator Richards said.

Manuel thought that the word *said* did not clearly express how the senator spoke. He wanted to use a more exact and more interesting word. He looked at the entry for *say* in the thesaurus.

Look at the thesaurus entry below. The entry word *say* is printed in boldface, or dark type. A sample sentence shows how the word is used. Notice that four synonyms are given for *say.*

say *v.* make known or express in words. Mel *said* that he wants to go home.
declare to make known publicly or formally. The mayor *declared* that the town needed more money.
speak to express an idea, fact, or feeling. Wendy *spoke* to us about the new shopping mall.
state to express or explain fully in words. Mr. Coombs *stated* his opinion during the meeting.
talk to express ideas or information by means of speech; to speak. Ken *talked* about his new model airplane.
See also tell.

Manuel chose to use the word *declared* in his sentence. He thought that it gave his audience a better picture of how Senator Richards spoke. If Manuel had not found a good synonym for *said* in this entry, where else might he have looked?

Practice

A. Write the answers to these items. Use the Thesaurus on pages 499-508 to help you.

1. Write two synonyms for *smile*.
2. Write the antonym for *shy*.
3. Write the part of speech for *bright*.
4. Write the definition of *cry*.
5. Write three antonyms for *neat*.
6. Write three synonyms for *quiet*.
7. Under which entry word is *small* listed?
8. Write the antonym for *strong*.
9. Write the part of speech for *tell*.
10. Write the sample sentence for *unusual*.

B. Use the Thesaurus on pages 499-508 to find a synonym for the underlined word in each sentence. Then rewrite the sentence, using the synonym.

11. Our dog, Spot, often needs a bath.
12. We have a big tub that we use to bathe him.
13. Be careful that the water is not hot.
14. It is hard to bathe Spot.
15. He does not let us catch him easily.
16. He is scared of getting wet.
17. He looks so sad standing in the tub.
18. Taking a bath must feel strange to him.
19. Our clothes are wet by the time we are finished giving Spot his bath.
20. It makes us laugh to see Spot run in circles and shake himself dry.

WRITING APPLICATION A Revision

Look back at the story you wrote. Choose five words that you think could be more interesting or more exact. Look these words up in a thesaurus. Replace each of the five words with a synonym. Keep your revision in your writing folder.

THE CURRICULUM CONNECTION

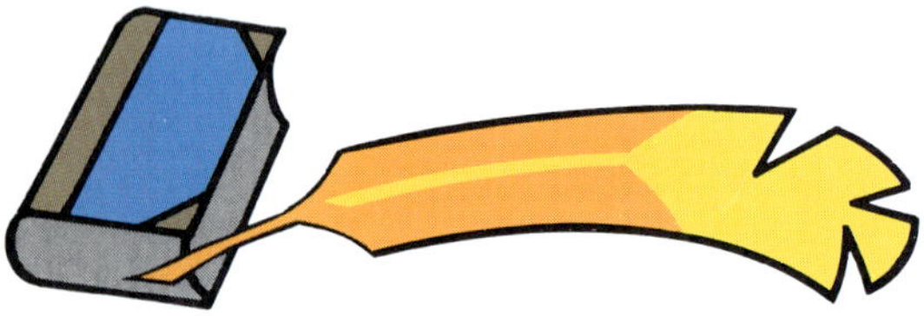

Writing About Literature

When Mr. Dobrow assigned a book report to Kiyoko's fourth grade class, she decided to write about one of her favorite books.

Behind the Attic Wall

by Sylvia Cassedy

INTRODUCTION

Strange things began to happen to Maggie when she came to live with her two great-aunts in their old stone house. Faint scrapings, tiny whispers, and stray words reached Maggie's ears as she sat alone in her room. What mystery did this house hold?

BODY

One day, Maggie heard her name called. She followed the voices to a hidden room in the attic. There was no one there, however, except for the two old dolls propped up on doll-sized chairs at a doll-sized table.

CONCLUSION

Can dolls talk? Why are they there? These are some of the questions you will find answers to as you follow Maggie's adventures behind the attic wall.

I thought this book was wonderful. It was scary, sad, and funny, all at the same time. Maggie became one of my favorite characters. I think you'll like her, too.

Writing a Book Report

A book report is a way to share your feelings about a book you have read. A good book report should have the following information.

1. **The title and the author**
2. **The introduction** should include:
- an opening sentence that will hold your reader's attention.
3. **The body of the report** should include:
- information about the setting and the main character
- a summary of the plot that tells about the problems the characters face without telling the whole story.
4. **The conclusion** should include:
- a clue about the ending of the book
- your opinion—why you did or did not like the book
- your recommendation to read or not to read the book.

ACTIVITIES

Write a Book Report Think of a book you have read. Write a report about it. Use the guidelines above to help you. A thesaurus can help you to find interesting words.

Send a Letter Write a letter to the author of a book that you enjoyed. Explain your feelings about the book. Describe what you liked about the book. If you wish, you can send your letter to the author in care of the book's publisher.

UNIT CHECKUP

LESSON 1 **Group Writing: A Story** (page 268) Read the story beginning below. Write a sentence that describes the main character and a sentence that describes the setting.

Kim couldn't wait to try out his new surfboard. Brushing his black hair from his eyes, he ran for the water. The waves were high today on this Hawaiian beach, and Kim felt fear as well as excitement.

LESSON 2 **Thinking: Understanding Sequence** (page 272) Read these story events. Write them in the correct order.

Lori and her sister Polly go alone on the train to Albany.
Lori runs back after Polly.
The train pulls into the station in Albany.
At the next stop they get off.
As they leave the train, Polly runs back to get her doll.
The train pulls away from the Albany station.

LESSON 3 **Writing a Story** (page 274) Look at your favorite comic strip in the newspaper. Write a story for your classmates about what happens in it. Make it as entertaining for your classmates as you can. Describe the characters and setting. Use dialogue.

LESSON 4 **Speaking and Listening: Telling a Story** (page 282) Think about the story, "Goldilocks and the Three Bears." Imagine that you will tell this story to a group of young children. Make a note card to use when you tell the story.

LESSON 5 **Writer's Resources: The Thesaurus** (page 284) Use the Thesaurus on pages 499-508 to find two synonyms for each word below. Write each word and its synonyms on a separate sheet of paper.

dry	let	cold
nice	cry	

THEME PROJECT A STORY TAPE

Many stories are told on tape. Taped stories are important to people who are sight-impaired or have trouble reading. They are also wonderful for those who just enjoy listening to a good storyteller. Taped stories are told dramatically, so the listener can imagine everything that is happening.

Think of a favorite story that you would like to tape. You can either read the story into the tape recorder or tell it in your own words.

- Practice the story before you tell it.
- Use a dramatic tone of voice.
- Use a different voice for each character.

GRAMMAR

UNIT 9

Adjectives

In this unit you will learn about adjectives. Adjectives are words such as *rainy* and *wet*. Adjectives add detail and color to what you say and write.

Discuss Read the poem on the opposite page. What do you see?

JOURNAL

Creative Expression The unit theme is *Pictures*. How might you picture your town in words? With a partner, write in your journal a description of your town. You could write a paragraph or song lyrics. You might even draw a picture.

THEME: *PICTURES*

I like the town on rainy nights
When everything is wet—
When all the town has magic lights
And streets of shining jet!

—Irene Thompson,
from "Rainy Nights"

GRAMMAR

1 WHAT IS AN ADJECTIVE?

An adjective is a word that describes a noun.

You describe people, places, and things every day. When you describe, you use adjectives. An adjective tells more about a noun. It can tell *what kind* or *how many.* An adjective usually comes just before the noun it describes.

A **chilly** breeze whistles through the pines.
Many animals shiver in the night.
One owl sits in a tree.

Read these sentences. Any word that fits in the blanks is an adjective. How many words can you think of to fill each blank?

A _____ rabbit sits quietly.
_____ squirrels climb the tree.

Guided Practice

Tell which word in each sentence is an adjective. Then tell which noun each adjective describes.

Example: The tall trees are in the forest. *tall* *trees*

1. Two trees stand near the lake.
2. A cold wind blows through the trees.
3. The moon shines on the white snow.
4. Several stars twinkle in the sky.

?! **THINK**

■ How can I decide if a word is an adjective?

G R A M M A R

REMEMBER

- An **adjective** is a word that describes a noun.
- An adjective tells *what kind* or *how many.*

More Practice

A. Write each sentence. Draw one line under each adjective. Draw two lines under the noun that the adjective describes.

Example: The dark forest is nearby.

5. Tall trees are everywhere.
6. Many shadows appear between the trees.
7. From behind the trees come quiet sounds.
8. A tiny owl hoots.
9. Three chipmunks hurry along the narrow path.
10. Dry leaves crackle on branches.
11. The forest is a peaceful place.
12. Some snowflakes fall in the forest.
13. The white flakes fall gently.

B. Complete each sentence. Use an adjective in each blank.

Example: I love my cabin in the _____ woods. *quiet*

14. My _____ cabin is a special place.
15. The fireplace gives off a _____ glow.
16. The _____ fire is cozy.
17. _____ chairs are comfortable.
18. A _____ blanket is on the back of the sofa.
19. My _____ books are in the bookcase.
20. _____ smells come from the kitchen.

Extra Practice, page 314

WRITING APPLICATION A Post Card

Imagine that you live in a cabin in the woods. Write a post card to a friend. Describe what you see from your window. Have a partner identify the adjectives in your post card.

2 ADJECTIVES AFTER LINKING VERBS

You know that an adjective is a word that describes a noun. Sometimes an adjective follows the noun it describes.

The classroom was **warm.** The students were **quiet.**
Joe is **happy.** The girls are **smart.**

When an adjective follows the noun it describes, the noun and adjective are connected by a linking verb. The linking verb is usually a form of the verb *be.*

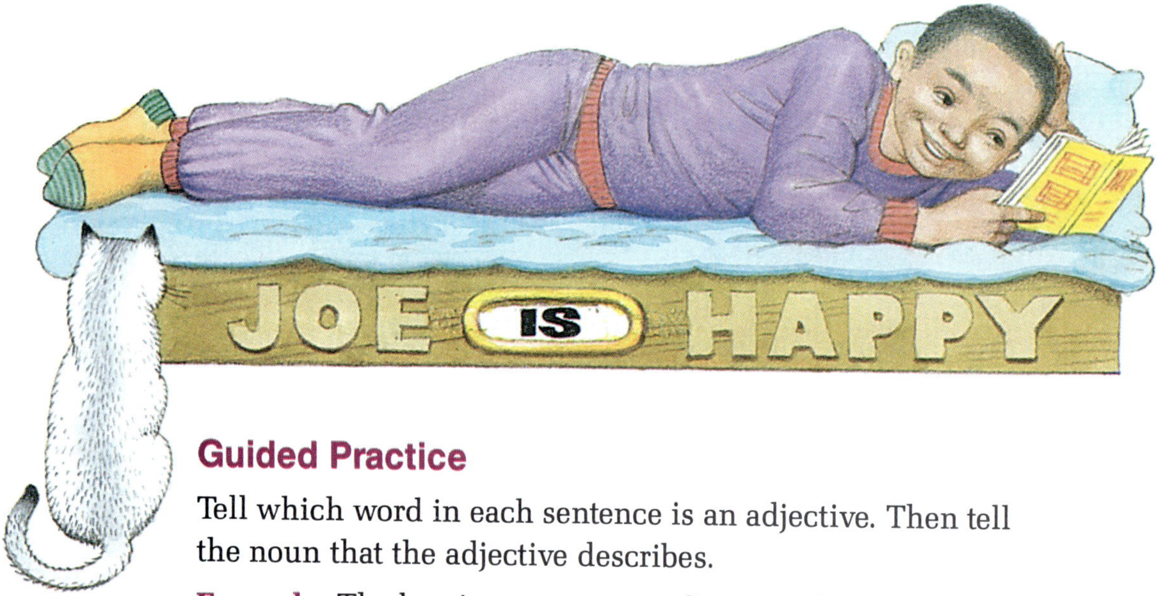

Guided Practice

Tell which word in each sentence is an adjective. Then tell the noun that the adjective describes.

Example: The bus is new. *new adjective bus noun*

1. The classroom is quiet.
2. The desks are brown.
3. Our room is bright.
4. The windows were clean.
5. Sometimes the bookcases are empty.

?! THINK

- How can I decide if an adjective should follow the noun it describes?

REMEMBER

- When an adjective comes after the noun it describes, the two are connected by a linking verb.

More Practice

A. Write each sentence. Draw one line under the adjective. Draw two lines under the noun it describes.

Example: The windows are clean.

6. The chalkboard is green.
7. Sometimes the erasers are dusty.
8. Our chalk is new.
9. A map of the world is big.
10. The map on the wall is brown.
11. The oceans on the map are blue.
12. My desk is full.
13. The classroom is large.

B. Write each sentence. Use an adjective in each blank to complete the sentence.

Example: The teacher's book is _____ . *new*

14. In the afternoon the classroom was _____ .
15. The posters on the wall are _____ .
16. Last year our classroom was _____ .
17. Yesterday I noticed that the teacher's desk was _____ .
18. The geography book was _____ .
19. The maps in our geography book are _____ .
20. The library corner was _____ .

Extra Practice, page 315

WRITING APPLICATION A Letter

Write a letter to a friend. Describe your classroom. Then, work in a small group to find all the adjectives that follow nouns.

COOPERATIVE LEARNING

3 ADJECTIVES THAT COMPARE

When you describe, you use adjectives. Sometimes you may want to use an adjective to compare two or more things.

The tree is **tall.**
This tree is **taller** than that tree.
That is the **tallest** tree in the woods.

- Add *er* to an adjective to compare two things.
- Add *est* to an adjective to compare more than two things.

Guided Practice

Find the adjectives that compare.

Example: The town is smaller than the city. *smaller*

1. The highway is wider than the country road.
2. This city is the biggest city in the state.
3. This country village is smaller than that city.
4. The farmhouse is older than the apartment building.
5. That city has the safest roads of all.

?! THINK

- How do I decide which form of an adjective I should use to compare?

REMEMBER

- Add **er** to most adjectives to compare two things.
- Add **est** to most adjectives to compare three or more things.

More Practice

A. Write each sentence. Underline the adjective that compares.

Example: This area is the busiest part of the city.

6. Country shops are smaller than department stores.
7. Traffic is heavier in the city than in the country.
8. Country breezes are cooler than city winds.
9. My pet is happier in the country than in the city.
10. The country is quieter than the city.
11. This city has the longest bridge in our state.
12. Fruits are fresher in the country than in the city.

B. Complete each sentence. Use the correct form of the adjective in parentheses ( ).

Example: This is the _____ town in the country. (busy)
This is the busiest town in the country.

13. That town is the _____ town in the state. (small)
14. The town square is _____ than the courthouse. (old)
15. The hotel is the _____ building in the town. (new)
16. The trees near the square are the _____ of all. (tall)
17. This spot is _____ than the spot under the tree. (cool)
18. Prices are _____ in the town than elsewhere. (low)
19. The inn is the _____ place in town. (quiet)
20. This inn has the _____ food in the state. (great)

Extra Practice, page 316

WRITING APPLICATION An Advertisement

Write an advertisement describing the city or the country. Read your advertisement to your classmates. Ask them to point out any adjectives that make comparisons.

4 SPELLING ADJECTIVES THAT COMPARE

You know that you can use adjectives to compare two or more things. Here are some spelling rules that will help you when you use adjectives to compare.

When the adjective ends in a consonant and *y*, change the *y* to *i* and add *er* or *est*.	happy happi**er** happi**est**
When the adjective ends in *e*, drop the *e* and add *er* or *est*.	cute cut**er** cut**est**
When the adjective has a single vowel before a final consonant, double the final consonant and add *er* or *est*.	big bi**gger** bi**ggest**

funny funni**er** funni**est**

Guided Practice

Add *er* and *est* to each adjective. Spell each adjective correctly.

Example: tiny *tinier* *tiniest*

1. jolly
2. short
3. strange
4. hot
5. friendly
6. wide
7. sleepy
8. tall

?! THINK

■ How can I remember the correct spelling of adjectives that compare?

REMEMBER

- When an adjective ends in a consonant and *y*, change the *y* to *i* and add *er* or *est*.
- When an adjective has a single vowel before a final consonant, double the final consonant and add *er* or *est*.

More Practice

A. Write each sentence. Use the correct form of the adjective in parentheses ( ).

Example: That was the (big) picnic of all.
That was the biggest picnic of all.

9. The reunion this year was (small) than last year's.
10. Uncle Will arrived in the (large) car I ever saw.
11. The cousins seemed (silly) than ever.
12. The sack race was the (funny) event of the day.
13. Laura was (clumsy) than Nan at the egg rolling contest.
14. The food seemed (tasty) this year than last year.
15. Mom's pies were the (sweet) of all the desserts.

B. Complete each sentence with an adjective that compares.

Example: Summer is _____ than winter.
Summer is warmer than winter.

16. Fourth of July at the lake is the _____ holiday of all.
17. The water in the lake is _____ than any other lake water.
18. The summer sun is _____ than ever before.
19. Our wooden raft is _____ than the float.
20. We swim until our arms feel _____ than lead.

Extra Practice, page 317

WRITING APPLICATION A Journal Entry

Imagine that you have just attended a family gathering. Write a description of the gathering as you would in a journal. Share your journal entry with a classmate. Have your classmate circle the adjectives in your description.

5 COMPARING WITH *MORE* AND *MOST*

You have learned how to form comparisons by adding *er* or *est* to adjectives. The words *more* and *most* are used with some longer adjectives to make comparisons.

Washington is a **popular** place.
Is Washington **more popular** than Boston?
Washington is the **most popular** place of all.

Use *more* to form a comparison when two nouns are compared. Use *most* to form a comparison when more than two nouns are compared.

When you use *more* or *most,* do not use the ending *er* or *est.*

Guided Practice

Tell whether *more* or *most* should be used to complete each sentence.

Example: That trip was the _____ popular of all. *most*

1. Our trip to Washington was _____ exciting than yours.
2. The trip was the _____ enjoyable of all.
3. Is the Capitol the _____ important place in the city?
4. The Capitol is a _____ recent building than the White House.

?! **THINK**

■ How do I decide whether to use *more* or *most* to make a comparison?

REMEMBER

- Use **more** to form a comparison when two nouns are compared.
- Use **most** to form a comparison when more than two nouns are compared.

More Practice

Complete each sentence with **more** or **most**.

Example: The buildings in Washington are the _____ outstanding in the world. *most*

5. The Jefferson Memorial is _____ interesting than the Capitol.
6. The Library of Congress is the _____ important library in the world.
7. I think that the cherry blossoms are the _____ beautiful sight in the city.
8. Washington is _____ crowded than it used to be.
9. Cars are _____ plentiful than parking spaces.
10. The _____ enjoyable park in Washington is Rock Creek Park.
11. The paths are _____ beautiful than in other parks.
12. The _____ famous street of all is Pennsylvania Avenue.
13. Washington's climate is _____ humid than the climate of New York City.
14. The Washington Monument is _____ impressive than the Eiffel Tower.
15. The National Gallery has one of the _____ valuable art collections in the world.

Extra Practice, Practice Plus, pages 318–320

WRITING APPLICATION A Talk

Imagine that you are a tour guide in Washington, D.C. Write a talk about the city. Give your talk to a group of students. Ask your classmates to point out any adjectives with *more* or *most* that you used.

6 USING ARTICLES

The words *a, an,* and *the* are special adjectives called **articles.**

Use *a* and *an* before singular nouns. Use *a* if the next word begins with a consonant sound.

Come join us for **a** trip under the sea.

Use *an* if the next word begins with a vowel sound.

It is **an** experience you will not forget.

Use *the* before a singular noun that names a particular person, place, or thing, and before all plural nouns.

The sea is amazing.
We will see **the** colorful creatures of **the** sea.

Guided Practice

Tell which word in the sentence is an article.

Example: Please show the slides. *the*

1. The sea is beautiful.
2. Many fish swim close to the surface.
3. Sometimes an octopus swims by.
4. The colors of underwater plants are striking.
5. A gray shark circles nearby.

?! THINK

■ How can I decide whether to use *a, an,* or *the?*

REMEMBER

- Use the articles **a** and **an** with singular nouns.
- Use the article **the** with singular nouns that name a particular person, place, or thing, and with all plural nouns.

More Practice

A. Write each sentence. Underline each article.

Example: A dolphin was sighted today.

6. That was the largest dolphin ever seen.
7. This is an excellent photograph of a reef.
8. We saw the school of fish swim by.
9. Divers have explored the ruins of sunken ships.
10. A ship from ancient times was discovered.
11. The underwater world is truly fascinating.

B. Write each sentence. Choose the article that best completes the sentence.

Example: The sea is (a, an) wonderful place.
The sea is a wonderful place.

12. Many creatures live on (a, an) coral reef.
13. Their delicate colors are (a, an) lovely sight.
14. The coral reef is (a, an) marvel of nature.
15. (A, An) ocean animal makes the reef its home.
16. (A, An) underwater scene may resemble a forest.
17. The reeds look like (a, an) group of trees.
18. The plants look like (a, an) overgrown jungle.
19. Will you see (a, an) unusual creature?
20. We will go on (a, an) sea voyage soon.

Extra Practice, page 321

WRITING APPLICATION A Poem

Write a short poem about an underwater scene. It can be a fantasy or a realistic description of diving. Exchange poems with a classmate. Discuss the use of articles in each other's poem.

GRAMMAR

7 MECHANICS: Capitalizing Proper Adjectives

You know that some nouns are called proper nouns. A proper noun names a particular person, place, or thing. An adjective formed from a proper noun is called a **proper adjective.**

Proper Noun	Proper Adjective
America	American
Alaska	Alaskan
Hawaii	Hawaiian
Mexico	Mexican
Canada	Canadian
Ireland	Irish

Notice that a proper adjective is always capitalized.

Guided Practice

Tell which word in each sentence is a proper adjective. Then tell which noun the adjective describes.

Example: The restaurant serves French food.
French   *French* describes *food.*

1. My neighborhood in San Francisco is well-known for its Italian restaurants.
2. Chinese newspapers are sold in Chinatown.
3. My town was settled by German immigrants.
4. San Francisco has many Japanese residents.
5. People come to this city from Asian countries.

?! **THINK**

■ Why is a proper adjective always capitalized?

REMEMBER

- **Proper adjectives** are formed from proper nouns.
- Proper adjectives are always capitalized.

More Practice

A. Write each sentence. Underline each proper adjective. Draw two lines under the noun that the adjective describes.

Example: Italian food is very good.

6. German neighborhoods grew early in our history.
7. Irish settlers came to America later.
8. Many Polish settlers were musicians.
9. Some neighborhood groups still do the old Russian dances.
10. Most Norwegian people went to the West.
11. There are many Swedish communities in the Midwest.
12. Colorful Chinese customs survive in many neighborhoods.

B. Write each sentence. Capitalize the proper adjective.

Example: The mexican dances are lively.
The Mexican dances are lively.

13. The spanish language is widely spoken here.
14. French is the language of haitian people.
15. Some cities have a large korean population.
16. Many Americans are of african descent.
17. Pastries are available in moroccan bakeries.
18. Clubs in many cities offer irish music.
19. We like spicy cuban food in the United States.
20. Performances of chinese operas are popular.

Extra Practice, page 322

WRITING APPLICATION A Summary

COOPERATIVE LEARNING

Work with a few classmates to find out about some special customs that come from other countries. Write a summary with your group. Ask a classmate to find proper adjectives in your summary.

GRAMMAR

8 VOCABULARY BUILDING: Synonyms and Antonyms

Synonyms are words that have the same, or almost the same, meaning.

We lived in a **big** house. We lived in a **large** house.

Antonyms are words that have opposite meanings.

This house was very **old.** That house was very **new.**

Some antonyms can be formed by adding the prefix *un.*

happy → unhappy   kind → unkind   true → untrue

Synonyms and antonyms for many words are given in the Thesaurus on pages 499-508.

Guided Practice

Tell which pairs are synonyms and which pairs are antonyms.

Example: hot and cold   *antonyms*

1. tall and short
2. pleased and happy
3. true and false
4. fast and quick
5. fat and thin
6. real and unreal

?! THINK

- How can I decide if words are synonyms or antonyms?

REMEMBER

- **Synonyms** are words that have the same, or almost the same, meaning.
- **Antonyms** are words that have opposite meanings.

GRAMMAR

More Practice

A. Write a synonym and an antonym for each underlined word.

Example: The house was small. *tiny* *large*

7. The front porch was big.
8. The windows were wide.
9. The roof was high.
10. The yard was clean.
11. The front door was heavy.
12. Everyone thought the house was beautiful.

B. Replace all underlined words with synonyms.

Example: We have a new library.
We have a modern library.

13. Elm Street was very broad.
14. Trees made the street seem peaceful.
15. The trees were very tall.
16. Neighbors were kind to one another.
17. Lovely flowers grew in the yards.
18. This quiet street was a clean place.
19. The neat lawns were lovely.
20. Several houses were large.

Extra Practice, page 323

WRITING APPLICATION A Brochure

All of the synonyms and antonyms in this lesson are adjectives. Work in small groups. Brainstorm to list some adjectives that are not in this lesson. Then think of synonyms or antonyms for your adjectives. Create a brochure. In it, describe your favorite place or your favorite food.

GRAMMAR AND WRITING CONNECTION

Choosing Vivid Adjectives

When you describe something, you want your audience to see what you see. By using vivid adjectives, you can add detail and color to your writing.

What is a vivid adjective? A vivid adjective is one that makes your word picture very clear. Compare these sentences.

An **interesting** oak tree grows in the city park.
A **majestic, old** oak tree grows in the city park.

The adjectives *majestic* and *old* are more precise or exact than the adjective *interesting*. A reader would know exactly what kind of oak tree grows in the park.

Working Together

COOPERATIVE LEARNING

With your classmates, talk about vivid adjectives. Supply as many vivid adjectives for each underlined adjective in the sentences below as you can. Use the Thesaurus on pages 499-508 if you wish.

Example: The small bird perches on the tree limb.
tiny, fragile, little

1. The nice squirrel sits below the tree.
2. The big fountain is filled with water.
3. The park is a great place.
4. Beautiful flowers grow everywhere.

Revising Sentences

Sue wrote these sentences to describe a city park. Help Sue revise her sentences by changing each underlined adjective to a more vivid one.

5. Tall skyscrapers surround the city park.
6. Inside the park nice plants grow everywhere.
7. Pretty paths wind through the park.
8. In spring interesting flowers bloom there.
9. In the center of the park is a great pond.
10. Small boats are docked at the edge of the pond.
11. The scene is quiet.
12. It is hard to believe a big city is nearby.
13. Near the pond is a good zoo.
14. The cute monkeys play in their cages.
15. Several noisy children watch the animals.
16. Children line up to ride on huge camels.
17. The camel's back is strong.
18. A shy fawn hides behind the mother deer.
19. The colorful birds are wonderful.
20. The thin tiger suns itself on the rock.
21. It is happy to feel the warm spring sun.
22. The seals' fur is shiny and wet.
23. The water in their pool is cold.
24. Seals are nice to watch.
25. We feel unhappy when it is time to leave the park.

WRITER AT WORK

Brainstorm to choose a place that you would like to describe. Will you describe a city street or a field of flowers? Write a description. Remember to create a clear picture for your audience. When you revise your work, make sure that you have used vivid adjectives.

UNIT CHECKUP

LESSON 1

What Is an Adjective? (page 292) Write each sentence. Underline each adjective.

1. Many cars lined the street.
2. A blue car stood out from the rest.
3. Its shiny surface glowed in the sunlight.
4. The silver tiger on the hood gleamed.
5. It was a beautiful car.

LESSON 2

Adjectives After Linking Verbs (page 294) Write each sentence. Underline each adjective.

6. In the summer the neighborhood is quiet.
7. The streets are peaceful.
8. The lights from the windows are cheery.
9. The evenings are cool.
10. The stars are bright in the sky.

LESSON 3

Adjectives That Compare (page 296) Complete each sentence. Use the correct form of the adjective in parentheses ( ).

11. This building is _____ than that one. (tall)
12. That building is the _____ of all. (small)
13. Is your house _____ than their house? (old)
14. The attic is the _____ room in our house. (warm)
15. My room is _____ than her room. (bright)

LESSON 4

Spelling Adjectives That Compare (page 298) Add *er* and *est* to each adjective. Spell each adjective correctly.

16. sad **17.** friendly **18.** short **19.** clumsy **20.** strange

LESSON 5

Comparing with *more* and *most* (page 300) Use the correct form of the adjective in parentheses ( ).

21. It was the _____ storm yet. (terrible)
22. The winds were _____ than before. (powerful)
23. The waves seemed _____ than ever. (threatening)
24. Our city had the _____ rescue team of all. (skillful)
25. It was the _____ time we ever had. (difficult)

LESSON 6

Using Articles (page 302) Write each sentence. Fill in the blank with *a, an,* or *the.*

26. We had fun at _____ Polk County fairgrounds.
27. We saw _____ old-fashioned rides.
28. Dad bought _____ tickets for our ride.
29. Seth rode on _____ elephant.
30. _____ lively tune played on the merry-go-round.

LESSON 7

Mechanics: Capitalizing Proper Adjectives (page 304) Write each sentence. Capitalize the proper adjectives.

31. It is wonderful to visit european countries.
32. The english countryside is beautiful.
33. We sailed down the Rhine, a german river.
34. We especially loved french food.
35. The swiss mountains were breathtaking.

LESSON 8

Vocabulary Building: Synonyms and Antonyms (page 306) Read each sentence. Follow the direction in parentheses ( ) to write a synonym or an antonym for the underlined word.

36. I will do my homework before school. (antonym)
37. Julian has a little white rabbit. (synonym)
38. Elaine is sad that summer is over. (antonym)
39. I felt scared when I saw the big dog. (synonym)
40. These flowers are a lovely gift. (synonym)

41.–50.

Writing Application: Adjective Usage (pages 292-305) The following paragraph contains 10 errors with adjectives. Rewrite the paragraph correctly.

A old cottage sat in the french countryside. An maple tree stood near the door. The tree was more taller than the house. In the tree was an nest of robins. One robin was smallest than the others. It was the more beautiful of all. A robins chirped all day long in their most small nest. Their song was the more beautiful I have ever heard.

ENRICHMENT

MAKE IT SNAPPY!

Play this game with a partner. Think of a word that would express a sound. For example, the word *snap* would express a sound. Tell your partner the word and ask him or her to add *ing* to it. Then, ask your partner to think of something the new word might describe—snapping fingers. Take turns. Think of as many sound words as you can. You can use these words in your writing.

AS SMOOTH AS GLASS

A **simile** is a type of comparison. A simile compares two different things by using the words *like* or *as*.

The ice was as smooth as glass.

By yourself or with a partner, create some similes. You can use the following or create some of your own.

an apple as ____ as ____
a rock as ____ as ____
a cloud as ____ as ____
a star as ____ as ____
a cat as ____ as ____

PICTURE THIS

Think of a place you have visited or would like to visit. Use your imagination. On a large piece of paper, draw a travel brochure for this place. Think of adjectives that appeal to the senses to describe the place. Decorate your drawing with the words.

CREATIVE EXPRESSION

February Twilight

I stood beside a hill
Smooth with new laid snow;
A single star looked out
From the cold evening glow.

There was no other creature
That saw what I could see—
I stood and watched the evening star
As long as it watched me.

—Sara Teasdale

TRY IT OUT!

"February Twilight" is a descriptive poem about a winter night. The poet has described a moment that was special or meaningful to her. What moment has she described? Write a brief descriptive poem. You might describe one of the seasons.

EXTRA PRACTICE

GRAMMAR

Three levels of practice

What Is an Adjective? (page 292)

LEVEL **A.** Write the adjective that describes the underlined noun.

1. Tall buildings stand in the city.
2. The shiny glass in the windows sparkles.
3. Many people crowd the sidewalks.
4. The loud horns honk all the time.
5. One woman walks three dogs.
6. The little dogs pull their leashes.
7. The young man runs away from the dogs.
8. A floppy hat falls off his head.
9. A polite teenager picks up the hat.
10. The happy man thanks the girl.

LEVEL **B.** Write each sentence. Draw one line under each adjective. Then, draw two lines under the noun that it describes.

11. The big buses drive along the streets.
12. The buses carry many passengers.
13. The driver has a loud voice.
14. She talks to the noisy passenger.
15. Several people leave the bus.
16. Happy passengers applaud the driver.
17. Some people even cheer loudly.
18. The proud driver takes a bow.

LEVEL **C.** Complete each sentence with an adjective.

19. My neighborhood is a _____ place.
20. _____ people live there.
21. _____ flowers grow in the window boxes.
22. The _____ children are everywhere.
23. _____ trees grow along the street.
24. The _____ cars sit in driveways.
25. _____ fences surround some of the houses.

EXTRA PRACTICE

Three levels of practice

Adjectives After Linking Verbs (page 294)

LEVEL A. In each sentence a noun is underlined. Write the adjective that describes the noun.

1. The forest is peaceful.
2. A rock was mossy.
3. The trees were green.
4. The lake was clear.
5. Its surface was smooth.
6. Nan is happy here.
7. The weather is mild.
8. The sky is cloudy.
9. The bees were busy.
10. A bird is blue.

LEVEL B. Write each sentence. Draw two lines under the adjective. Draw one line under the noun it describes.

11. The hikers are alert
12. Their footsteps are gentle.
13. The air is cool.
14. The squirrels were cute.
15. The branches were thick.
16. Some leaves were brown.
17. The sunflowers are lovely.
18. The stalks were heavy.

LEVEL C. Complete each sentence with an adjective that follows the linking verb.

19. That mountain is _____ .
20. The view from the top was _____ .
21. The sun is _____ .
22. The return trip was _____ .
23. The hikers are _____ .
24. Their hike was _____ .
25. The trails were very _____ .

EXTRA PRACTICE

Three levels of practice

Adjectives That Compare (page 296)

LEVEL **A.** Write each sentence. Underline the adjective that compares.

1. Our new house is larger than our old house.
2. It is the nicest house on the block.
3. The back door is smaller than the front door.
4. The living room is the brightest room of all.
5. My bedroom is cozier than my brother's room.
6. The kitchen is the warmest room in the house.
7. The basement is quieter than the den.
8. The den is messier than the living room.

LEVEL **B.** Complete each sentence. Choose the correct adjective from the pair in parentheses ( ).

9. We are (closer, closest) to town than we were.
10. Dad drives a (shorter, shortest) distance to work than before.
11. The school is (nearer, nearest) our house than yours.
12. Our garden is the (bigger, biggest) of all.
13. Our lawn is the (sunnier, sunniest) one on the street.
14. Our street is the (quieter, quietest) one in town.
15. Is your house (larger, largest) than mine?
16. I think our house is (smaller, smallest) than yours.
17. This is the (prettier, prettiest) block of all.

LEVEL **C.** Write each sentence. Use the correct form of the adjective in parentheses ( ).

18. This house is _____ than our last house. (cool)
19. The dining room is _____ than the other rooms. (light)
20. Our house is the _____ of all. (new)
21. The shutters upstairs are _____ than those downstairs. (plain)
22. Meg was _____ than I in fixing up her room. (quick)
23. She is _____ in the new house than I am. (happy)
24. Our old house was _____ than this one. (nice)
25. We had the _____ rooms of all there. (big)

EXTRA PRACTICE

Three levels of practice

Spelling Adjectives That Compare (page 298)

LEVEL **A.** Write each sentence. Underline the adjective that compares.

1. Andrew is the smartest boy in our class.
2. The beagle is friendlier than the spaniel.
3. The runt of the litter is the smallest puppy.
4. The roses smell the sweetest after a rain.
5. The planes sound closer on a rainy day.
6. The box was heavier than the suitcase.
7. My suitcase was sturdier than his.
8. Is your computer smaller than mine?

LEVEL **B.** Complete each sentence with the correct spelling of the adjective in parentheses ( ).

9. The thunderstorm is (nearer, nearrer) than it was a moment ago.
10. Saturday was the (hotest, hottest) day of the summer.
11. Today the librarian is (busier, busyer) than he was yesterday.
12. Those are the (fluffyest, fluffiest) clouds I have ever seen.
13. Mr. Jordan is (thinner, thiner) than Mr. Smith.
14. The pitcher threw the (fasttest, fastest) pitch of the game.
15. We picked the (cuteest, cutest) puppy in the store.
16. Was that trip (shorter, shortter) than the last?

LEVEL **C.** Write each sentence. Use the correct form of the adjective in parentheses ( ).

17. Is it (rainy) here on the mainland than elsewhere?
18. The sky is (dark) than it was this morning.
19. That is the (fierce) wind I have ever seen!
20. Today the weather will be (dry) than it was yesterday.
21. This is the (warm) evening of the spring.
22. Each day seems (hot) than the last one.
23. The climate is (wet) than elsewhere.
24. This island is the (small) I've visited.
25. Is this vacation (long) than last year's?

EXTRA PRACTICE

Three levels of practice

Comparing with *more* and *most* (page 300)

LEVEL **A.** Write *more* or *most* to complete each sentence.

1. We just had our _____ enjoyable vacation ever.
2. We had a _____ carefree trip than last year.
3. We all felt _____ relaxed on this vacation.
4. I bought the _____ detailed maps I could find.
5. They were _____ useful than any we have had before.
6. Niagara Falls was the _____ stunning sight we saw.
7. It was the _____ powerful waterfall we had ever seen.
8. We cannot think of a _____ beautiful spot.
9. We had the _____ marvelous time there.
10. The trip was the _____ outstanding I have taken.

LEVEL **B.** Write each sentence. Use *more* or *most* to complete the sentence.

11. Driving over the mountains was the _____ difficult part of the whole trip.
12. We had to be _____ careful there than elsewhere.
13. Dad is a _____ experienced driver than many others are.
14. He felt _____ tired than usual after this trip.
15. I was _____ eager than Mom to take pictures.
16. The mountains gave us the _____ exciting views possible.
17. I am a _____ patient photographer than my mother is.
18. I took the _____ terrific photographs.

LEVEL **C.** Write each sentence. Use *more* or *most* with the adjective in parentheses ( ).

19. California has _____ scenery than Kansas has. (varied)
20. It was sometimes _____ to rest than to drive. (pleasant)
21. I found the small towns _____ than the cities. (interesting)
22. The _____ food was in San Francisco. (delicious)
23. The _____ sight we saw was the Grand Canyon. (amazing)
24. Traveling is the _____ way to spend a vacation. (satisfying)
25. It is _____ than staying in one place. (appealing)

PRACTICE + PLUS

Three levels of additional practice for a difficult skill

Comparing with *more* and *most* (page 300)

LEVEL **A.** Write each sentence. Use *more* or *most* to complete each sentence.

1. This is the (more, most) wonderful trip we have taken.
2. Joe is a (more, most) skillful tour guide than Dan.
3. He is the (more, most) interesting speaker in the group.
4. The rose looks (more, most) beautiful than the daisy.
5. The orchard is filled with the (more, most) enormous apples I have seen.
6. The seashore is (more, most) popular than the mountains are.
7. Is the ocean (more, most) special than the mountains are?
8. The ocean is one of the (more, most) fascinating places on earth.
9. Are the mountains (more, most) majestic than the ocean?
10. No, the ocean is the (more, most) impressive sight of all.
11. Our trip to the city will be (more, most) exciting this year than last.
12. We will see the (more, most) pleasant scenery of all.
13. Is the view (more, most) outstanding than others you have seen?
14. Yes, the swaying trees are the (more, most) graceful of all.
15. This sunset is the (more, most) magnificent in the world.
16. Are you (more, most) comfortable on the bus than on the train?
17. This trip was (more, most) enjoyable than the trip last year.

LEVEL **B.** Write each sentence. Use *more* or *most* to complete the sentence.

18. *The Circus* was the _____ enjoyable movie of all.
19. Jack looks _____ comfortable than John.
20. The lamb was _____ playful than its mother.
21. The shark is the _____ dangerous creature of all.
22. The hammer is _____ useful than the saw.
23. The baby was the _____ interesting person at the party.
24. The famous actor was _____ boring than anyone else.
25. The food was the _____ satisfying part of the evening.

PRACTICE + PLUS

26. Were the desserts _____ exciting than the salads?
27. Our collie is _____ playful than our kitten.
28. The kitten is the _____ lovable of our pets.
29. The garden is the _____ peaceful place of all.
30. My friend Dan is _____ musical than Pam.
31. Pam is the _____ helpful guest at the party.
32. Sue is _____ careful about serving the guests than Bob is.

LEVEL C. Complete each sentence. Use an adjective with *more* or *most*.

33. The waves became _____ when the wind blew.
34. Amy is _____ than her sister.
35. That room looks the _____ of all.
36. Lena has the _____ eyes in the family.
37. That movie was the _____ I've ever seen.
38. Was that singer _____ than the other singer?
39. The acting was _____ than the singing.
40. The last scene was the _____ in the movie.
41. Did you find the pen _____ than the pencil?
42. The sunset was _____ than the sunrise.
43. Sam is the _____ person I know.
44. The baby kitten is _____ than the older cat.
45. One clown was _____ than the other clown.
46. The candidate was the _____ person in the room.
47. The character in the mystery was the _____ of all.
48. Fruits are the _____ source of vitamins.
49. The stars are _____ than the planets.
50. Is the view from the skyscraper _____ than from anywhere else?

EXTRA PRACTICE

GRAMMAR

Three levels of practice

Using Articles (page 302)

LEVEL A. Read each sentence. Write each article and the noun that follows it.

1. We visit a bakery early in the morning.
2. The bakers have been working all night.
3. One baker kneads the dough.
4. Another baker puts loaves into an oven.
5. A smell of freshly-baked bread fills the bakery.
6. We will buy a loaf of whole wheat bread.
7. A cake looks especially good.
8. It just came out of the oven.
9. We will buy the cake, too.
10. What else is in the oven?

LEVEL B. Write each sentence. Choose the article that best completes the sentence.

11. This bakery is in (a, an) old building.
12. The bakers work in (a, an) huge kitchen.
13. One baker is making (a, an) apple pie.
14. She uses (a, an) rolling pin.
15. There is (a, an) large pie plate on the table.
16. This will be (a, an) excellent pie.
17. The pie is baked in (a, an) antique oven.
18. The oven is (a, an) reminder of the past.

LEVEL C. Complete each sentence.

19. The dough must rise for about an _____ .
20. It must be in a _____ .
21. The _____ sit on long, shiny trays.
22. Flour is an _____ ingredient in bread.
23. The _____ loaf comes out of the oven.
24. Let's get a _____ loaf of this delicious bread.
25. We will have the _____ bread with our dinner.

EXTRA PRACTICE

Three levels of practice

Mechanics: Capitalizing Proper Adjectives (page 304)

LEVEL **A.** In each sentence a noun is underlined. Write the proper adjective that describes the noun.

1. This museum has many Greek vases.
2. Have you seen the African masks?
3. There are Nigerian sculptures nearby.
4. Many rooms contain Egyptian art.
5. The Mayan carvings are beautiful.
6. Did you notice the delicate Turkish tiles?
7. The Roman coins were fascinating.
8. I liked the Mexican art.

LEVEL **B.** Write each sentence. Capitalize the proper adjective.

9. We learned about the history of italian art.
10. Rembrandt was a famous dutch painter.
11. This english painting shows a country scene.
12. Do you like chinese art?
13. This is an example of danish furniture.
14. Picasso was a spanish artist.
15. The paintings by french artists were lovely.
16. The american exhibit was fascinating.

LEVEL **C.** Complete each sentence. Use a proper adjective made from the noun in parentheses ( ).

17. This old book contains _____ letters. (Egypt)
18. That animal head is from a _____ ship. (Norway)
19. Here is an interesting _____ statue. (Spain)
20. This room has works by _____ artists. (France)
21. Outside is a _____ garden. (Japan)
22. Who is the best-known _____ artist? (Germany)
23. I think that _____ painter is very famous. (England)
24. Who is your favorite _____ painter? (Italy)
25. The _____ vases are beautiful. (China)

EXTRA PRACTICE

GRAMMAR

Three levels of practice

Vocabulary Building: Synonyms and Antonyms (page 306)

LEVEL A. Write each pair of words. Then write **synonyms** or **antonyms** after each pair.

1. deep/shallow
2. dull/boring
3. loud/soft
4. brave/courageous
5. tight/loose
6. serious/important
7. below/under
8. strong/weak
9. big/large
10. noisy/quiet

LEVEL B. Read each sentence. Then write a synonym for each underlined word.

11. When will you complete your report?
12. A funny idea came to my mind.
13. This is a difficult test.
14. Please shut the door.
15. That is the correct answer.
16. The concert will begin on time.
17. Will you want a big meal?

LEVEL C. Read each sentence. Then write an antonym for each underlined word.

18. I always leave a light on at night.
19. This glass is empty.
20. Did you lose your mittens?
21. They will arrive at 10 o'clock.
22. Amy is always first in line.
23. Bick ran up the stairs.
24. Is Jane happy about the news?
25. Tell Amy to close the window.

UNIT 10

Writing Descriptions

Read the quotation and look at the picture on the opposite page. Talk with your classmates about the quotation and about what you see in the photograph. Describe the scene in the picture aloud.

Writing a description is much like telling one aloud. You want your **audience** to share your experience. You want your **reader** to see what you see.

Focus Descriptive writing creates a clear and vivid picture of a person, place, or thing.

What would you like to describe? On the following pages you will find a story and interesting pictures of places. You can use them to give you ideas for descriptive writing.

THEME: *PICTURES*

. . . Remember always to look, won't you? At the world, I mean. Soak it up—smell, listen, feel. Look at everything!

—Eleanor Cameron

LITERATURE

Reading Like a Writer

AWARD WINNING SELECTION

Think about your neighborhood. What do you like about it?

Jeannie has just moved to a new neighborhood. She and her sister Marguerite are somewhat bored by their new surroundings.

As you read the selection, look for the details that the author uses to help you see the neighborhood as Jeannie first saw it.

THE HOUSE ACROSS THE STREET

from Circle of Giving
by Ellen Howard

THE SUMMER before my tenth birthday, our family moved to California because, "It's the land of opportunity," Daddy said. "There are jobs," said Mother.

The setting is introduced.

"I thought California would be glamorous," said my sister Marguerite. "I thought there'd be movie stars and stuff." But the closest thing our neighborhood had to a movie star was Mr. Dooley, who was a bookkeeper at Metro-Goldwyn-Mayer. No one glamorous came to live on Stanley Avenue . . . until the Hanisians moved into the house across the street.

FROM the very first day, we were irresistibly drawn to the Hanisians.

A LARGE VAN turned onto our street right after breakfast one Saturday morning late in the spring. I was sitting on the front steps, picking a scab on my knee and waiting for someone to come out to play. I could hear the Dooley baby crying from the far end of the block, and Mrs. Lord, shrill over the whir of Mr. Lord's lawn mower, hollering from her porch. Through an open window, Mrs. Sisson's piano rang forth with Sammy Benjamin's laborious, but loud, rendering of "Flow Gently, Sweet Afton."

The van stopped, and I was on my feet in an instant. Something interesting was going to happen today. Someone was moving into the house across the street!

"Marguerite," I yelled, running into the house. "Marguerite, come and see. The new people across the street are here!"

Marguerite had been spending a lot of time fooling with her hair ever since she turned twelve in January. I had a pretty good idea where to find her, and sure enough, she was at our dressing table, mooning into the mirror, when I ran into our room that morning. But at my news, she jumped right up and came out to join me on the steps.

We watched, squinting against the morning sun, as the moving men, clad in overalls, let down the ramp on the back of the van and opened the big doors. We could not see inside, but we could imagine what was there—chairs and tables and a sofa and beds and boxes, piles and piles of boxes!

Marguerite and I had gotten expert at guessing the size and character of a new family, just from their belongings. "Kids," Marguerite would say if a box of toys was carried in, or "A baby," if we saw a high chair or a crib. "They like to read," I would announce if I saw the moving men strain under heavy boxes of books. It was me who guessed Mrs. Lord was a good cook, just from the number and variety of her pots and pans, before we even saw how plump the whole family was.

BUT THIS morning, the moving men seemed to take forever to begin unloading our new neighbors' things. Marguerite and I could hear them grunting and heaving at something heavy in the back of the van. There were thumps and scufflings, and the van swayed a little with the activity inside it.

"Maybe they've got a pet elephant," I said, trying to make a joke, but Marguerite acted as if she hadn't heard me. She was gazing down the street toward Mrs. Sisson's house, her head cocked to hear the music that floated from the window. Mrs. Sisson must be playing now, I thought, because Sammy sure wasn't that good. I looked up and down Stanley Avenue, feeling bored and a little sad.

All the houses on Stanley Avenue looked alike. They were new and shiny white, with red tile roofs. The real estate man had called them "Spanish bungalows," and Marguerite and I had thought that sounded terribly romantic. "But it's not," said Marguerite when we first saw our new house. "It's not romantic at all, Jeannie. It's *ordinary* and just like all the rest."

Details give a clear picture of the neighborhood.

Our house sat on its own little square of new green lawn, as all the houses did. A row of scraggly palm trees marched along the parking strip in front, and the sidewalk ran between the lawns and

parkings like a smooth gray ribbon. "Great for skating, I bet," I told Marguerite, trying to cheer her up when we first saw it. I patted my skate key, hanging from a string around my neck.

IT WAS GOOD for skating, we soon found out—smooth and bumpless —but that didn't cheer Marguerite. "Not a crack in it," she would shout as we whizzed along, side by side, holding hands. "It's dull!" she would say. "Just like the houses, just like the people, just like us!" And her arm would wave about in despair, pointing out the square white houses, the thin green lawns, the straight rows of skinny palms, until she unbalanced us and sent me, arms flailing, shooting off the walk to fall in a heap on the grass.

She was right, in a way. The houses were ordinary and all alike, and until the Hanisians came, we and our neighbors seemed ordinary and very nearly alike as well.

Thinking Like a Reader

1. Jeannie and Marguerite think their neighborhood is boring. How would you describe it?
2. If you lived in their neighborhood, what would you think of it? How does it compare with your own neighborhood?

Write your responses in your journal.

Thinking Like a Writer

3. How does the author let you know what Jeannie and Marguerite think of their new neighborhood?
4. Which details did the author use to do that?
5. Which details do you like best?

Write a list of the details you like best.

Responding to LITERATURE

Brainstorm *Vocabulary*

In "The House Across the Street," Jeannie mentions "thin green lawns" and "skinny palms." Think of a place you know. It might be your neighborhood or a place you have visited. In your journal write all the images that come to mind as you think about the place. Begin to create a personal vocabulary list. You can use these words and phrases in your writing.

Talk It Over
Describe the Neighborhood

When you compare, you tell how things are alike. Jeannie compares the sidewalk to a smooth gray ribbon. Imagine that you have just moved into your neighborhood. With a partner, imagine that you are on the telephone with a friend. Describe your new surroundings. You might want to include a comparison in your description.

Quick Write
Write an Ad

Now that you have been thinking about a place you would like to describe, try writing a description of one object in that place. Write the description as if you were writing a "For Sale" advertisement. Here's an example:

> For sale. One very shiny red bike. It has ten speeds, a padded seat, and is made of light aluminum. This bike moves like the wind when it is ridden by a pro. Only reasonable offers will be considered.

Keep your description in your writing folder.

Idea Corner *Think of Places*

You probably have some ideas about places to describe. In your journal write whatever ideas come to mind. You might write a topic idea, such as "My Bedroom," or a comparison, such as "moves like a feather floating on the breeze." You might sketch a small picture and label certain parts.

PICTURES SEEING LIKE A WRITER

Finding Ideas for Writing

Look at the pictures. Think about what you see.
What ideas for descriptive writing do the pictures give you?
Write your ideas in your journal.

WRITING TOGETHER

COOPERATIVE LEARNING

1 GROUP WRITING: A Description

The **purpose** of a description is to create a clear and vivid picture. Writers of description think of their **audience.** What will make a picture clear and vivid for their audience?

- An Overall Impression
- Sensory Details
- Logical Order

An Overall Impression

Read the following paragraph. Think about what makes the underlined sentence special.

> At dusk the skyscraper looked like a glittering giant robot. Two tall towers on the top of the building reached toward the sky. Bright red lights flashed from the towers. Below the towers a huge balcony reached like arms all around the building. White lights from thousands of windows beneath the balcony twinkled brightly. At the bottom of the giant building, two golden lions guarded the doors.

The underlined sentence gives a general idea, or overall impression, of the skyscraper. All of the details tell more about the overall impression.

Guided Practice: Stating an Overall Impression

As a class, agree on a place to describe. Decide on an audience. Use the list below or your journal for ideas. Write a sentence that gives an overall impression of that place.

Example: The library was cool and peaceful.

the schoolyard	the lunchroom	the playground
your classroom	the art room	the gym

Sensory Details

The details in descriptive writing are often sensory details. Sensory details tell more about how things look, sound, taste, feel, or smell. In the paragraph that describes the skyscraper, the sensory details help to give you an overall impression. They help you to create a picture in your mind of the skyscraper just as the writer saw it. Look back at that paragraph.

- Which words help you see that the skyscraper is glittering?
- Which words help you see that the skyscraper is like a giant?

Logical Order

Look at the paragraph on page 334 again. Notice that the skyscraper is described from top to bottom. Words such as *top of the building* and *below the towers* show top-to-bottom order.

- What is at the top of the building? What is at the bottom?
- What location words did the writer use?
- In what other order might the writer have chosen to describe the skyscraper?

When you arrange details in logical order, you help your reader to see a clear picture.

Guided Practice: Charting Sensory Details

Recall the place you have chosen to describe. Think of sensory words to describe it. Look in your journal for ideas. As a class, make a chart like this one. Write sensory words that tell about the overall impression of the place.

SOUND	SIGHT	SMELL	TOUCH	TASTE
whir	green	fresh	rough	sour

Putting a Description Together

With your classmates you have written a sentence that gives an overall impression of a place. You have listed some sensory words about that place, too.

Think about your overall impression sentence. Then, look at your chart of sensory words. It is now time to make some choices. Which sensory details will you include in your description?

Here is one student's overall impression sentence. Look at the sensory words that she checked.

The city street was like a noisy carnival.

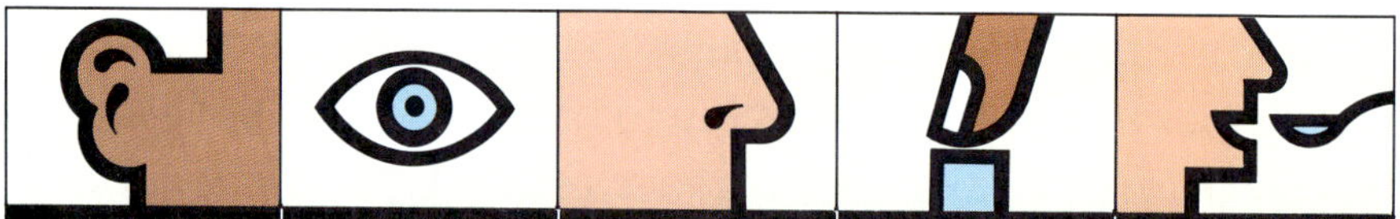

SOUND	SIGHT	SMELL	TOUCH	TASTE
whir	green	fresh	rough	sour
✓ squeal	✓ cars	stale	soft	✓ sweet
✓ crash	✓ people	✓ like apples	prickly	✓ spicy
✓ bang	red		✓ smooth	salty

This student chose details that would tell more about the city street that was like a noisy carnival.

Guided Practice: Writing a Description

Write three or four detail sentences to add to your overall impression sentence. In your detail sentences, include sensory words from your chart. Choose the words that will help to give your reader a clear overall impression of the place you have chosen. Be sure to use a logical order for your detail sentences.

Share your description with a friend. Ask your friend to suggest ways to make your description clearer and more vivid.

Checklist: Descriptive Writing

When you write a description, you will want to keep some points in mind. A checklist will remind you of the things that you want to include in your descriptive writing.

Look at this checklist. Some points need to be added. Make a copy of the checklist and complete it. Keep a copy of it in your writing folder. You can use it when you write your description.

CHECKLIST

- ✓ Purpose and audience
- ✓ Overall impression
- ✓ Sensory details
- ■ Sound
- ■ ____________________
- ■ ____________________
- ■ ____________________
- ■ ____________________
- ✓ ________________ order

2 THINKING AND WRITING: Classifying Sensory Details

You know that descriptive writing creates a clear and vivid picture. In some ways, a description is like a photograph. A description gives the reader a "picture" in words.

A writer gets to choose just how that picture will look. A writer does this by first deciding on an overall impression. Then, the writer chooses certain details to tell more about that impression. Look at this page from a writer's journal. The writer plans to write a description of the place where her family washes clothes. On the page, many details are listed.

big washing machines
spinning dryers
a telephone outside
the smell of clean clothes
cars passing on the street
bags of laundry everywhere

Thinking Like a Writer

■ Which details do you think are important to the overall impression?

The writer needs to make a choice. Here, two details do not fit—the cars passing and the telephone. They do not add to the overall impression of a place where clothes are washed.

When you write a description, you will have to make choices, too. You will have to decide which details are important. As you choose the details to include, keep in mind the five senses. Details that appeal to sight, sound, smell, touch, and taste will make your description vivid.

THINKING APPLICATION Classifying Sensory Details

COOPERATIVE LEARNING

Each of the writers named below is planning to write a description. Help each writer to decide which details to include. Write the details to include on a separate piece of paper. You may wish to discuss your thinking with other students. In your discussions, explain your choices to each other.

1. Paula's paragraph will describe a campfire. She wants to create an overall impression that the fire is cozy and warm. Which details should she include?

the orange flames	the sound of a nearby bird
the smell of burning wood	the heat of the fire

2. Dean's paragraph will describe a hockey rink. He wants to create an overall impression of the inside of the rink. Which details should he include?

the parking lot	the smoothness of the ice
the cold air	the voices of the hockey players

3. Caridad's poem will describe her basement. She wants to give a very clear picture of what is in her basement. Which details should she include?

the old oil burner	the cold cement floor
a smell from the kitchen	the pipes

4. Jim's letter will describe his backyard. He wants to create an overall impression that the yard is lovely and peaceful. Which details should he include?

soft green grass	round flower beds
small fruit trees	a bicycle near the garage

3 INDEPENDENT WRITING: A Description

Prewrite: Step 1

You have learned some important ideas about description. Now you are ready to choose a topic of your own for writing. Lee, a student your age, wanted to write a description for his classmates. He chose a topic in this way.

Choosing a Topic

1. First, he wrote a list of places that he would like to describe.
2. Next, he thought about how he would describe each place.
3. Last, he decided on the place that he could describe best.

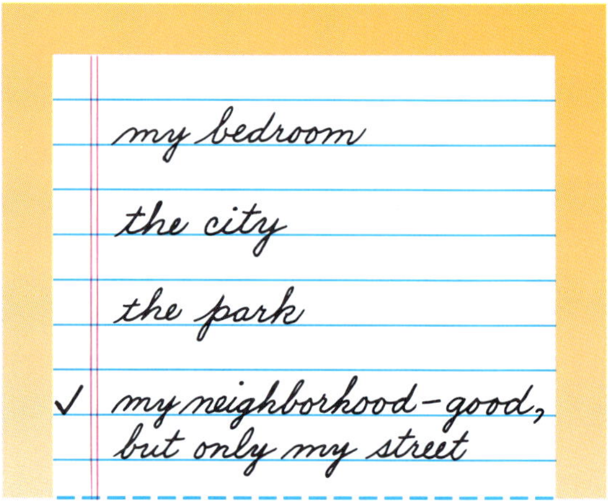

Lee liked the last place on his list best. He thought he would like to narrow the topic of his neighborhood to just his street.

Lee explored his topic by making a **cluster.** Here is what Lee's cluster looked like.

Exploring Ideas: Clustering Strategy

Lee thought he had some good ideas. He knew that his **purpose** for writing was to describe his street so that his classmates could see it as he did.

Before beginning to write, Lee closed his eyes and imagined his street. He did this to get a clear picture. At this point, he even added some more details to his cluster.

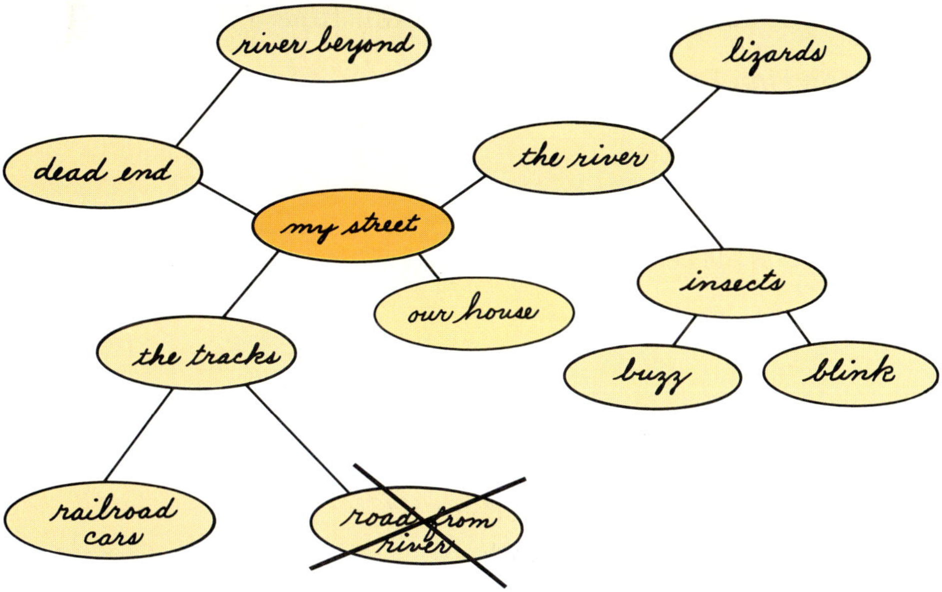

Thinking Like a Writer

- What did he add?
- What did he decide to cross out?
- Why do you think he crossed out that part?

YOUR TURN

JOURNAL

Think of a place you would like to describe. Choose an audience for your writing. Use **Pictures** or your journal for ideas. Follow these steps.

- Make a list of places.
- Choose the one you like best.
- Narrow your topic if it is too broad.
- Think of an overall impression of your place.
- Think about your purpose and audience.

Make a cluster. Remember, you can add to or take away from the cluster at any time.

Write a First Draft: Step 2

Lee knows what his description should include. He used a planning checklist. Lee is now ready to write his first draft. He will not worry about errors at this time.

Lee's First Draft

I live on a street that is a dead end. If you drive passed my house, you reach the closest river. A dirt road goes along the river. It ends up at the railroad tracks. the railroad cars sit there. At night near the river, the insects blink in different colors. They also make sounds.

YOUR TURN

Write your first draft. As you prepare to write, ask yourself these questions.

- What will my audience want to know about the place?
- How can I best express my overall impression?

TIME-OUT You might want to take some time out before you revise. That way you will be able to revise your writing with a fresh eye.

Planning Checklist

- Remember purpose and audience.
- Include an overall impression.
- Use sensory words and details.
- Use logical order.

Revise: Step 3

After he finished his first draft, Lee read it over to himself. Then he shared his writing with a classmate. He wanted some suggestions for improvement.

Lee then looked back at his planning checklist. He noticed that he had forgotten one point. He checked it off so that he would remember it when he revised. Lee now has a checklist to use as he revises.

Lee made changes to his paragraph. Notice that he did not correct small errors. He knew he could fix them later.

The revisions Lee made changed his paragraph. Turn the page. Look at Lee's revised draft.

Revising Checklist

- Remember purpose and audience.
- Include an overall impression.
- ✓ Use sensory words and details.
- Use logical order.

Lee's Revised Draft

I live on a ~~street that is a~~ dead end. If you
drive passed my house, you reach the ~~closest~~
and
river. A dirt road goes along the river. ~~It~~ ends
up at the railroad tracks. the railroad cars
looking like long forgotten dinosaurs.
sit there. At night near the river, the
—some yellow, some red, some blue.
insects blink in different colors. They also
hum quietly. My street is not fancy, but it is special to me.
~~make sounds.~~

Thinking Like a Writer

WISE WORD CHOICE

- Which words about sights and sounds did Lee add? How do they improve the paragraph?
- Which sentences did he combine? How does combining them improve the paragraph?

YOUR TURN

Read your first draft. Make a checklist. Ask yourself these questions.

- How can I improve the overall impression?
- How can I add details to make my description clearer?
- How can I make the order of my details more logical?

If you wish, ask a friend to read your paragraph and make suggestions. Then revise your paragraph.

Proofread: Step 4

Lee knew that his work was not complete until he proofread his paragraph. He used a proofreading checklist while he proofread.

Lee's Proofread Draft

¶ I live on a street that is a dead end. If you
past
drive passed my house, you reach the closest
and
river. A dirt road goes along the river. It ends
up at the railroad tracks. the railroad cars
looking like long-forgotten dinosaurs.
sit there. At night near the river, the
—some yellow, some red, some blue.
insects blink in different colors. They also
hum quietly. My street is not fancy, but it is special to me.

YOUR TURN

Proofreading Practice

Below is a paragraph that you can use to practice your proofreading skills. Find the errors. Write the paragraph correctly on a separate piece of paper.

> I have my bedroom very carefully arranged. My bed is agenst the wall that has a window. I like to look outside when I wake up My nice new desk is near my Bookshelves so that I do not have to go far to find a book. My dog's bed is in the corner near the heater. She likes to stay more warmer.

Proofreading Checklist

- Did I indent my paragraph?
- Did I spell all words correctly?
- What punctuation errors do I need to correct?
- What capitalization errors do I need to correct?

Applying Your Proofreading Skills

Now proofread your description. Read your checklist again. Review **The Grammar Connection** and **The Mechanics Connection,** too. Use the proofreading marks to show changes.

THE GRAMMAR CONNECTION

Remember these rules about adjectives.

- Use *more* or *most* before most adjectives that have two or more syllables.
- *More* compares two things. *Most* compares more than two things.

  One house is **more** beautiful than the next.
  That house is the **most** beautiful of all.

Check your descriptive paragraph. Have you used *more* and *most* correctly?

THE MECHANICS CONNECTION

Remember this rule about using commas.

- Use a comma between adjectives that describe the same noun.

  A white**,** fluffy rabbit sat near the fence.

Check your descriptive paragraph. Have you used commas between adjectives correctly?

Proofreading Marks

¶ indent
∧ add
ℓ take out
≡ capital letter
/ make a small letter

Publish: Step 5

Lee made a neat, final copy and posted it on the class bulletin board. Several of his classmates read his work. They told him he was lucky to live by the river.

YOUR TURN

Make a neat, final copy of your descriptive paragraph. Think of a way to share your description. You might want to use one of the ideas in the **Sharing Suggestions** box below.

SHARING SUGGESTIONS

Create a book of descriptions. Illustrate your book.	Include your description in a letter to a relative.	Make a tape recording of your description.

4 SPEAKING AND LISTENING: Describing a Place

You have just written a description of a place that you know. Your description probably included an overall impression of the place. It included some sensory details, too. Now you can use what you know about writing a description to give a short talk. In your talk, you will tell your **overall impression.**

First, choose a topic. Narrow your topic if it is too broad. You may want to explore your topic by making a cluster. This will help you decide which details you will include in your talk.

Next, you will want to make a note card to use for your talk. You do not have to write everything on your note card. The note card should include only the main points and some details. Look at this note card.

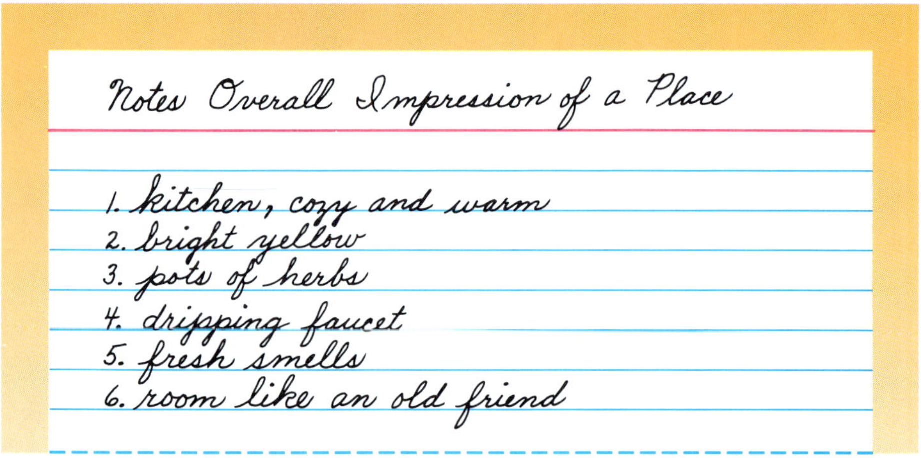

Notice that the overall impression is listed on the note card. What other points are listed? How do the details support the overall impression?

When you give a talk, it will help you to keep your **purpose** and **audience** in mind. The speaking guidelines on page 349 will help you to focus your talk.

SPEAKING GUIDELINES: Describing a Place

1. Remember your **purpose** and **audience.**
2. Make a note card. Practice using your note card.
3. Tell an overall impression. Include sensory details. Use logical order.
4. Look at your listeners.
5. Speak in a clear voice that your audience can hear.

- Why are sensory details important when I am telling about a place?
- How does describing in logical order help my audience?

SPEAKING APPLICATION Describing a Place

Think of a place that is special to you. Prepare a note card to use to give a short description of this place. Use the speaking guidelines to help you prepare. Your classmates will be using the following guidelines as they listen to your description.

LISTENING GUIDELINES: Describing a Place

1. Listen to "see" the image.
2. Listen for sensory details.
3. Listen for an overall impression.

5 WRITER'S RESOURCES: The Encyclopedia

In this unit, you have written descriptions of places. You may have used many resources—photographs, poems, stories, or your own imagination—to find ideas for your writing.

Another useful resource for a writer is the encyclopedia. An **encyclopedia** is a set of books that contains information about many subjects. Each book, or volume, in the set has articles that are arranged in alphabetical order. Encyclopedia articles give information about people, places, things, and events.

Notice that the volumes are labeled with one or more letters. Each volume includes subjects beginning with those letters. For example, an article about *deserts* would be in volume 5. An article about *photography* would be in volume 15.

Every encyclopedia has an **index** that lists all the subjects written about in the encyclopedia. The index in the encyclopedia on this page is in volume 22.

WRITING EXTENSION

Practice

Use the encyclopedia on the opposite page. Write each subject below on a sheet of paper. Then write the number of the volume that would have an article about that subject.

1. Niagara Falls
2. Christopher Columbus
3. rain forests
4. pueblo life
5. silver mines of America
6. Amazon River
7. Inca ruins
8. Japan
9. mapmaking
10. Sacajawea
11. Brazil
12. Hernando De Soto
13. fiords
14. Rio Grande River
15. the Great Plains
16. Tampa
17. Mount Washington
18. the Everglades
19. Grand Canyon
20. pampas
21. The Declaration of Independence
22. Great Britain
23. West Virginia
24. Plymouth Rock
25. Thomas Jefferson

WRITING APPLICATION A Summary

Use an encyclopedia to look up information about a place that interests you. Write a short **summary** of some information that interests you. Keep your summary in your writing folder. You will use it in **The Curriculum Connection** on page 352.

Writing About Geography

When you think of geography, you probably think of maps. Maps are important tools for the geographer. But geography is more than the making and reading of maps. Geography is the study of places. It is also the study of the earth's features and the ways that people live.

The word *geography* comes from the Greek word that means "earth description." Geographers try to describe our earth in a number of ways. They draw maps to show where things are located. They take photographs. They interview people and record their words. They also write descriptions that are included in encyclopedias, magazines, textbooks, and government reports. Geographers help to create an accurate picture of our world.

ACTIVITIES

Visualize a Place Look at the summary you wrote about the place you looked up in the encyclopedia. Based on your summary, draw a picture. Under the picture, write sentences that describe the place.

Describe a Photograph Look at the photograph on the opposite page. Think of how you would describe the place that is pictured there. Write a letter to a friend who has never seen the photograph. Tell your friend about what you see. Start by jotting down ideas. Remember to use sensory words. Use your imagination to think of sensory words for hearing and touching.

Respond to Literature The following description is taken from the diary of the explorer Robert E. Peary. After reading the description, write a response. Your response may be a letter to Peary and his team, or a poem about their trip.

From the Diary of Robert E. Peary

Peary describes his feelings on the day he had chosen to start the assault, which was March 1, 1909.

When I awoke before light on the morning of March 1, the wind was whistling around the igloo. . . . I looked through the peephole of the igloo and saw that the weather was still clear, and that the stars were . . . like diamonds. . . . After breakfast, with the first glimmer of daylight, we got outside the igloo and looked about . . . the ice fields to the north, as well as the lower part of the land, were invisible in that gray haze which, every experienced Arctic traveler knows, means vicious wind. . . . Some parties would have considered the weather impossible for traveling . . . (but) we were all in our new and perfectly dry fur clothes and could bid defiance to the wind.

UNIT CHECKUP

LESSON 1

Group Writing: A Description (page 334) Read the paragraph below. On a separate sheet of paper, write the sentence that states the overall impression.

From my window seat, the earth below looked like a patchwork quilt. There were perfectly square fields of golden wheat right next to fields of green grasses. Now and then, a plowed field of rich, dark soil completed the pattern.

LESSON 2

Thinking: Classifying Sensory Details (page 338) Imagine that you are planning to write a description of a beach. You wish to create the overall impression that the beach is busy and crowded. Which of the following details would you include? Write those details on a separate sheet of paper.

1. hundreds of people
2. rows of beach towels
3. planes flying above
4. many beach chairs
5. several volleyball nets
6. a boat offshore

LESSON 3

Writing a Description (page 340) Imagine that you are a successful author. The story that you have written is set in a mysterious old house. Write a description of the house for the book jacket.

LESSON 4

Speaking and Listening: Describing a Place (page 348) Work with a partner. Describe a room in your house or a room in your school to your partner. Give an overall impression. Include sensory details. Ask your partner to tell you the impression he or she has gotten of the place you described.

LESSON 5

Writer's Resources: The Encyclopedia (page 350) Select a topic. Use an encyclopedia to find information about the topic. Write a short summary of your findings.

THEME PROJECT A STAGE SET

Think about the kinds of pictures you know. There are moving pictures, or movies, photographs, and paintings. There is the picture on your television or video screen.

Look at the picture below. This picture shows a stage set. It is the kind of picture you would see when the curtain rises at a play. Talk with your classmates about all the things you see in the stage set.

Think of a favorite story or create one of your own. Imagine that the story will be made into a play.

- Design a stage set for the play.
- Begin by brainstorming for ideas.
- Make a list of what you will include.
- You may want to draw a picture of your stage set, or you may want to create a model.

GRAMMAR

UNIT 11

Pronouns

In Unit 11 you will learn about pronouns. Pronouns are words that take the place of nouns. When you want to avoid repeating a noun, you can use a pronoun.

Discuss Read the poem on the opposite page. Why do we sometimes take the world around us for granted? Talk over your ideas with a partner.

Creative Expression The unit theme is *Decisions*. How do you make a difficult decision? Sometimes writing a list of reasons for and against the decision helps. Try this strategy out with a partner. Write your list in your journal.

JOURNAL

THEME: *DECISIONS*

One day I listened to the earth.
One day I stopped taking everything for granted.
Ears of mine, I said, I will teach you something new.
Eyes, I will teach you to see what no one has seen.

—Claudia Lewis, from "Listen to the Unheard"

GRAMMAR

1 WHAT IS A PRONOUN?

A pronoun is a word that takes the place of one or more nouns.

A noun names a person, place, or thing. A good writer does not use the same noun over and over. A **pronoun** takes the place of one or more nouns. When you write, think about how you can use a pronoun to replace a noun.

> **Lisa** visits **Lisa's** grandmother every summer.
> **She** visits **her** grandmother every summer.

Like nouns, pronouns are singular or plural. Singular pronouns take the place of singular nouns. Plural pronouns replace plural nouns or a group of nouns.

> **Ted and Kim** go camping with **Paul.**
> **They** go camping with **him**.

Singular Pronouns: I, you, he, she, it, me, him, her

Plural Pronouns: we, you, they, us, them

Notice that the pronoun *you* may be singular or plural.

Guided Practice

Tell which word in each sentence is a pronoun. Then tell whether the pronoun is singular or plural.

Example: We decided to visit Alaska this year. *We plural*

1. Are you excited about the trip, Larry?
2. Will we see any polar bears?
3. Tim showed me slides of animals in Alaska.
4. He has pictures of bears, seals, elk, and moose.

?! THINK

■ How can I decide if a word is a pronoun?

REMEMBER

- A **pronoun** takes the place of one or more nouns.
- A pronoun may be singular or plural.

More Practice

A. Write each sentence. Draw a line under each pronoun. Then write whether it is singular or plural.

Example: Ana told us about Mexico. *plural*

5. It is a large and beautiful country.
6. "You can climb the pyramids," Ana told Gary.
7. The Mayans built them many hundreds of years ago.
8. They still stand in the jungle today.
9. Emily said, "I would like to see Mexico City."
10. Someday we will visit Mexico.
11. "You will love Mexico," Ana said to the children.

B. Write each sentence. Then write the pronoun that takes the place of each underlined word or words.

Example: The Lees drove to Sequoia National Park. *They*

12. Sequoia National Park is in California.
13. "The Lees will photograph the sequoias," Mr. Lee said.
14. A ranger guided the Lees through the huge park.
15. The sequoias are among the oldest living things on earth.
16. Many of these trees are more than one thousand years old.
17. The oldest sequoia is about 3,500 years old.
18. The sequoias are named after Sequoya, a Cherokee man.
19. Sequoya invented a written alphabet for the Cherokee.
20. A statue of Sequoya is in Washington, D.C.

Extra Practice, page 378

WRITING APPLICATION A Letter

Write a letter to persuade a foreign pen pal to visit the United States. Suggest some interesting places to visit. Ask a classmate to underline the pronouns in your letter.

2 SUBJECT PRONOUNS

A **subject pronoun** is a word that is used as the subject of a sentence. It tells whom or what the sentence is about. Like a noun, a subject pronoun may be singular or plural.

Martha practices the piano.
She practices the piano.

Mom and I sing duets.
We sing duets.

Dad and Joe play the violin.
They play the violin.

Subject Pronouns
Singular: I, you, he, she, it **Plural:** we, you, they

Notice that only the pronouns in the box may be used as subjects.

Guided Practice

Tell which word is the subject pronoun in each sentence. Tell whether the pronoun is singular or plural.

Example: I decided to join the orchestra in school.
I singular

1. I play cello in the orchestra.
2. We watch the conductor, Ms. Kelly.
3. She helps the students.
4. Julie and I work hard at practice sessions.
5. It is time for a rehearsal now.

?! THINK

- How do I decide which pronoun to use as the subject of a sentence?

REMEMBER

- *I, you, he, she, it, we,* and *they* are **subject pronouns.**

More Practice

A. Write each sentence. Underline the subject pronoun. Then write whether it is singular or plural.

Example: Jerry, you should join the orchestra. *singular*

6. We will perform in two weeks.
7. I enjoy our rehearsals and concerts.
8. We practice together twice a week.
9. We need another clarinet player.
10. Robert and I play the flute.
11. We played a march by John Philip Sousa.
12. He wrote many marches.
13. They are my favorite pieces.

B. Write each sentence. Use a subject pronoun in place of each underlined word or words.

Example: Lynn and I study the oboe. *She*

14. The oboe is a difficult instrument.
15. Juan and I play the bassoon.
16. Sometimes bassoons sound very funny.
17. Ben said to Kim, "Kim should come to the concert."
18. The concert is on Friday.
19. "Ted and Ben love concerts," said Ben.
20. "Tanya and Nicole will meet you there," said Nicole.

Extra Practice, page 379

WRITING APPLICATION A Descriptive Paragraph

What is the name of your favorite musical group? Write a paragraph describing the group. Tell about the musicians in the group. Describe the kind of music they play. Exchange paragraphs with a partner. Underline the subject pronouns in your paragraphs.

GRAMMAR

3 OBJECT PRONOUNS

You have learned that a subject pronoun may be used as the subject of a sentence. An **object pronoun** is a pronoun that is used in the predicate of a sentence. It may follow an action verb or a word such as *in, into, to, with, by, for,* or *at.*

Bill found **the injured bird.** Bill found **it.**
Bill showed the bird to **Sue.** Bill showed the bird to **her.**
The bird saw **Bill and Sue.** The bird saw **them.**

Object Pronouns
Singular: me, you, him, her, it **Plural:** us, you, them

Bill found it.

Guided Practice

Tell which word is the object pronoun in each sentence.

Example: Bill carried it into the classroom. *it*

1. "We should adopt the bird," Jenny told us.
2. The class agreed with her.
3. Jenny's argument convinced them.
4. I gave it a sunflower seed.
5. The bird looked at Ms. Dabney and me.

?! THINK

■ How do I decide if a word is an object pronoun?

REMEMBER

- An **object pronoun** is used after an action verb or a word such as *in, into, to,* or *with.*
- *Me, you, him, her, it, us,* and *them* are object pronouns.

More Practice

A. Write each sentence. Underline the object pronoun in each sentence.

Example: We put it in a large cardboard box.

6. Bill built a nest for it.
7. Rosa worked with him on the nest.
8. The sewing teacher gave us some rags.
9. The class thanked her.
10. We used them in the nest.
11. Let's put it in the nest.
12. "The bird winked at me," said Tara.

B. Write each sentence. Use an object pronoun in place of each underlined word or words.

Example: Mark and Gloria feed the bird every day. *it*

13. Mark asked Gloria to help him.
14. The bird sings for Mark and Gloria.
15. "The bird watches Mark and Gloria," said Gloria.
16. We asked Mr. Ward for a book about birds.
17. We learned how to care for the bird.
18. The bird likes the students.
19. People should be kind to animals.
20. The teacher told us, "I'm proud of the class."

Extra Practice, page 380

WRITING APPLICATION A Poster

Make a poster that shows how people can help protect animals. Your poster should have a picture and a caption. Ask your classmates to find the object pronouns in your caption.

COOPERATIVE LEARNING

4 POSSESSIVE PRONOUNS

You use a special kind of pronoun to show who or what owns something. This pronoun is called a **possessive pronoun.** A possessive pronoun takes the place of one or more possessive nouns.

Tim's life preserver is in the boat.
His life preserver is in the boat.

The Browns' sailboat has red sails.
Their sailboat has red sails.

Possessive Pronouns
Singular: my, your, his, her, its
Plural: our, your, their

Notice that possessive pronouns do not have an apostrophe.

Guided Practice

Tell which word is the possessive pronoun in each sentence.

Example: The players listened to their coach. *their*

1. Jane carries her uniform into the gym.
2. My brother never misses basketball practice.
3. Does your team meet after school?
4. Our team won the tournament.
5. The team chose Jon as its captain.
6. He takes his job seriously.

?! THINK

■ How do I decide when to use a possessive pronoun?

REMEMBER

- A **possessive pronoun** shows who or what owns something.

More Practice

A. Write the possessive pronoun in each sentence.

Example: My family plays tennis together. *My*

7. Swimming is my favorite form of exercise.
8. Our school has an excellent gym.
9. The students choose their exercise programs.
10. Greg is known for his speed as a runner.
11. Yvette practices her backstroke in the pool.
12. I jump rope in my exercise program.
13. Each sport has its rewards.

B. Write each sentence. Use a possessive pronoun in place of the underlined word or words.

Example: Baseball fans know Jackie Robinson's name.
Baseball fans know his name.

14. Robinson was baseball's first major league black player.
15. Jackie's first year as a Brooklyn Dodger was difficult.
16. Some Dodgers did not want a black player on the Dodgers' team.
17. Mr. Rickey told Jackie, "Don't show Jackie's anger."
18. "Yes, I won't lose Jackie's temper," Jackie said.
19. Before long everyone knew that Jackie would soon be one of baseball's greatest players.
20. Matt and Erika say, "Jackie Robinson was Matt and Erika's favorite player."

Extra Practice, page 381

WRITING APPLICATION A Sports Article

Write a short article about your favorite sports figure. Explain why you believe this person is a good athlete. Then, underline the possessive pronouns in your article.

GRAMMAR

5 USING *I* AND *ME* CORRECTLY

Sometimes it is difficult to decide whether to use *I* or *me* in a sentence. Always use **I** in the subject of a sentence. Use **me** after an action verb and words such as *in, into, to, with, by,* or *at.*

Subject	Object
Dora and **I** will attend the party.	Ina invited Roy and **me.**
Roy and **I** will dress up as bears.	No one will recognize **me.**

One way to decide which pronoun is correct is to say the sentence using only *I* and *me*.

Gina and **I** made costumes.	**I** made costumes.
Jeff helped her and **me.**	Jeff helped **me.**

When you talk about other people as well as yourself, it is polite to name yourself last.

Guided Practice

Tell which word or words in parentheses ( ) complete each sentence correctly.

Example: Ina told Gina and (I, me) to come at 5 P.M. *me*

1. Tim and (I, me) will surprise everyone.
2. The costumes will fit Maura and (I, me).
3. (Dan and I, I and Dan) will have fun.

?! THINK

■ How do I decide whether to use *I* or *me* in a sentence?

REMEMBER

- Always use **I** in the subject of a sentence.
- Use **me** after an action verb or words such as *in* or *with.*

More Practice

A. Write the correct word or words to complete each sentence.

Example: (Luis and I, Luis and me) are good friends.
Luis and I are good friends.

4. Luis and (I, me) will walk to the party together.
5. Will you come with (I, me), too?
6. You and (I, me) will wear long robes.
7. Mrs. Chin gave (Lynn and me, me and Lynn) tall hats.
8. (She and I, I and she) will put them on.
9. Some monsters scared (me and her, her and me).
10. (Marnie and I, I and Marnie) enjoyed the party.

B. Write each sentence. Use **I** or **me** to complete the sentence.

Example: Ted, Nina, and _____ are planning our party. *I*

11. Ted, she, and _____ will have a costume party.
12. Nina and _____ will dress up as frogs.
13. She and _____ will hop around the floor.
14. Everyone will laugh at her and _____ .
15. Where can Bob and _____ buy the masks?
16. He and _____ have looked everywhere.
17. Mr. Smith gave masks to Peg and _____ .
18. Len and _____ thought the costumes were funny.
19. Bill, Jean, and _____ will dress as robots.
20. Please show Terry and _____ your costume.

Extra Practice, page 382

WRITING APPLICATION An Invitation

COOPERATIVE LEARNING

Imagine that you are giving a costume party. Write an invitation to your friends. Read the invitation to a classmate. Check that you used the pronouns *I* and *me* correctly.

6 MECHANICS: Pronoun Contractions

A **contraction** is a shortened form of two words. Some contractions are formed from a pronoun and a verb. Look at the apostrophe in each contraction below. It takes the place of one or more letters.

Contraction	Meaning	Contraction	Meaning
I'm	I am	we're	we are
I've	I have	we've	we have
I'd	I had/would	we'd	we had/would
I'll	I will	we'll	we will
he's	he is/has	you're	you are
she's	she is/has	you've	you have
it's	it is/has	you'd	you had/would
he'd	he had/would	you'll	you will
she'd	she had/would	they're	they are
he'll	he will	they've	they have
she'll	she will	they'd	they had/would
it'll	it will	they'll	they will

Notice that ***'s*** can stand for *is* or *has*, and ***'d*** can stand for *had* or *would*.

Guided Practice

Tell what contraction you can form with each pair of words.

Example: I would *I'd*

1. we are
2. it is
3. she will
4. they have
5. you would
6. I am

?! THINK

■ How do I form a contraction using a pronoun and a verb?

REMEMBER

- A **contraction** is a shortened form of two words. One or more letters are left out, and an apostrophe takes their place.

More Practice

A. Write the two words that were joined to form each underlined contraction.

Example: Sometimes it's hard to choose a career. *it is*

7. You'll learn about some job choices on Career Day.
8. Betty says she's interested in animals.
9. Maybe she'll be a veterinarian.
10. Many students say they'll study computers.
11. We'd like more information about that.
12. You're welcome to join our group.
13. We'll listen to a career counselor.

B. Write each sentence, using a contraction for the underlined words.

Example: We have planned a Career Day at school.
We've planned a Career Day at school.

14. The students say they are excited.
15. I am hoping that many students will attend.
16. Carl's mother said she would talk to us.
17. She is the head of the Parks Department.
18. It will be a fascinating discussion.
19. She has worked hard in her position.
20. I have been looking forward to her speech.

Extra Practice, Practice Plus, pages 383–384

WRITING APPLICATION A Job Description

Think about a job you would like to have. Then, write a paragraph describing what you would do in the job and why you would like it. Exchange papers with a friend. Have your friend point out the contractions you have used.

GRAMMAR

7 VOCABULARY BUILDING: Homophones/Homographs

Many words in English sound alike but have different spellings and different meanings. These words are called **homophones.**

The **plane** landed on the **plain.**
I wonder **whether** planes fly in stormy **weather.**

Other words are spelled the same but have different meanings and often have different pronunciations. These words are called **homographs.**

I **saw** the boy **saw** wood for the kite frame.
As the **wind** blows, we **wind** the kite string.

You must read or listen carefully to know which meaning of a homophone or homograph is being used.

Guided Practice

Tell which words in each sentence look or sound alike. Tell whether those words in the sentence are **homophones** or **homographs.**

Example: It's fun to watch my hamster use its exercise wheel.
It's its homophones

1. Barney ate eight grapes.
2. They're waiting for their school bus.
3. She was in tears when she saw the tears in her painting.
4. Do you think the bus fare is fair?
5. I can't stand to stand in line.
6. I cannot bear to meet that scary bear.
7. Can you strip the paint from that strip of wood?

?! **THINK**

- How do I decide which meaning of a homophone or homograph is being used?

REMEMBER

- Use the other words in the sentence to help you decide which meaning of a **homophone** or **homograph** is being used.

More Practice

A. Write the correct homophone.

Example: Ron feels (weak, week) after his illness. *weak*

8. This report is due next (weak, week).
9. Would you like a (peace, piece) of bread?
10. The two countries signed a (peace, piece) treaty.
11. That book is on (loan, lone) from the library.
12. A (loan, lone) tree stood in the field.
13. (Your, You're) invited to my party on Sunday.
14. Bring (your, you're) bathing suit and a towel.
15. This bridge is made of (steal, steel).
16. Don't leave the food (their, there) on the table.
17. My cat will (steal, steel) food from the table.

B. Write the meaning of the underlined homograph.

Example: The doctor wound a bandage around the cut. *b*
a. an injury b. wrapped

18. A seal uses its flippers to swim.
a. an animal b. close tightly
19. Dad tried to hide the package behind his back.
a. animal skin b. keep out of sight
20. All the actors bow to the audience.
a. weapon b. bend at the waist

Extra Practice, page 385

WRITING APPLICATION A Riddle

Many of the riddles you know use homographs.

What did the mayonnaise say to the refrigerator?
"Close the door. I'm *dressing*!"

Write your own riddle, using homographs or homophones.

GRAMMAR AND WRITING CONNECTION

Combining Sentences

Remember that you can sometimes make your writing clearer by combining sentences that have similar ideas. Varying the length of sentences can also make your writing more interesting.

When you combine two or more sentences, you may list several words in a row. This list is called a **series**. Words in a series are separated by commas. Place the word ***and*** or ***or*** before the last word in the series.

Will, Terry, **and** I ate lunch.
Do I want salad, spaghetti, **or** meat loaf?

Working Together

COOPERATIVE LEARNING

Talk about the sentences below with your classmates. Tell how you would combine each pair to make a single sentence. Discuss whether you would add the word *and* or *or* to the series of words in your sentence.

Example: Stevie ran for class president. Tina and Meg also ran for class president.
Stevie, Tina, and Meg ran for class president.

1. Kim and I worked on Stevie's campaign. Beth worked on Stevie's campaign, too.
2. Stevie wants to raise money for a class trip and a garden. He wants to raise money for library books.
3. We could hold a bake sale or a raffle. We could hold a dance.

Revising Sentences

Martin wrote these sentences in his journal. Help Martin revise his work by combining his sentences.

4. Should Rudy and Lily run for vice-president? Should Martha run for vice-president, too?
5. We made posters and flyers. We made advertisements for the campaign.
6. Nan and Cindy ran for treasurer. Tom also ran.
7. Beth and I worked hard for Stevie. Kim worked hard, too.
8. Will Stevie or Tina win the election? Will Meg win?
9. The class chose Stevie and Martha. They chose Cindy, too.
10. Stevie thanked me after the election. Stevie thanked Beth and Kim, too.
11. I was happy that Stevie won the election. Beth and Kim were also happy.
12. I know that Stevie will work hard at his job. I'm sure that Martha and Cindy will work hard, too.

WRITER AT WORK

Think about an election in your school or town. Write a brief news article about the election. When you revise your article, combine any sentences you can by joining words in a series. Make sure that you use *and* or *or* when you join the words. Use commas to separate words in the series.

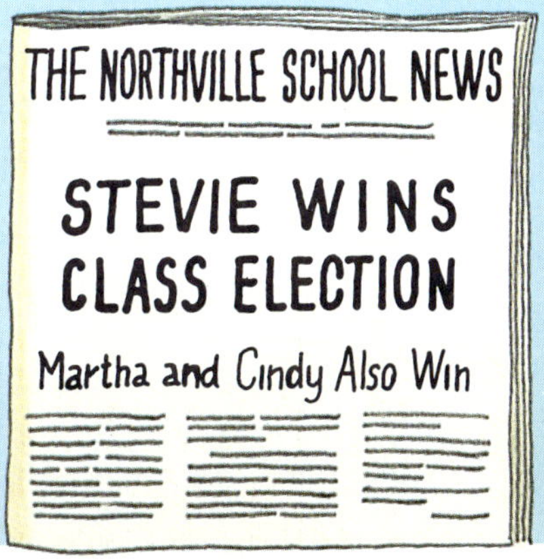

UNIT CHECKUP

LESSON 1

What Is a Pronoun? (page 358) Write each pronoun.

1. Will you play with me, Kit?
2. We could play catch outside.
3. Joan and Sal said they will join us.
4. I like them very much.
5. She and I are good friends.
6. I stay at her house overnight.

LESSON 2

Subject Pronouns (page 360) Use a subject pronoun in place of each underlined word or words.

7. Karen wants a pet dog.
8. She and George go to the pet store.
9. Mr. Benson is the owner of the pet store.
10. "Karen would like this dog," he tells Karen.
11. "Karen will buy the little puppy," said Karen.
12. Karen will be kind to the puppy.

LESSON 3

Object Pronouns (page 362) Write each sentence. Underline the object pronoun in each sentence.

13. Mr. Benson showed us the puppy.
14. He gave it to Karen.
15. George helped her with the puppy.
16. The puppy likes them.
17. "We'll take you home," they said.
18. "We'll make a sturdy bed for you," Karen said.

LESSON 4

Possessive Pronouns (page 364) Use a possessive pronoun in place of the underlined word or words.

19. Max's pet is a green frog.
20. Carmen's and my hamster is cute.
21. "Is that Josh's cat?" I asked Josh.
22. Wes and Jane's dog is friendly.
23. Lynn brought Lynn's turtle to school.
24. "Is that Patty's parrot?" I asked Patty.

LESSON **5**

Using *I* and *me* Correctly (page 366) Write each sentence. Use *I* or *me* to complete the sentence correctly.

25. Terri and _____ went to a record store.

26. Jim showed an album to Terri and _____ .

27. Jim and _____ wanted the album.

28. Terri, Jim, and _____ like this group.

29. Tell Jim and _____ about the album you want.

30. Next week Ruth will come with Jim and _____ .

LESSON **6**

Mechanics: Pronoun Contractions (page 368) Use a contraction in place of the underlined words.

31. We are shopping for a new car.

32. Mom says she would like a station wagon.

33. Dad says he will compare the prices of two cars.

34. It is going to be a hard decision.

35. I am sure we will find a great car.

36. You are invited to come on our first drive.

LESSON **7**

Vocabulary Building: Homophones/Homographs (page 370) Write each sentence, using the correct word from the pair in parentheses ( ).

37. The dog (chews, choose) on its bone.

38. (Its, It's) time for lunch.

39. Our guide (lead, led) us down the trail.

Write the correct meaning of the underlined homograph.

40. Kermit stirred the batter with a spoon.
a. baseball player b. cake mixture

41. Those dogs make a terrible racket.
a. noise b. tennis equipment

Writing Application: Pronoun Usage (pages 360–371) The following paragraph contains 9 errors with pronouns. Rewrite the paragraph correctly.

42.-50.

Julio decided to come with me and Ingrid to the mall. Your invited, too. Well meet Helene their. Im planning to buy presents for Rick and Gail. Me and Julio are going to they're party. Its on Saturday. Julio's dad will drive him and I to the party.

ENRICHMENT

CONTRACTION CARDS

Play this game with a small group. Write each pronoun-verb pair from the chart in Lesson 6 on a separate card. Put the cards in a pile. Players should take turns drawing a card. When it is your turn, say and spell the contraction for the pronoun and verb on the card you picked. Score one point for each correct answer.

Homophone Humor

My dog can't* write *a letter
Although he tries and tries.
***If he could ever do it* right**
He'd win a special prize.

—Bernice Kohn Hunt

The poet is having a good time with homophones. She plays with the words *write* and *right* in order to create a humorous poem. Think of several pairs of homophones. Then, imagine an event such as a dog writing a letter that would work with one of the pairs. Write a four-line poem using both of the homophones in the pair you chose. Illustrate your poem.

PICTURE YOU **Make a picture diary of yourself at different times of the day. Draw four or five pictures showing what you do or would like to do at each time. Write a sentence under each picture to tell what is happening. Use the pronouns *I* and *me* in your sentences.**

CREATIVE EXPRESSION

Poets choose their words carefully. Sometimes a poet uses several words in a line or a stanza that begin with the same sound. Repeating the same sound at the beginning of words is called **alliteration**. Say this well-known line to yourself:

She sells seashells by the seashore.

Did you hear the swish and rush of waves in this line? The sound of the words is very important in any poem. Alliteration is one way a poet helps the reader to hear and enjoy the sounds of words. Notice the alliteration in the poem below. How many examples of alliteration can you find?

Don't Ever Cross a Crocodile

Don't ever cross a crocodile
However few his faults.
Don't ever dare
A dancing bear
To teach you how to waltz.

Don't ever poke a rattlesnake
Who's sleeping in the sun
And say the poke
Was just a joke
And really all in fun.

Don't ever lure a lion close
With gifts of steak and suet.
Though lion-looks
Are nice in books
Don't ever, ever do it.

—Kaye Starbird

TRY IT OUT!

"Don't Ever Cross a Crocodile" is a poem that has alliteration. Write a short poem of your own. Include some words that begin with the same sound.

EXTRA PRACTICE

Three levels of practice

What Is a Pronoun? (page 358)

LEVEL A. Write the pronoun or pronouns in each sentence. Then write whether each pronoun is singular or plural.

1. It was springtime at last.
2. I helped Dad in the garden.
3. He used a big shovel.
4. Together we worked hard.
5. Carrie and Lew joined us.
6. They turned over the earth with spades.
7. Carrie said she would plant carrots.
8. "What vegetables will you plant?" she asked me.
9. "You can look in the seed catalog," Dad told us.

LEVEL B. Write each sentence. Then write the pronoun that takes the place of each underlined word or words.

10. Roger decided he would plant a garden.
11. Tina said she would help Roger.
12. "May we help, too?" Becky and Sue asked.
13. Roger watered the seeds to help them grow.
14. "Will you plant corn?" Becky asked Roger.
15. "I will plant flowers," Roger said.
16. Becky and Tina said they love flowers.
17. The garden will be beautiful.

LEVEL C. Write each sentence. Replace each underlined word or words with a pronoun.

18. Anne and Tony love tomatoes.
19. "Juan and Dora will plant beans," said Juan and Dora.
20. Anne says, "Anne will weed the garden."
21. Dora thanked Anne for helping.
22. "Thanks for helping Juan and Dora," Dora said.
23. Tony will water the garden.
24. The vegetables will be delicious.
25. The garden provides us with food for the winter.

EXTRA PRACTICE

GRAMMAR

Three levels of practice

Subject Pronouns (page 360)

LEVEL A. The subject in each sentence is underlined. Write the pronoun or pronouns that are part of the subject.

1. Nick and she plan their report.
2. Judy and he will report on penguins.
3. They and the teacher find these birds fascinating.
4. Betty and you will do research.
5. Barbara and I cannot decide on a topic.
6. Ellen and we will work together.
7. You and I will give our report to the class.
8. Linda's group and we will report tomorrow.
9. They and we will make covers for our reports.

LEVEL B. Write each sentence. Underline the subject pronoun in each sentence.

10. We are going to the library today.
11. David said he will go, too.
12. You may come with us.
13. It is quiet there.
14. I will ask the librarian for information.
15. She finds all the right books.
16. They will help us.
17. Will you meet us there?

LEVEL C. Write each sentence. Use a subject pronoun in place of each underlined word or words.

18. Jason plans to write a report on camels.
19. Camels can be angry animals.
20. The report will interest the class.
21. "Kareem will read about bats," said Kareem.
22. "Fay chose a good topic," Kirk told Fay.
23. Jerry and I started our work yesterday.
24. Julie has finished her report.
25. The students enjoy writing their reports.

EXTRA PRACTICE

Three levels of practice

Object Pronouns (page 362)

LEVEL **A.** Write the object pronoun that is part of the underlined predicate in each sentence.

1. Jay is giving a party for her.
2. He told Perry and me about the plan.
3. Jay asked him to bring something.
4. Marla will go shopping with you.
5. Please help us fix up the room.
6. Ken bought balloons to decorate it.
7. We will hang them on the walls.
8. Marge will tell us when to come.
9. We will call you tonight.

LEVEL **B.** Write each sentence. Underline the object pronoun in each sentence.

10. We planned the party for him.
11. Jay invited them by telephone.
12. Perry and Marla made a cake for her.
13. They put raisins in it.
14. Ken taught us a new party game.
15. I'll show the game to you.
16. You'll like playing it.
17. Rob played it with me all afternoon.

LEVEL **C.** Write each sentence. Use an object pronoun in place of each underlined word or words.

18. Rex and Carol bought a book for Judy.
19. They brought the book to the party.
20. Judy thanked Rex and Carol for the present.
21. She told Rex all about the book.
22. "I think this is a good book for Rex," she told Rex.
23. "Show the book to Jay," said Jay.
24. Marla liked the pictures in the book.
25. "This book interests Ken and Marla," said Marla.

EXTRA PRACTICE

GRAMMAR

Three levels of practice

Possessive Pronouns (page 364)

LEVEL **A.** Complete each sentence with the correct possessive pronoun in parentheses ( ). Use the underlined word or words as a clue.

1. The class is putting on (its, her) play.
2. I worked hard to learn (his, my) lines.
3. Norma studied (her, their) part, too.
4. "Is (her, your) part hard?" Chris asked Norma.
5. "I like (its, my) part," said Inez.
6. Sam learned (his, their) part quickly.
7. Victor and Ray play (their, our) parts well.
8. The class is happy with (your, its) show.
9. We thanked Ms. O'Brien, (our, their) director.

LEVEL **B.** Write each sentence. Underline the possessive pronoun in each sentence.

10. Our director tells us what to do.
11. Her instructions are very clear.
12. My job is to paint the sets.
13. What is your job?
14. This play has its problems.
15. One actor must change his costume quickly.
16. The actors practice their lines every day.
17. We want to make our play a success.

LEVEL **C.** Write each sentence. Use a possessive pronoun in place of the underlined word or words.

18. The audience laughed at Jim's character.
19. Janet's and Laura's costumes were striking.
20. Susan's posters for the play were beautiful.
21. "Tom's family bought six tickets," said Tom.
22. "Did Dawn's family like the play?" I asked Dawn.
23. "Dawn's parents applauded the loudest," said Dawn.
24. Mr. Goh set out cookies for the students' families.
25. "We are proud of the school's students," Mr. Goh said.

GRAMMAR

EXTRA PRACTICE

Three levels of practice

Using *I* and *me* Correctly (page 366)

LEVEL **A.** Complete each sentence with the correct word in parentheses ( ).

1. June and (I, me) started a softball team.
2. The players met with her and (I, me).
3. Carl and (I, me) want new uniforms.
4. He and (I, me) discussed the cost of the uniforms.
5. The team and (I, me) will raise the money.
6. June told Carl and (I, me) about her idea.
7. June and (I, me) talked about uniform colors.
8. Carl and (I, me) went to tell the other players.
9. They agreed with Carl and (I, me) about the plan.

LEVEL **B.** Use *I* or *me* to complete each sentence correctly.

10. Cam, Carl, and _____ will walk the dogs.
11. Mrs. Brown hired Tad and _____ as errand runners.
12. That seems like a good job for Tad and _____ .
13. Tim, you and _____ could wash windows.
14. My parents can use Roz and _____ at the car wash.
15. Diane and _____ will run a lemonade stand.
16. She and _____ will raise money that way.
17. The lemonade will taste good, especially to Diane and _____ .

LEVEL **C.** Write each sentence. Choose the correct group of words in parentheses ( ) to complete each sentence.

18. (Emma and I, Me and Emma) want blue uniforms.
19. Rachel asked (her and me, me and her) for red ones.
20. (I and she, She and I) found it hard to choose.
21. (Me and Jon, Jon and I) went to the mall.
22. Emma came with (Jon and I, Jon and me).
23. (Emma and I, Emma and me) picked the uniforms.
24. (Jon and I, I and Jon) hope the team will like them.
25. The team thanked (Emma, Jon, and I; Emma, Jon, and me) for our help.

EXTRA PRACTICE

Three levels of practice

Mechanics: Pronoun Contractions (page 368)

LEVEL **A.** In each sentence a contraction is underlined. Write the two words that were joined to form each contraction.

1. Jen says she's chosen a new hobby.
2. She'll learn to do magic tricks.
3. It's something everyone likes.
4. We're invited to her first magic show.
5. Lenny says he'll come, too.
6. I know you'll enjoy it.
7. You've an interesting hobby.
8. I'd like to raise tropical fish, too.
9. It'll be fun to watch them.

LEVEL **B.** Write each sentence. Underline the contraction. Then write the two words that form the contraction.

10. I'd like a collection of shells.
11. They're pretty and unusual.
12. Rick says he's found a big conch shell.
13. I've found a lovely purple shell.
14. It's the prettiest shell in my collection.
15. Perhaps we'll trade shells.
16. My sister said she'd buy me a big shell.
17. We've seen fascinating shells in the museum.

LEVEL **C.** Write each sentence, using a contraction for the underlined words.

18. We are going on a hike.
19. They will join us.
20. He will take a map of the forest.
21. You had better wear comfortable shoes.
22. I will bring a picnic lunch.
23. It will be a long hike.
24. We have never walked this far before.
25. We will be home by dark.

GRAMMAR

PRACTICE + PLUS

Three levels of additional practice for a difficult skill

Pronoun Contractions (page 368)

LEVEL **A.** Write each sentence. Underline the contraction. Then write the two words that form the contraction.

1. I'm happy about our move to California.
2. We'll live near the ocean.
3. I've never seen the Pacific Ocean before.
4. It's bigger and colder than the Atlantic.
5. I'll watch the surfers.
6. They've a lot of courage.
7. We're a family that loves the beach.
8. My sister says she'll swim every day.
9. I'd like that, too.

LEVEL **B.** Write each sentence. Replace the underlined words with a contraction.

10. <u>I will</u> be glad when we reach Tulsa.
11. <u>It is</u> the home of my friend, Nathan.
12. <u>He is</u> the best friend I ever had.
13. In Vermont, <u>we would</u> always play together.
14. <u>We have</u> been apart for two years.
15. I wonder if <u>we will</u> still like each other.
16. <u>He has</u> made many new friends in Tulsa.
17. Perhaps <u>they will</u> be his best friends now.

LEVEL **C.** Complete each sentence with a pronoun contraction.

18. ______ be happy when school is out.
19. ______ made a lot of plans for summer.
20. ______ visit my grandmother.
21. ______ my favorite relative.
22. ______ work in her garden.
23. ______ the best garden I have ever seen.
24. ______ let me pick apples from the tree.
25. ______ taste delicious.

EXTRA PRACTICE

GRAMMAR

Three levels of practice

Vocabulary Building: Homophones/Homographs (page 370)

LEVEL **A.** Write the words in each sentence that look or sound alike. Then write whether they are **homophones** or **homographs.**

1. Be careful not to squash that squash.
2. We rode down the road on our bikes.
3. Do you want to come, too?
4. We have four books for you.
5. Can you open this can?
6. Please write the letter right away.
7. We can't hear you from here.
8. It only took a second to eat my second sandwich.

LEVEL **B.** Write each sentence, using the correct homophone from the pair in parentheses ( ).

9. That (ring, wring) has a beautiful stone.
10. I will (ring, wring) out these wet clothes.
11. Bart (threw, through) out the trash.
12. Are you (threw, through) with your homework?
13. Have you (heard, herd) the news?
14. Mr. Brown sold his (heard, herd) of cows.
15. The (hole, whole) school is going on a picnic.
16. Be careful of the (hole, whole) in the sidewalk.

LEVEL **C.** Choose the correct meaning of the underlined homograph. Write **a** or **b**.

17. The boy climbed the palm to get a coconut.
    a. tropical tree   b. part of the hand
18. We've had a spell of hot weather.
    a. period of time   b. name the letters of
19. I like to loaf on a hot summer day.
    a. mass of bread   b. relax
20. Ernesto wound the rope around the pole.
    a. a deep cut   b. wrapped

WRITING

UNIT 12

Writing Persuasive Paragraphs

Read the quotation and look at the picture on the opposite page. Talk about the ways you can make your opinion known.

When you write to persuade, you present your ideas in a way that will persuade your audience to feel the way you feel.

Focus Persuasive writing encourages an audience to share the writer's beliefs.

What do you have a definite opinion about? How could you persuade someone to share your opinion? On the following pages you will read a story about a girl who has definite opinions. You will find some photographs, too. You can use both the story and the photographs to give you ideas for writing.

THEME: *DECISIONS*

. . . there are no pat solutions, but rather, growth and discovery, with more struggles ahead to be met, one hopes, with greater strength and insight.

—Myron Levoy

LITERATURE

Reading Like a Writer

AWARD WINNING SELECTION

Think about a time when you felt proud. What made you feel that way?

Noreen loves her father, but she does not feel good about his fish store and the way it looks. She wants to be proud of her father and his shop. She wants her father to feel proud, too.

As you read the selection, pay attention to the example Noreen sets for her father and how Noreen's father changes as a result.

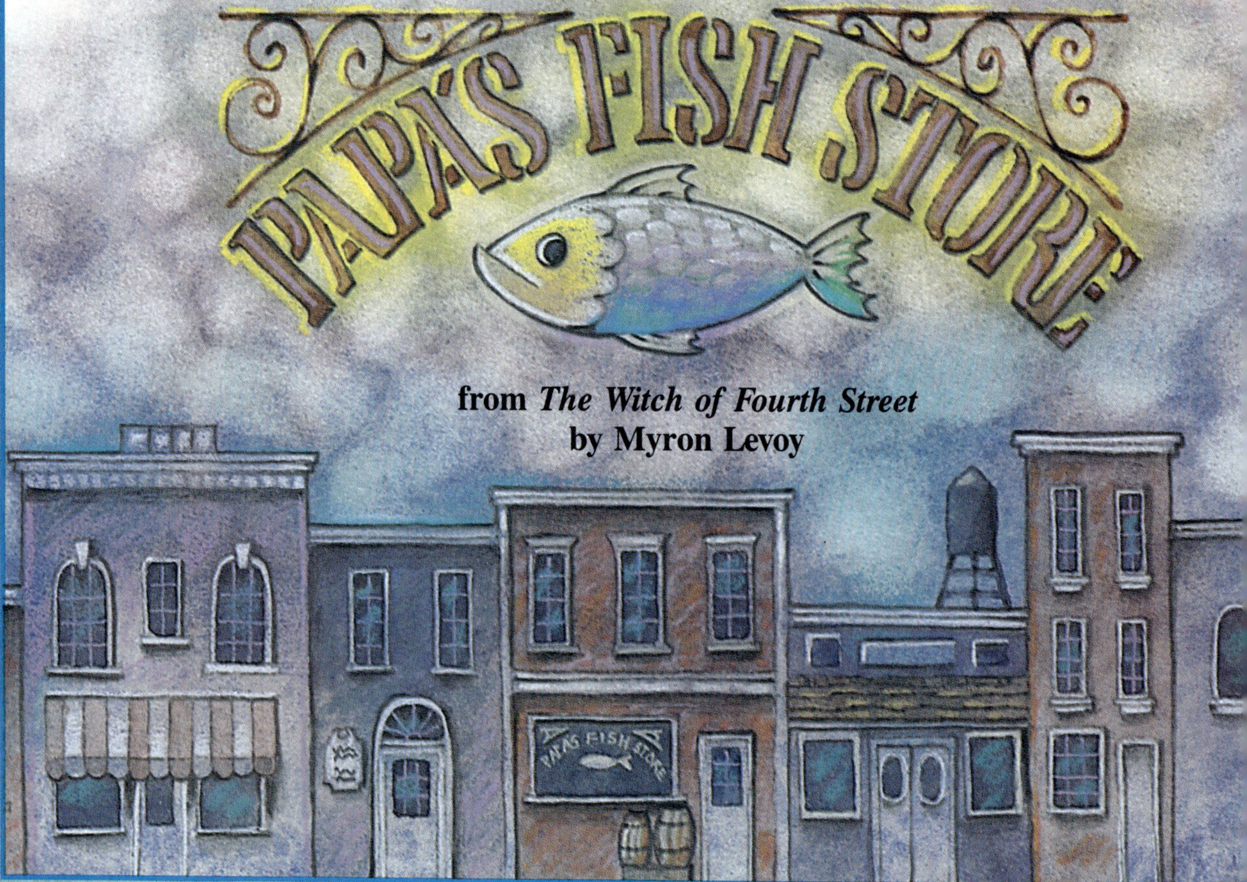

from *The Witch of Fourth Street*
by Myron Levoy

Noreen Callahan was convinced that her father's fish store on Second Avenue was, without a doubt, the ugliest fish store on the East Side. The sawdust on the floor was always slimy with fish drippings; the fish were piled in random heaps on the ice; the paint on the walls was peeling off in layers; even the cat sleeping in the window was filthy. Mr. Callahan's apron was always dirty, and he wore an old battered hat that was in worse shape than the cat, if such a thing were possible. Often, fish heads would drop on the floor right under the customer's feet, and Mr. Callahan wouldn't bother to sweep them up. And as time passed, most of his customers went elsewhere for their fish.

The writer introduces the character and setting.

Mr. Callahan had never wanted to sell fish in a fish store. He had wanted to be an actor, to do great, heroic, marvelous things on the stage. He tried, but was unsuccessful, and had to come back to work in his father's fish store, the store which was now his. But he took no pride in it; for what beauty was possible, what marvelous, heroic things could be done in a fish store?

Noreen's mother helped in the store most of the week, but Saturday was Noreen's day to help while her mother cleaned the house. To Noreen, it was the worst day of the week. She was ashamed to be seen in the store by any of her friends and classmates, ashamed of the smells, ashamed of the fish heads and fish tails, ashamed of the scruffy cat, and of her father's dirty apron. To Noreen, the fish store seemed a scar across her face, a scar she'd been born with.

Noreen's feelings are described here.

And like a scar, Noreen carried the fish store with her everywhere, even into the schoolroom. *Fish Girl! Fish Girl! Dirty Fish Girl!* some of the girls would call her. When they did, Noreen wished she could run into the dark clothes closet at the back of the room and cry. And once or twice, she did.

But pleasant things also happened to Noreen. A few weeks before Christmas, Noreen was chosen to play an angel in the church pageant, an angel who would hover high, high up on a platform above everyone's head. And best of all, she would get to wear a beautiful, beautiful angel's gown. As beautiful as her mother could make it.

Mrs. Callahan worked on the angel's gown every night, sewing on silver spangles that would shine a thousand different ways in the light. And to go with the gown, she made a sparkling crown, a tiara, out of cloth and cardboard and gold paint and bits of clear glass.

On the day of the pageant, Noreen shone almost like a real angel, and she felt so happy and light that with just a little effort she might have flown like a real angel, too. And after the pageant, Noreen's mother and father had a little party for her in their living room. Mr. Callahan had borrowed a camera to take pictures of Noreen in her angel's gown. "To last me at least a year of looking," he said.

For though Mr. Callahan hated his fish store, he loved Noreen with a gigantic love. He often told Noreen that some children were the apple of their father's eye, but she was not only the apple of his eye, but the peach, pear, plum, and apricot, too.

And Noreen would ask, "And strawberry?"

"Yes," her father would say. "You're the fruit salad of m'eye, that's what you are. Smothered in whipped cream."

And so he took picture after picture with the big old camera that slid in and out on a wooden frame. Noreen had a wonderful time posing with her friend Cathy, who had also been an angel in the pageant. But the party came to an end as all parties must, and it was time to take off the angel's gown and the tiara, and become Noreen Callahan again. How heavy Noreen felt after so much lightness and shining. Into the drawer, neatly folded, went the heavenly angel. "Perhaps next year," her mother said, "we'll have it out again."

That night, Noreen dreamed that she was dancing at a splendid ball in her dress of silver and her crown of gold. Round and round the ballroom she went, as silver spangles fluttered down like snow, turning everything into a shimmering fairy's web of light. And then she was up on her toes in a graceful pirouette. Everyone watched; everyone applauded. As she whirled, her dress opened out like a great white flower around her and . . . suddenly she felt herself sliding and skidding helplessly. She looked down; the silver spangles had changed to fish scales. The floor was covered with fish heads and fish tails and slimy, slippery sawdust. And everyone was calling: *Fish Girl! Fish Girl! Fish Girl!*

Noreen awoke, not knowing quite where she was for a moment. Then she turned over in bed and cried and cried, till she finally fell asleep again.

The next week passed in a blur of rain and snow that instantly turned to slush. Every day, when she came home from school, Noreen looked at the dress lying in the drawer. *Wear me, wear me,* it seemed to say. But Noreen just sighed and shut the drawer, only to open it and look again an hour later.

And then, all too soon, it was Saturday. The day Noreen dreaded. Fish store day. How she wished she could turn into a real angel and just fly away.

Noreen finds a solution to her problem.

Suddenly Noreen sat down on her bed. She knew it was decided before she could actually think. The angel gown! How could anyone wait a year to have it out again? She would wear it now. Now! In her father's store. And then people would know that she had nothing to do with that dirty apron and filthy floor. And perhaps those children would stop calling her Fish Girl. She would be a Fish Angel now.

Mrs. Callahan saw the gown under Noreen's coat, as Noreen was about to leave the house. She rarely scolded Noreen, but this was too much! It was completely daft! That gown would be ruined; her father would be very angry. Everyone would laugh at her; everyone would think she was crazy! But Mrs. Callahan saw that nothing, absolutely nothing, could stop Noreen. And she finally gave in, but not before warning Noreen that next year she would have to make her own dress. An angel's gown in a fish store! Why it was almost a sin!

When Noreen arrived at the fish store and took off her coat, Mr. Callahan was busy filleting a flounder. But when he saw Noreen he gasped and nicked himself with the knife.

"Aggh!" he called out, and it was a cry of surprise at the gown, and anger at Noreen, and pain from the cut, all in one. He nursed his finger, not knowing what to say to Noreen in front of all those customers.

"What a lovely gown," said a woman.

"What happened?" asked another. "Is it a special occasion?"

"His daughter," whispered a third. "His daughter. Isn't she gorgeous?"

And Mr. Callahan simply couldn't be angry anymore. As the customers complimented him on how absolutely beautiful his daughter looked, he felt something he hadn't felt for a long, long time. He felt a flush of pride. Perhaps marvelous things, even heroic things *could* be done in a fish store.

Mr. Callahan watched Noreen as she weighed and wrapped the fish, very, very carefully so as not to get a single spot on her dress. Wherever she moved, his eyes followed, as one follows the light of a candle in a dark passage.

And toward the end of the day, Mr. Callahan took off his filthy apron and his battered hat. He went to the little room in the back of the store, and returned wearing a clean, white apron.

Christmas came and passed, and New Year's, and Noreen wore her gown and tiara every Saturday. And more and more customers came to see the girl in the angel gown. Mr. Callahan put down fresh sawdust twice a day, and laid the fish out neatly in rows, and washed and cleaned the floors and window. He even cleaned the cat, and one night in January he painted the walls white as chalk. And his business began to prosper.

The writer describes the outcome of the story here.

The children who had called Noreen *Fish Girl* called her nothing at all for a while. But they finally found something which they seemed to think was even worse. *Fish Angel,* they called her. *Fish Angel.* But Noreen just smiled when she heard them, for she had chosen that very name for herself, a secret name, many weeks before.

And Saturday soon became Noreen's favorite day of the week, for that was the day she could work side by side with her father in what was, without a doubt, the neatest, cleanest fish store on the East Side of New York.

Thinking Like a Reader

1. How did Mr. Callahan change at the end of the story?
2. What did Noreen do to cause her father to change? Have you ever tried to get someone to change? What did you do?

Write your responses in your journal.

Thinking Like a Writer

3. How does the author show that Noreen has successfully changed her father's attitude about the store?
4. Which details help you to clearly see the change in Mr. Callahan's feelings?

Make a list of the details you like best.

Responding to

LITERATURE

Brainstorm

Vocabulary

In "Papa's Fish Store" the author shows that people often feel strongly about something. Noreen felt that the store was "without a doubt, the ugliest fish store." Saturday became "the worst day of the week." Think of some things about which you feel strongly. In your journal write words and phrases that describe your feelings. Begin to create a personal vocabulary list. You can use these words and phrases in your writing.

Talk It Over

Take Pride

Noreen is proud of her costume. Play this game in a circle. Start by saying what makes you proud: "I am proud of my writing." Call on someone to go next. He or she might say, "I am proud of the way I play basketball." Continue until everyone has had a turn.

Quick Write

Write a Speech

Imagine that you have been asked to give a one-minute speech about something that makes your town feel proud. Write a beginning paragraph for your speech. Include three reasons why people are proud. Here is an example:

> Our town park is beautiful. The grass and flowers are well cared for. There are many litter baskets. You will not find empty cans and bottles lying about in *our* park. We are all very proud of it.

Idea Corner

Think About Things You Feel Strongly About

You have been thinking about things that you feel strongly about, things about which you might like to persuade others to feel as you do. In your journal make two lists. Label one "Things I Feel Good About." Your second list should be labeled "Things I Don't Like."

PICTURES SEEING LIKE A WRITER

Finding Ideas for Writing

Look at the pictures. Think about what you see. What ideas for writing a persuasive paragraph do the pictures give you? Write your ideas in your journal.

NIGERIA
MÉXICO IS READY...
LONDON

BALLOT BOX

DON'T BUG ME
Have incoming fruit inspected...please.

WRITING TOGETHER

1 GROUP WRITING: Persuasive Paragraphs

COOPERATIVE LEARNING

The **purpose** of persuasive writing is to persuade an **audience** to feel the way the writer does. What makes persuasive writing convincing?

- Opinions Clearly Stated
- Order of Reasons
- Facts That Support the Opinions

Opinions Clearly Stated

Read the following paragraph. Think about what makes the underlined sentence special.

> Our class should fix up the vacant lot next to our school. It will be a wonderful way for us to show that we care about our environment. Planning the project will help us learn to work together. Fixing up the lot would not be expensive. It would cost only $10 for us to buy seeds and fertilizer to make a beautiful garden there. We could borrow gardening tools from our families and neighbors. This will also keep our expenses low. Perhaps we can set an example for others to follow. We will all work together toward a cleaner community.

The writer begins with a topic sentence that states her opinion clearly. The other sentences give strong and exact reasons that support her opinion. Did you notice the persuasive words such as *wonderful, only,* and *beautiful*?

Guided Practice: Writing a Topic Sentence

With your class, complete the topic sentence below.

It is a good idea to _____ .

Example: It is a good idea to eat a balanced diet.

Order of Reasons

In a persuasive paragraph, the topic sentence usually states an opinion. It is followed by reasons that support it.

In the paragraph about a class project, the writer mentions that fixing up the lot is a wonderful way to show concern for the environment. Because that is her most important reason, she gives it first. Look back at the paragraph.

- What other reasons does the writer mention?
- Do these reasons support her main idea?
- How does she end her paragraph?

Facts That Support the Opinions

In the paragraph the writer gives facts that support her opinion. A **fact** can be proved or checked. It is possible to check how much seeds and fertilizer cost. It can be proved that borrowing tools instead of buying them will save money. An **opinion** tells what a speaker or writer believes. An opinion cannot be checked. Which reasons given in the paragraph cannot be proved?

It is a good idea to back up your opinions with facts. Facts may help you to convince your audience that your opinion is sound.

Guided Practice: Listing and Ordering Reasons

Recall the topic sentence that you created on page 398. As a class, list reasons to support your topic sentence. Write the reasons in complete sentences. Vote on the best order in which to list those reasons.

Examples: Reason 1: Good health depends on the foods you eat.
Reason 2: Some foods give you a lot of energy.
Reason 3: Others provide the protein you need to build strong bones.
Reason 4: Different vitamins are found in different foods.

Putting a Persuasive Paragraph Together

With your classmates, you have begun to write a persuasive paragraph. You have written a topic sentence. You have listed reasons that support the topic sentence, and have arranged your reasons in the order of their importance.

Now you can complete your paragraph. Look at the paragraph on page 398 again. Reread the last sentence. The writer ended her paragraph with a strong and convincing statement summing up her reasons for wanting to clean up the lot.

Guided Practice: Writing a Persuasive Paragraph

Complete your persuasive paragraph. Think about your purpose and your audience. Have you listed strong reasons that will convince your audience? Remember to give your strongest reason first. Make sure that you back up your opinions with facts. Use persuasive language in your paragraph. Add a final sentence that makes a convincing statement.

Share your paragraph with a classmate. Ask your classmate to suggest where you might have used more facts or given your reasons in a more logical order.

Checklist: Persuasive Writing

When you write a persuasive paragraph, you will want to keep some points in mind. You can use a checklist to remind yourself of the things you will want to include in your paragraph.

Look at this checklist. Some points need to be added. Make a copy of the checklist and finish it. Keep the copy in your writing folder. You can use it when you write your persuasive paragraph.

CHECKLIST

- ✓ Purpose and ______
- ✓ Good topic sentence
- ✓ Opinions clearly stated
- ✓ Order of reasons
- ■ ______
- ■ ______
- ■ ______
- ✓ Facts that support ______
- ✓ Persuasive language
- ✓ Convincing final ______

2 THINKING AND WRITING: Telling Fact from Opinion

You know that good persuasive writing clearly states what a writer believes, and gives reasons to support that opinion. The writer often includes facts to convince his or her audience.

Remember that a **fact** is a statement that can be proved or checked. It is always true for everyone. An **opinion** is something that is believed by someone. It may not be true for everyone all of the time. An opinion cannot be proved or checked.

Look at this page from a writer's journal.

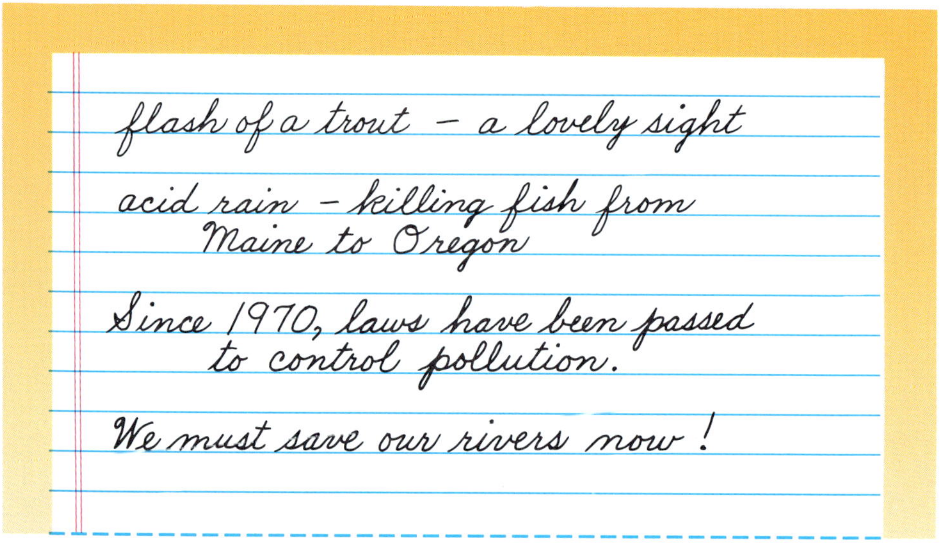

Thinking Like a Writer

- Which facts could the writer use to convince his audience that it is important to stop the pollution of America's rivers?

The second and third items are facts. They can be proved. When you write a persuasive paragraph, you may use facts, opinions, or both, to support your topic sentence. It is usually a good idea, however, to use facts to back up your opinions. A reader is more likely to be persuaded by facts or a combination of facts and opinions than by opinions alone. You should also decide which reasons are the most important and the most likely to convince your audience.

THINKING APPLICATION Telling Fact from Opinion

COOPERATIVE LEARNING

Each of the writers named below is planning to write a persuasive paragraph. They have written topic sentences and have listed several reasons that support their topic sentences. Help each writer decide which reasons are facts and which are opinions. Write each topic sentence and the reasons that support it on a separate sheet of paper. Then write **fact** or **opinion** next to each reason. You may wish to discuss your thinking with other students. In your discussions, explain how you decided whether a statement was a fact or an opinion.

1. James: Crowds of tourists are destroying many of our national parks.

   The number of visitors to our national parks increases every year.
   People always are careless when they are on vacation.
   City dwellers do not know how to behave in the wild.
   When hikers leave the trails, many wildflowers and other plants are crushed.
   Visitors to national forests start more than five thousand forest fires a year.

2. Jeanne: National parks are a good place in which to see wildlife.

   Bald eagles are beautiful to watch.
   Whales have been spotted from the shores of Glacier Bay National Park.
   Nothing is as much fun to watch as a grizzly cub.
   Some rare animals live in Badlands National Park, which is located in South Dakota.
   Alligators sun themselves in the swamps of Everglades National Park.

WRITING PROCESS

3 INDEPENDENT WRITING: Persuasive Paragraphs

Prewrite: Step 1

At this point, you have learned many things about writing a persuasive paragraph. Now, you are ready to write a persuasive paragraph of your own. Marisa, a student your age, wanted to convince her classmates that helping other people would be a good class project. She chose her topic this way.

Choosing a Topic

1. First, Marisa wrote down a list of the kinds of things students can do to help others.
2. Next, she thought about each activity and how it would help people.
3. Last, she decided on the activity that she thought would most interest her classmates.

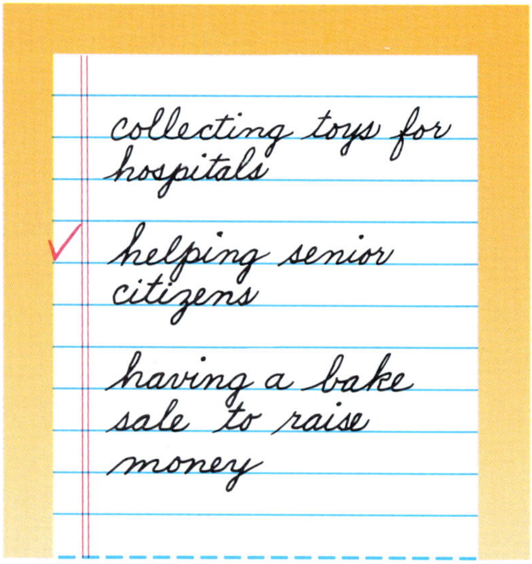

Marisa decided that her classmates would like the second activity best. She narrowed her topic to one way of helping. She chose to write about doing errands for senior citizens.

Exploring Ideas: Brainstorming Strategy

Marisa knew that her purpose for writing was to persuade her classmates to choose a class project that would help others. Before beginning to write, she brainstormed for sound reasons that would support her opinion. She tried to think of as many reasons as possible. She wrote these reasons on a chart under the headings *Facts* and *Opinions*.

After Marisa finished her chart, she made some changes. She numbered her reasons in the order of their importance. She crossed out one reason.

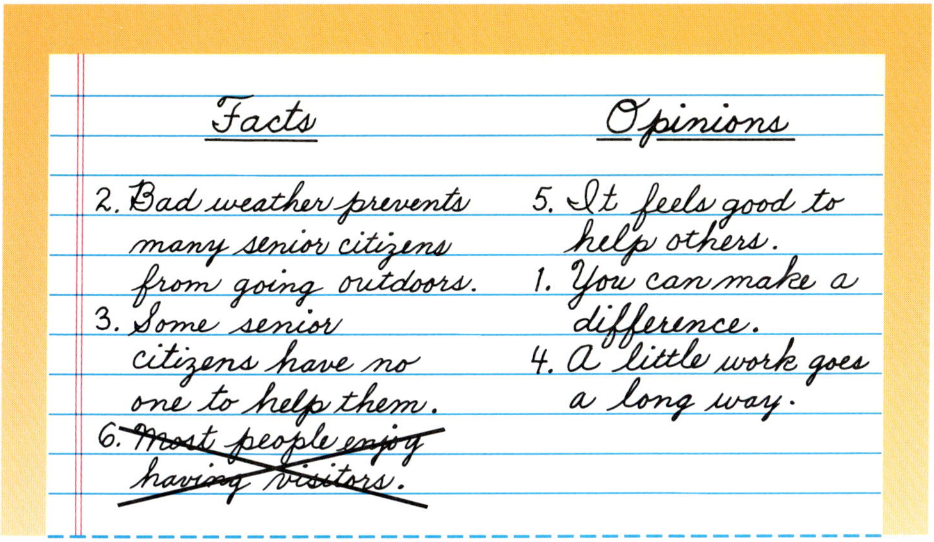

Thinking Like a Writer

- What reason does Marisa believe is the most important?
- What did she cross out? Why do you think she did this?

YOUR TURN

JOURNAL

Think of something about which you feel strongly. It should be something that you would like others to feel the same way about. Use **Pictures** or your journal for ideas. Follow these steps.

- Make a list of possible topics.
- Choose the one you like best.
- Narrow your topic if it is too broad.
- Brainstorm for a topic sentence and reasons to support it.
- Think about your purpose and audience.

Make a fact and opinion chart. Remember, you can add to or take away from your chart at any time.

WRITING PROCESS

Write a First Draft: Step 2

Marisa knows how to put a persuasive paragraph together. She used a planning checklist. Marisa is now ready to write her first draft.

Marisa's First Draft

A good project for our class would be running errands for senior citizens. You can make a difference. In bad weather many senior citizens can not go out. Many have no one to help them. A little work on you're part can go a long way toward making their lives easier.

While Marisa was writing her first draft, she did not worry about errors. She will revise her paragraph later.

Planning Checklist
- Remember purpose and audience.
- Begin with a topic sentence.
- Write reasons in order of importance.
- Include facts to support opinions.
- Use persuasive language.
- End with a convincing statement.

YOUR TURN

Write your first draft. As you prepare to write, ask yourself these questions.

- What will my audience want to know?
- What reasons should I give to persuade my audience to feel as I do?

TIME-OUT You might want to take some time out before you revise. That way you will be able to revise your writing with a fresh eye.

Revise: Step 3

After she finished her first draft, Marisa read it over to herself. Then she shared her writing with a classmate. She wanted some suggestions for improvement.

Marisa then looked back at her planning checklist. She had forgotten the point about ending with a convincing statement. She checked it off so that she would keep it in mind when she revised her paragraph. Marisa now has a checklist to use as she revises.

Marisa made changes in her paragraph. She did not correct small errors. She knew she could fix them later.

The revisions Marisa made changed her paragraph. Turn the page. Look at Marisa's revised draft.

Revising Checklist

- Remember purpose and audience.
- Begin with a topic sentence.
- Write reasons in order of importance.
- Include facts to support opinions.
- Use persuasive language.
- ✓ End with a convincing statement.

Marisa's Revised Draft

A good project for our class would be running errands for senior citizens. You can make a difference. In bad weather many senior citizens can not go out~~. Many~~ and have no one to help them. A little work on you're part can go a long way toward making their lives easier. It feels good to help others. Try it!

Thinking Like a Writer

WISE WORD CHOICE

- Which sentences did Marisa add? How does adding these sentence improve her paragraph?
- Which sentences did Marisa combine? How does combining them improve the paragraph?

YOUR TURN

Read your first draft. Make a checklist. Ask yourself these questions.

- Will my paragraph persuade my audience?
- Is my topic sentence supported by reasons?
- How can I improve my paragraph? Can I improve my paragraph by adding facts or by changing the order of my reasons?

If you wish, ask a friend to read your paragraph and make suggestions. Then, revise your paragraph.

Proofread: Step 4

Marisa knew that her work was not complete until she proofread her paragraph. She used a proofreading checklist while she proofread.

Marisa's Proofread Draft

¶ A good project for our class would be running errands for senior citizens. You can make a difference. ! In bad weather many senior citizens can not cannot go out . and Many have no one to help them. A little work on you're your part can go a long way toward making their lives easier. It feels good to help others. Try it!

YOUR TURN

Proofreading Practice

Below is a paragraph that you can use to practice your proofreading skills. Find the errors. Write the paragraph correctly on a separate piece of paper.

> Its always a good idea to follow traffic rules when you ride a Bike. If you ride against traffic, cars mite not see you. if you ignore lights, you could hurt someone who is walking across the street. Their were four accidents on main street last year, and all of them involved Bike riders.

Proofreading Checklist

- Did I indent my paragraph?
- Did I spell all words correctly?
- Which punctuation errors do I need to correct?
- Which capitalization errors do I need to correct?

WRITING PROCESS

Applying Your Proofreading Skills

Now proofread your persuasive paragraph. Read your checklist again. Review **The Grammar Connection** and **The Mechanics Connection,** too. Use the proofreading marks to mark changes.

THE GRAMMAR CONNECTION

Remember these rules about pronouns.

- *I, you, he, she, it, we,* and *they* are subject pronouns.
- *Me, you, him, her, it, us,* and *them* are object pronouns.

Check your persuasive paragraph. Have you used pronouns correctly?

THE MECHANICS CONNECTION

Remember this rule about contractions.

- Use an apostrophe to stand for the letters that are left out in a contraction.

  it is — it's   you will — you'll

Check your persuasive paragraph. Have you used apostrophes correctly?

Proofreading Marks

¶ indent
∧ add
℮ take out
≡ make a capital letter
/ make a small letter

Publish: Step 5

Marisa made a neat, final copy. She pinned it on the class bulletin board next to the Suggestions Corner. Many of Marisa's classmates said that they would vote for her suggestion. Marisa had persuaded her classmates to feel the way she did.

YOUR TURN

Make a neat, final copy of your persuasive paragraph. Think of a way to share your paragraph. You might want to use one of the ideas in the **Sharing Suggestions** box below.

SHARING SUGGESTIONS

Send your paragraph to your school newspaper.	Read your work aloud to your classmates.	Make a poster that will persuade people to feel as you do.

4 SPEAKING AND LISTENING: Listening for Persuasive Techniques

When you write to persuade, you use facts and opinions to persuade people to feel the way you do. People who write advertisements and commercials also write to persuade. They use persuasive language as well as facts and opinions to persuade people to buy a certain product.

Read these statements from a commercial.

1. For the best chicken, you can't beat Chicken Pete.
2. Everyone you know eats at Chicken Pete.
3. Chicken Pete is the king of Bar-B-Q.

The statements above may look like facts, but they would be very hard to prove. Statement 3, in addition, uses persuasive language. It contains a **charged word.** Charged words are often used in advertisements to persuade an audience. They are words that create strong feelings in listeners. The word *king* in this sentence is a charged word. You know that a king has the highest position in a country. The writer of the commercial is trying to convince you that Chicken Pete is the best Bar-B-Q restaurant in the land. Can you think of some other charged words? Look for words that make a person, place, or product appear to be all good or all bad.

When you listen to advertisements and commercials, pay attention to the statements that are made. If you listen carefully, you can tell the difference between facts and opinions. You will recognize when the writer is using persuasive language.

- How can careful listening make me a better consumer?

SPEAKING APPLICATION A Commercial

Think of a product you would like to persuade your classmates to buy. Write a short commercial for the product. It may be funny or serious. Use persuasive language and as many charged words in your ad as you can. Read your commercial aloud. Remember that you are trying to persuade your audience to buy your product. Emphasize the important words. Speak with strong feeling. Your classmates will be using the guidelines below as they listen to your commercial.

LISTENING GUIDELINES: A Commercial

1. Listen closely to the speaker's words.
2. Remember that the speaker's purpose is to persuade.
3. Listen for statements that sound like facts but would be very hard to prove.
4. Listen for statements of opinion that use charged words.

WRITING EXTENSION

5 WRITER'S RESOURCES: The Atlas and the Almanac

You know that when you write a persuasive paragraph, you should support your opinions with facts. Using a reference book is a good way to find the specific facts you need. Two reference books that you will find particularly helpful are the atlas and the almanac.

An **atlas** is a book of maps. It usually contains several kinds of maps for one area. For example, you might find a political map, a rainfall map, a relief map, and a map that shows the natural resources of the United States all in one atlas.

An **almanac** contains many kinds of information. A new almanac is published every year. Therefore, it provides fairly up-to-date information. It gives facts about populations, current events, famous people, sports, elections, and many other subjects.

Professor Gruber is writing an article about Atlantis, an ancient Greek island that is supposed to have sunk into the sea many centuries ago. The professor wants to convince people that Atlantis was once connected to the Greek island of Thira. He believes that part of Thira sank after a volcano erupted.

Professor Gruber wonders whether any volcanoes are still active in Greece. He looks up *volcanoes* in an almanac. You will see one of the tables he finds on page 415.

Active Volcanoes—Europe		
Country	**Volcano**	**Last Activity**
Norway	Beerenberg	1985
Iceland	Helgafell	1973
Italy	Stromboli	1986
Italy	Etna	1987

From this table Professor Gruber can see that no volcanoes have erupted recently in Greece. Which country had a volcanic eruption in 1987?

Practice

Professor Gruber has some more questions. Copy the number of each question on a separate piece of paper. Write **atlas** or **almanac** next to each to tell which reference book the professor should use to find the answers.

1. How far is Thira from Athens?
2. Is Thira the smallest island in the Aegean?
3. Does Greece have many mountains?
4. What lies due west of Thira?
5. What is the current population of Greece?
6. Is Thira north or south of Rhodes?
7. What is the average rainfall in Greece during the month of January?
8. What kind of money do Greeks use?
9. Did any Greek athlete win a gold medal in the 1988 Olympics?
10. Who is the American ambassador to Greece?

WRITING APPLICATION Research Questions

Think of a country you would like to visit some day. Write ten questions about the country. Decide which ones could be answered using an atlas or an almanac. Save the list in your writing folder. You will use it in the **Curriculum Connection** on the next page.

Writing About Social Studies

People are social. They live in small family groups, larger community groups, and still larger groups as nations. Social studies is mainly the study of people—where they live, what they believe, what work they do, what kind of government they have, and what they did in the past.

The writers who write about social studies usually write history books or biographies. However, a newspaper reporter who writes about a court case is writing about social studies. A speech writer, who writes for a political candidate, is writing about social studies, too.

ACTIVITIES

Atlas/Almanac Search Use an atlas and an almanac to answer the questions you wrote in the last lesson. Share your answers with the class. If you cannot find the answers, check an encyclopedia.

Summarize a News Story Read the front page of your local newspaper. Find a story that you think will be important in the history of the United States. Write a summary of the story.

Respond to Literature The following description is taken from the book *About Us*. People everywhere are both different and the same all at once. After reading the description, write a response. Your response may be a letter to a Dyak boy or girl telling about your own home and family. Perhaps you'd like to write a paragraph comparing and contrasting your town with the Dyak village. Tell what you would like or not like about life in a Dyak longhouse.

Many families—One house

In most villages around the world, you'll find lots of houses. But on the island of Borneo, a Dyak village may have only one house! That's because the house is a village all by itself!

A Dyak house, called a longhouse, may be a block long. And it may be the home for as many as 50 families. Sometimes these families are all related to one another. Each family has its own sleeping room and place to work. The rest of the house is one enormous room, which the families share. There is also a porch on one side of the house.

During the day, almost everyone in the longhouse does some kind of job. The men and older boys hunt, fish, or mend tools. Women work on the longhouse farm, or make baskets, clothes, and blankets. Children gather food for the pigs and chickens. But at night, everyone takes it easy. The families eat together. Then the big room of the longhouse becomes filled with the sounds of music, dancing, and laughter until bedtime.

UNIT CHECKUP

LESSON 1

Group Writing: A Persuasive Paragraph (page 398)

Write five persuasive phrases that could support the topic sentence below.

In towns, people should walk their dogs on a leash.

LESSON 2

Thinking: Telling Fact from Opinion (page 402)

Copy each sentence. Write **fact** or **opinion** next to each.

1. People should only drink bottled water.
2. Tap water may contain rust or dirt.
3. Rio Blanco water is delicious.
4. Bottled water costs more than tap water.
5. Every citizen has the right to clean water.

LESSON 3

Writing a Persuasive Paragraph (page 404)

Imagine that you work for the Chamber of Commerce in your town. Your job is to persuade people to move to your town. Write a persuasive paragraph for a brochure called *Move to Our Town.*

LESSON 4

Speaking and Listening: Listening for Persuasive Techniques (page 412)

List two things that you should listen for when you hear a commercial.

LESSON 5

Writer's Resources: Atlas and Almanac (page 414)

Write **atlas** or **almanac** to tell where you would find the answers to these questions

1. Who is the Egyptian head of state?
2. Which countries border Egypt?
3. Is Egypt next to Saudi Arabia?

THEME PROJECT A DEBATE

The people in the picture below are holding a **debate.** They have different opinions on important issues. Each would like to persuade the audience that he or she is right. The people in the audience will make their own decision. One person is guiding the debate. That person is the **moderator.** The moderator's job is to keep the debaters on the topic and to allow each person a chance to speak.

Think of a topic that you and a group of your classmates would like to debate. Your class will be the audience.

- There are two sides in every debate. Decide who will talk in favor of and who will speak against the topic.
- Research the topic. Get all the facts.
- Choose a moderator to guide the debate.
- Ask your audience to decide which side has presented the more persuasive argument.

UNIT 13

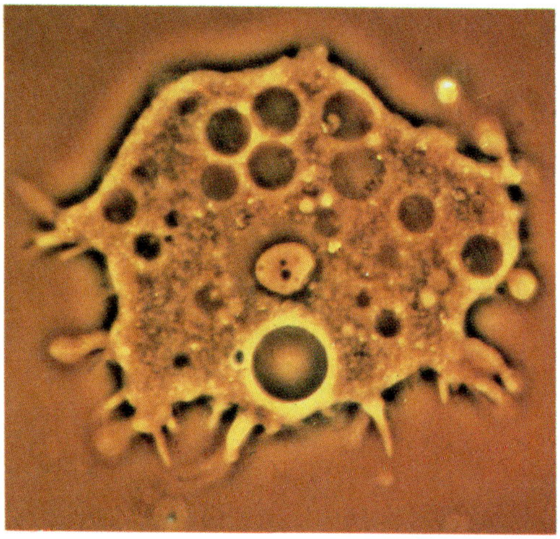

Adverbs

In this unit you will learn about adverbs. Adverbs add detail to what you say and write. You can use adverbs to tell *where, when,* and *how.*

Discuss Read the poem on the opposite page. What do you think the poet is looking for?

Creative Expression The unit theme is *Searches.* What would you do if you discovered that something important to you was missing? Write a list in your journal of the steps you would need to take to conduct a search.

JOURNAL

THEME: *SEARCHES*

Searching,
forever searching,
Looking,
but never finding.
Day and night,
my eyes roam the world.

—Alonzo Lopez,
from "Endless Search"

1 WHAT IS AN ADVERB?

An adverb is a word that tells more about a verb.

You know that a verb expresses action. An adverb tells *how, when,* or *where* an action takes place. Many adverbs end with *ly*.

	Tim searches.
how?	Tim **carefully** searches.
when?	**Today,** Tim searches.
where?	Tim searches **everywhere.**

Guided Practice

Tell which word in each sentence is an adverb. Then tell which verb each adverb describes.

Example: Bette sits sadly in the chair. *sadly sits*

1. Bette's book suddenly disappeared.
2. She saw it yesterday.
3. She looks upstairs.
4. Finally, she finds it.
5. She carefully returns the book to the shelf.

?! **THINK**

- How do I decide if a word is an adverb?

GRAMMAR

REMEMBER

- An **adverb** tells more about a verb.
- An adverb tells *how, when,* or *where.*

More Practice

A. Write each sentence. Draw two lines under each adverb. Then draw one line under the verb that the adverb describes.

Example: Bob recently started a detective agency.

6. Lisa once lost a pen.
7. She called Bob immediately.
8. He patiently questioned Lisa and her friends.
9. Lisa described the pen carefully.
10. She used that pen daily.
11. Bob quickly looked at his notes.
12. He searched the house thoroughly.
13. Finally, he found the lost pen.
14. Lisa happily thanked him.

B. Write each sentence. Underline each adverb. Then write whether the adverb tells **how, when,** or **where.**

Example: Often people find lost items in strange places. *when*

15. Once a man caught a large fish.
16. Inside he found a diamond ring.
17. My dog, Pepper, always hides her bones.
18. She secretly finds new hiding places.
19. Pepper never fools us.
20. Sometimes we find a bone under the bed.

Extra Practice, page 442

WRITING APPLICATION A Skit

COOPERATIVE LEARNING

Work in a small group to write a short skit about finding something that was lost. Perform your skit for the class. Ask your classmates to jot down the adverbs as you use them.

2 MORE ABOUT ADVERBS

You have learned that an adverb is a word that tells more about a verb. It tells *how, when,* or *where.* An adverb can be put at the beginning of a sentence, before or after the verb, or at the end of a sentence.

Quickly, Jason ran to the store.
Jason ran **quickly** to the store.
Jason **quickly** ran to the store.
Jason ran to the store **quickly.**

Guided Practice

Tell whether the underlined adverb tells **how, when,** or **where.**

Example: Jimmy walked slowly through the stores in the mall.
how

1. He looked carefully for his little brother.
2. Stan never stayed in one place.
3. Loudly, Jimmy shouted Stan's name.
4. Finally, Jimmy found Stan.
5. He was there next to the toy counter.

?! THINK

- How can I decide whether a word is an adverb or an adjective?

REMEMBER

- An **adverb** tells more about a verb, while an adjective describes a noun.

More Practice

A. Write each sentence. Write whether the underlined adverb tells **how, when,** or **where.**

Example: Darryl always enjoys watching birds. *when*

6. Eagerly, Darryl joined the bird-watchers' club.
7. The group often hikes and climbs.
8. They hiked high into the mountains.
9. Red-shouldered hawks soared upward.
10. Downy woodpeckers scratched noisily.
11. The group members usually carry binoculars.
12. The binoculars greatly magnify the birds.
13. Darryl can clearly see markings on each bird.

B. Write each sentence. Choose the adjective or adverb in parentheses ( ) that correctly completes the sentence.

Example: Each spring I wait (eager, eagerly) for the first robin.
Each spring I wait eagerly for the first robin.

14. The robins that nest under our eaves return (regular, regularly).
15. (Careful, Carefully), they choose bits of twigs and straw.
16. They chirp (loud, loudly) in their nests.
17. They sit on their (delicate, delicately) eggs.
18. (Slow, Slowly), the eggshells crack.
19. The chicks are (helpless, helplessly).
20. One day they will fly (confident, confidently).

Extra Practice, page 443

WRITING APPLICATION A Letter

Make a list of the birds you saw this week. Use your list to write a letter to a friend describing the birds. Have a partner find three adverbs in the letter.

3 USING ADVERBS TO COMPARE

Remember that an adjective can compare two or more nouns. An adverb can also be used to make comparisons.

Dan ran **fast.**
Amy ran **faster** than Dan.
Noah ran the **fastest** of all.

Add *er* to a short adverb to compare two actions. Add *est* to a short adverb to compare more than two actions.

The words *more* and *most* are usually used to form comparisons with adverbs that end in *ly* and with longer adverbs.

Dan ran **quickly.**
Amy ran **more quickly** than Dan.
Noah ran the **most quickly** of all.

Use *more* to compare two actions. Use *most* to compare more than two actions. When you use *more* or *most,* do not use the ending *er* or *est.*

Guided Practice

Tell which form of the adverb in parentheses ( ) correctly completes the sentence.

Example: This year the treasure hunt began (earlier, earliest) than last year. *This year the treasure hunt began earlier than last year.*

1. Ann's team started (sooner, soonest) than mine.
2. The first clue was hidden the (more, most) carefully.
3. Lynn solved it (more, most) quickly than I.
4. Sal searched the (harder, hardest) of all.

?! **THINK**

- How can I decide which form of an adverb to use when making a comparison?

REMEMBER

- Add *er* or use *more* when two actions are compared.
- Add *est* or use *most* when more than two actions are compared.

More Practice

Write each sentence. Use the correct form of the adverb in parentheses ( ) to complete the sentence.

Example: On our team, who worked the (faster, fastest) of all?
On our team, who worked the fastest of all?

5. The next clue was the (harder, hardest) of all.
6. Of all the trees, which grows the (taller, tallest)?
7. Mark climbed (higher, highest) than anyone else.
8. The last clue puzzled us the (more, most) deeply.
9. Juan answered this (more, most) easily than I.
10. Barry cheered the (louder, loudest) of us all.
11. The Phoenicians sailed the (more, most) skillfully of all.
12. Their ships crossed the sea (faster, fastest) than any other.
13. Columbus tried the (harder, hardest) to find a route to India.
14. Ponce de León searched the (more, most) unsuccessfully.
15. He looked (longer, longest) than anyone else for the Fountain of Youth in Florida.
16. Cortés treated the Aztecs (more, most) cruelly than others.
17. Robert Peary reached the North Pole (sooner, soonest) of all.
18. No one in the Lewis and Clark expedition crossed the Rockies (more, most) joyfully than Sacajawea.
19. Jacques-Yves Cousteau has shown us undersea life (more, most) clearly than any other diver.
20. He has journeyed (deeper, deepest) into the ocean than others.

Extra Practice, page 444

WRITING APPLICATION A Set of Clues

Imagine that you are planning a treasure hunt. Write some clues. Then identify the adverbs that compare.

4 USING *GOOD* AND *WELL* CORRECTLY

You know that an adjective describes a noun, and an adverb tells more about a verb. Be careful not to confuse the adjective *good* with the adverb *well*.

Good is an adjective. It describes a noun. It may come before the noun, or it may follow a linking verb. *Well* is usually an adverb. It tells more about a verb.

Adjective
Bill reads a **good** book.
The book is **good.**

Adverb
Bill reads **well.**
The author writes **well.**

Guided Practice

Tell which word in parentheses ( ) correctly completes the sentence.

Example: Bill wanted a (good, well) topic for his report.
Bill wanted a good topic for his report.

1. This book gives a (good, well) account of the Gold Rush.
2. The author knows the subject (good, well).
3. Bill studies the book (well, good).
4. He is a (good, well) student.
5. The book is a (good, well) introduction to an interesting subject.

?! **THINK**

■ How do I decide when to use *good* or *well?*

REMEMBER

- *Good* is an adjective. Use it to describe a noun.
- *Well* is often an adverb. Use it to tell more about a verb.

More Practice

A. Write each sentence. Choose the word in parentheses ( ) that correctly completes the sentence.

Example: The Gold Rush makes a (good, well) story.
The Gold Rush makes a good story.

6. The writer Bret Harte described it (good, well).
7. It is a (good, well) example of how eagerly people search for riches.
8. California in 1848 is a (good, well) starting point for the story.
9. One man had (good, well) luck; he found gold.
10. The newspapers reported this event (good, well).
11. People left (good, well) jobs to go West.
12. They hoped that their luck would be (good, well).
13. The Gold Rush was (good, well) for many businesses.

B. Complete each sentence with either **good** or **well.**

Example: People in the mining camps didn't live _____ . *well*

14. _____ food was frequently not available.
15. Sanitary conditions were seldom _____ .
16. The chances of finding gold, however, were not _____ .
17. Californians knew very _____ that the gold could not last forever.
18. Those who found gold lived _____ .
19. They settled _____ into their new lives.
20. The Gold Rush brought many _____ things to California.

Extra Practice, page 445

WRITING APPLICATION A Narrative

Write a paragraph about searching for gold or silver. Your paragraph will be more exciting if you describe some dangers in the search. Be sure you use *good* and *well* correctly.

G R A M M A R

5 NEGATIVES

Some sentences include the word *no,* or other words that mean "no." These words are **negatives.** Some negatives contain the word *no.*

nothing, nobody, nowhere, none, no one

Others include the contraction *n't.*

can't, don't, won't, couldn't, wouldn't

Never use two negatives in a sentence. You will need to change one of the negatives without changing the meaning of the sentence.

INCORRECT: He **didn't** tell **no one** where the treasure is.
CORRECT: He **didn't** tell **anyone** where the treasure is.

INCORRECT: We **won't never** discover it.
CORRECT: We **won't** ever discover it.
We will **never** discover it.

Notice that there is often more than one way to correct a sentence that has two negative words.

Guided Practice

Find the negative in each sentence.

Example: There is nothing new under the sun. *nothing*

1. The search for new inventions never stops.
2. Nobody can predict the future.
3. Not every invention is very useful.
4. We can't stop progress.
5. We wouldn't want it any other way.
6. Our world wouldn't be the same without inventions.

?! **THINK**

- How do I decide whether I have used too many negatives in a sentence?

REMEMBER

■ Never use two **negatives** in the same sentence.

More Practice

A. Write each sentence. Then underline the negative in each one.

Example: No invention was more important than the wheel. *No*

7. The wheel does not exist in nature.
8. Don't underestimate the importance of the wheel.
9. Further progress wasn't possible without it.
10. Before the Stone Age, people didn't have tools.
11. Nobody knows who invented these early tools.
12. Records and diagrams are nowhere to be found.
13. The alphabet had not yet been invented.

B. Write each sentence. Choose the correct word in parentheses ( ) to complete the sentence.

Example: There isn't (no, any) limit to our imagination. *There isn't any limit to our imagination.*

14. We won't (ever, never) stop needing new ideas.
15. (Can, Can't) we find no new sources of energy?
16. We don't make full use of solar power (anywhere, nowhere).
17. We (must, mustn't) never forget water power.
18. We (should, shouldn't) never ignore the use of windmills.
19. Someday no car (will, won't) be without a solar battery.
20. We shouldn't overlook (any, no) promising invention.

Extra Practice, Practice Plus, pages 446–447

WRITING APPLICATION Instructions

Plan an invention that will make daily life easier. Write a description of your invention and instructions for how to use it. Include some warnings about what *not* to do when using it.

GRAMMAR

6 MECHANICS: Punctuating Titles

When you write, you may need to name a book or story that you have read. When you write titles, there are certain rules to follow.

The first, last, and all important words in a title should be capitalized. Underline titles of books, magazines, and newspapers. Use quotation marks to punctuate titles of articles, stories, songs, and poems.

Book: Little House on the Prairie	Article: "All About Ants"
Magazine: Ranger Rick	Story: "The Fun They Had"
Newspaper: My Weekly Reader	Song: "America, the Beautiful"
	Poem: "Rain in the City"

Guided Practice

Tell which words in each book title should be capitalized.

Example: a lion to guard us *A Lion to Guard Us*

1. citizen of the galaxy
2. beyond the divide
3. bridge to terabithia
4. a sound of chariots
5. henry and the clubhouse
6. soup in the saddle

THINK

■ How do I decide which words to capitalize in a title?

REMEMBER

- Capitalize the first, last, and all important words in a title.

More Practice

A. In each of the following sentences, a title is underlined. Write each sentence, and capitalize the title correctly.

Example: Look for a bear called Paddington in the library.
A Bear Called Paddington

7. Susie looked for u.s.a. today at the library.
8. Bob asked the librarian about the magazine sports and fitness.
9. The librarian told Lisa about the book demo and the dolphin.
10. She thought Tina would enjoy a cricket in times square.
11. Marcia found encyclopedia brown takes the case.
12. Then she read the book a light in the attic.
13. Beryl enjoyed the magazine called world of photography.
14. She saw beautiful pictures in a book called the rain forest.
15. Dan read about bats in the magazine science for everyone.
16. Zach found my side of the mountain.
17. My favorite book is the search for delicious.

B. Write each of the following titles correctly.

Example: if once you have slept on an island (poem)
"If Once You Have Slept on an Island"

18. over the top (poem)
19. sing a song (song)
20. the washington post (newspaper)
21. newsweek (magazine)
22. national parks (article)
23. scope (magazine)
24. it's a small world (song)
25. never on time (poem)

Extra Practice, page 448

WRITING APPLICATION A Review

Write a short review of a book or magazine you enjoyed reading. Be sure that you have written the title correctly.

G R A M M A R

7 VOCABULARY BUILDING: Borrowed Words

The English language has many words that come from other languages. Some of these words came across the sea when people from different countries settled here. With time, the words became part of our own language. Several Native American words entered English as well. We call these words **borrowed words.** A dictionary often will tell you from which language a borrowed word comes.

Here are some examples of borrowed words.

mesa (Spanish)
avenue (French)
pasta (Italian)
banjo (African)
raccoon (Native American)
piano (Italian)

Guided Practice

Tell which word from the list above best completes each sentence.

Example: Far in the distance across the plain we saw the flat-topped _____ . *mesa*

1. We call a large street an _____ .
2. A _____ looks something like a guitar.
3. A _____ has a bushy striped tail.
4. Dora loves _____ with tomato sauce.
5. On stage the musician sat down at the large musical instrument called a _____ .

?!

THINK

- How can I find out from which language a borrowed word comes?

REMEMBER

- A dictionary often tells you from which language a **borrowed word** comes.

GRAMMAR

More Practice

A. Write each sentence. Complete the sentence with the correct word from the list below. Use a dictionary if you need help.

tepees	chef
kimono	ukulele
koala	

Example: Janet strummed a Hawaiian instrument called a ____ . *ukulele*

6. The French word for a master cook is _____ .
7. Some Native Americans lived in tents called _____ .
8. Carrie wore a Japanese robe called a _____ .
9. A _____ is an animal found in Australia.

B. The names for the foods below have come into English as borrowed words. Write each food name. Then write the letter of the correct description.

Example: yogurt *a*

10. pretzel **11.** tortilla **12.** spaghetti

a. A Turkish food made from milk
b. The Italian name for a long, thin type of pasta
c. The Spanish name for a pancake made from cornmeal
d. The German name for a bread stick shaped like a knot

Extra Practice, page 449

WRITING APPLICATION A Short Report

COOPERATIVE LEARNING

Work with a partner to find the origin of one of these borrowed words: *kowtow, fez, igloo, crepe, karate.* Using a dictionary, write a short report about the word.

GRAMMAR AND WRITING CONNECTION

Combining Sentences

Writers frequently use words and phrases that tell *how, when,* or *where.* These words add detail and color to descriptive writing and help the reader to see what is happening. When you use words and phrases in your own writing that tell *how, when,* or *where,* look for ways to combine sentences that have similar ideas.

Look at the sentences below. Notice how the two short sentences have been combined to make a more exact and more interesting sentence.

The train left the station. It left at noon.
The train left the station at noon.

Working Together

COOPERATIVE LEARNING

With your classmates, talk about each group of sentences. Then tell how you would combine them to make a single sentence.

Example: Lina came to Kathy's house. It was one o'clock.
Lina came to Kathy's house at one o'clock.

1. Lina looked for Kathy. She looked everywhere.
2. Kathy had left the house. She had left early.
3. Lina waited for Kathy. She waited patiently.

Revising Sentences

Joel wrote these sentences for a story about two friends. Help him revise his sentences by combining each group of sentences. Join words in each group that tell *how, when,* or *where.*

4. Then Lina became worried. She ran outside.
5. She knew that Kathy liked to go to the caves. She went there often.
6. Lina found the caves. She found them easily.
7. She called into the caves. She called Kathy's name loudly.
8. A voice answered faintly. It came from inside.
9. Lina climbed into the cave. She went cautiously.
10. Kathy sat on the cave floor. She sat unharmed.
11. Lina saw Kathy and ran to her. She ran quickly.
12. "I had forgotten all about the time," Kathy said. She said it quietly.

WRITER AT WORK

Imagine that you are a television news reporter. You must write a news report about a search for a group of campers who are lost in a forest. When you revise your report, combine any sentences you can. Be sure that your sentences tell in a clear and interesting way *how, when,* and *where* the events took place.

UNIT CHECKUP

LESSON 1

What Is an Adverb? (page 422) Write each sentence. Draw two lines under each adverb. Draw one line under the verb.

1. Once, we lost our parakeet.
2. We looked everywhere for it.
3. We searched the room carefully.
4. Suddenly, we heard a familiar sound.
5. Happily, we opened the closet door.
6. There was our bird, safe and sound.

LESSON 2

More About Adverbs (page 424) Choose the word in parentheses ( ) that correctly completes the sentence.

7. Inez looked through the (powerful, powerfully) telescope.
8. A star shone (bright, brightly) in the sky.
9. It was the (large, largely) planet, Venus.
10. The moon sank (slow, slowly) from sight.
11. (Sudden, Suddenly), a comet streaked by.
12. Inez followed it (close, closely) with the telescope.

LESSON 3

Using Adverbs to Compare (page 426) Use the correct form of the adverb in parentheses ( ) to complete each sentence.

13. Bill uses the library (oftener, more often) than I do.
14. He can find books (faster, fastest) than I can.
15. Our library is arranged (more, most) simply than others are.
16. Finding books takes (long, longer) than finding magazines.
17. I read fiction (more, most) frequently than nonfiction.

LESSON 4

Using *good* and *well* Correctly (page 428) Write either **good** or **well** to complete each sentence.

18. A _____ detective asks many questions.
19. Sorting out the clues must be done _____ .
20. This is an example of _____ detective work.
21. Descriptions of lost objects must be _____ .
22. The detective must search the area _____ .
23. If the search is done _____ , the object will reappear.

LESSON 5

Negatives (page 430) Choose the correct word in parentheses ( ) to complete each sentence.

24. Some questions don't have (any, no) answers yet.
25. Doesn't (anybody, nobody) know about life on other planets?
26. We don't have (any, no) cure for some diseases.
27. Nobody (has, hasn't) been able to control the weather.
28. We won't (ever, never) have all the answers.
29. We (should, shouldn't) not stop our search.

LESSON 6

Mechanics: Punctuating Titles (page 432) Write each of the following titles correctly.

30. the new york times (newspaper)
31. snow white and rose red (story)
32. how to install a telephone (article)
33. a tale of two cities (book)
34. sweet betsy from pike (song)
35. young miss (magazine)

LESSON 7

Vocabulary Building: Borrowed Words (page 434) Each word in the left-hand column is borrowed from another language. Write each word. Next to it, write the letter of the correct description.

36. kimono	a. a word for a cook
37. tepee	b. a type of pasta
38. spaghetti	c. a Native American tent
39. chef	d. an Australian animal
40. koala	e. a Japanese robe

Writing Application: Adverb Usage (pages 422–431) The following paragraph contains ten errors with adverbs. Rewrite the paragraph correctly.

41.–50. I searched impatient for a present for my sister. It was more late than I thought. I had not planned good. I looked quick at toys. None was well. Then I thought sudden of a book I used to like. She could read it easy. She reads most fast than others in her class. That book would definite be well.

ENRICHMENT

ADVERB MADNESS

Two or more students can play this game.

The first player says aloud a simple sentence that includes an adverb: "Jim laughed happily."

The second player repeats the sentence and adds an adverb: "Jim laughed happily and loudly."

The next player might say: "Jim laughed happily, loudly, and long."

When a player forgets the sentence or can't add to it, that player is "out."

STUMP THE EXPERTS

Have a group of students use the dictionary to make a list of words that come from other languages, such as *dachshund, opera, menu,* and *sombrero.*

Another group will be the "experts." They must give the meaning of each word and use it in a sentence. Score one point for each correct meaning and sentence. The highest-scoring "expert" wins. Then, the first group should tell the language from which each word comes.

Imagine that you are a book publisher. Make a list of new books that you will publish this year. They can have silly titles and funny names of authors. For example:

I Don't Get It by Ida Noe
Yawn by R.U. Tired
Slow and Steady by E.Z. Duzit

A World of Adverbs

Make a humorous drawing, with people, animals, or things performing a variety of actions. Label the figures with "signs" that include a verb in the *ing* form and an adverb.

CREATIVE EXPRESSION

Oh, Susanna
I come from Alabama
With a banjo on my knee,
I'm going to Louisiana,
My true love for to see.

Chorus
Oh, Susanna,
Oh, don't you cry for me,
I come from Alabama
With my banjo on my knee.

It rained all night the day I left,
The weather it was dry;
The sun so hot I froze to death;
Susanna, don't you cry.

Chorus
Oh, Susanna,
Oh, don't you cry for me,
I come from Alabama
With my banjo on my knee.

—Stephen Foster

Like poems, the lyrics of songs have a steady beat or rhythm. Usually the lines in a song end with words that rhyme.

The song on this page is probably familiar to you. It is made up of several verses and a chorus. The verses and the chorus are each four lines long. Notice that in each of them the second and fourth lines rhyme. In a song the verses change but the chorus remains the same. The second verse of this song is a "nonsense" verse. First, the words say one thing, and then they say the opposite; the verse does not make sense. As you read the lyrics of "Oh, Susanna," think about the rhythm and the rhymes.

TRY IT OUT!

Try writing another verse for "Oh, Susanna." Your verse should fit the melody, and it should be followed by the chorus. You might want to write a "nonsense" verse, or you might tell a story. Remember to make the second and fourth lines rhyme.

EXTRA PRACTICE

Three levels of practice

What Is an Adverb? (page 422)

LEVEL **A.** A verb in each of the following sentences is underlined. Write each sentence. Draw two lines under the adverb that describes the underlined verb.

1. We carefully searched for the house.
2. Earlier, we had lost the address.
3. We knew exactly what the house should look like.
4. Jeremy glanced quickly around the neighborhood.
5. Suddenly, he stopped and stared at a building.
6. "This is it," he told us excitedly.
7. We quickly walked to the front door.
8. The bell rang loudly.
9. Soon, the door opened.
10. "Grandpa," we shouted noisily, "we love your new house."

LEVEL **B.** Write each sentence. Draw two lines under each adverb. Then draw one line under the verb it describes.

11. Jill and Pete really love birds.
12. They trotted quickly through the park.
13. "Look hard for the woodpeckers," said Jill.
14. They searched carefully, but found no birds.
15. Finally, Pete understood the problem.
16. "We are walking noisily," he said.
17. They stood quietly and waited.
18. Soon, many beautiful birds appeared.

LEVEL **C.** Write each sentence. Underline each adverb. Then write whether the adverb tells **how, when**, or **where.**

19. We sometimes overlook the simplest answers.
20. Mrs. Troob frantically searched for her eyeglasses.
21. She had dropped them carelessly.
22. Wendy looked everywhere for her coat.
23. Later, she found it in the closet.
24. Mark sadly cried because his dog was lost.
25. The dog was sleeping happily in the doghouse.

EXTRA PRACTICE

GRAMMAR

Three levels of practice

More About Adverbs (page 424)

LEVEL A.

Write each sentence. Write whether the underlined adverb tells **how, when,** or **where.**

1. Sherri arrived at the baseball game early.
2. She waited eagerly for the first pitch.
3. The team had won many games lately.
4. The first batter hit the ball upward.
5. The shortstop caught it easily.
6. Loudly, the crowd cheered.
7. The next batter swung at the ball smoothly.
8. The center fielder ran hurriedly toward the ball.
9. Then, he stood and watched it fly over the fence.
10. "A home run," Sherri thought sadly.

LEVEL B.

Write each sentence. Choose the word in parentheses ( ) that correctly completes each sentence.

11. (Recent, Recently), Phil made dinner for his family.
12. He prepared the food (happy, happily).
13. The soup he made was (thick, thickly).
14. The stew was (delicious, deliciously).
15. He set the table (nice, nicely).
16. The family ate (hungry, hungrily).
17. They enjoyed the meal (great, greatly).
18. Everyone (quick, quickly) cleared the table.

LEVEL C.

Write each sentence. Fill in the blank with an adverb of your own that tells *how, when,* or *where.*

19. Julius started his garden _____ . (when)
20. He dug the soil _____ . (how)
21. The sun shone on his garden _____ . (how)
22. _____ , tiny shoots broke through the soil. (when)
23. The vegetables grew _____ . (how)
24. He picked them and brought them _____ . (where)
25. We will cook them _____ . (when)

EXTRA PRACTICE

Three levels of practice

Using Adverbs to Compare (page 426)

LEVEL **A.** Write each sentence and underline the form of the adverb that shows a comparison.

1. People fly more often than they used to.
2. An airplane travels faster than a train does.
3. The Concorde flies the fastest of all.
4. Passengers fly more comfortably in large planes.
5. Airports are planned more carefully now.
6. Air traffic has increased more rapidly than expected.
7. Planes take off from Chicago more frequently than from Miami.
8. Planes leave Atlanta the most frequently of all.
9. Passengers move more quickly on moving sidewalks than on foot.
10. Trams carry people the most quickly of all.

LEVEL **B.** Write each sentence. Use **more** or **most** to complete the sentence.

11. Airports are used (more, most) heavily in the summer.
12. Which airport is used the (more, most) heavily of all?
13. Air traffic in our area has increased (more, most) steadily than in other areas.
14. Airports near a city are reached (more, most) easily than those farther away.
15. Do travelers use airplanes (more, most) readily than they use cars?
16. Some people fly (more, most) eagerly than others.
17. Perhaps pilots fly the (more, most) happily of all.

LEVEL **C.** Write each sentence. Use the correct comparative form of the adverb in parentheses ( ).

18. Kim lives _____ to the airport than I do. (close)
19. Planes fly _____ over her house than over mine. (low)
20. Planes fly the _____ possible near the airport. (low)
21. Kim sees planes _____ than most people do. (clearly)
22. She can identify them _____ than I can. (accurately)
23. She flies the _____ of all her friends. (frequently)
24. Planes interest her _____ than anything else does. (deeply)
25. She reads _____ about airplanes than about any other topic. (often)

EXTRA PRACTICE

GRAMMAR

Three levels of practice

Using *good* and *well* Correctly (page 428)

LEVEL **A.** Each of the following sentences contains the adjective *good* or the adverb *well.* Write each sentence. Then underline the noun that *good* describes or the verb that *well* describes.

1. Columbus was a good navigator.
2. "There is a good chance that the world is round."
3. "With good luck I could sail around the world."
4. Columbus planned his voyage well.
5. He prepared well for the journey.
6. He chose three good, sturdy ships.
7. He outfitted them well.
8. Queen Isabella treated Columbus well.
9. She gave him money to pay for good sailors.
10. "I'll repay you well," Columbus told her.

LEVEL **B.** Write each sentence. Use **good** or **well** to complete the sentence.

11. Columbus's idea was (good, well).
12. A new route to the East would be (good, well).
13. His ships sailed (good, well).
14. The crew was trained (good, well).
15. They were provided with (good, well) food.
16. Columbus knew that a hungry sailor would not work (good, well).
17. The crew must be in a (good, well) mood.

LEVEL **C.** Write each sentence. Write either **good** or **well** to complete the sentence correctly.

18. There was _____ weather most of the time.
19. The ships performed _____ during the storms.
20. The crews were made up of _____ sailors.
21. They did their jobs _____ .
22. The trip's length, however, was not _____ for them.
23. They wondered whether their captain's judgment was _____ .
24. A view of land was _____ for their spirits.
25. The trip turned out _____ after all.

EXTRA PRACTICE

GRAMMAR

Three levels of practice

Negatives (page 430)

LEVEL **A.** Write each sentence. Then underline the negative in each one.

1. Frank can't locate his skates.
2. He couldn't find them in the closet.
3. Nobody has seen them.
4. None of his friends has seen them.
5. "You weren't careful," says his sister.
6. "That's not much help," Frank answers.
7. "They are nowhere to be found," Frank tells Alan.
8. "I won't be able to play hockey today."
9. "Isn't it possible that you left them in school?"
10. "I've never left them there before," says Frank.

LEVEL **B.** Write each sentence. Choose the correct word in parentheses ( ) to complete the sentence.

11. Craig never loses (anything, nothing).
12. He doesn't ever fail to return (any, no) library books.
13. He isn't (ever, never) forgetful.
14. He won't go (anywhere, nowhere) without careful planning.
15. I haven't ever met (anyone, no one) like him.
16. None of my other friends (is, isn't) like that.

LEVEL **C.** Each of the following sentences has a double negative. Rewrite each sentence correctly. There may be more than one correct way to rewrite each sentence.

17. We couldn't find our dog, Feather, nowhere.
18. Feather wasn't never lost before.
19. She had never even caused no mischief.
20. Nobody didn't see Feather for days.
21. Finally, she returned when none of us wasn't around.
22. We don't have no idea where she had gone.
23. She won't go nowhere again.
24. We don't let her stay outside alone no more.
25. It isn't no fun to lose a pet.

PRACTICE + PLUS

Three levels of additional practice for a difficult skill

Negatives (page 430)

LEVEL **A.** Write each sentence. Then draw a line under the negative in each one.

1. Stan has never gone to a football game.
2. He doesn't like the game.
3. "It is not easy to understand," Stan says.
4. "I don't know why people enjoy it so much."
5. "Nowhere else in the world is football so popular."
6. None of Stan's friends agrees with him.
7. "Wouldn't you like us to explain the plays?" they ask.
8. "The rules aren't hard to learn."
9. "Stan, won't you come to a game with us?"
10. "No," said Stan, "I'd rather stay at home."

LEVEL **B.** Write each sentence. Choose the correct word in parentheses ( ) to complete the sentence.

11. Nobody in Carrie's family (would, wouldn't) eat the food she made.
12. She wasn't (any, no) good as a cook.
13. No one ever liked (any, none) of her meals.
14. The spices weren't (ever, never) right.
15. Don't (any, none) of her dishes ever taste good?
16. Carrie doesn't listen to (anybody, nobody).
17. She (will, won't) never learn the right way to cook.

LEVEL **C.** Read each sentence. Next to each sentence that is correct, write **correct.** Rewrite each incorrect sentence.

18. Hannah didn't never play a sport.
19. She said she didn't like sports.
20. She wasn't no good at softball.
21. Nobody never taught her how to play.
22. None of Hannah's friends liked sports either.
23. They never went to no school games.
24. "You don't know how much fun sports can be," said Mrs. Perez.
25. "You won't never know unless you give them a try."

EXTRA PRACTICE

Three levels of practice

Mechanics: Punctuating Titles (page 432)

LEVEL A. In each of the following sentences, a title is underlined. Write each sentence, and capitalize each title correctly.

1. My favorite book is <u>the wind in the willows</u>.
2. Don's mother writes for <u>the miami herald</u>.
3. <u>How to train your parakeet</u> is a useful book.
4. Our textbook is called <u>macmillan language arts today</u>.
5. Leila subscribes to <u>better homes and gardens</u>.
6. I read <u>cheaper by the dozen</u> for my report.
7. I would recommend that you read <u>dear mr. henshaw</u>.
8. Debbie reported on the book <u>and now miguel</u>.
9. I enjoyed reading <u>arthur for the very first time</u>.
10. Did you like <u>james and the giant peach</u>?

LEVEL B. Write each of the following titles correctly.

11. the los angeles times (newspaper)
12. the cry of the crow (book)
13. the care of tropical fish (article)
14. sports illustrated (magazine)
15. a simple song (song)
16. daddy fell into the pond (poem)
17. the fox and the goat (story)
18. stopping by woods on a snowy evening (poem)
19. why there are four seasons in the year (story)

LEVEL C. Write each sentence. Capitalize each title correctly. Add quotation marks or underline where they are needed.

20. Every week Jenny reads the magazine newsweek.
21. Have you seen my book, alice in wonderland?
22. The westwood daily is an excellent newspaper.
23. Kay has read the book charlotte's web twice.
24. The pictures in the article birds of the world are beautiful.
25. Does the library have the book mr. revere and i?

EXTRA PRACTICE

GRAMMAR

Two levels of practice

Vocabulary Building: Borrowed Words (page 434)

LEVEL **A.** Write each sentence. Complete the sentence with the correct word from the list below. Use a dictionary if you need help.

bazaar	sherbet	bronco	rouge	pecan
mosquito	mayonnaise	tepee	macaroni	hamburger

1. The Turkish word for a frozen desert is _____ .
2. The Spanish called an untamed horse a _____ .
3. The Persians called an outdoor market a _____ .
4. A _____ is a Native American tent.
5. Order _____ on your sandwich, and you're using a French word.
6. The Spanish name for a small insect is _____ .
7. One kind of Italian pasta is called _____ .
8. The name of a kind of makeup, _____ , comes from the French word for red.
9. Native Americans called a kind of nut a _____ .
10. A chopped meat patty, or _____ , is named after a German city.

LEVEL **B.** Each of the words in the left-hand column is borrowed from another language. Write each word, and next to it write the letter of the correct description from the right-hand column.

11. tea	a. an Algonquian name for a small animal
12. barbecue	b. perfumed water named after a German city
13. pajamas	c. a Chinese name for a drink made from leaves
14. skunk	d. German for a school for young children
15. bouquet	e. Hindi for a loose-fitting shirt
16. cologne	f. a Caribbean style of outdoor cooking
17. umbrella	g. a bunch of flowers, in French
18. omelet	h. a Latin word for a doorway
19. exit	i. a French dish made with eggs
20. kindergarten	j. an Italian word for something that protects you from the rain

MAINTENANCE

UNIT 1: Understanding Sentences

Subjects and Predicates (pp. 8, 10, 12) Write each sentence. Then, draw a line between the complete subject and the complete predicate. Next, draw one line under the simple subject and two lines under the simple predicate. Finally, if a group of words is not a sentence, write **not a sentence.**

1. The new school opened this year.
2. The children walk to the school.
3. My friends peeked into our class.
4. The books on the tables.

Compound Subjects and Predicates (p. 14) Write each sentence. Then, draw a line between the subject and the predicate. Finally, underline the two main words in the compound subject and the compound predicate.

5. The coach and team walked and jogged to the starting line.
6. Parents and friends cheered loudly and waved from the bleachers.
7. Knees and hands bent and flexed at the starter's voice.
8. The starter's arm and hand rose and signaled the racers.

Correcting and Punctuating Run-on Sentences (pp. 16, 18) Write the sentences below. Rewrite each run-on sentence correctly as two sentences.

9. Set out the glasses our guests are arriving.
10. How many people are coming what fun a surprise party is!
11. Please help me with these sandwiches where are the plates
12. Jamal will be here soon we must all quietly hide and yell "Surprise!"

Using Context Clues (p. 20) Write the meaning of the underlined word in each sentence. Then write the word or words that you used as context clues.

13. In ancient times people made paper from <u>papyrus</u>, which grew by rivers.
    a. plants b. dirt
14. Egypt <u>exported</u> its papyrus to other countries.
    a. bought from b. sold to
15. European <u>scribes</u> frequently wrote on paper made from the skins of animals.
    a. speakers b. writers

UNIT 3: Using Nouns

What Is a Noun? (p. 76) Write each sentence. Capitalize each proper noun. Then underline all the nouns.

16. The library has several books on florida.

17. Did diane choose this state for a report in class?

18. Pictures of plants and animals in the everglades are wonderful.

19. The teacher has set aside twenty minutes for each talk.

Singular and Plural Nouns (pp. 78, 80, 82) Write the plural of each noun. Then write the singular and possessive form of each noun.

20. city

21. man

22. goose

23. mouse

24. sheep

UNIT 5: Using Action Verbs

Action Verbs, Main Verbs, and Helping Verbs (pp. 152, 154) Write each sentence. Draw one line under the action or main verb. Draw two lines under the helping verb.

25. I am buying a pig.

26. My grandfather has kept pigs on his farm for many years.

27. I have read many books about them.

28. I will learn even more.

Verb Tenses and Using Irregular Verbs (pp. 156, 158, 162, 164) Write the verb in each sentence. Then write the present form of the verb.

29. A glass maker invented eyeglasses around 1286.

30. Glasses brought better vision to many people.

31. We have seen great improvements in eye care since 1286.

32. Many people have begun to wear contact lenses in place of eyeglasses.

Subject-Verb Agreement (p. 160) Write each sentence. Choose the correct form of the verb in parentheses ( ) to complete the sentence.

33. Snow (form, forms) in cold clouds.

34. Then the crystals (fall, falls) to the ground as they become heavy.

35. Frozen rain (drop, drops) in the form of hail.

36. A bucket of water (weigh, weighs) more than a bucket of snow.

MAINTENANCE

Using the Comma (p. 168) Write each sentence. Use commas where they are needed.

37. Clams scallops and snails make their homes in seashells.

38. In this book Jody you can see a clam opening its shell.

39. Yes giant pearls may grow in these clams.

40. Snails outgrow their shells and move into larger ones.

UNIT 7: Using Linking Verbs

Past- and Present-Tense Linking Verbs (pp. 226, 228) Write and complete each sentence by choosing the correct verb in parentheses ( ).

41. Canals, waterways across land, (was, were) important ways to travel long ago.

42. It (is, are) possible to travel from lakes to rivers, for example, through canals.

43. Perhaps the most famous American canal (was, were) the Erie Canal.

44. Canal boats (is, are) still in operation for tourists along many of the old canals.

Contractions with *not* (p. 232) Write a contraction for each pair of words.

45. will not

46. have not

47. has not

48. would not

Using Quotation Marks (p. 234) Write each sentence. Add quotation marks where they are needed.

49. Do you want to see the Statue of Liberty? Aiko asked.

50. Russ said, The boat is here.

51. How much are the tickets? he asked.

52. How large the statue looks up close! Mindy exclaimed.

Suffixes (p. 236) Write and complete each sentence by substituting a word with a suffix for the words in parentheses ( ).

53. That astronaut is the (one who leads) of the space flight.

54. The bunks that the crew sleep in look (capable of comfort).

55. Every part of the ship is checked (with care) before takeoff.

56. I wonder what it feels like to be (without weight) in space.

UNIT 9: Using Adjectives

Adjectives, Adjectives After Linking Verbs (pp. 292, 294) Write each sentence. Then, draw one line under each adjective in the sentence and two lines under the noun it describes. Finally, write the linking verb in each sentence.

57. The moon is full tonight.
58. The twinkling stars are bright.
59. Those pictures of the planets were amazing.
60. The surface of Mars is rocky.
61. You can find Mars easily because it is red.

Adjectives That Compare, Comparing with *more* and *most* (pp. 296, 298, 300) Write and complete each sentence, using the correct comparative form of the adjective in parentheses ( ).

62. The Empire State Building in New York City was once the _____ skyscraper. (tall)
63. It was the _____ building of its time. (modern)
64. The two towers of the World Trade Center are even _____ . (high)
65. The Chicago Sears Tower is currently the _____ skyscraper of all. (high)
66. Is it possible that a skyscraper might be built that will be _____ than these buildings? (tall)

Using Articles (p. 302) Write each sentence. Then fill in the blank with the article *a, an,* or *the.*

67. An elephant is _____ enormous animal.
68. _____ African elephant may weigh six tons.
69. _____ trunk of an elephant is very sensitive.
70. The elephant can pick up _____ coin with its trunk.
71. Elephants eat grass, shrubs, and _____ leaves of trees.
72. _____ elephant may ram down a tree to get its leaves.
73. Elephants live _____ average of 60 years.

Synonyms/Antonyms (p. 306) Use the direction in parentheses ( ) to write a synonym or an antonym for the underlined word in each sentence.

74. This book is <u>funnier</u> than the last one I read. (antonym)
75. The main character took a <u>short</u> time finding her dog. (antonym)
76. Her dog was <u>huge</u>. (synonym)
77. They <u>traveled</u> far together. (synonym)
78. They saw many <u>boring</u> sights. (antonym)
79. The girl and her dog were <u>sad</u> as they traveled around the country. (antonym)

MAINTENANCE

UNIT 11: Using Pronouns

Subject and Object Pronouns

(pp. 360, 362) Write each sentence. Use a subject pronoun or an object pronoun in place of the underlined word or words in the sentence.

80. Tony and Fran worked on a science project together.
81. Tony said the project was fun.
82. Fran agreed with Tony.
83. Fran found a book on solar energy in the library.
84. The librarian told Fran where to look for the book.

Possessive Pronouns (p. 364)

Write each sentence. Use a possessive pronoun in place of the underlined word or words in the sentence.

85. Kenji said, "I entered Kenji's cat in the pet contest."
86. Tina wanted to know if that was Kenji's orange cat.
87. Rob and Dave entered Rob and Dave's cat, too.
88. Linda is leaving Linda's dog home this year.
89. June, will you bring June's dog to the contest?
90. Tony's kitten plays happily in the kitten's cage.

Using *I* and *Me* correctly (p. 366)

Write each sentence. Use the correct pronoun in parentheses ( ) to complete the sentence.

91. Tanya and (I, me) will go downtown on Saturday.
92. Janet wants to come with Tanya and (I, me).
93. Janet, Tanya, and (I, me) are good friends.
94. Janet will call Tanya and (I, me) if she can go.

Pronoun Contractions, Homophones/Homographs

(pp. 368, 370) Write each sentence using the correct word in parentheses ( ).

95. Dan realized he had to (we'd, weed) his garden.
96. He said to Jo, "(We've, Weave) let it go far too long."
97. Dan studied the plants on the (right, write).
98. "Don't you see that (their they're) leaves are yellow?"
99. "That means (their they're) not getting enough sunlight," said Dan.
100. "I think (your, you're) right."
101. Jo continued, "Get (your, you're) tools and let's begin."

UNIT 13: Using Adverbs

What Is an Adverb? (pp. 422, 424) Write each sentence. Then underline the adverb in each one. Finally, write **how, when,** or **where** to show what the adverb in the sentence tells.

102. Mac gladly joined the scavenger hunt.
103. He began looking earlier than the other searchers.
104. He looked here in the barn.
105. Then, he moved quickly on to the backyard.
106. He found what he needed there.
107. Happily, Mac began to search for the next item on his list.

Using Adverbs to Compare (p. 426) Write and complete each sentence, using the correct comparative form of the adverb in parentheses ( ).

108. Gail can skate _____ than Bill. (fast)
109. This year, she won the race _____ than last year. (easily)
110. She hopes to skate _____ next year. (strongly)
111. She practices _____ than the other skaters in her class. (often)
112. Gail learns new routines _____ than most skaters. (quick)
113. I believe that she will reach the top _____ than other people. (soon)

Using *good* and *well* Correctly (p. 428) Write each sentence. Use *good* or *well* to complete the sentence.

114. My sister Abby sings _____ .
115. It certainly helps to have _____ music.
116. She also has a very _____ teacher.
117. She hopes to do _____ in the talent show.
118. I know she will be _____ at whatever she does.
119. She does _____ in all her school subjects, too.

Negatives (p. 430) Rewrite each sentence using only one negative. Remember that there may be more than one correct way to write the sentence.

120. Don't never give up learning new things.
121. You won't learn nothing unless you try.
122. Benjamin Franklin didn't discover nothing after only one attempt.
123. Thomas Edison wouldn't have gotten nowhere if he had given up.
124. Don't let no idea go before you test it.
125. You don't never how how much you can accomplish.

UNIT

14

Writing Research Reports

Look at the picture and read the quotation on the opposite page. What does Byrd Baylor want to know? What kinds of things do you want to know more about?

When you write a research report you become a detective. You must find, organize, and then present information for your audience.

Focus A research report summarizes information about a subject. The information in a research report comes from many different sources. The purpose of a research report is to inform.

What would you like to learn more about? On the following pages you will find a story and some photographs. You can use both the selection and the photographs to give you ideas for writing.

THEME: *SEARCHES*

I want to know the things that hawks and horned toads know. I want to understand dust devils and falling stars. I want to follow coyote trails wherever they go.

—Byrd Baylor

LITERATURE

Reading Like a Writer

AWARD WINNING SELECTION

Have you ever had a great idea and begun to work on it without thinking it through?

The cotton crop had failed, and farmers were in trouble. Because Professor Carver of Tuskegee Institute knew that planting goobers (peanuts) was good for the soil, he suggested that farmers plant them. However, what was to be done with a bumper crop of goobers?

The selection is *biographical*, which means that it tells facts about a real person. As you read, watch for ways the author has made the facts interesting and the characters real.

A POCKETFUL of PEANUTS

from A Pocketful of Goobers

by Barbara Mitchell

Little by little, the farmers began to follow Professor Carver's advice. One crisp October evening, Professor Carver heard a soft tap at his door. It was the widow from a neighboring farm. "I did just as you said," she told the Professor. "I planted my land in goobers. Now I've put by all I can use in a year and given my hired man the same. Tell me, Professor, what am I to do with the rest?"

Professor Carver made a fast tour around the countryside. Macon County had indeed produced a bumper goober crop. He saw goobers, goobers, and more goobers. They were piled everywhere, right up to the rickety cabins that sat in the middle of them. The awful truth of it all suddenly washed over him. There was not a thing to do with all those goobers.

Professor Carver's problem is introduced here.

The Professor went back to his room and shut the door. He pulled up a chair and sat down, sick at heart. "*Why* did you not think this whole thing through!" he asked himself. The Macon County farmers were worse off now than ever before.

At last he got up and went to bed, but sleep would not come. The guilt he felt weighed on him far into the night.

At dawn he went for his daily walk in the woods. He threw himself down on the mossy ground and began to pray. "I had a little talk with my Creator," he said afterward. To Professor Carver, talking to God was as natural as talking to his students. Years later, when he was much in demand as a speaker, he liked to recall how the answer to the perplexing goober problem had come to him in the stillness of the morning. "The Creator gave me a pocketful of goobers," he would say, "and together we went back to the lab and got down to work."

The writer presents the facts in an interesting way.

On that morning in October 1915, Professor Carver had gone to the Tuskegee goober patch and then straight to the lab. He locked himself in, put on his flour-sack apron, and shelled the pocketful of goobers. He ground some of the nuts, heated them, and put them under a press. Out came a cupful of oil. The Professor got to work on it.

In what seemed like no time at all, a knock came at the door. It was a worried student. "Your lunch, Prof." Professor Carver had not appeared at either breakfast or lunch.

"Set it down, set it down. Thank you," he said absently. He went on working. The goober oil was wonderful stuff. It blended easily with other substances and was easier to break down than animal fat.

Next he took the dry cake left from the pressed oil. He added a little water and set up an artificial digestion process. By imitating the human digestive system, he would be able to discover the nutritional value of the goober. The little goober cake was packed full of protein, he found. It had more carbohydrate value than potatoes and more vitamins than beef liver.

Professor Carver went back to the remaining ground-up nuts. Out came a fluid that looked like milk. He added a pinch of salt and a little sugar. He tasted the result. "Well, I declare!" he exclaimed. It *was* milk.

Another knock came at the door. "Your supper, Prof. Prof, are you all right?"

"Yes, yes. Thank you," Professor Carver answered. He ate the supper and the cold lunch and got back to work. He worked on

through the night, stopping only to go out to the field for more goobers.

In the morning, he looked at the glass of goober milk. Cream had formed on top. Professor Carver whipped it. Up came a plump pat of butter. He worked on, for a total of two days and two nights, recombining the goober by-products at different temperatures and under different pressures. At last he took off his apron and stepped out into the coolness of a new morning. He was exhausted, but pleased. He had found fats and oils, gums and resins, pectins and proteins. The goober could easily be broken down for use in margarine, cooking oil, rubbing oil, even cosmetics. The milk it yielded was every bit as nutritious as cow's milk, and it took only a handful of goobers to make a glassful. Professor Carver's several days in the lab had given birth to twenty uses for the goober. His farmers would have no trouble selling their goobers now.

The solution to the problem is given here.

Thinking Like a Reader

1. Why did Professor Carver feel responsible for helping the farmers of Macon County?
2. Do you think Professor Carver's discoveries helped people other than the farmers? Explain your answer.

Write your responses in your journal.

Thinking Like a Writer

3. Professor George Washington Carver was a real person. How does the author show you what kind of person he was?
4. Copy into your journal some of the details that the author uses to make Professor Carver come alive.
5. Name some other people in history whom you find interesting.

Write about them in your journal.

Responding to

LITERATURE

Brainstorm

Vocabulary

In "A Pocketful of Peanuts," the author uses some technical words. Some examples are *digestion, carbohydrate, nutritional,* and *proteins.* Think of some technical terms that you have learned in science or social studies. Begin to create a personal vocabulary list of technical words and phrases.

Talk It Over

Giving Instructions

When scientists plan an experiment, they arrange the steps in a logical order. Then, they write out each step clearly so that other people can repeat the experiment. Work in a group of five. Think of a set of directions for an everyday activity to give to the class. For example, you might explain how to make a peanut butter sandwich. One of you should tell the first step in the process; the next student should tell the next step, and so on. Anyone in the class may challenge you by giving a step that you have left out.

Quick Write

Write an Autobiography

You have been reading about the life of a real person. Your own life story is your *autobiography.* How would you begin your autobiography? Remember, present the facts in an interesting way. Write the opening paragraph of your autobiography. Here is an example.

> Few people who know me now would guess that I was the tiniest baby born in 1980 at Wynn Memorial Hospital. I weighed barely 3 pounds 5 ounces. When my mother saw me for the first time, she burst into tears, or so they tell me. I was not really paying much attention.

Idea Corner

Hall of Fame

You will soon write a report about some historical person. You will want to include interesting details to capture your reader's attention. As you read and study, make notes in your journal about interesting people. List as many facts about them as you can. You will use this information as you write.

PICTURES SEEING LIKE A WRITER

Finding Ideas for Writing

Look at the pictures. Think about what you see. What ideas for writing a research report do the photographs give you? Write your ideas in your journal.

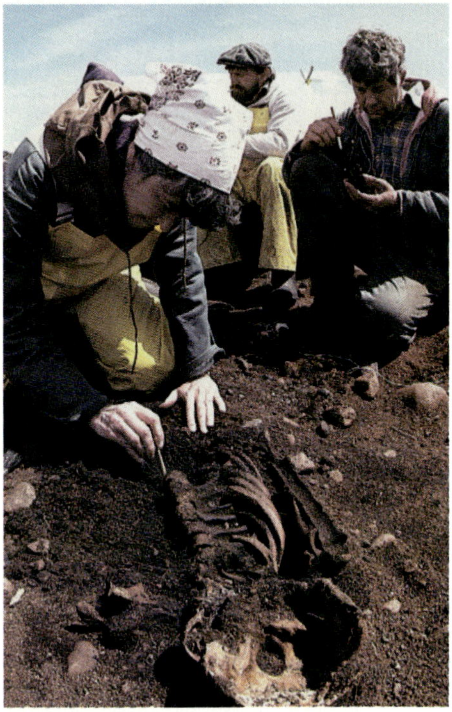

1 GROUP WRITING: A Research Report

COOPERATIVE LEARNING

The **purpose** of a research report is to give information to an **audience** about a specific topic. What steps does a writer need to follow when writing a report?

- Note Taking
- Outlining
- Organizing Information Logically

Note Taking

Joanne went to the library to find information on Margaret Mead. She read an encyclopedia article and a short biography. She took notes on her reading.

Taking notes will help you to remember what you have read. Keep your notes short. Write only main ideas and important details. Here are Joanne's notes.

studied youth in Pacific Islands
compared them to Americans in well-known
book Coming of Age in Samoa
anthropology: study of humans and
their society
worked at Museum of Natural History -
taught at Columbia University
revisited New Guinea in 1967 to see changes

Guided Practice: Taking Notes

As a class, find an article in a book or an encyclopedia about one of these scientists. Read the article and take notes on what you find.

Marie Curie   Louis Pasteur   Jonas Salk

Outlining

An outline helps you to organize a report. Use your notes to list items in the order in which you wish to discuss them. Each numbered item, or **main topic,** will be a paragraph. Each capital letter is followed by a **subtopic.** A period follows each Roman numeral and capital letter. Which words did Joanne capitalize in her outline? What is the title of the outline?

Margaret Mead

I. *Who she was*
   A. *Famous anthropologist*
   B. *Summary of her work*

II. *What she did*
   A. *The early years in the Pacific*
   B. *Writing and teaching*
   C. *Return to New Guinea*

III. *Why she is important*
   A. *Her discoveries*
   B. *Her pioneering spirit*

- How many paragraphs will be in this report?
- How many subtopics will paragraph II have?

Organizing Information Logically

A research report should be organized in a logical manner so that the reader can easily follow your ideas. Most of the time you will probably arrange your report in time order.

Guided Practice: Making an Outline

Make an outline for a three-paragraph report. Use your class notes about the scientist you chose. Remember to add a title.

Putting a Research Report Together

Now it is time to write your research report. Remember that each main topic in your outline will become a paragraph. Each paragraph will need a topic sentence. The words in your main topic will help you to form a topic sentence. Here is part of Joanne's outline and the topic sentences she wrote from her outline.

Margaret Mead

I. *Who she was*
   A. *Famous anthropologist*
   B. *Summary of her work*

II. *What she did*
   A. *The early years in the Pacific*
   B. *Writing and teaching*

Topic Sentence 1: Margaret Mead was a famous anthropologist.

Topic Sentence 2: The years she spent in the Pacific led Dr. Mead to a new career as a professor at Columbia University.

The subtopics in your outline will become the supporting details in your paragraphs.

Guided Practice: Writing a Research Report

Use the numbered items in your class outline to write topic sentences for the three paragraphs of your report. Use the lettered items in the outline to write the detail sentences.

Share your report with a classmate. Have your classmate point out ways to make your topic sentences more interesting.

Checklist: Research Report

When you write a research report, you will want to keep some points in mind. A checklist will remind you of the things you will want to include in your report.

Look at this checklist. Some points need to be added. Make a copy of the checklist and finish it. Keep the copy in your writing folder. You can use it when you write your research report.

CHECKLIST

- ✔ Purpose and audience
- ✔ Note taking
- ✔ ______________________
- ■ Main topics
- ■ Subtopics
- ✔ Organizing information
- ______________________

2 THINKING AND WRITING: Summarizing

The topic sentence tells the main idea of a paragraph. A **summary** tells the most important ideas in a piece of writing. A summary is short. It gives only the main ideas and facts that the audience will need to know.

Read the article from a scientific magazine below. Then read the summary written by a reporter for a local newspaper. Notice that the main idea is stated in the **topic,** or first, sentence in the summary. The other sentences give the most important details.

Researchers from the Fish and Wildlife Service are exploring parts of the tundra from Bethel northeast, tracking the nesting curlews *(Numenius tahitiensis)* for the Yukon Delta National Wildlife Refuge. To date 42 pairs have been banded and released. Researchers will track the birds in their winter migrations to islands off the coast of Oahu, Hawaii, for a period of five years.

The research crew was joined this year by students from the University of Washington. Sixteen researchers worked for ten weeks during the first part of the project. Of these, eight will travel to Hawaii to study the winter habits of this rare bird.

Anchorage—A team of researchers studying the nesting curlews have banded 42 pairs of the birds so far this summer. Researchers and college students tracked the pairs on the tundra northeast of Bethel. Some researchers will follow the birds to Hawaii during their winter migrations. The project will take five years.

Thinking Like a Writer

- Which details did the reporter leave out? Why do you think she did this?

The reporter is writing for people who do not know much about birds. She explains what the project is and what the researchers have done. The other details are not needed by this audience.

When you summarize information, keep your audience and purpose in mind. Choose only those details that will interest your audience and are most important for your audience to know.

THINKING APPLICATION Summarizing

Imagine that you are a reporter for your school newspaper. Write a short summary of this news report for your schoolmates.

May 12—The City Council voted today to search for a good location for a new housing project. The project must contain six buildings of ten apartments each in order to receive additional money from the state. Several possible places were suggested. These included the former site of Old Farm Inn, which burned down last year; a six-acre site north of Jeeves Park; and the parking lot next to Kress Hardware. None of these locations seemed entirely suitable. A search committee was formed to look for more sites. Roy Leeds and Rowena May will head the committee. Ms. May was the chairperson for the search committee that found a site for the new electric plant last year. The committee has until August 1 to find a location for the housing project. The meeting ended at 7 P.M.

3 INDEPENDENT WRITING: A Research Report

Prewrite: Step 1

You have learned some important ideas about writing a research report. Now you are ready to choose a topic for writing your own report. Matthew, a student your age, wanted to write a report about someone in history for his classmates. He chose a topic in this way.

Choosing a Topic

1. First, he listed people he would like to know more about.
2. Next, he decided which person or group of people interested him most.
3. Then, he narrowed his topic.

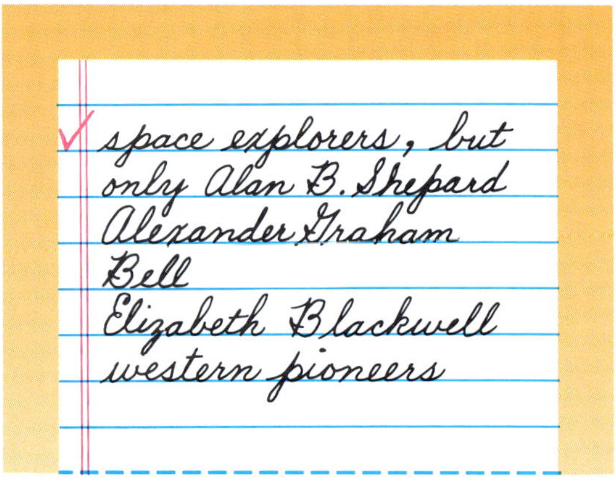

Matthew liked the first topic on his list best. He thought that he would enjoy learning more about the men and women who have journeyed into space. He decided, however, to narrow the topic to Alan B. Shepard, the first American in space.

Matthew went to the school library. He read several articles about Alan Shepard. He made notes about what he had read. Now he is ready to organize his report by writing an outline.

Exploring Ideas: Outlining Strategies

Matthew read through his notes. He thought that he had found some interesting facts about Alan Shepard. He knew that his **purpose** for writing was to give information to his classmates so that they, too, would learn more about Shepard's career.

The First American in Space

I. Who is Alan B. Shepard?
  A. Birthdate and early life
  B. Chosen for astronaut program

II. His most famous flight
  A. *Freedom 7*
  B. Facts about the flight

III. His later accomplishments
  A. *Apollo 14*
  B. Rear Admiral

Thinking Like a Writer

- In which paragraph will Matthew discuss *Freedom 7*?
- Will Matthew's report be in time order? Is using time order a logical way to organize this report? Explain.

YOUR TURN

JOURNAL

Think of a person about whom you would like to write a report. Use **Pictures** or your journal for ideas. Follow these steps.

- Make a list of people who interest you. Choose the person you like best.
- Find information about that person in the library. Use at least two sources.
- Narrow your topic if it is too broad. Take notes.
- Think of your purpose and audience.

Organize your notes into an outline. Remember, you can add to or change your outline at any time.

Write a First Draft: Step 2

Matthew's planning has helped him to write a first draft.

Part of Matthew's First Draft

The First American in space

If you read The Right Stuff, you know the name Alan B. Shepard. When he was born in New Hamshire in 1923, his parents never dreamed that he would grow up to become the first american in space.

In 1947 he became a Navy test pilot. He learned to fly at high altitudes. He also learned to fly under great stress. Then, he was chosen to be among the first group of astronauts.

Planning Checklist

- Remember purpose and audience.
- Write paragraphs based on the main topics in your outline.
- Write detail sentences based on the subtopics.
- Make your facts interesting.

While Matthew was writing his first draft, he did not worry about errors. He was interested in putting his major ideas into paragraphs.

YOUR TURN

Write your first draft. Ask yourself these questions.

- Who is my audience? What do they want to know?
- How can I make the facts interesting for my audience?

TIME-OUT You may want to take some time out now. Then you will be able to revise your writing with a fresh eye.

Revise: Step 3

After he finished his first draft, Matthew read it over. He shared his report with his friend Katy. He asked Katy to suggest ways he could improve his work.

Matthew then looked back at his planning checklist. He noticed that he had forgotten the last point. He checked it off so that he would remember it when he revised. Matthew will use his checklist as he revises.

Matthew made changes in his report. Notice that he did not correct small errors. He knew that they could be fixed later.

The revisions Matthew made changed his paragraph. Turn the page. Look at Matthew's revised draft.

Revising Checklist

- Remember purpose and audience.
- Write paragraphs based on the main topics in your outline.
- Write detail sentences based on the subtopics.
- ✓ Make your facts interesting.

Part of Matthew's Revised Draft

The First American in space

If you read The Right Stuff, you know the name Alan B. Shepard. When he was born in New Hamshire in 1923, his parents never dreamed that he would grow up to become the first american in space. *Shepard loved to fly.*

In 1947 he became a Navy test pilot *and* ~~He~~ *he* learned to fly at high altitudes. He also learned to fly under great stress. Then, he was chosen

Thinking Like a Writer

WISE WORD CHOICE

- Which sentences did Matthew combine? How does combining them improve his writing?
- Which words did Matthew add? How does this added detail make his report more interesting?

YOUR TURN

Read your first draft. Ask yourself these questions.

- Am I writing paragraphs based on my outline?
- Is my report arranged in a logical order?
- How can I add facts or details to make the report more interesting?

If you wish, ask a friend to read your report and make suggestions. Then revise your report.

Proofread: Step 4

Matthew used a proofreading checklist while he proofread.

Part of Matthew's Proofread Draft

The First American in space

If you read The Right Stuff, you know the name Alan B. Shepard. When he was born in New ~~Hamshire~~ Hampshire in 1923, his parents never dreamed that he would grow up to become the first american in space. Shepard loved to fly. In 1947 he became a Navy test pilot, and ~~He~~ he

YOUR TURN

Proofreading Practice

Below is a paragraph that you can use to practice your proofreading skills. Find the errors. Write the paragraph correctly on a separate piece of paper.

> After a volcano explodes, scientists frequent study it. They hope to learn how to predict when a Volcano will erupt. A special machine, the seismograph, is used to measure rumbles deep in the earth. Will a volcano rumble most violently when it is ready to erupt. scientists want to find this out. A good book to read about volcanoes is The restless Earth by Patricia Lauber

Proofreading Checklist

- Did I indent my paragraphs?
- Did I spell all words correctly?
- What punctuation errors do I need to correct?
- What capitalization errors do I need to correct?

Applying Your Proofreading Skills

Now proofread your research report. Read your checklist again. Review **The Grammar Connection** and **The Mechanics Connection**, too. Use the proofreading marks to mark changes.

THE GRAMMAR CONNECTION

Remember these rules about adverbs.

- Use *more* or *most* before adverbs that end with *ly* or have two or more syllables.
- *More* compares two actions. *Most* compares more than two actions.

Corn grows **more** slowly than radishes grow.
Potatoes grow the **most** slowly of all.

Check your report. Have you used adverbs correctly?

THE MECHANICS CONNECTION

Remember these rules about punctuating titles.

- Capitalize the first letter of each important word in a title.
- Underline titles of books, newspapers, and magazines. Use quotation marks around the titles of stories, articles, songs, and poems.

I recommend that you read The Wind in the Willows.

Check your report. Have you written all titles correctly?

Proofreading Marks

¶ Indent
∧ Add
ℯ Take out
≡ Make a capital letter
/ Make a small letter

Publish: Step 5

Matthew shared his report by reading it aloud to his class. He read slowly and carefully but allowed his excitement about the report to show. After he finished reading, Matthew answered questions about his report.

YOUR TURN

Make a neat, final copy of your research report. Think of a way to share your work. Some ideas are given in the **Sharing Suggestions** box below.

SHARING SUGGESTIONS

Illustrate your report and post it on the bulletin board.	Put your report into a binder and add it to the classroom library.	Read your report aloud to another class.

4 SPEAKING AND LISTENING: Giving an Oral Report

Matthew chose to read his research report aloud to his class. He might have decided to give an oral report instead. When you give an oral report, you do not read your report aloud. You use a note card or an outline to remind yourself of what you want to say.

Nora will give an oral report to her classmates about Queen Isabella I of Spain. She has decided to use an outline for her talk.

Nora looked in the encyclopedia for information about Queen Isabella. She also looked in the card catalog, and found several books that had sections about Spain during Isabella's reign. She took notes on what she had read.

Queen Isabella I of Spain

I. *Kingdom*
   A. *Castile and Leon (1474–1504)*
   B. *Aragon (1479–1504) (show map)*
II. *United Spain*
   A. *Controlled nobles*
   B. *Took over the Inquisition*
III. *Enlarged Spain*
   A. *Invaded Granada*
   B. *Paid for Columbus's voyage*

Nora reread her notes. She wrote only her main points and some details in her outline. She arranged the main points in a logical order. What visual aid is Nora planning to use? How will using a visual aid make her oral report more interesting?

When you give a talk, it will help you to keep your **purpose** and **audience** in mind. These speaking guidelines will help you to focus your talk.

SPEAKING GUIDELINES: An Oral Report

1. Remember your purpose and audience.
2. Make a note card or an outline. Practice using it.
3. Be sure that your report is organized logically.
4. Look at your listeners.
5. Speak in a clear voice that your audience can hear.
6. Be prepared to answer questions when you finish.

- How does organizing my report in a logical order help my audience?

SPEAKING APPLICATION An Oral Report

Think of a topic that interests you. Prepare an outline to use for a short oral report. Use the speaking guidelines to help you to prepare. Your classmates will be using the following guidelines as they listen to your report.

LISTENING GUIDELINES: An Oral Report

1. Pay attention to the speaker.
2. Write down any questions that you wish to ask.
3. Save your questions until the speaker finishes.

5 WRITER'S RESOURCES: Graphs, Tables, and Maps

You have learned that books, magazines, and encyclopedia articles are excellent resources to use when writing a report. Writers also consult other special resources to locate facts. Some possible resources are graphs, tables, and maps.

Imagine that Teeburg University would like to persuade scientists to join their staff. It publishes a report for scientists to read that contains graphs, tables, and maps. **Graphs** and **tables** are good ways of showing information about numbers.

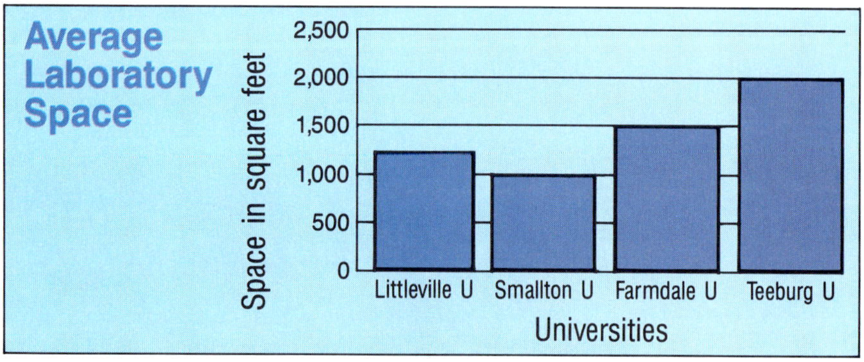

This bar graph shows that Teeburg University has more laboratory space than Littleville, Smallton, or Farmdale universities do.

The Science Departments at Teeburg University		
DEPARTMENT	TEACHERS	STUDENTS
Biology	**12**	**192**
Chemistry	**8**	**126**
Physics	**6**	**96**

What information does the table above give you?

Maps also give facts. They show where things are and how far one place is from another. This map can help you to find the buildings in the science area of Teeburg University.

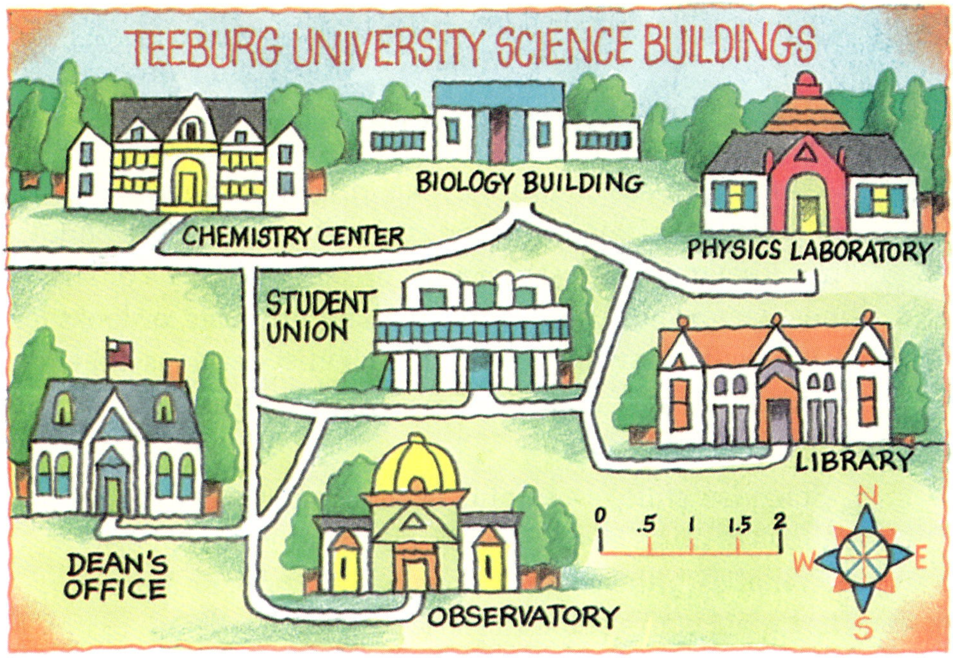

Practice

Use the graph, table, and map in this lesson to answer the following questions.

1. How many students are in the Chemistry Department?
2. How many more square feet does the average laboratory at Teeburg have than the average lab at Smallton?
3. Dr. Zarkoff leaves the Biology Building and heads for the Library. In which direction does he walk?

WRITING APPLICATION A List

Find a graph, table, or map in your science book. List five facts that are given in the resource that you find. Save the list in your writing folder. You will use it in **The Curriculum Connection** on page 484.

THE CURRICULUM CONNECTION

Writing About Science

When scientists conduct an experiment, they follow some of the steps that you use when you write a research report. First, a scientist chooses an area, or subject, that he or she finds interesting. The scientist then experiments, or looks for facts, about the subject. Next, the scientist develops a theory based on his or her observations. Finally, the scientist writes a report about the theory.

Scientists study everything from tiny atoms to stars billions of miles away. Some scientists work for colleges or universities. Others work in businesses, zoos, or museums. They write books and articles about their work.

ACTIVITIES

Summarize Facts Look at the list of facts that you gathered from the graph, table, or map in your science book. Use the facts to write a paragraph explaining what you learned from the resource.

Plan an Experiment For each of the theories below, think of a way to look for facts to support it. For example, for **Theory 1** you might set up thermometers in different parts of the world.

Theory 1: The temperature of the earth is rising.
Theory 2: Babies can communicate with each other.
Theory 3: Wolves share their food with the pack.

Respond to Literature The following paragraphs are taken from *Science in a Vacant Lot* by Seymour Simon. You might read this kind of book to find information for a research

report, or just to learn how scientists find out more about the world we live in. After reading the paragraphs, write a response. You might want to report on what you have learned by watching animals.

Insects and Other Creeping Crawlers

Turn over a large flat rock and look beneath it. You will probably find a number of crawling, creeping, and wiggling animals. Beneath your feet in the soil of a vacant lot live many different kinds of insects, spiders, centipedes, millipedes, snails, earthworms, pill bugs, mites, and many other living things too small to see without a microscope.

Look for these animals beneath rocks, old logs, and pieces of rotting wood. Put your eyes close to the ground and look for ants and spiders making their way through the tangled plants. Listen for the sounds of insects on a hot summer day.

Spread out several sheets of newspaper on the ground. With a shovel, dig up a square foot of soil to a depth of six inches. Spread the soil out on the newspapers. Look for movement in the soil. Count the number of different animals you find. You may be surprised to find out how many there are.

UNIT CHECKUP

LESSON 1 **Group Writing: A Research Report** (page 466) Turn to page 485 and reread the paragraphs about insects in a vacant lot. Take notes on the paragraphs as though you were planning to write a report on that topic.

LESSON 2 **Thinking: Summarizing** (page 470) Write a two- or three-sentence summary of this news report.

Paris—A new tour sponsored by the Ministry of Education allows tourists to "live" the history of France. For a mere $5,000 a daring tourist can follow Napoleon's path to glory and defeat, retrace the footsteps of Joan of Arc, or trade places with Charlemagne. Thirty people may join each group. Groups leave Paris on July 2 and August 15. There are separate tours for speakers of French, English, Italian, and Japanese.

LESSON 3 **Writing a Research Report** (page 472) Imagine that you work for NASA. You are part of a team searching for signs of life on other planets. Find information, take notes, and make an outline. Write a three-paragraph report about the planets for your team.

LESSON 4 **Speaking and Listening: An Oral Report** (page 480) List three guidelines to remember when listening to an oral report.

LESSON 5 **Writer's Resources: Graphs, Tables, and Maps** (page 482) Use library resources to find these facts. Tell whether you found each fact in a graph, a table, or a map.

1. the leading wheat-growing area in the world
2. the percentage (%) of protein in whole wheat flour

THEME PROJECT — A MAP

People have always had the urge to travel to new places. Marco Polo journeyed by land to distant China. Columbus sailed across an ocean searching for a direct water route to the Far East. Think about how much easier it would have been for these early travelers if good maps had been available. With what kinds of maps are you familiar?

Look at the map below. It is the map of a building. It tells the map reader where he or she is standing and how to find other parts of the building.

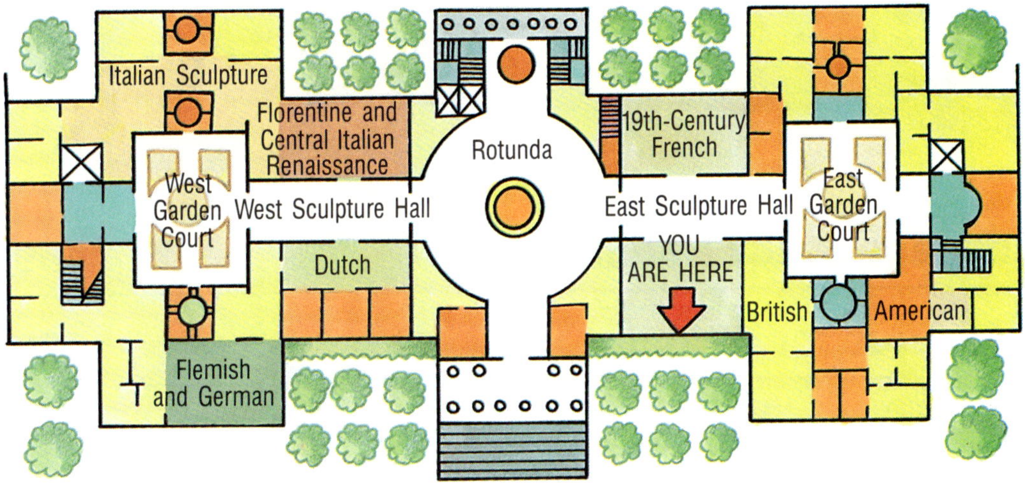

The National Gallery of Art, Washington, D.C.

Think about your school building. Which rooms and offices might a visitor want to locate?

- Make a YOU ARE HERE map of the first floor.
- Begin by brainstorming what you will include.
- Decide where you will hang the map. Be sure to draw a YOU ARE HERE arrow.

Writer's Reference

CONTENTS

LANGUAGE STUDY HANDBOOK

GRAMMAR

Sentences

A **sentence** expresses a complete thought. A sentence contains a subject and a predicate.

complete subject **complete predicate**
A Native American woman/guided the expedition.

A **simple subject** tells what the sentence is about. The subject may be one word or more than one word.

Jack saw Jill. **Jack** and **Jill** went up the hill.

A **simple predicate** tells what the subject does or is. The simple predicate is the verb. The predicate may be one word or more than one word.

Jack **walked** slowly. Jack **was watching** the sunset.

There are four sentence types. Notice the end punctuation of each type.

I am a firefighter.	(Declarative—ends with a period)
What do I do?	(Interrogative—ends with a question mark)
Ask me questions.	(Imperative—ends with a period)
My career is terrific!	(Exclamatory—ends with an exclamation mark)

A **run-on sentence** contains two or more complete thoughts.

My dog jumped up the visitor fell down and tore his shirt.

Divide a run-on sentence into two or more sentences.

My dog jumped up. The visitor fell down and tore his shirt.

A **sentence fragment** is an incomplete thought.

The bright golden sunshine.	(fragment: no predicate)
Felt like warm rain on my face.	(fragment: no subject)

Add a subject or a predicate to complete a sentence fragment.

The bright golden sunshine was wonderful.
The sun's rays felt like warm rain on my face.

Nouns

A **noun** is a word that names a person, place, or thing.

uncle	city	dog

A **singular noun** names one person, place, or thing.

boy	school	cat

A **plural noun** names more than one person, place, or thing. Add ***s*** to most singular nouns to make them plural.

boys	schools	cats

If a singular noun ends in ***s, z, x, sh,*** or ***ch,*** add ***es*** to form the plural.

loss—losses	tax—taxes	bush—bushes

Some nouns are irregular. You must memorize the plurals of irregular nouns.

sheep—sheep	child—children	mouse—mice

A **possessive noun** is a noun that shows ownership.

A **singular possessive noun** shows what one person owns. Usually, ***'s*** is added to singular nouns to form a singular possessive noun.

Jack's pail	Luis's school

A **plural possessive noun** shows what more than one person owns. If a plural noun ends in ***s,*** an **apostrophe** is added to form the plural possessive noun.

workers' tools	drivers' seats

If a plural noun does not end in ***s, 's*** is added to the plural noun to form the plural possessive noun.

children's toys	geese's beaks

Verbs

A **verb** is a word that expresses action or tells what something is or is like.

walk walked	is was

The **time** of a verb is called its **tense.**

Present tense expresses action that is happening now.

I open the box.

Past tense expresses action that has already happened.

I opened the box yesterday.

Future tense expresses action that will happen at a later time.

I will open the box tomorrow.

Most verbs add ***ed*** to form their past tense. If a verb ends in **e,** drop the **e,** and add ***ed.***

love—loved ask—asked

An **irregular verb** is a verb that does not add ***ed*** to form its past tense. You must memorize the irregular verb forms.

Present	**Past**	**Past with *has, have, had***
see	saw	seen
go	went	gone
come	came	come
run	ran	run
give	gave	given
eat	ate	eaten
write	wrote	written
drive	drove	driven
ride	rode	ridden
take	took	taken
fly	flew	flown
draw	drew	drawn
sing	sang	sung
swim	swam	swum
begin	began	begun
do	did	done
grow	grew	grown
throw	threw	thrown
bring	brought	brought
make	made	made

Adjectives

An **adjective** is a word that describes a noun. An adjective tells **what kind** or **how many**.

yellow car   **several** bowls   **loud** noise

Articles

A, an, and ***the*** are special adjectives called **articles.**

Use ***a*** before a singular noun beginning with a consonant.
Use ***an*** before a singular noun beginning with a vowel.
Use ***the*** before plural nouns and before singular nouns that name a particular person, place, or thing.

a place in **the** sun   **an** apple   **a** day on top of **the** world

Adverbs

An **adverb** is a word that tells more about a verb. An adverb tells **how, where,** or **when.**

He walks **carefully.** (how)   She lives **there.** (where)
They will arrive **soon.** (when)

To make an adjective into an adverb, add ***ly.***

sad—sad**ly**   quick—quick**ly**

Pronouns

A **pronoun** takes the place of a noun.

Subject pronouns are used in the subject part of a sentence.

Subject Pronouns	I, you, he, she, it, we, they

Object pronouns are used after verbs and after words such as *into, of, with,* and *to.*

Object Pronouns	me, you, him, her, it, us, them

Possessive pronouns are pronouns that show ownership.

Possessive Pronouns	my, your, his, her, its, our, their

MECHANICS

PUNCTUATION

End Punctuation

Use end punctuation to end a sentence.

A **period (.)** ends a **statement** (declarative sentence) or a **command** (imperative sentence).
A **question mark (?)** ends a **question** (interrogative sentence).
An **exclamation mark (!)** ends an **exclamation** (exclamatory sentence).

This exercise is easy.	(statement)
Finish each page.	(command)
Is my work improving?	(question)
I made a perfect score!	(exclamation)

Periods

Use a period to show the end of an abbreviation.

Mr. Mrs. Dr. St.

Use a period with initials.

John F. Kennedy Susan B. Anthony

Colons

Use a colon to separate hours and minutes in time.

2:45 12:15 3:30

Apostrophes

Use an apostrophe **(')** in a contraction to show where letters are missing.

don't we'll aren't

Use apostrophes with nouns to show possession.

Add **'s** to singular nouns and to plural nouns that do not end in **s**.

Bill's book Charles's pen children's stories

Add an **'** to plural nouns ending in **s**.

balloons' strings clowns' smiles

HANDBOOK

HANDBOOK

Commas

Use commas between the names of cities and states.

Chicago, Illinois   Dallas, Texas

Use commas between the day and the year in dates.

October 12, 1492   July 4, 1776

Use commas to separate words in a series.

Our flag is red, white, and blue.
Wynken, Blynken, and Nod are characters in a poem.

Use commas after the greeting and closing in a letter.

Dear Shirley,   Sincerely,

Use commas after introductory words or phrases in a sentence.

Yes, your answer is correct.
In fact, it is the best answer of all.

Use commas to separate exact words from explanatory words in quotations.

"Is this," he asked, "the way to California?"

Quotation Marks

Put quotation marks before and after the **exact** words of a speaker.

Do **not** put quotation marks unless you use the exact words.

"I have just begun to fight," said John Paul Jones.
Jones said that he had just begun to fight.

Do not put quotation marks around words that tell who is speaking.

"I have just," said Jones, "begun to fight."

Put quotation marks before and after the title of a short story, a song, a poem, or a chapter.

"Jack and the Beanstalk"   "The Star-Spangled Banner"

Capitalization

Capitalize the names of specific persons, places, or things.

Harriet Tubman   Alaska   Old Glory

Capitalize titles of respect that are part of a specific name.

President Lincoln   Doctor Martin Luther King, Jr.

Always capitalize the pronoun **I.**

Capitalize the first word and all important words in the title of a book, song, poem, play, short story, or movie.

The Wizard of Oz "The Farmer in the Dell" *Fiddler on the Roof*

Capitalize family names if they refer to specific people.

I asked Mother for a glass of water. The mother wolf fed her cubs.

Capitalize the days of the week and the months of the year.

Monday Thursday August April September

Capitalize the names of holidays and religious days.

Halloween April Fool's Day Independence Day

Capitalize the names of specific cities, states, countries, and other geographic locations.

Houston Georgia United States Mount Rushmore

Capitalize the titles of specific clubs and organizations.

American Society for the Prevention of Cruelty to Animals

Capitalize proper adjectives.

French American African Chinese

Capitalize the first word in a sentence.

Capitalize the first word in a quotation.

He said, "This must be the place."

Capitalize all words in the greeting of a letter.

Dear Friend,

Capitalize only the first word in a letter's closing.

Very truly yours,

Capitalize and put a period after abbreviations of titles of respect.

Dr. Ms. Prof.

Capitalize and put a period after abbreviations of addresses.

St. Ave. Blvd.

Capitalize and put a period after abbreviations for days and months.

Mon. Fri. Nov. Jan.

Use the **United States Postal Service** abbreviations for state names. Notice that each abbreviation consists of two capital letters. No period follows these abbreviations.

AL	(Alabama)	LA	(Louisiana)	OH	(Ohio)
AK	(Alaska)	ME	(Maine)	OK	(Oklahoma)
AZ	(Arizona)	MD	(Maryland)	OR	(Oregon)
AR	(Arkansas)	MA	(Massachusetts)	PA	(Pennsylvania)
CA	(California)	MI	(Michigan)	RI	(Rhode Island)
CO	(Colorado)	MN	(Minnesota)	SC	(South Carolina)
CT	(Connecticut)	MS	(Mississippi)	SD	(South Dakota)
DE	(Delaware)	MO	(Missouri)	TN	(Tennessee)
FL	(Florida)	MT	(Montana)	TX	(Texas)
GA	(Georgia)	NE	(Nebraska)	UT	(Utah)
HI	(Hawaii)	NV	(Nevada)	VT	(Vermont)
ID	(Idaho)	NH	(New Hampshire)	VA	(Virginia)
IL	(Illinois)	NJ	(New Jersey)	WA	(Washington)
IN	(Indiana)	NM	(New Mexico)	WV	(West Virginia)
IA	(Iowa)	NY	(New York)	WI	(Wisconsin)
KS	(Kansas)	NC	(North Carolina)	WY	(Wyoming)
KY	(Kentucky)	ND	(North Dakota)		

USAGE

Pronouns

Use a **subject pronoun** as the subject of a sentence.

I went on the treasure hunt with Sheila.

She was happy about the adventure.

Use an **object pronoun** after an action verb and after words such as *to, with, for,* and *at*.

Sheila gave **me** a treasure map.

I gave the compass to **her.**

When you use a pronoun such as *I* or *me* with another noun, remember to name yourself last.

Sheila and **I** looked for the treasure.

The prize was handed to Sheila and **me.**

Adjectives

If an adjective compares two nouns, the adjective usually ends in ***er.***

The collie is **bigger** than the poodle.

If an adjective compares more than two nouns, the adjective usually ends in ***est.***

The **smartest** of these three dogs is the beagle.

Some adjectives use ***more*** and ***most*** to show comparison. Use ***more*** to compare two nouns. Use ***most*** to compare more than two nouns.

Diane is **more** careful than Sally.
Stan is the **most** careful of the children.

Verbs

A verb must **agree** with the subject of the sentence. If a subject is singular, the verb must be singular. If a subject is plural, the verb must be plural.

The **cat chases** its tail. (singular subject and verb)
The **cats chase** their tails. (plural subject and verb)

Double Negatives

Negatives are words that mean ***no.*** Some examples of negatives are ***no, never, none, not,*** and ***nothing.*** Use only one negative in a sentence.

I have **not** seen **nothing.** (incorrect) I have **not** seen **anything.** (correct)

Troublesome Words

Some words or word pairs are easy to confuse. Look at the rules below.

good—well

Good is an adjective. *Well* is usually an adverb.

This is a **good** book. The author writes **well.**

bad—badly

Bad is an adjective. *Badly* is an adverb.

He is a **bad** tennis player. They play tennis **badly.**

Use *good* and *bad* when talking about health.

I feel **good** today. However, I felt **bad** yesterday.

HANDBOOK

let—leave

Let means "to allow or permit."

I will **let** you go to the movie.

Leave means "to let stay" or "to go away from."

I will not **leave** this book when I **leave** the house.

its—it's

Its is a possessive pronoun. Do not use an apostrophe with a possessive pronoun.

Did the dog find **its** bone?

It's is a contraction meaning "it is."

I think **it's** the biggest dog in the neighborhood.

your—you're

Your is a possessive pronoun meaning "belongs to you."

This is **your** life!

You're is a contraction meaning "you are."

You're going to love this joke.

their—there—they're

Their is a possessive pronoun meaning "belongs to them."

My uncle and aunt have a tree in **their** yard.

There is an adverb that tells "where."

That is the house over **there.**

They're is a contraction meaning "they are."

They're planting another tree this week.

two—too—to

Two is a number.

I have **two** sisters.

Too means "also" or "very."

They have two sisters, **too!** This is **too** complicated.

To is a direction word meaning "toward."

We walk **to** school together.

THESAURUS

What Is a Thesaurus?

A **thesaurus** is a reference that can help you when you write. It provides synonyms for many common words. Synonyms are words that mean the same or almost the same thing.

The thesaurus can help you choose more interesting words and more exact words. For example, you may write this sentence.

Joey **walked** across the street.

Walked is not a very interesting word, and it says very little about Joey. If you look up the word ***walk*** in the thesaurus, you will find these words: ***march, stride, stroll, strut.*** Using one of these words would make your sentence more interesting and more exact.

Using the Thesaurus

The words in a thesaurus often are listed in alphabetical order. You would look up words in a thesaurus as you would in a dictionary. Look at the entry for the word *beautiful* below.

part of speech (→ *adj.*)

main entry word → **beautiful** *adj.* full of beauty; having qualities that are pleasing. ← definition

sample sentence → Those flowers are *beautiful.*

synonyms →
- **gorgeous** extremely beautiful or richly colored. What a *gorgeous* sunset!
- **lovely** beautiful in a comforting way. This is a *lovely* room.
- **pretty** pleasing or attractive, especially said of something small or dainty. What a *pretty* doll!

antonyms → **antonyms:** ugly, hideous

Cross-references

Sometimes you will find cross-references in the thesaurus. The cross-reference for ***allow*** tells you to look under ***let.***

cross-reference entry — **allow** *See* let.

A

allow *See* let.

angry *adj.* feeling or showing anger. Don's remark made me *angry*.
enraged filled with rage; angry beyond control. The *enraged* lion growled loudly.
furious extremely angry. Marty was *furious* at me.

answer *v.* to give a spoken or written response. I asked her, but Jan did not *answer*.
respond to give an answer. Are you going to *respond* to my question?
reply to say in response. "I feel fine," Ted *replied*.
antonyms: ask, inquire

ask *v.* to put a question to. I will *ask* Dad if he knows.
question to try to get information (from someone). The police officer began to *question* the witness.
inquire to seek information by asking questions. You will have to *inquire* at the desk.
antonyms: *See* answer.

awful *adj.* causing fear, dread, or awe. The storm was *awful*.
terrible causing terror or awe. We saw a *terrible* accident today.

B

beautiful *adj.* full of beauty; having qualities that are pleasing. What a *beautiful* sunset!
gorgeous extremely beautiful or richly colored. What a *gorgeous* sunset!
lovely beautiful in a comforting way. This is a *lovely* room.
antonyms: ugly, hideous

big *adj.* of great size. He works on a *big* farm.
huge extremely big. That is a *huge* tree!
enormous much greater than the usual size. We saw an *enormous* elephant at the zoo.
large of great size; big. What *large* feet you have!
antonyms: *See* little.

brave *adj.* willing to face danger; without fear. The *brave* firefighter raced into the burning house.
bold showing courage; fearless. The *bold* explorer walked into the dark jungle.
courageous having courage. A *courageous* woman dove into the icy water to save the child.
daring willing to take risks. The *daring* boy stood ready at the edge of the cliff.
antonyms: afraid, fearful

bright *adj.* filled with light; shining. The sun was so *bright* I had to wear sunglasses.
brilliant shining or sparkling with light. The sky was filled with *brilliant* stars.
shiny shining; bright. I could see the *shiny* coin in the water.
antonyms: dark, dull

C

cold *adj.* having a low temperature; lacking warmth or heat. The desert has hot days and *cold* nights.
chilly uncomfortably cool. The first day was wet and *chilly.*
icy very cold. An *icy* wind stung our cheeks.
antonyms: *See* hot.

collect *v.* to gather or bring (things) together. Tom *collected* soda cans to raise money.
assemble to gather or bring together, especially people. The mayor *assembled* the council.
compile to collect and put together (information), as in a list or report. Nancy *compiled* a list of members.
gather to bring together in one place or group. Ray *gathered* all the team members for a photo.

cry *v.* to shed tears. Julie did not know what to do when the baby started to *cry*.
sob to cry with short gasps. Tina *sobbed* as she told us what had happened.
weep to show grief, joy, or other strong emotions by crying. James will *weep* no more.
antonyms: *See* laugh.

D

do *v.* to carry out. Mrs. Riley will *do* the job right.
execute to complete, often when told to do so. The soldier *executed* his orders.
perform to carry out to completion. The doctor *performed* the operation.

dry *adj.* not wet; free of moisture. Please bring me a *dry* towel.
arid dry as a result of having little rainfall. The Gobi Desert is *arid.*
parched dried out by heat. It was so hot that my throat was parched.
antonyms: *See* wet.

F

far *adj.* a long way off; not near. Steve's house is *far* from here.
distant extremely far. Pluto is a *distant* planet.
remote far away, in an out-of-the-way place. We visited a *remote* village in Africa.
antonyms: near, close

fast *adj.* moving or done with speed. We rode on a *fast* train.
quick done in a very short time. That was a *quick* game.
swift moving with great speed, often said of animals or people. The *swift* horse flew by us.
antonym: slow

funny *adj.* causing laughter. Dick told us a *funny* joke.
amusing causing smiles of enjoyment. That story was *amusing.*
comical causing laughter through actions. The clowns were *comical*.
hilarious very funny and usually noisy. That movie was *hilarious.*

get/hurt

G

get *v.* to go for and return with. Please *get* me a sandwich.
acquire to come into possession of through effort. He *acquired* a new house.
obtain to get as one's own, often with some difficulty. Lily worked hard to *obtain* her job.

good *adj.* above average in quality; not bad. This is a *good* book.
excellent extremely good. Marie always does *excellent* work.
fair somewhat good; slightly better than average. Jeremy did a *fair* job.
fine of high quality; very good. She made a *fine* dinner for us.
antonyms: bad, poor

great *adj.* of unusual quality or ability. Mark Twain was a *great* writer.
remarkable having unusual qualities. That was a *remarkable* movie.
superb of greater quality than most. She is a *superb* singer.

H

happy adj. having, showing, or bringing pleasure. Today, Mr. Carson is a *happy* man.
glad feeling or expressing joy or pleasure. Tony was *glad* to meet Mrs. James.
joyful very happy; filled with joy. Danny was *joyful* when he heard his father was coming home.
merry happy and cheerful. Christmas was a *merry* occasion.
pleased satisfied or content. Harry was *pleased* with his new coat.
antonyms: *See* sad.

hard *adj.* not easy to do or deal with. Mowing the lawn is *hard* work.
difficult hard to do; requiring effort. Steering the ship through the storm was a *difficult* task.
tough difficult to do, often in a physical sense. Catching wild horses is a *tough* job.
antonym: easy

help *v.* to provide with support; be of service to. Will you *help* me clean this floor?
aid to give help to (someone in trouble). The police *aided* us in finding the lost child.
assist to help, often in a cooperative way. Ned *assisted* his brother in painting the house.

hot *adj.* having a high temperature; having much heat. The oven is *hot*.
fiery as hot as fire; burning. The spaceship flew toward a *fiery* sun.
scalding hot enough to burn, often said of liquids. A pot of *scalding* water fell on the floor.
antonyms: *See* cold.

hurt *v.* to cause pain or damage. Did you *hurt* your knee?
harm to do damage to. A good rider would never *harm* a horse.
injure to cause physical damage. Jon fell and *injured* his leg.

I

interesting *adj.* arousing or holding interest or attention. It was an *interesting* book.
captivating capturing and holding the attention of by beauty or excellence. Grandpa told us a *captivating* ghost story.
fascinating causing and holding interest of through a special quality or charm. The snake charmer's act was *fascinating.*
antonyms: dull, boring

L

large *See* big.

laugh *v.* to make the sounds and facial movements that show amusement. He *laughs* at my jokes.
chuckle to laugh softly, especially to oneself. Carla *chuckled* when she read my note.
giggle to laugh in a silly, high-pitched, or nervous way. Jill *giggled* and turned red.
guffaw to laugh loudly. Henry *guffawed* so hard he had to hold his sides.
antonyms: *See* cry.

let *v.* give permission to. Mom won't *let* me go to the game.
allow to grant permission to or for, usually in relation to rules. The police do not *allow* fishing at the beach.
permit to allow (a person) to do something. He will *permit* you to use the pool if you ask him first.
antonyms: refuse, deny, forbid

like *v.* to take pleasure in (something); to feel affection for (someone). I *like* to go walking in the rain.
admire to have affection and respect for (someone). Johnny *admires* his grandfather.
enjoy to take pleasure in (something). She *enjoys* music.
love to like (something) very much; to feel great affection for (someone). Mary *loves* to go sailing.
antonyms: dislike, hate

little *adj.* small in size; not big. Vanna found a *little* puppy.
small not large. Wally needs a *small* box for his gift.
tiny extremely small. We saw three *tiny* birds in the nest.
antonyms: *See* big.

look *v.* to see with one's eyes. She *looked* at the moon.
glance to look quickly. Kenny only *glanced* at the book.
peer to look closely. Moe *peered* at the map to find the town.
stare to look at for a long time with eyes wide open. Sue was so surprised she just *stared* at me.

loud *adj.* having a strong sound. We heard a *loud* crash overhead.
deafening loud enough to make one deaf. The dam broke with a *deafening* roar.
noisy full of sounds, often unpleasant. The crowd was *noisy.*

M

mad See angry.

many *adj.* consisting of a large number. Dave has *many* socks.
numerous a great many. I have asked you *numerous* times.
several more than a few but less than many. Cheryl has played in *several* games this season.
plenty (of) enough, or more than enough, suggesting a large number. We have *plenty* of plates.
antonym: few

mean *adj.* lacking in kindness or understanding. Joe was really *mean.*
nasty resulting from hate. That was a *nasty* trick he played on us.
selfish concerned only about oneself. Kelly is too *selfish* to care about how I feel.
spiteful filled with ill feelings toward others. Pat is a *spiteful* person.
antonyms: *See* nice.

N

neat *adj.* clean and orderly. His clothes are always *neat.*
tidy neat and clean, often said of a place. She likes to keep this room *tidy.*
well-groomed carefully dressed and groomed. Marvin always looks *well-groomed.*
antonyms: messy, untidy, sloppy

nice *adj.* agreeable or pleasing. Lynn is a *nice* person.
gentle mild and kindly in manner. He is so *gentle* with the children.
kind good-hearted. Uncle Bob was very *kind* to send you a gift.
pleasant agreeable; giving pleasure to. She has a *pleasant* way of talking.
sweet having or marked by agreeable or pleasing qualities. Jenny has a *sweet* personality.
antonyms: *See* mean.

O

often *adv.* many times; again and again. Theo *often* visits his sister.
frequently happening again and again. Sarah *frequently* works late.
regularly happening at fixed times. Mrs. Day *regularly* takes the bus.
antonyms: seldom, rarely

old *adj.* having lived or existed for a long time. The vase is *old.*
aged having grown old. Minnie helps take care of her *aged* aunt.
ancient very old; of times long past. Dr. Tyrell found an *ancient* coin.
antonym: young

P

plain *adj.* not distinguished from others in any way. The villagers are *plain,* hard-working people.
common average; not special. He lives like any *common* person.
ordinary plain; average; everyday. It's just an *ordinary* newspaper.

antonyms: special; *See also* unusual.

proud *adj.* having a sense of one's own worth, usually in a positive way. He was very *proud.*
conceited having too high an opinion of oneself, in a negative way. Shelly is too *conceited* to talk to me.
haughty having or showing much pride in oneself. He is a *haughty* football hero.
antonym: humble

Q

quiet *adj.* with little or no noise. The house was *quiet* after everyone had gone.
calm free of excitement or strong feeling; quiet. Everyone was *calm* after the mayor left the room.
peaceful calm; undisturbed. The camp is so *peaceful* in early morning.
still without sound; silent. The forest was *still.*
antonyms: loud, noisy.

R

ready *adj.* fit for use or action. Everything is *ready* for the party.
prepared ready or fit for a particular purpose. Jim was *prepared* for the test.
set ready; prepared to do something. Willie was all *set* to go to school.

really *adv.* in fact. What *really* happened at the store today?
actually in fact; really. Dan *actually* got a job yesterday!
indeed really; truly. I was *indeed* waiting for you at the park.
truly in fact; really. He *truly* did earn ten dollars.

right *adj.* free from error; true. Every single answer was *right.*
accurate without errors or mistakes. His description was *accurate.*
correct agreeing with fact or truth. He found the *correct* way to solve the puzzle.
antonyms: wrong, mistaken

rude *adj.* not polite; ill-mannered. Jack made a *rude* remark to me.
discourteous without good manners. You have no reason to be *discourteous* to Mr. Braun.
impolite not showing good manners. They were *impolite* to everyone at the party.
antonyms: polite, courteous

S

sad *adj.* feeling or showing unhappiness or sorrow. Jake was *sad* when he lost his dog.
downcast low in spirits; sad. She was *downcast* when she did not make the team.
miserable extremely unhappy. Mary was *miserable* after her brother left home.
antonyms: *See* happy.

say *v.* make known or express in words. Mel *said* that he wants to go home.
declare to make known publicly or formally. The mayor *declared* that the town needed more money.
speak to express an idea, fact, or feeling. Wendy *spoke* to us about the new shopping mall.
state to express or explain fully in words. Mr. Coombs *stated* his opinion during the meeting.
talk to express ideas or information by means of speech; to speak. Ken *talked* about his new model airplane.
See also tell.

scared *adj.* afraid; alarmed. She got *scared* when she heard a noise.
afraid feeling fear, often in a continuing way or for a long time. Jerry is *afraid* of the dark.
fearful filled with fear. Donna was *fearful* of the thunder.
frightened scared suddenly, or for a short time. When the lights went out, he was *frightened.*
terrified extremely scared; filled with terror. Pete was *terrified* when he heard the scream.

shy *adj.* uncomfortable in the presence of others. Paula is too *shy* to stand in front of the class.
bashful easily embarrassed; very shy. Carl was too *bashful* to step out from behind the chair.
timid showing a lack of courage; easily frightened. The *timid* little boy would not go near the cows.
antonym: bold

sick *adj.* having poor health. Ted was *sick* in bed all week.
ill not healthy; sick. Mark stayed home because he was *ill.*
unwell not feeling well. Stan has been *unwell* for a month.
antonyms: well, healthy

small *See* little.

smart *adj.* intelligent; bright; having learned a lot. Tommy is a *smart* boy for his age.
clever mentally sharp; quick-witted. He is a *clever* fellow.
intelligent able to learn, understand, and reason. Shana is an *intelligent* girl.
wise able to know or judge what is right, good, or true. The chief was a *wise* old man.
antonym: stupid

smile *v.* to have, show, or give a smile, in a happy or friendly way. May Li *smiled* when she saw the puppy.
grin to smile broadly, with great happiness or amusement. Keith *grinned* when he saw my costume.
smirk to smile in a silly or self-satisfied way. Pat *smirked* at him because she knew the answer.
beam to smile radiantly or joyfully. The happy mother *beamed* whenever she looked at her new baby.
antonyms: frown, scowl

strange *adj.* differing from the usual or the ordinary. That is a *strange* little dog.
odd not ordinary. She has some very *odd* clothes.
weird strange or odd, in a frightening or mysterious way. A *weird* man came out of the house.
See also unusual.

strong *adj.* having great strength or physical power. Football players have to be *strong*.
muscular having well-developed muscles; strong. Neil has become *muscular* from lifting weights.
powerful having great strength, influence, or authority. The governor is a *powerful* woman.
antonym: weak

sure *adj.* firmly believing in something. Pam is *sure* that our team will win.
certain free from doubt; very sure. Russ is *certain* of his answer.
confident firmly trusting; sure of oneself or of another. Mac is *confident* that he'll get the job.
definite positive or certain, often in a factual way. It is *definite* that the school will be closed on Friday.
antonyms: doubtful, unsure

surprised *adj.* feeling sudden wonder. Joan was *surprised* when she heard the news.
amazed overwhelmed with wonder or surprise. I was *amazed* when the dog did as I asked.
astounded greatly surprised; stunned. Lynn was so *astounded* that she could not move.

T

talk *See* say.

tell *v.* to put or express in written or spoken words. Mandy *told* us about summer camp.
announce to state or make known publicly. Mrs. Grimes *announced* that she would be leaving.
narrate to tell about events, especially a story. The camp leader *narrated* a ghost story.
relate to tell or report events or details. Paul *related* the story of how we got lost in the woods.
See also say.

thin *adj.* not fat. He was small and *thin* until he was ten years old.
lean with little or no fat, but often strong. A runner must have a *lean* body.
slim thin, in a good or healthy way. Dennis has gotten *slim* since he started exercising.
antonyms: fat, plump, chubby

think *v.* to have in the mind as an opinion or attitude. Kim *thinks* we should have a picnic.
believe to accept as true or real. She *believes* my story.
consider to think to be; believe. The coach *considers* him the best player on the team.

U

unusual *adj.* not usual, common, or ordinary. Her eyes are an *unusual* color.
extraordinary very unusual; beyond the ordinary. That painting is an *extraordinary* work of art.
rare seldom happening, seen, or found. Bald eagles are *rare* birds.
uncommon rare or unusual. Snowstorms are *uncommon* in this area.
See also strange.
antonyms: usual, common

upset *adj.* feeling uneasy; distressed. Tina was *upset* when no one came to the party.
concerned troubled or worried. Mom was *concerned* when my brother did not come home for supper.
worried uneasy or troubled about something. Jack was *worried* that the river would flood.
antonym: calm

W

walk *v.* to move or travel on foot. Ruth *walked* across the street.
march to walk with regular steps. The band *marched* down the street.
stride to walk with long steps, usually with a purpose. We watched him *stride* down the hall.
stroll to walk in a relaxed or leisurely manner. Amy and Sally *strolled* through the park.
strut to walk in a vain or very proud way. Joe likes to *strut* up and down in his new clothes.

want *v.* to have a desire or wish for. Lenny *wanted* to have lunch.
crave to want badly, often in an uncontrollable way. Sue *craved* ice cream so much she ran all the way to the store.
desire to have a strong wish for. Molly *desired* a lot of money.
wish to have a longing or strong need for. Gary *wished* he had blond hair.
yearn to feel a strong and deep desire. Grandpa *yearned* for the warm days of summer.

wet *adj.* covered or soaked with water or other liquid. Her hair was *wet* after she went swimming.
damp slightly wet. Our bathing suits are still *damp*.
moist slightly wet; damp. Use a *moist* cloth to wipe up the dust.
sopping extremely wet; dripping. Lisa's clothes were *sopping* by the time she got home.
antonyms: *See* dry.

whole *adj.* made up of the entire amount, quantity, or number. Did you eat that *whole* pizza?
complete having all its parts. Is that a *complete* set of crayons?
entire whole; having all its parts. The *entire* class had to stay after school.
total whole, full, or entire, often referring to numbers. Did you pay the *total* amount?

LETTER MODELS

Look carefully at the letter models for a thank-you note and an invitation below. They show you the correct form to use when you write a friendly letter. Notice where commas are used in the heading, greeting, and closing of each letter. You can use these models to help you when you write.

THANK-YOU NOTE

157 Sylvan Avenue
Asheville, North Carolina 28806
August 13, 19-- — **HEADING**

Dear Aunt Mary, — **GREETING**

Thank you so much for the beautiful necklace that you sent me. The purple stones will match my new dress. Whenever I wear my new necklace, I will think of you. — **BODY**

Love, — **CLOSING**

Joanne — **SIGNATURE**

INVITATION

214 Oaktree Lane
Tampa, Florida 33612
May 5, 19-- — **HEADING**

Dear Greg, — **GREETING**

Please come to my birthday party on Saturday, May 23, at 2:00 p.m. The party will be at my house. My address is at the top of this invitation. Wear casual clothes. — **BODY**

Your friend, — **CLOSING**

Louis — **SIGNATURE**

SPELLING STRATEGIES

When you write, it is very important that you spell every word correctly. Read the spelling strategies below. Following them will help you to improve your spelling.

1. Learn the basic spelling rules.
2. Learn the correct spellings of commonly misspelled words.
3. Check your work carefully when you have finished writing.
4. Whenever you have a question about how a word should be spelled, use a dictionary to check the spelling.

Spelling Rules

Study the rules below. They will help you to spell many words correctly.

Words with *ie* and *ei*

Spell the word with ***ie*** when the sound is /ē/, except after ***c***.

Sound is /ē/: chief, believe, piece

Except after *c*: receive, ceiling, deceive

Spell the word with ***ei*** when the vowel sound in the word is /ā/.

Sound is /ā/: neighbor, weigh, eight

There are some exceptions to the rules above. It is best to memorize the spelling of the following words.

Exceptions: either, neither, seize, weird, friend

Adding *s* and *es*

In most cases, add ***s*** to a noun to make it plural.

Examples: club + s = clubs   day + s = days

If a noun ends in ***s, ch, sh, x,*** or ***z,*** add ***es*** to spell the plural.

Examples: bus + es = buses   match + es = matches
brush + es = brushes   fox + es = foxes

If a noun ends in ***f*** or ***fe***, change the ***f*** to ***v*** when adding ***s*** or ***es*** to spell the plural.

Examples: leaf leaves life lives

If a noun ends in a consonant and a ***y***, change the ***y*** to ***i*** before adding ***es*** to spell the plural.

Example: story stories

Adding *ed, ing, er,* and *est*	If a word ends in a consonant and a ***y***, change the ***y*** to ***i*** before adding an ending that does not begin with ***i***.				
	Examples:	worry	worried	tiny	tiniest
	In most cases, if a one-syllable word has a single vowel before a final consonant, double the final consonant when adding an ending that begins with a vowel.				
	Examples:	trip	tripped	rub	rubbing
		sad	sadder	big	biggest
	If a word ends in a silent ***e***, drop the ***e*** when adding an ending that begins with a vowel.				
	Examples:	dive	diving	hike	hiked
		pale	paler	large	largest
Adding prefixes and suffixes	When a prefix is added to a base word, the spelling of the base word remains the same.				
	Example:	re+write = rewrite			
	When a suffix is added to a base word, the spelling of the base word may change. If the base word ends in a silent ***e***, drop the ***e*** when adding a suffix that begins with a vowel or a ***y***.				
	Examples:	shine+y = shiny		love+able = lovable	
	For most words ending in silent ***e***, keep the ***e*** when adding a suffix that begins with a consonant.				
	Examples:	pave+ment = pavement			
Homophones	Homophones are often misspelled. Knowing the meanings of homophones will help you to choose—and spell—them correctly.				
	Examples:	ate	heal	break	hole
		eight	heel	brake	whole
Contractions	Use an apostrophe in a contraction.				
	Examples:	it's	you're	they're	
Possessives	Do not use an apostrophe with a possessive pronoun.				
	Examples:	its	your	their	

OVERVIEW OF THE WRITING PROCESS

In this book you have learned that writing is a process. When you write, you follow certain steps. Sometimes you move back and forth between steps, but basically you proceed from the beginning to the end of the process.

Prewriting

- Decide on a **purpose** and **audience** for your writing.
- Choose a topic that would be suitable for your purpose and audience.
- Explore ideas about your topic. You could **brainstorm, cluster,** or **list.**
- Narrow your topic if it is too large for you to cover it well.

Writing a First Draft

- Use your prewriting ideas to write your draft.
- Do not worry too much about making errors. Get your ideas on paper.

Revising

- Read your draft. Share it with someone else to get a response.
- Ask yourself these questions about your draft.

  What else will my audience want to know? What details can I add?
  How can I make my purpose clearer?
  How can I make my writing easier to understand?
  How can I improve the organization of my writing?

Proofreading

- Read your revised draft.
- Ask yourself these questions about your revised draft.

  Have I followed correct paragraph form?
  Have I used complete sentences?
  Have I used capitalization and punctuation correctly?
  Have I spelled all words correctly?

Publishing

- Make a clean copy of your revised and proofread draft.
- Share your writing with the audience for whom you wrote it.

STUDY STRATEGIES

Studying is an important part of learning. You often will need to study written material, and sometimes you will have to take a test. These study strategies will help you to study effectively.

General Study Guides

1. Plan your time carefully.
2. Keep a list of assignments.
3. Decide how much time to spend on each task.
4. Find a quiet, comfortable place to work.
5. Keep study materials handy.

Helpful Study Methods

There are many different ways to study. Two methods, SQ3R and PROTO, are described below. You can decide which method fits your needs.

SQ3R The name stands for the five steps you should follow when you read a unit or chapter.

1. **Survey** the selection to find out what it is about.
2. Think of **Questions** to ask to help you understand the selection.
3. **Read** the material. Look for answers to the questions you made up, and note the important points in what you read.
4. **Record** answers to the questions and list the important points by writing them down.
5. **Review** the selection and group or underline the notes that you have written.

PROTO The name stands for the five steps you should follow when you study all kinds of material.

1. **Preview.** Preview the material to identify the general idea. Look at the title and the major headings.
2. **Read.** Read the material. Look at the headings again before you read each part. Then, read each part carefully. Identify the most important points in each section.
3. **Organize.** After you have read the material once, figure out how the most important points should be organized. Important information may be organized by time order, classification, cause-and-effect, or comparison-and-contrast.

4. **Take Notes.** Use the method of organization to take notes. Write down the important points in what you have read. You may want to write down each major idea or title, and then write notes under each idea. You may want to use an outline, a picture, or a time line.
5. **Overview.** Finally, read through your notes and the list of important ideas again to form an overview or summary of what you have read.

Special Study Tips

Follow Directions Carefully

1. Identify the steps you should follow.
2. Ask questions about steps you do not understand.
3. Follow directions step by step.

Set a Purpose for Studying

1. Before you begin studying, identify the purpose of your work.
2. Sometimes you will want to find out why something happened or to compare two similar events or people.
3. Use the directions to help you to identify your purpose.
4. Keep your purpose in mind as you work.

Outline Your Material

1. Make an outline of what you are studying.
2. Organize your outline according to the important points you noted.

Map Your Material

1. Use a diagram or picture to outline what you are studying.
2. You might use a map, a time line, or a flow chart to indicate what information is important and how it is organized.

Memorize Your Material

1. Say what you want to remember aloud. Then write it down.
2. Think of a way to classify what you want to memorize. You might classify information in alphabetical order or into categories such as people, places, or things.
3. Invent memory joggers. A memory jogger might be a funny word or sentence that helps you to remember something. For example, if you want to remember the primary colors—red, blue, and yellow—you might make up the sentence Rough Babies Yell. The first letter of each word in the sentence is the first letter of one of the colors.
4. Repeat things as many times as you can. Repeating information will often help you to remember it.

Taking Tests

Taking tests is an important part of your schoolwork. Tests are helpful in showing you and your teacher what you have learned. The best approach to taking a test is to study well ahead of time. Then, on the night before the test, get plenty of rest. You can use many of the study skills you have learned to make test taking easier.

1. **Preview the test.** Look through the test quickly to see what it covers and how long it is.
2. **Plan your time.** Your teacher will tell you how much time you have. Decide how much time to spend on each part of the test. Some parts may take longer than others. Writing a paragraph, for example, will usually take longer than punctuating sentences correctly. Keep track of the time as you work.
3. **Follow directions.** Listen to any directions your teacher gives you. Then, read the test directions carefully before you begin the test. As you work through the test, read any directions you see at the beginning of each new section.
4. **Read questions carefully.** Read each test question carefully. Figure out exactly what the question means. Use key words to figure out what kind of answer is required. (Key words might include *why, when, who, because, after,* and *what.*) Then, decide on your answer.
5. **Outline answers to essay questions.** When you need to write a paragraph or more to answer a test question, make a rough outline to help you organize your thoughts. Write the outline quickly on scrap paper. Then use the outline to write a complete and logical answer.
6. **Do easy questions first.** Work through the test and finish every question for which you know the answer. Leave the difficult questions for last. Then, go back and work on each difficult question.
7. **Mark your answers carefully.** If you are taking a multiple-choice test, fill in only one bubble for each question and fill it in completely. If you are writing your answers, write each one clearly and neatly so that the teacher can read it.
8. **Answer all questions.** Even if you are not sure of the answer to a question, you should try to answer it. In a multiple-choice test, your guess may be correct. In a short-answer or essay test, your answer may receive a few points. On the other hand, an answer left blank will earn you no points at all.
9. **Check your work.** When you have answered all the questions, use the time you have left to go back and check your work. Make sure you have answered each question.

SENTENCE STRUCTURE: Diagraming Guide

A sentence diagram uses lines to show how the words in a sentence go together. A diagram always begins with the most important words in the sentence. At the beginning, you will diagram only **some** of the words in the sentences. You will learn how to diagram other words in later lessons.

Simple Subject and Simple Predicate (pages 10–12)

A sentence diagram puts the simple subject and the simple predicate on a straight line called a **base line.** An up-and-down line separates the simple subject from the simple predicate.

Find the simple subject and simple predicate in this sentence.

Dogs bark.

Look at the diagram below. You can see how the simple subject and simple predicate are diagramed.

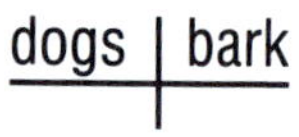

Now find the simple subject and the simple predicate in this sentence.

The black and white puppy yipped excitedly.

Look carefully at the diagram below. Which two words from the sentence are written on the base line? These words are the simple subject and the simple predicate of the sentence.

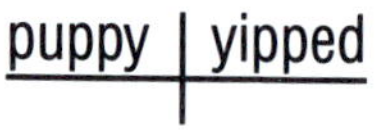

Practice Make a sentence diagram of the simple subject and the simple predicate in each sentence.

1. Some dogs make no noise.
2. I learned about these dogs.
3. These dogs lived in Egypt.
4. People call them *saluki*.
5. Ted owns a saluki.
6. He named his dog King Tut.
7. King Tut runs very fast.
8. Saluki are hunting dogs.
9. I have a collie.
10. Collies herd sheep.

Compound Subjects (page 14)

A sentence with a compound subject has two or more subjects. Each of the subjects is placed on a separate line in the sentence diagram. The word **and, or,** or **but** is written on a dotted up-and-down line that connects the compound subjects.

Look at this sentence. Find the two words that make up the compound subject.

Students and teachers went to the zoo.

Look at the diagram. Notice how the compound subject is diagramed.

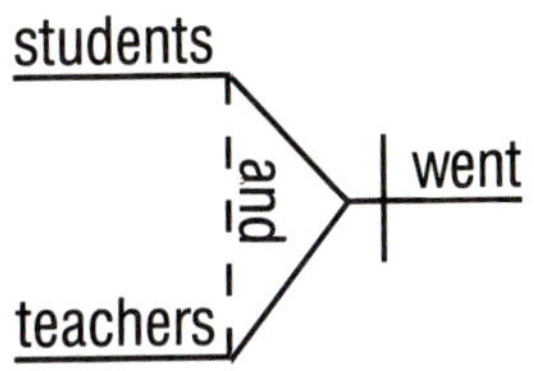

There may be more than two words in a compound subject. Find the compound subject in this sentence.

Lions, tigers, and bears interested the group.

Look carefully at the diagram of this sentence. Which words make up the compound subject? Notice where *and* is placed in the diagram.

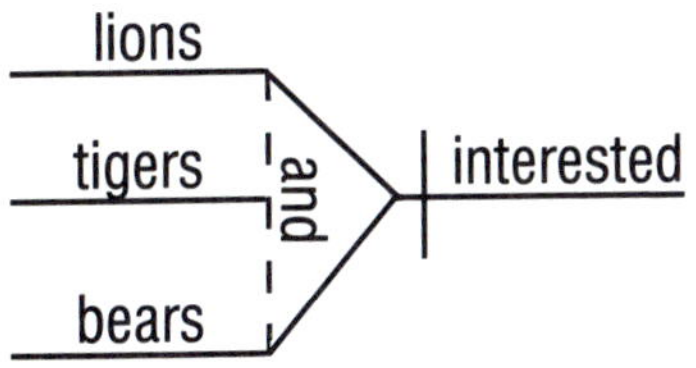

Practice Diagram each sentence. Be sure you show each part of the compound subject.

1. Lions and tigers are called big cats.
2. Panthers or leopards are other big cats.
3. Zoos, preserves, and parks protect these animals.
4. India, Africa, and Asia have many big cats.
5. Bears or tigers appear rarely in Africa.
6. Parrots and tucans live in tropical climates.

7. Macaws, cockatoos, and parakeets are part of the parrot family.
8. Cockatoos and lories live in Australia.
9. Fruits, nuts, and seeds form the diet of most parrots.
10. Parrots and mockingbirds imitate sounds easily.

Compound Predicates (page 14)

A sentence with a compound predicate has two or more verbs. Each verb appears on a separate line in a diagram. The word **and, or,** or **but** is written on a dotted up-and-down line that connects the compound verbs.

Look at this sentence. Find the words that make up the compound predicate.

My class studied and learned about Ben Franklin.

Look at this sentence diagram. Notice how the compound predicate is diagramed.

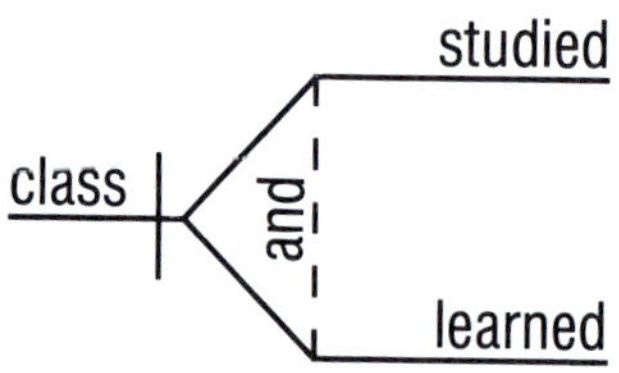

How many words make up the compound predicate in the sentence below?

Franklin wrote, edited, and printed a newspaper.

Look at the diagram of this sentence. Which words make up the compound predicate? Notice how *and* is placed in the compound subject.

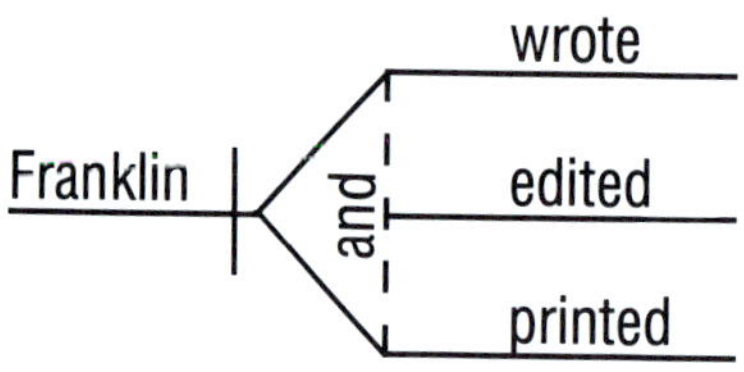

Practice Diagram each sentence. Show the subject. Be sure you show each part of the compound predicate correctly.

1. Franklin lived and worked in Philadelphia.
2. He was born and raised in Boston, however.
3. Franklin wrote, experimented, and traveled widely.
4. He liked England and traveled in France.
5. We wrote, printed, and sold a newsletter.

6. We delivered or mailed the newsletter to our customers.
7. Angie designed and illustrated the newsletter.
8. Suzanne revised and proofread the articles.
9. Many people requested and bought advertising space.
10. Some customers wrote, telephoned, or faxed for extra copies.

Adjectives (pages 292–302)

Adjectives are diagramed on a line that slants below the words they describe.

Look at this sentence. Find the adjective.

Golden sunshine warmed the earth.

Now look carefully at the diagram. Notice how the adjective is added to the base line.

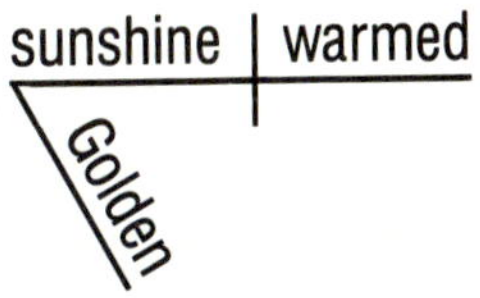

Often more than one adjective in a sentence may describe the same noun. Find the adjectives in this sentence. Remember that the words *a, an,* and *the* are special adjectives.

The bright, golden sunshine warmed the earth.

Look at the diagram. Notice how the adjectives are added to the sentence diagram.

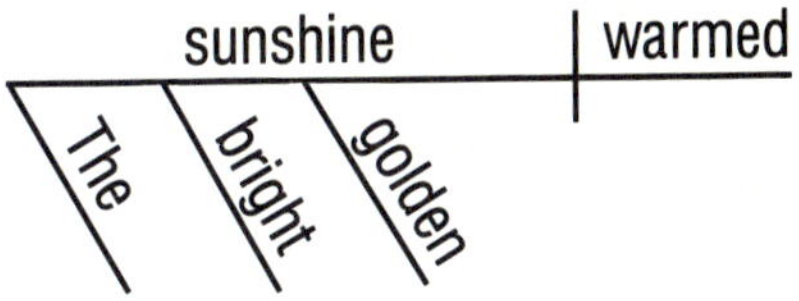

Some sentences have adjectives in a series. Find the adjectives in this sentence.

A big, colorful, and new kite pulled at its string.

Look at the diagram of this sentence. Notice how *and* is placed in the series of adjectives.

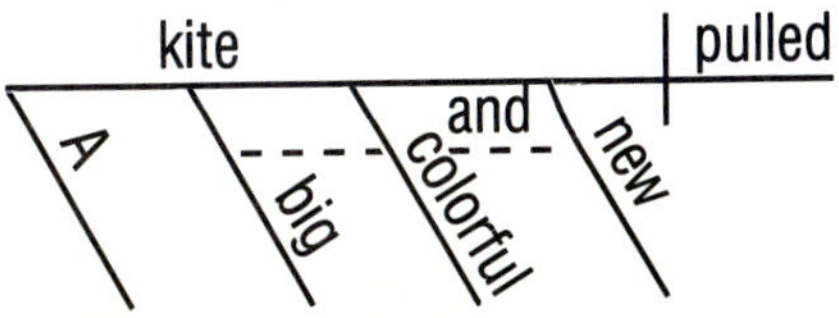

Practice Diagram each sentence. Show the simple subject, the simple predicate, and all the adjectives.

1. An old kite lay at my feet.
2. The torn, dirty, and faded paper needed repairs.
3. The twisted and knotted string tore easily.
4. A large, new, and expensive kite arrived today.
5. The small and faded kite was stuck in a tree.
6. Blue, red, and orange kites filled the air.
7. A large, silk kite danced in the breeze.
8. The howling wind lifted the kites high into the sky.
9. The long tails snapped merrily.
10. Six Chinese kites flew above the the trees.

Remember that an adjective may follow a linking verb. These adjectives are diagramed in a special way.

Find the linking verb and the adjective that follows it in the sentence below.

The video is interesting.

Look carefully at the diagram. Notice how each adjective is added to the diagram. The adjective that follows the linking verb is written on the base line. A slanting line that points back toward the subject comes between the verb and the adjective. Where is the article *the* written?

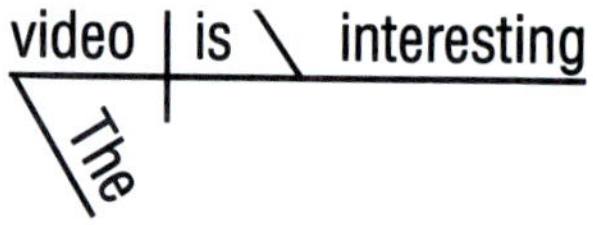

Practice Diagram each sentence. Show the simple subject, the linking verb, and all the adjectives.

1. The new movie was exciting.
2. The actors were good.
3. One actress is well-known.
4. Her colorful costumes were unusual.
5. The photography was beautiful, too.
6. Videos are fun to watch.
7. The store that sells videos is large.
8. Weekends are busy there.
9. The aisles are crowded.
10. Many tapes are missing from the shelves.

Adverbs (pages 422–430)

Adverbs describe a verb. When an adverb describes a verb, it is placed on a slanted line below the verb.

Read this sentence. Find the adverbs.

The busy children talked loudly and happily.

Look at the diagram. Where are the adverbs added to the sentence diagram? Notice how the word *and* connects two adverbs.

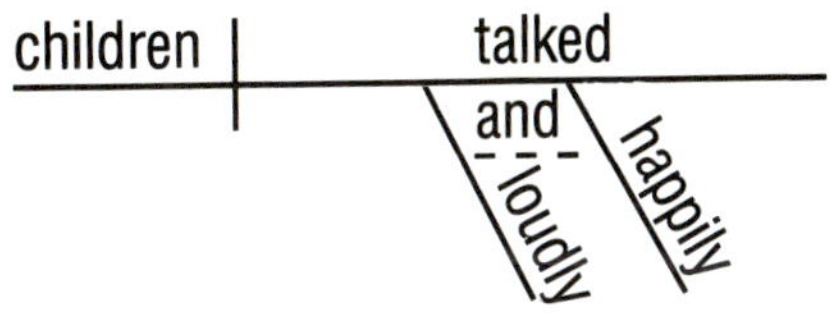

Remember that an adverb may appear anywhere in a sentence. It does not always follow the verb. However, all adverbs in a sentence are written below the verb in the sentence diagram.

Look at this sentence. Find the adverb.

Quietly the children walked into the room.

Look at the diagram.

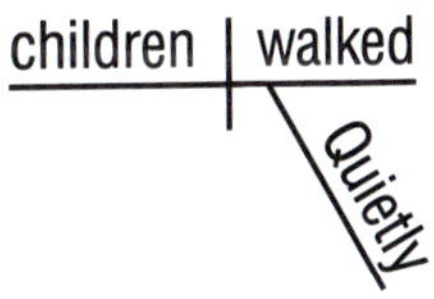

Practice Diagram each sentence. Show the simple subject, the simple predicate, and all the adverbs.

1. They quickly painted colored flags.
2. A tall boy laughed loudly and often.
3. A short girl carefully reached for paint.
4. A common color appeared frequently.
5. Bright flags flapped merrily.
6. Neatly the paints were put away.
7. Many people saw the flags there in the schoolyard.
8. Soon a photographer speedily snapped pictures.
9. Proudly and happily the children showed the flags.
10. One child excitedly told about the flags.

Compound Sentences (pages 22–23)

Compound sentences are two sentences connected by **or, and,** or **but.** Each sentence is diagramed. The connecting word is written on a line between the two sentences. Dotted lines connect this word to each sentence.

Read the compound sentence. Notice how it is diagramed.

Warm weather arrived, and flowers bloomed brightly.

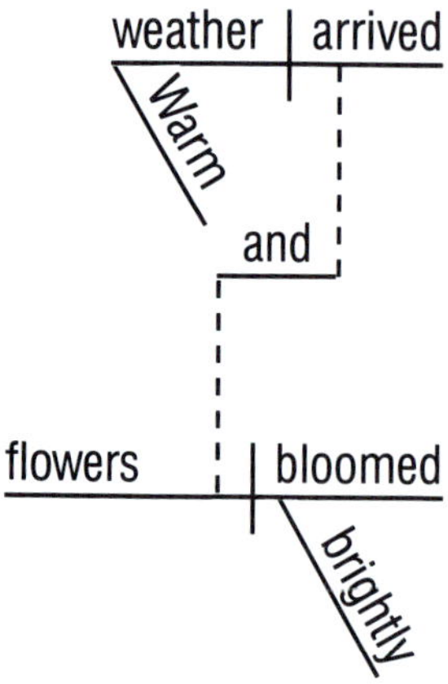

Practice Diagram all the words in these compound sentences.

1. Tulips appeared early, but purple lilacs bloomed later.
2. Rain sometimes falls, but I always water frequently.
3. Neighbors wave happily, and I smile brightly.
4. The sun shines, and the young birds sing cheerfully.
5. I work slowly and carefully, but the little garden grows quickly.
6. Soon seeds arrive, and I plant neatly.
7. The tiny seeds sprout, and now the weeds are tall.
8. Radishes grow fast, but potatoes take longer.
9. Later I harvest, and the family eats well.
10. Tasty soups simmer, and I cook happily.

GLOSSARY

OF WRITING, GRAMMAR, AND LITERARY TERMS

WRITING TERMS

audience — the reader or readers for whom a composition is written

detail sentences — sentences that tell more about the main idea of a paragraph

first draft — the first version of a composition, in which the writer gets his or her basic ideas down on paper

main-idea sentence — the sentence that states the overall point of a paragraph

overall impression — the general idea or feeling expressed in a description

personal narrative — a piece of writing in which the writer tells about something that has happened in his or her life

prewriting — the stage in the writing process in which the writer chooses a topic, explores ideas, gathers information, and organizes his or her material before writing a first draft

prewriting strategies — particular ways of gathering, exploring, planning, and organizing ideas before writing the first draft of a composition

• **charting** a way to gather ideas under different headings—especially useful in comparing and contrasting

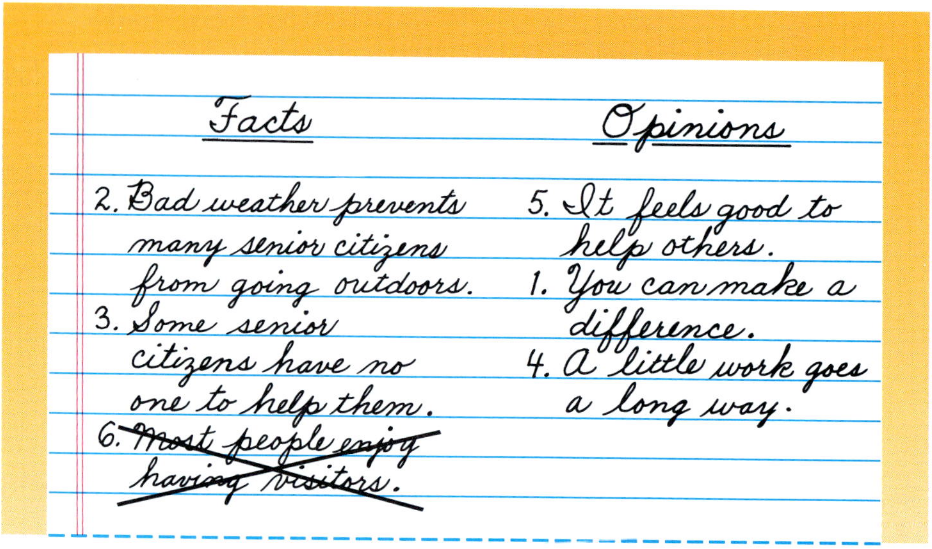

Problem	Solution	Steps to follow
How will I earn extra money?	Sell brownies.	1. Buy brownie ingredients. 2. Bake brownies. 3. Sell brownies at Little League games. 4. Save money.

• **clustering** a way to explore ideas by gathering details related to the writing topic

- **listing** a way to gather supporting reasons and details—especially useful in persuasive writing

Nature Camp	Baseball Camp
wildlife walks	special training
swimming	arts and crafts
campfires	swimming
arts and crafts	

- **outline** a way to organize topic-related ideas in the order in which they will be discussed—especially useful in drafting a research report

The First American in Space

I. Who is Alan B. Shepard?
  A. Birthdate and early life
  B. Chosen for astronaut program

II. His most famous flight
  A. Freedom 7
  B. Facts about the flight

III. His later accomplishments
  A. Apollo 14
  B. Rear Admiral

- **story organizer** — a way to gather ideas and details under headings important for story writing

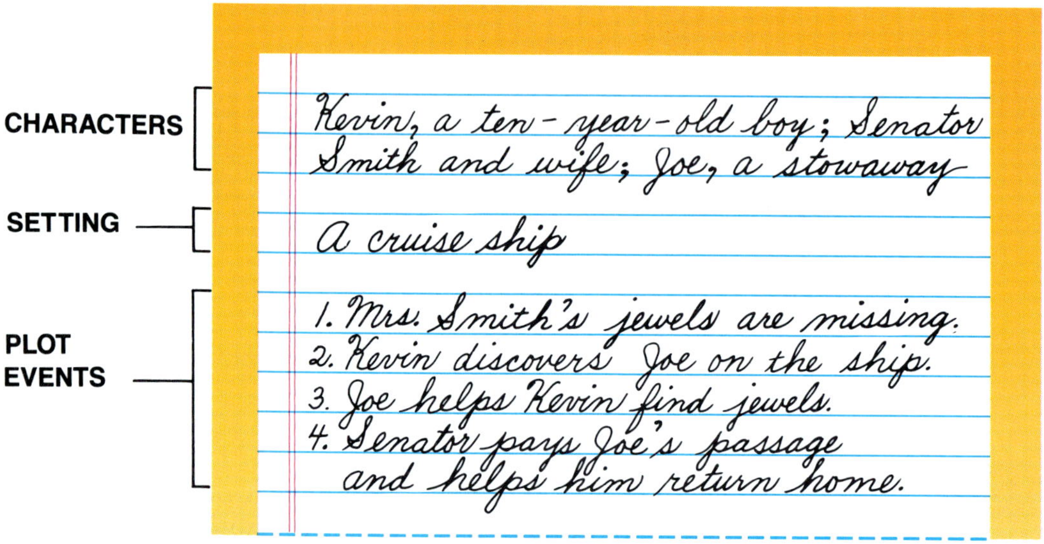

- **time line** — a way to organize the events in a narrative in time order

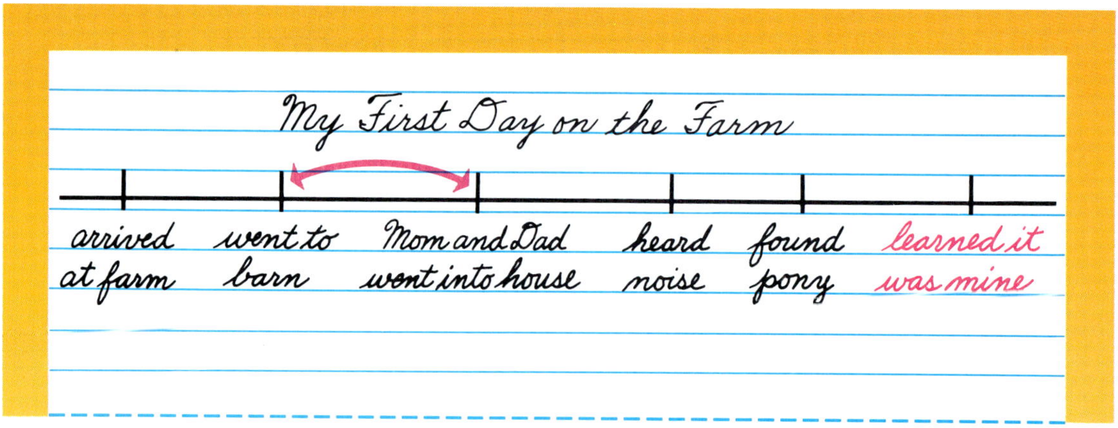

proofread — to correct errors in punctuation, capitalization, spelling, and grammar in a writing draft

publish — to share a composition with an audience

purpose — the writer's reason for writing a composition—for example, to explain, to entertain, or to persuade

revise	to improve the first draft of a composition by adding or taking out information, combining and reordering sentences, or changing word choice according to the purpose and audience
sensory details	in a description, the details that appeal to the reader's five senses—sight, hearing, touch, taste, and smell
supporting details	facts, examples, or sensory details that give more information about the main idea of a paragraph
time order	the arrangement of events in a composition according to when they occur in time
topic sentence	another name for the **main-idea sentence**
transition words	words or phrases that link sentences in a paragraph, such as *next* and *finally*
writing conference	a meeting in which a writer asks and answers questions about his or her writing with the purpose of improving it
writing process	the steps for writing a composition, including prewriting, writing a first draft, revising, proofreading, and publishing

GRAMMAR TERMS

action verb	a word that expresses action Dogs often *bark* at strangers.
adjective	a word that describes a noun or a pronoun Joanne has many *interesting* friends.
adverb	a word that tells more about a verb We *cheerfully* planned for the party.
article	the word *a*, *an*, or *the* *The* book is on *a* shelf.

common noun a noun that names any person, place, thing, or idea

Dr. Kang has an *office* in the *city.*

complete predicate all the words that tell what the subject of a sentence does or is

The tired child *slept in her mother's arms.*

complete subject all the words that tell whom or what a sentence is about

The dark and cloudy sky made us leave the park.

compound sentence a sentence that contains two sentences joined by a comma and the word *and, or,* or *but*

It rained hard, and the reservoirs filled.

future tense the form of a verb that shows something that has not yet happened

Tara *will buy* a new bicycle next spring.

helping verb a verb that helps the main verb to show an action

Karen *has* started her swimming lessons.

irregular verb a verb that does not form the past tense by adding *d* or *ed*

Joey *took* a ride on his bicycle.

linking verb a verb that connects the subject of a sentence to a noun or an adjective in the predicate

New Jersey *is* on the ocean.

main verb a verb that tells what the subject does or is

Dana *visits* her grandmother on Thursday.

noun a word that names a person, place, thing, or idea

The *picnic* was canceled.

object pronoun a pronoun that is used as the object of an action verb or after words such as *to, for, with, in,* and *at*

Laura will attend the concert with *me.*

past tense	the form of a verb that expresses action that has already happened Pete and Brenda *debated* in class last week.
possessive noun	a pronoun that shows ownership What is the *cat's* name?
possessive pronoun	a pronoun that shows who or what owns something Jeanine used *our* basement for band practice.
present tense	the form of a verb that tells that something is happening now The bird *sings* at my window.
pronoun	a word that takes the place of one or more nouns and the words that go with the nouns *It* sings early in the morning.
proper adjective	an adjective formed from a proper noun Marla likes to eat *Japanese* food.
proper noun	a noun that names a particular person, place, thing, or idea *Julio* is from *Cuba.*
run-on sentence	two or more sentences that have been joined together incorrectly *I have a new wool sweater it is very comfortable.*
sentence	a group of words that expresses a complete thought *Our music teacher plays many instruments.*
sentence fragment	a group of words that does not express a complete thought *Has a long tail and bright feathers.*
simple predicate	the main word or words in the complete predicate of a sentence Ray *drove* to Colorado last summer.

simple subject	the main word or words in the complete subject of a sentence The colorful *umbrella* shielded us from the sun.
subject pronoun	a pronoun that is used as the subject of a sentence *They* laughed at the clown's tricks.

LITERARY TERMS

alliteration	the repetition of the same first letter or initial sound in a series of words—for example, "Leonard likes little lizards."
autobiography	the story of a person's life written by himself or herself
biography	the story of a real person's life
characters	the people in a story or play
dialogue	the conversations that people have in a story or a play
fiction	written works such as novels and short stories that tell about imaginary characters and events
haiku	a poem that has three lines and usually seventeen syllables, and that frequently describes something in nature
images	pictures suggested by a description or a comparison, such as "The stars formed a glittering road in the sky."
nonfiction	written works that deal with real situations, people, or events, such as biographies
plot	the sequence of events in a story
setting	the time and place in which the events of a story happen

INDEX

INDEX

D

E

M

N

O

P

Q

R

T

U

V

W

Y

Brief quotation by Gordon Parks from *Gordon Parks* by Midge Turk (Thomas Y. Crowell). Copyright © 1971 Midge Turk. Reprinted by permission of Harper & Row, Publishers, Inc.

Brief quotation by Eleanor Cameron is from *A Room Made of Windows* by Eleanor Cameron. Copyright © 1971 by Eleanor Cameron. Used by permission of Little, Brown and Company.

Brief quotation by E. B. White from *More Books by More People* by Lee Bennett Hopkins. Copyright © 1974 by Lee Bennett Hopkins. Reprinted by permission of Curtis Brown, Ltd.

Excerpt from "Listen to the Unheard" from *Poems of Earth and Space* by Claudia Lewis. Copyright © 1967 by Claudia Lewis. Reprinted by permission of the publisher, E. P. Dutton, a division of NAL Penguin, Inc.

Excerpt from *Beginning Dictionary*, edited by William D. Halsey. Copyright © 1987 Macmillan Publishing Company. Reprinted by permission of the publisher.

"When You Walk" from *Collected Poems* by James Stephens. Copyright 1926 by Macmillan Publishing Company. Renewed 1954 by James Stephens. Reprinted with permission of Macmillan Publishing Company. Reprinted by permission also of The Society of Authors on behalf of the copyright owner, Mrs. Iris Wise.

Quotes by Byrd Baylor, Ezra Jack Keats, Marianna Mayer, and Cynthia Rylant are reprinted by the Imprints of Macmillan Children's Book Group.

Excerpt from "Insects and Other Creeping Crawlers" in *Science in a Vacant Lot* by Seymour Simon. Copyright © 1970 by Seymour Simon. Reprinted by permission of the author.

Excerpt from "Whispers" and the entire poem are from *Whispers and Other Poems* by Myra Cohn Livingston. Copyright © 1958 by Myra Cohn Livingston. Reprinted by permission of Marian Reiner for the author.

Brief quotation by Clyde Robert Bulla from *Books Are by People* by Lee Bennett Hopkins. Copyright © 1969 by Scholastic Magazines, Inc. Published by Citation Press. Reprinted by permission of Scholastic, Inc.

Excerpt from "Rainy Nights" and the entire poem are from *Come Follow Me* by Irene Thompson. Published by Evans Bros. and reprinted by kind permission of Unwin Hyman, Ltd.

Excerpt on soccer from the article "Soccer" in *The World Book Encyclopedia*. Copyright © 1988 World Book, Inc. Reprinted by permission of the publisher.

Excerpt from "The Frozen World" by Thayer Willis in the *Encyclopedia of Discovery and Exploration*. Copyright Aldus Books Limited, London 1971.

"Solving Problems" from *Childcraft—The How and Why Library*, Vol. 13. Copyright © 1982 U.S.A. by World Book-Childcraft International, Inc.

Myron Levoy quote is from *Something About the Author Autobiography Series:* Volume 4. Edited by Anne Commire. Copyright © 1987 by Gale Research Company. All rights reserved. Reprinted by permission of the publisher.

ILLUSTRATION CREDITS: Alex Bloch 86, 173, 192, 193, 194, 195, 196, 197, 237, 287, 294, 309, 349, 362, 366, 419M, 437, 481. Andrea Eberbach 100. Len Ebert 326, 327, 328, 329, 330, 331. Simon Galkin 232, 239, 296, 350, 364, 373, 424, 431. Marilyn Janovitz 258, 259, 260, 261, 262, 263, 264, 265. Bernie Karlin 176, 177, 312. Richard Loehle 458, 459, 460, 461, 462, 463. Loretta Lustig 242, 243, 376, 377. Carl Molno 97, 140, 216, 221M, 298, 414, 483, 487M. Nancy Munger 42, 43, 44, 45, 46, 47. Jan Pyk 2B, 3, 4, 5, 6BR, 7, 8, 9T&B, 10B, 11T&BL, 12B, 13, 14B, 15, 16, 17, 18B, 19, 20T&BL, 25, 55, 65, 67, 69, 70, 73T, 76, 77, 78BR, 79, 80B, 81, 82B, 83, 84, 85, 86BR, 87, 88B, 89, 90B, 91, 92B, 93, 94B, 95, 99, 124, 131, 134B, 141, 143, 145, 146, 149, 152B, 153, 154BR, 155, 156BR, 157, 158B, 159, 160, 161, 162, 163, 164, 165, 166, 167, 168B, 169, 170BR, 171, 175, 198, 205, 215, 217, 218, 221T, 224, 225, 226, 227, 228, 229, 230B, 231T&BR, 232BR, 233, 234, 235, 236, 237L, 266, 283, 285, 286, 289T, 292, 293, 294B, 295, 296B, 297, 298B, 299, 300, 301, 302, 303, 304, 305, 306, 307, 311, 332, 335, 336, 339, 349B, 351, 352, 355, 358, 359, 360, 361, 362B, 363, 364, 365, 366B, 367, 368, 369, 370, 371, 375, 396, 403, 413, 415, 416, 419, 422B, 423, 424B, 425, 426B, 427, 428B, 429, 430, 431BL, 432B, 433, 434, 435, 439, 464, 471, 481B, 484B, 484, 487T. Richard Steadham 388, 389, 390, 391, 392, 393, 394, 395. Fred Thomas 118, 119, 120, 121, 122, 123. Sy Thomas 9, 14, 21, 23, 78, 80, 142, 154, 156, 158, 168, 204, 214, 230, 289, 398, 412, 413, 422, 426, 428, 432. Joe Veno 26, 27, 440, 441. Lane Yerkes 2M, 6, 10, 12, 18, 73, 82, 88, 90, 92, 94, 152, 170.

PHOTO CREDITS: Clara Aich: 150, 203, 206, 209, 212, 213, 271, 274, 277, 280, 281, 338, 372, 373, 386, 401, 404, 407, 410, 411, 469, 472, 475, 478, 479. Animals Animals: Dan Baliotti 124; Patti Murray 19, 128R; Robert Pearcy 3; L. L. Rue III 425. Ira Block 353. The Bettmann Archive: 11, 231, 233. The British Tourist Authority (Compliments of): 239TR. Bruce Coleman, Inc.: Jeff Foott 257; E. R. Degginger 165, 223. Comstock: Michael Stucky 40; Mike & Carol Werner xii. © The Cousteau Society, a member-supported, non-profit environmental agency 427. Leo De Wys, Inc.: Buddy Jenssen 224; Randy G. Taylor 235. DRK Photo: Jim Brandenberg 457; Stephen J. Krasemann 356; Don & Pat Valenti 456. Steve Elsmore 333TL, 333B. Earth Scenes: Michael Habicht 200; Breck Kent 465; Tom Vanderschmidt 116. Myrleen Ferguson: 370. Tony Freeman: 464. Richard Hutchings: 387. The Image Bank: Murray Alcosser 48, 266; Bullaty/Lomeo 23TL, 238; Sonja Bullaty 75; D. Carroll 267; Luis Castañeda 22; Alain Choisnet 267T, 359; Dan Coffey 270; Mel Di Giacomo 173TL; G. V. Faint 23TR, 308; Cliff Feulner 172; Mitchell Funk 54; Gary Gladstone 161; Jay Grayson 74; David W. Hamilton 309TL; John Kelly 268; William

(Acknowledgments continued on page 532.)

Kennedy 49TR; Charles Krebs 49TL; David Maenza 334; Richard & Mary Magruder 306L; Patti McConville 5, 306R; Burton McNeely 402; Michael Melford 125B; Colin Molyneux 85; Paul Nehrenz 239TL; Marc Romanelli 272; Guido Alberto Rossi 351; Michael Salas 324; Isy Schwart 302; Chris Thomson 485; Anne van der Vaeren 125TR; Hans Wendler 77, 309TR. Richard Haynes, Jr. 337, 340, 343, 346, 347. Institute for International Studies Inc.: 466. The Metropolitan Museum of Art, Bequest of Mrs. H. O. Havemeyer, 1929. The H. O. Havemeyer Collection. (29100370) 16. Lawrence Migdale: 50, 52, 53, 56, 59, 62, 63, 64, 66, 96, 97, 129, 130, 132, 135, 138, 139, 141, 149. Monkmeyer Press: Michal Heron 291. National Aeronautics and Space Administration: 219. Gordon Parks: 71. PhotoEdit: Mary Kate Denny 151, 199T; Bill Thomas 101. Photo Researchers: Biophoto Associates/Science Source 420; William Curtsing 465; Dr. Fred Espenak 229; V. Englebert 417; Carl Frank 225; Robert Goldwitz 163; Eunice Harris 267BL; Stephen J. Krasemann 358; Calvin Larsen 256; Tom McHugh 49B, 333TR, 397BR; National Audubon Society 465; Bruce Roberts 199BL; R. Van Nostrand 470. Rainbow: Linda K. Moore 222. Ron Scherl: 355. The Stock Market: Joe Bator 313; Tibor Bognár 128L; Mark E. Gibson 293; Stephen Green-Armytage 125TL; Albano Guatti 290; Brownie Harris 117; David Hundley 48; Chris Jones 126; Barbara Kirk 41, 191, 227; Charles Krebs 49TL; Harvey Lloyd 153, 400; Guy Mancuso 435; J. T. Miller 8; Roy Morsch 423; Jeffry W. Myers 198; Peter Salutos 437TR; Chris Sorensen 437TL; Maggie Steber 360; Joan Teasdale 1. The Stock Shop: Clyde Smith 436; Antonio Suarez 147. Time Magazine: Terry Ashe 300; Johan Elbers 305. The United Nations: 69. UPI/Bettmann Newsphotos: 365, 467. Woodfin Camp & Associates, Inc.: Jim Anderson 169; Craig Aurness 190, 357; Robert Frerck 434; George Hall 173TR; Michal Heron 396; Martin Rogers 397BL; Bill Ross 325.

ADDITIONAL ILLUSTRATION CREDITS:
Roger Chandler xii-xix.

ADDITIONAL PHOTO CREDITS: PhotoDisc, Inc. © 1997, xii, xiii, xiv, xv, xvi, xvii, xviii, xix.